Contents

West Country
Page 1
Cornwall
Devon
Somerset

Central Southern England
Page 26
Dorset
Hampshire
Isle of Wight
Oxfordshire
Wiltshire

London & the South
Page 47
London
East Sussex
Kent
Surrey
West Sussex

East of England
Page 76
Bedfordshire
Cambridgeshire
Hertfordshire
Norfolk
Suffolk

Heart of England
Page 89
Derbyshire
Gloucestershire
Herefordshire
Leicestershire
Lincolnshire
Northamptonshire
Nottinghamshire
Shropshire
Warwickshire
Worcestershire

North West
Page 124
Cheshire
Cumbria
Greater Manchester
Lancashire

Yorkshire & North East
Page 152
Cleveland
County Durham
Northumberland
Yorkshire

Wales
Page 178
Aberconwy
Carmarthenshire
Gwynedd
Monmouthshire
Pembrokeshire
Powys
Vale of Glamorgan

Scotland
Page 205
Aberdeenshire
Argyll and Bute
Dumfries and Galloway
East Lothian
Edinburgh
Glasgow
Fife
Highland
Perth & Kinross
Scottish Borders

Channel Islands
Page 231
Guernsey, Herm
Jersey, Sark

Ireland
Page 244
Co. Clare
Co. Cork
Co. Donegal
Co. Dublin
Co. Kerry
Co. Offaly
Co. Tipperary

Hotels by facilities
Page 263

Hotels by county
Page 267

Hotels listed alphabetically
Page 275

Maps
Page 279

Signpost Guide 2003
How to use the guide

Choose a region
There is a map of the regions at the beginning of the guide. If you want to look up the hotels in a particular region, simply turn to the relevant regional colour-coded section.

Alternatively, turn to the colour maps starting on page 279
The numbers on the maps refer to the pages in this guide on which **Signpost** approved hotels are described.

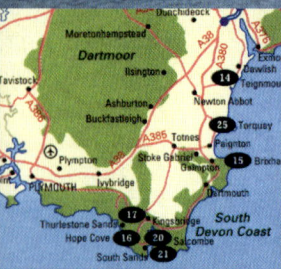

Fact File
Each regional section is prefaced by an illustrated guide to places of interest, walks, and historic houses and museums in the area, together with a unique diary of events that take place. All designed to give you a feel for the area.

Select a hotel
The hotel entries for each region follow and most hotels have a page to themselves. There is a large colour photograph of each hotel and a description of its situation, local attractions and general ambience to give you an idea of its character.
This is followed by a list of the hotel's facilities, number of bedrooms, dining options, leisure and sporting opportunities and opening times.

Single room including breakfast from £62.00
Double room including breakfast from £90.00

Check the room rates
Room rates are clearly shown as well as details of any special offers for weekend breaks etc.

Find out how to get there
To help you find the hotel, there is an area map which shows the hotel location and the surrounding roads and motorways.

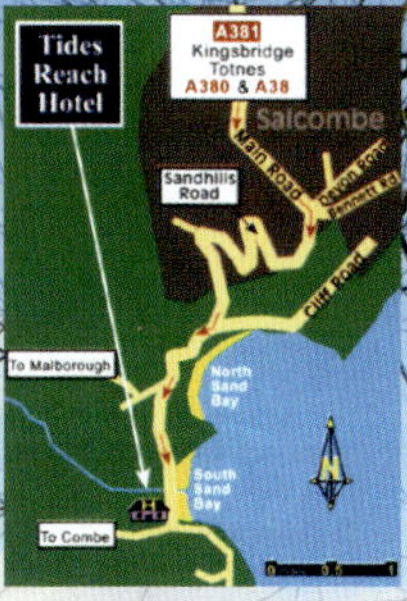

SIGNPOST member hotels make an annual contribution towards the costs of our inspections and a range of members services we provide.

Signpost Guide 2003

How to book a hotel

By phone or fax
You can book your hotel by phoning the number given in the guide or alternatively you could fax a reservation request.

Internet

Reservations and enquiries can be made directly via our INTERNET site on:

www.signpost.co.uk

Watch this site also for special offers from individual hotels throughout the year.

Advantage Card 2003 EDITION

Get up to 10% off your bill at many of the 250 top class hotels in this book. Simply present the card to receive your discount or room upgrade See page 277 for full details and an application form.

Signpost Guide 2003
Our standards

Signpost is the oldest established colour accommodation guide - now in its 64th year of publication!

Signpost Inspector Dan Walker (left) with proprietor Chris Robins at the Hotel Petit Champ, Sark.

Carrying on the work of the original founders, our inspectors check hotels every year personally, trying to stay or eat at each one to make sure that the highest standards are maintained and that the Signpost criteria continue to be met: **individual style, good value, friendly service and a personal welcome** .

We are looking for fine cuisine, using the best fresh produce. Bedrooms should be furnished with style and have all the comforts you need away from home. The hotel should be located in an interesting area, with plenty of opportunity for sport and leisure.

Signpost Inspector Olof White (left) with General Manager John Edwards at Tides Reach Hotel, South Sands, near Salcombe.

Above all hotels should be welcoming, places you want to return to again and again.

The Signpost sign. Your guarantee of a top quality hotel

Signpost Guide 2003

West Country

Fact File
Illustrated Guide to
Historic Houses, Gardens & Sites
Diary of Events

Hotels in	PAGE
Cornwall	**8**
Devon	**13**
Somerset	**22**

2 The West Country

Historic Houses, Gardens & Parks

Bath & North-East Somerset
Clevedon Court, Clevedon
Sally Lunn's House

Cornwall
Cotehele House, St Dominic Saltash
The Eden Project, St Austell
Glendurgan Garden, Mawnan Smith
Kit Hill Country Park, Callington
Lanhydrock House, Bodmin
Mount Edgcumbe House & Park, Torpoint
Trebah Garden, Mawnan Smith
Trelissick Garden, Truro
Trengwainton Garden, Penzance
Trerice, Newquay

Devon
Arlington Court, Barnstaple
Bicton Park & Gardens, E Budleigh
Overbecks Museum & Garden, Salcombe
Rosemoor RHS Garden, Gt Torrington
Saltram House, Plympton
Ugbrooke House & Park, Newton Abbot

Somerset
Barrington Court Gardens, Ilminster
Clapton Court Gardens
Fyne Court, Broomfield, Bridgwater
Hestercombe Gardens, Fitzpaine, Taunton
Lytes Cary Manor, Charlton Mackrell, Somerton
Montacute House
Tintinhull House Garden, Nr Yeovil

Walks & Nature Trails

Bath & Northeast Somerset
Cotswold Way (starts at Bath)
West Mendip Way (starts at Uphill)

Cornwall
The Camel Trail from Padstow to Poley's Bridge
The North Cornwall Heritage Coast

Devon
Dartmoor National Park Guided Walks
The Tarka Trail

Somerset
Exmoor National Park Country Walks
West Somerset Mineral Railway, from Watchet to Washford

Historical Sites & Museums

Bath & North-East Somerset
American Museum, Claverdon, Bath
Museum of Costumes, Bath
Pump Room, Bath
Roman Baths Museum, Bath

Bristol
Bristol City Museum & Art Gallery
Harveys Wine Museum, Bristol

Cornwall
Launceston Castle
Restormel Castle, Lothwithiel
St. Catherine's Castle, Fowey
St. Mawes Castle
St. Michael's Mount, Marazion
Tintagel Castle

Devon
Buckfast Abbey, Buckfastleigh
Buckland Abbey, Yelverton
Castle Drogo, Drewsteignton, Exeter
Compton Castle, Marldon, Paignton
Dartmouth Castle
Okehampton Castle
Powderham Castle, Kenton, Nr. Exeter
Royal Albert Memorial Museum, Exeter

Watermouth Castle, Berrynarbor, llfracombe

Somerset
Cleeve Abbey, Washford, Watchet
Dunster Castle
Glastonbury Abbey
Nunney Castle
Taunton Cider Mill
Wells Cathedral

Entertainment Venues

Bristol
Bristol Zoological Gardens

Cornwall
Cornish Seal Sanctuary, Gweek, Helston
Flambards Victoria Village Theme Park, Helston
Land's End, Penzance
Newquay Zoo
Paradise Park, Hayle
World in Miniature, Truro

Devon
City Museum & Art Gallery, Plymouth
Combe Martin Wildlife & Dinosaur Park
Dartmoor Wild Life Park & West Country Falconry Centre, Sparkwell, Plymouth
Kents Cavern Showcaves, Torquay
Paignton & Dartmouth Steam Railway, Paignton
Paignton Zoological & Botanical Gardens
Plymouth Dome, Plymouth
Riviera Centre, Torquay
Torquay Museum

Somerset
Cheddar Showcaves, Cheddar Gorge
Haynes Motor Museum Sparkford, Yeovil
The Tropical Bird Gardens, Rode
West Somerset Railway, Minehead
Wookey Hole Caves & Papermill

Right: Powderham Castle, Kenton, Nr. Exeter
Middle column. Top: American Museum, Bath
Middle: Tintagel, Cornwall

The West Country

DIARY OF EVENTS

January

1. **National Hunt Horse Racing**, Exeter Racecourse, Kennford, Exeter.
10-12. **Outdoor Leisure Show.** Shepton Mallet. Somerset.

February

1-2. **24th Bristol Classic Car Show.** Royal Bath & West Showground, Shepton Mallet.
8. **Devon County Antiques Fair.** The Matford Centre, Marsh Barton, Exeter.
7-9. **Bournemouth Int'l Holiday Show.** Bournemouth ExC
10. **St Ives Feast & Hurling of the Silver Ball.** Trad annual event, St Ives, Cornwall.
14-16. **Bournemouth Wedding Exhibition.** Bournemouth ExC Drewsteignton, Exeter.

March

1-9. **Bath International Literature Festival.** Various venues, Bath, Somerset.
2*. **Great Days Out Fair.** Assembly Rooms, Bath.
8-22. **Mid-Somerset Competitive Festival Concerts**, Bath.
6. **N H Racing** at Wincanton.
15-30*. May. **Cornwall's Festival of Spring Gardens.** Var Venues thr't Cornwall.
29. **Spring Show** of Asburton & District Garden Assoc'n.
25-25.8. **Bude Horticultural Show.** Bude, Cornwall.
31-31.7. **St Endellion Music Festival**, Port Isaac, Cornwall.

April

1. **N H Racing.** Taunton, Som.
15. **N H Racing.** Exeter, Devon
20-21. **Easter Egg Safari.** Paignton Zoo, Devon.
24-27.**Knit & Stitch Creative Crafts Show**, Shepton Mallet
27. **Trevithick Day.** Camborne, Cornwall.

May

3-5*. **Bath** Annual Spring Flower Show.
6,19.30. **Flat Racing.** Bath
15-17. **Devon County Show.** Clyst St Mary, Devon.
16 May-June 1. **Bath International Music Festival.** Var. venues in & around Bath,Som't
16-Sept 10*.**The Minack Drama Festival.**The Minack, Porthcurno, Penzance, Cornwall
20. **Concert. Endellion Quartet.** Taunton, Somerset.
29-31. **Royal Bath & West Show.** Shepton Mallet Show'd
29. **Ecumenical Rally & Service.** Busveal, Cornwall.

June

1-31.7*. **Exeter Festival.** Various venues, Exeter.
3,9,13,21.28. **Racing** at Newton Abbot, Devon.
4,14,25. **Racing** at Bath.
5-7. **Royal Cornwall Show.** Wadebridge, Cornwall.
7-8. **Ivybridge Vintage Rally.** Smithaleigh, Devon.
12***Liskeard Show.** The Showground, Liskeard, Cornwall
14-15. **Murdoch Weekend.** Redruth, Cornwall.
14, 25. **Racing at Bath.**
14-22. **South Brent Carnival** South Brent, Devon.
20-29. **Golowan Festival.** inc. Mazey Day, Penzance, Corn'll
29. **Longleat Amateur Radio Rally.** Longleat, Somerset.

July

12. **Glastonbury Pilgrimage.** Glastonbury, Somerset
14. **Stithians Show.** The Showground, Truro.
14,27,30. **NH Racing** at Newton Abbot, Devon.
19. **Pilton Green Man Festival.** Barnstaple, Devon.
22-27. **Chulmleigh Old Fair.** Chulmleigh, Devon.
20-27*. **Dartmouth Town Week.** Dartmouth, Devon.
20-27* **SWEB Bristol Harbour Festival.** City Centre, Bristol.
27-2.8*. **Sailing.** Dinghy Regatta. Salcombe Yacht Club, Salcombe, Devon.
26-27. **South Devon Fuchsia & Pelagonium Society Annual Show.** Torquay, Devon.
27-3.8. **Stoke Gabriel Carnival Week.** Totnes, Devon.

August

1*. **RAF St Mawgan Intl Air Day.** St Mawgan, Newquay.
1-8. **Sidmouth Int'l Festival.** Sidmouth, Devon.
4, 12, 25. **NH Racing** at Newton Abbot, Devon.
5, 17 & 22. **Racing** at Bath.
7. **Honiton Agricultural Show** Honiton, Devon.
9-10. **Yeovil Festival of Transport.** Yoevil, Somerset.
10-16. **Falmouth Regatta Week.** Helford River, Carrick Rds & Falmouth Bay, Cornwall.
16. **Summer Show.** Ashburton & Dist Garden Assoc, Devon.
16-25. **The Moorland Exhibition.** Princetown, Devon.
23-27. **Torbay Royal Regatta.** Torquay, Devon.
28-30.**Port of Dartmouth Royal Regatta.** Dartmouth, Devon.
23-30*. **Bude Jazz Festival.** Various venues, Bude, Cnwll.
23-26*. **Wadebridge Folk Festival.** Town Hall, Cornwall.

The West Country

September

5-20. **Exmouth Art Group 57th Annual Summer Exhibition.** Exmouth, Devon.
8,15,29. **Racing** at Bath.
10*. **Widecombe Fair.** Old Field, Widecombe-in-the-Moor, Devon
17-20***Barnstaple Ancient Char-tered Fair.** Barnstaple, Devon.
27. **South Molton Carnival.** South Molton, Devon.

October

5. **West of England Transport Collection Annual Open Day.** Winkleigh, Devon.
8. **NH Racing** at Exeter.
8. **Tavistock Goose Fair.**
9 & 26. **Racing** at Wincanton.
18. **Wincanton Carnival.** Wincanton, Somerset.
19. **Trafalgar Day Service.** Exeter, Devon.

November

4 & 21. **Racing** at Exeter.
5. **Cruise: Bonfire Night.** Exmouth, Devon.
5 & 18. **Racing** at Newton Abt
5. **Old Custom: Rolling of the Tar Barrels.** Ottery St Mary, Devon.
7-17. **Bridgwater, North Petherton, Highbridge & Burnham-on-Sea, Glastonbury Guy Fawkes Festivals.**

December

1. **Cruise: Santa Special.** Exmouth, Devon.
5 & 18. **National Hunt Racing** at Kennford, Exeter, Devon.
6. **Sidmouth Christmas Carnival.** Sidmouth, Devon
16-17*.**Carols /Christmas Music Concert.** Bristol Cathedral.
20*. **Music for Christmas.** Pump Room, Bath.
* *denotes provisional dates.*

For further information contact:

TOURIST BOARD

South West Country Tourism
Woodward Park, Exeter,
Devon EX2 4WT
Tel: 0870 442080/01392 360050
Web:www.westcountrynow.com

England's West Country

The counties of Cornwall, Devon, Somerset, Dorset and Wiltshire comprise England's West Country. Adminstratively the **Scilly Islands** fall under Cornwall's jurisdiction. These are Britain's most south-westerly islands, stretching out into the Atlantic Ocean. Their climate is traditionally subtropical and this enables plants to grow, for example on Tresco, one of the smaller islands, which are not found anywhere else in Europe.
The popularity of the region owes much to its geography and landscape. The coastline alone offers great variety and choice for the holiday maker. Around the coast you can also seek out the little ports and villages where visitors rub shoulders with the fishermen. If imposing scenery and bracing cliff walks are for you, then make for North **Cornwall**. The north coast is famous for its surfing beaches, whereas the south coast has the picturesque tree-lined Helford River and its subsidiary Gillan Creek. There is the historic county town of Bodmin, the cathedral city of Truro and Launceston, once the ancient capital of Cornwall. Plymouth, the largest city in **Devon**, is a happy blend of holiday resort, tourist centre, historic and modern city. The famous Hoe has its associations with Sir Francis Drake and the Barbican with the Pilgrim Fathers. Exeter is the cultural capital of the county with its university, theatre,

Tresco Abbey Gardens, Isles of Scilly

The West Country

medieval cathedral and Maritime Museum. 19th-century dramatist Richard Ford wrote: "This Exeter is quite a capital, abounding in all that London has, except its fog and smoke".

Inland are the two magnificent National Parks of Dartmoor and Exmoor. Dartmoor lies in the south of Devon, 365 square miles of great natural beauty and rugged grandeur where you can sense the history and legend and discover peace and quiet. From the sparkling streams of the outskirts to the starker granite tors of the *high moor*, new pleasures unfold. The wild heather moorland and deep, wooded valleys are the home of red deer and of the legendary Doones of R D Blackmore's novel. Exmoor, in the north of Devon is famous for its ponies. It is a place for relaxation, for walking perhaps, or resting in one of the sleepy villages.

The West Country also suits those who look for activity on their holiday. Fishing, for example - whether sea, game or coarse, is available in the five counties. The varied coastline is ideal for all watersports, with much opportunity for surfing, windsurfing, sailing and diving. Golf, with over 80 courses on breezy cliffs, amid the dunes, in parkland or on the moor, the West Country is a paradise for the golfer. The walker can choose to follow part of the Southwest Peninsula Coast Path, 515 miles of the finest coastal scenery, or try a long distance path like the Ridgeway in Wiltshire or the West Mendip Way, from Weston-super-Mare along the Mendips down to Wells in Somerset. Details of shorter nature trails and walks around historic cities are available from Tourist Information Centres.

Bristol, the largest city in the West Country, is steeped in history. You can stroll down cobbled King Street, famous for its Theatre Royal, Almshouses and Llandoger Trow. The city docks are of great interest, providing a home for the SS Great Britain, Brunel's famous iron ship, the Industrial Museum and The Watershed shopping area.

A few miles up the river Avon is Britain's oldest and most famous spa, the City of Bath. Bath's 2000-year old fame started with its popularity as a resort for the Romans, who discovered its hot springs, still operative today. A second great era dawned in the 18th century Regency period, characterised by the Assembly Rooms, Royal Crescent, Circus, Lansdowne

Crescent and other notable architecture. Tea in the Regency *Pump Room*, with a string quartet playing, should not be missed.

The county town of **Dorset** is Dorchester, founded by the Romans and later to become the fictional "Casterbridge" of Thomas Hardy's novels. Judge Jeffreys lodged in High West Street during his Bloody Assize. There are fine walks around Chesil Beach and on the Studland peninsula, part of the 7000-acre Corfe Castle estate. Bournemouth, with a population of 160,000 is the largest town in Dorset, representing a quarter of the county's population, is famous for its multitude of hotels and guesthouses, its theatre and concert hall with one of the few permanent non-Metropolitan orchestras of Britain in residence, its exhibition centre, its English Language Schools and for some reason often the highest priced fruit and vegetables in National comparative surveys!

6 *The West Country*

In **Somerset**, visit the city of Wells, dominated by the great cathedral, with its magnificent west front. And do not miss Vicar's Close, one of the oldest medieval streets in Europe, and the moated Bishop's Palace. On the West coast of he county are the resorts of Weston-super-Mare and Minehead. Cheddar Gorge and the Wookey Hole caves in the Mendip Hills should not be missed. Glastonbury Tor, another Druidic site and now home to an annual popular music festival, is also striking.

Also dominated by its cathedral with its 404 ft spire, is Salisbury in **Wiltshire,** and around it, set back from the close, are many fine historic buildings. 20 miles north of the city is Stonehenge, one of the most visited Druidic sites of Britain, dating back 3000 years. Amesbury, with its Roman burial mound and seemingly random stones, dates form the same period.

Every county in the West Country has its share of stately homes and gardens (see *Historic Houses, Gardens and Parks* on page 4). With a coastline of 650 miles, the West Country is to this day strongly influenced by the sea.

England is a nation of garden lovers and the mild climate, which makes the West Country so popular with tourists, offers a long growing season. Some gardens, like Abbotsbury and Tresco (in the Scillies) specialise in subtropical plants. Spring is the best time for visiting the gardens of the Southwest. Few sights can compare with the flowering of the rhododendrons and azaleas across the lake at Stourhead. At gardens like Killerton, with its hardwood trees, the warm tones of Autumn create another riot of colour to reward the late visitor.

Newly opened in 2001 in a former tin mine near St Austell in Cornwall was the Eden Project. This consists of three *Biomes* (huge domes) which reproduce the conditions respectively of a Humid Tropic Zone, A Temperate Zone and a Warm Mediterranean Zone. As well as the plants, there are lectures, sculpture, performance art and restaurants in the complex.

Photographs reproduced by kind permission of the West Country Tourist Board. This page, top to bottom: Roman Baths at Bath, Wells, The eden Project, Westbury White Horse. Previous page Bowermans Nose, Hells Mouth, Clifton Suspension Bridge, Bristol.

Henry Matthews
Explorer

When I was 5, it was holidays with my parents

At 11, holidays with the school

At 21, holidays with the lads

At 35, holidays with my kids

Now I'm going somewhere on my own

LONG LIVE DREAMS™

Whatever the situation, medical, legal or financial, American Express Cards come with a helpline number that you can call in an emergency. Good to know when you're out there alone. For peace of mind before you go, go to www.americanexpress.co.uk

CARDS   INSURANCE SERVICES   FINANCIAL SERVICES   TRAVEL SERVICES   TRAVELLERS CHEQUES

Meudon Hotel

Mawnan Smith, Falmouth,
Cornwall TR11 5HT
Tel: (01326) 250541; Fax: (01326) 250543
E-mail: wecare@meudon.co.uk
Website: www.meudon.co.uk

Nestling on the south Cornish coast in thickly wooded countryside between the famous 'Packet' harbour of Falmouth and the romantic Helford estuary, Meudon is a unique family run luxury hotel set in a timeless sub-tropical valley leading to its own private sea beach at Bream Cove. Originally a country mansion built at the turn of the century, it then incorporated two 17th-century former coastguards' cottages and now has a large modern bedroom wing. Public rooms furnished with antiques, fine paintings and fresh flowers and all bedrooms overlook the fantastic gardens. The award winning restaurant, under the supervision of chef Alan Webb, specialises in local seafood, lobster, crab and oysters which are delivered daily by local fishermen. By car it is possible to reach Cornwall's many resorts, castles and gardens, including the Eden Project. Golf on six local courses is free to residents and riding, sailing and Cornwall's coastal path and many attractions are on the doorstep. Mr & Mrs Harry Pilgrim developed the hotel and their son Mark now manages it, representing the third generation - truly a Pilgrim's Progress of fine Cornish hotel-keeping.

Rates: Room, breakfast & dinner from £80 single, £160 double/twin. Cottage (sleeps 4/5) from £475.
Leisure breaks. Winter Warmers Nov-end Feb, three nights, dinner, b & b for two, sharing, £300. Xmas/New Year Breaks - on application

● 29 en suite bedrooms, all with direct dial telephone, colour TV, hairdryer, laundry/valet service, tea/coffee making, fax/modem points, trouser press. ♿ rooms available.
● 5-cse tdh dinner £27.50. Alc, lunch & diets available. last orders 9.00 p.m.
● Snooker, fishing, golf, sea bathing, hotel's own yacht available for skipper's charter. Tennis, riding, shooting nearby.
● Open 1st February-2nd January.
● Hair salon.
🅿 50; car rental, taxi service.
AMERICAN EXPRESS & Visa, Diners Mastercard acc'd

Falmouth 5,
Helston 8,
Redruth 12,
Truro 13,
Land's End 40,
London 259.

Cornwall, Lizard Peninsula

Polurrian Hotel

Mullion, Lizard Peninsula, Cornwall
TR12 7EN
Tel: (01326) 240421; Fax: (01326) 240083
E-mail: Polurotel@aol.com
Website: www.Polurrianhotel.com

Three hundred feet above Polurrian Cove and surrounded by wonderful National Trust coastline, the Polurrian Hotel enjoys an enviable position overlooking some of Cornwall's loveliest scenery. Steps lead down from the hotel to the sandy beach where bathing is safe and clean, or there is an alternative of indoor swimming or outdoor heated swimming pools. The hotel's leisure club includes a hairdressing and beauty salon, sauna and solarium, a gym for the more energetic, a tennis court and light snacks can be enjoyed in the Aqua Bar. An inviting 18-hole golf course is nearby. Small children can enjoy a safe play area within the hotel's gardens, an indoor activity room, and, during my visit, a conjuror! The attractive restaurant romantically overlooks the sea. The dishes are expertly cooked and presented and seafood is a speciality. Early rising guests can help with the catch! The bedrooms are luxurious, some having four-posters. The Polurrian Hotel also has its own self-catering apartments and bungalows. A great place for a family holiday.

Rates: Dinner, room & breakfast from £55 + VAT
Leisure Breaks: For a special occasion or a break from the stress of life, our Feature Breaks and Leisure Breaks in this unspoiled part of Cornwall will provide you with a memory to treasure. 3-day breaks - dinner, bed & breakfast from £120 per person

● 39 en suite bedrooms (8 ground floor), all with direct dial telephone and TV, room service, baby listening, night service.
● Last dinner orders 9.00 pm; diets catered for.
● Children welcome; dogs accepted, conferences to 100
● Games room, snooker/billiards, outdoor & indoor heated swimming pools, leisure centre, sauna, solarium, spa pool, gymnasium, squash, tennis, sea bathing 200 yards, golf ½ mile, shooting/fishing ½ mile, sailing & boating 5 miles.
● & all major credit cards accepted.
● Open all year;
The Lizard 4½, Helston 4, Penzance 22, Truro 26, London 323

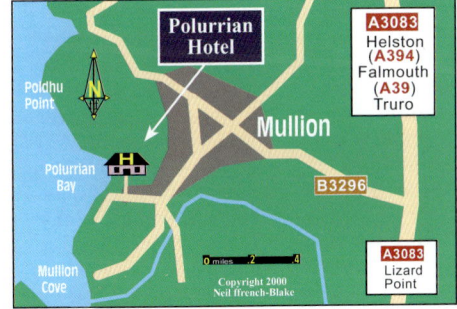

Cornwall, Looe

Hannafore Point Hotel

Marine Drive, West Looe, Cornwall
PL13 2DG
Tel: (01503) 263273; Fax: (01503) 263272
E-mail: hannafore@aol.com
Website: www.hannaforepointhotel.com

Marine and Hotel Leisure, a small family owned West Country Hotel Group who also own the Berry Head (page 22) and The Polurrian (page 10) hotels, took over this spectacularly situated hotel in 1999. With panoramic views of sea, cliffs and St George's Island, the hotel is conveniently placed for sandy beaches, the town of Looe, and, naturally, the facilities for deep sea fishing for which the area is famous. Should the weather not be conducive for indulging these activities, the hotel has comfortable public rooms in which to relax, a complete leisure centre with indoor heated swimming pool, a restaurant offering à la carte and table d'hôte menus and two bars. The public rooms can accommodate 100 for a conference or 160 for a wedding or private function. Hannafore Point is an excellent venue for a family holiday. Golf can be booked at discounted rates at St Enodoc, Lanhydrock and Looe courses. Hannafore is on the southwest coastal path and there are several gardens nearby including the Lost Gardens of Heligan, the Eden Project and Cotehele. In addition the famous Looe to Polperro walk starts just outside the hotel.

Rates: Room with breakfast from £40 per person; room, breakfast and dinner from £50 per person.
Leisure breaks: Two nights, dinner, bed & breakfast from £75

● 37 en suite bedrooms, all with colour TV, hairdryer, trouser press, tea/coffee making.
● Headland restaurant with table d'hôte and à la carte menus; last orders 9pm. Lunch & special diets available. Raffles Lounge Bar and Island Bar.
● Heated indoor swimming pool, sauna, steam room, spa pool, squash court, gymnasium, indoor games. Massage & hydrotherapy by appt. Golf, diving, fishing, watersports & sailing nearby.
● Conferences to 100; receptions to 160.
● Open all year
● & all major credit cards accepted.

Liskeard 9,
Plymouth 19,
Bodmin 16,
Fowey 18,
St Austell 23,
London 228.

Cornwall, Penzance

Queens Hotel

The Promenade, Penzance, Cornwall
TR18 4HG
Tel: (01736) 362371; Fax: (01736) 350033
E-mail: enquiries@queens-hotel.com
Website: www.queens-hotel.com
Discover Britain Hotel of the Year 2000-2002

The Queens Hotel enjoys pride of place on the sea front promenade of Penzance, with majestic views sweeping across Mount's Bay from Mousehole Point to the Lizard peninsular and St Michael's Mount. A warm welcome awaits you at the Queens, which combines Victorian elegance with modern comforts, gracious and comfortable rooms, excellent cuisine and attentive service. The Sun Lounge serves Cornish cream teas or pre-dinner drinks. The restaurant serves the best local produce - fresh vegetables, locally caught fish and lobster and crab landed at Newlyn and St Ives. The area around Penzance is steeped in history, with ancient monuments, Stone Age villages, rugged moorlands and spectacular seascapes. Nearby are sub-tropical gardens and famous beaches like Porthcurno where the famous Minack open air theatre is situated. Well known National Trust properties are located in West Cornwall, including St Michael's Mount and the magnificent coastal footpaths.

Rates: Single room with breakfast from £55; double room from £110. Seaview supp't + £8 per pers p nt.
Leisure breaks: Autumn/Winter Break £50 dinner, b & b per person per night; Summer Break £60 pppnight. Min. two nights.

- 70 en suite bedrooms, all with colour TV+sat, ddtel, hairdryer, laundry/valet service, 24-hr room service, tea/coffee making, radio/alarm clock, fax/modem points. ✁ rooms available.
- Tdh dinner £16.95; lunch & diets available; last orders 2045.
- Sea bathing, fishing, watersports, sailing, squash, indoor pool nearby. Open all year. ₪ 50.
- 4 conference rooms/function rooms - capacity 150
- & all major credit cards accepted.

St Ives 8, Land's End 10, Helston 13, Redruth 17, Truro 25, Eden Project 35, London 281.

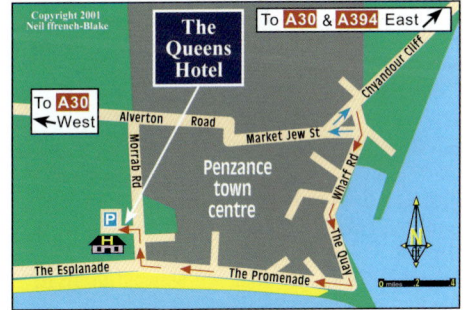

The Garrack Hotel & Restaurant

Burthallan Lane, St. Ives, Cornwall
TR26 3AA
Tel: 01736 796199; Fax 01736 798955
E-mail: garrack@accuk.co.uk
Website: www.garrack.com

The discerning traveller seeking a classic small country house hotel could hardly do better than to stay in the family-run Garrack with its spectacular views over the old town of St. Ives and the sea. It has two acres of gardens, is near a coastal footpath and its excellent leisure centre caters for most eventualities. The personal touch and friendliness of the Garrack is reflected in the main lounge with its log fire in winter, books, magazines and board games. In addition there is a small TV lounge and a bar lounge. Whilst the bedrooms in this the main house are traditional as befits the building, an extension houses additional rooms of more modern design and equally comfortable. Some rooms have four posters, others whirlpool baths. There are family rooms and a room for the disabled. The hotel restaurant is justifiably renowned for its seafood with lobsters fresh from the hotel's storage tank, as fresh as is the other locally produced food with many of the vegetables coming from the garden. It would take several weeks to work through the wine list. The Garrack is a rarity - one of those places which it was a delight in itself to visit - and so hard to leave.

Single room including breakfast from £65.50.
Double room with breakfast from £131.
Leisure breaks available November to end March

● 18 en suite bedrooms with TV, direct-dial telephone, hairdryer on request. Morning tea service. One room for disabled. Baby monitoring.
● AA 2 rosetted restaurant. Last dinner orders 21.00.
● Conferences for up to 25 guests.
● Indoor swimming pool, sauna, solarium and fitness area. Access to fishing, riding, shooting (clay), golf, water sports, squash and tennis.
● Airport pick-up and car rental by arrangement. Car parking for 30 cars.
● & all major credit cards accepted.
● Open all year.

Penzance 10, Redruth 14, Truro 25, London 319.

Devon, Ashwater

THE WEST COUNTRY

Blagdon Manor Hotel & Restaurant

Ashwater, Beaworthy, Devon EX21 5DF
Tel: 01409 211224; Fax: 01409 211634

E-mail: stay@blagdon.com
Website: www.blagdon.com

Blagdon Manor was mentioned in the Domesday Book of 1086 but the present establishment dates back to the 17th century. It is a beautiful Grade II listed building surrounded by rolling Devonshire countryside and with uninterrupted views of Dartmoor's rugged spaces. Today the hotel retains the warmth and atmosphere of the manorial home it used to be. Heavy oak beams and worn slate flagstones combine with hand-stitched soft furnishings, the scent of summer flowers and, in winter, the hint of wood smoke to create a beguiling and tranquil charm. Steve and Liz Morey welcome guests to share their home. Steve runs the kitchen, using all the very best of locally sourced products with some fruit, vegetables and herbs being grown in his own kitchen garden and orchard. Liz runs the front of house with the emphasis on high quality and attentive service. There are 20 acres of grounds in which to stroll before heading off to visit the many stately homes and gardens nearby and explore the wider pleasures of the West Country. Blagdon Manor is one of those hidden gems, ideal for a getaway break.

Double room including breakfast from £90. Single occupancy £72.

● 7 en suite bedrooms (five double, two twin) with colour TV, direct-dial telephone, hairdryer, tea/coffee making, radio/alarm clock.
● Tdh dinner £25 Tues-Sat (7 days per week for residents); lunch available Wed-Sun. Spec. diets available. Last dinner orders 9 pm.
● Meeting room for eight. Parking for ten cars.
● Children over 12 and dogs welcome.
● Croquet lawn, garden. Fishing, golf, sailing and riding within 10 miles.
● Closed two weeks in January and two weeks in November.
● Visa, Mastercard, Switch, Solo accepted.

**Holsworthy 5,
Launceston 8,
Bideford 25,
Exeter 43,
London 218.**

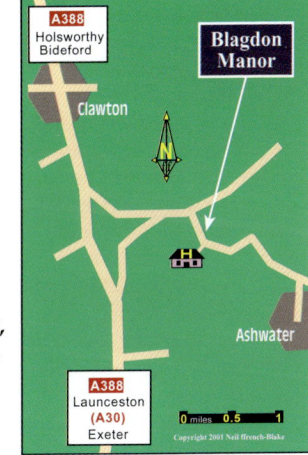

Devon, Brixham

The Berry Head Hotel

Berry Head Road, Brixham,
Devon TQ5 9AJ
Tel: (01803) 853225; Fax: (01803) 882084
E-mail: Berryhd@aol.com
Website: www.berryheadhotel.com

The Berry Head Hotel is set in a superb water's edge position in six acres of its own gardens and woodland, in the seclusion of the Berry Head Country Park, which is noted for its bird life and rare wild flowers. The hotel is steeped in history. It was built as a military hospital in the Napoleonic Wars, and was later the home of the Reverend Francis Lyte, who wrote the famous hymn *Abide with Me* at the hotel, no doubt inspired by the glorious sunsets. The historic fishing port of Brixham, where William of Orange first landed on English soil, is only a short walk away. The hotel offers relaxing accommodation and all the en suite bedrooms have colour television, radio and tea and coffee making facilities. The comfortable lounge and the restaurant, which overlook the terrace, enjoy spectacular views of Torbay and the Devon coast. The emphasis here is upon good food, wine and company in a very special setting. Set in national parkland at the water's edge, with miles of coastal walks, fishing, birdwatching and sailing, yet close to the major resort of Torquay, this is an ideal hideaway for a short break.

Room and breakfast from £40.00, and dinner, room and breakfast from £50.00 including VAT. Leisure breaks: Two nights, dinner, bed and breakfast from £75.00

- 32 en suite bedrooms all with direct dial telephone, TV; hairdryer; tea/coffee facilities; room service; baby listening; night service.
- Last orders for dinner 9.30p.m; bar meals until 9.30p.m; special diets; children welcome.
- Dogs accepted; conferences 100 max.
- Boules; sea bathing 30 yds; indoor heated swimming pool; outdoor seawater pool 200 yds; squash courts 1/2 mile; sailing and boating, shooting and fishing 1/4 mile; tennis one mile; golf and riding two miles.
- Visa and Mastercard accepted.
- Open all year.

Torquay 8, Exeter 30, Plymouth 32, Bristol 100, Birmingham 200, London 230.

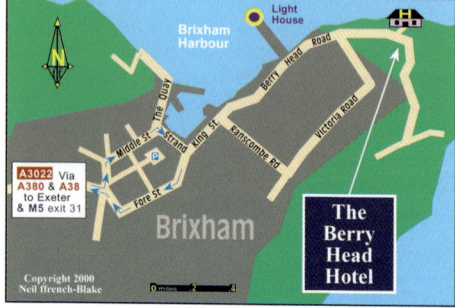

Devon, Exmouth   15

THE WEST COUNTRY

The Royal Beacon Hotel

The Beacon, Exmouth, Devon EX8 2AF
Tel: (01395) 264886; Fax: (01395) 268890
E-mail: reception@royalbeaconhotel.co.uk
Website: www.royalbeaconhotel.co.uk

The Royal Beacon has long been established as a premier hotel. An elegant building, it was originally a Georgian posting house and both Lady Nelson and Lady Byron used to live in the same terrace. The early traditions of hospitality, good fare and comfort have continued throughout the years, adapting to meet the expectations of today's discerning guests. The hotel has recently changed hands but has only had four proprietors in its 260-year existence. It has wonderful views over its own well tended gardens and along the Devon coastline to Lyme Bay and the red cliffs of Orcombe Point. Most of the refurbished bedrooms have a sea view. The restaurant overlooks the sea and offers both à la carte and table d'hôte menus, attractively presented. Traditional Devon cream teas are served in the afternoon and packed lunches can be arranged. Exmouth, with its good road, rail and air links, is an ideal centre for exploring this fascinating part of South Devon. It is rich in natural and man-made beauty, from the flocks of seabirds inhabiting the estuary to the beautiful flower and tree displays at nearby Bicton Gardens and the fascination of Exeter Maritime Museum and Exeter Cathedral.

Rates: *Single room with breakfast from £45. (Dinner, b & b fm £62). Double room inc. b'fst from £85. (Dinner, b & b from £120.)*
Leisure breaks *available in the winter. Please write for details. Special Activity Breaks available all year round.*

● 30 en suite bedrooms, all with direct-dial telephone, colour TV, radio, tea/coffee making, hairdryer, trouser press, room service. ✄ rms available.
● Tdh dinner £19; Last orders for dinner 9 pm; lunch available. ● Ballroom, capacity up to 150.
● Children welcome; dogs accepted.
● Gym, jacuzzi, watersports, riding, sailing, squash, swimming pools, tennis $^1/_2$ mile; croquet, fishing within 4 miles. ● Open all year.
● Mastercard, Visa, Switch, Diners, Delta cards accepted.

Airport 10, Exeter 11, Honiton 17, Axminster 26, Lyme Regis 27, London 170.

Devon, Hope Cove

The Cottage Hotel

Hope Cove, Kingsbridge, South Devon
TQ7 3 HJ
Tel: (01548) 561555; Fax: (01548) 561455
E-mail: info@hopecove.com
Website: www.hopecove.com

The Cottage Hotel enjoys a superb position, overlooking the picturesque harbour and cove, with spectacular sea views and sunsets. The gardens descend to the beach, where you can bathe in safety. The hotel is delightful and has 35 beautifully furnished bedrooms, with 25 of them having private bathrooms /showers. I always enjoy visiting The Cottage; it has a happy and relaxing atmosphere thanks to the owners, John and Janet, Sarah and William Ireland, who personally care for this pleasant and comfortable haven. The enticing dining room, which has lovely views of the cove and coast, offers table d'hôte and à la carte menus. I chose the former, which was excellent, cooked with great interest and attention, served by cheerful, efficient and courteous staff of many years' standing. The meal was supported by a selective wine list. This hotel still remains one of the best family hotels I visit, well illustrated by the preponderance of sun-tanned, well-fed families.

Rates: Dinner, room and breakfast £50-75.
Leisure breaks are available from 1st November to April inclusive. 2-night stay £31.00-£47.50; 7-night stay from £32.00-£46.50 according to room. Prices are per person per night and include accommodation, 6-course dinner plus coffee, full English breakfast, service and VAT.

● 25 en suite bedrooms (7 ground floor), all with direct-dial telephone and colour TV, room service, baby listening. 10 other bedrooms.
● Last orders for dinner 8.30 pm; bar meals 12-1. 30 pm. ● Conferences, max. 50
● Children welcome; dogs accepted.
● Games room, sea bathing, sailing/boating, riding three miles, golf four miles, tennis & squash six miles.
● Hotel closed 2-30th January. Debit cards acc'd.

Totnes 18, Torquay 21, Plymouth 25, Exeter 36, London

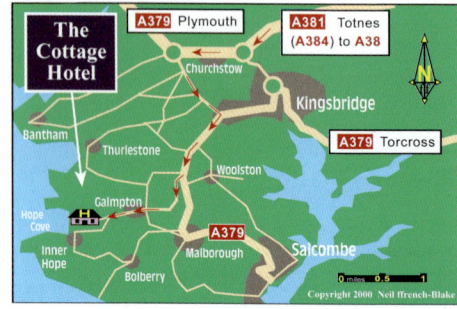

Devon, Nr. Kingsbridge

Thurlestone Hotel

Thurlestone, Nr. Kingsbridge,
South Devon TQ7 3NN
Tel: (01548) 560382; Fax: (01548) 561069
E-mail: enquiries@thurlestone.co.uk
Website: www.thurlestone.co.uk
AA, RAC, ETC ★★★★ ⊙ Food. RAC 2 dining awards.
Voted Best West Country Hotel for *England for Excellence* (ETC)
RAC Merit Awards for hospitality, service and comfort.

This luxurious hotel has been owned and run by the Grose family for over 100 years and during that time they have gained a 72% AA 4-star award - the highest graded hotel in the district. The standard of rooms, especially the beautifully appointed suites, testify to this. The AA have also awarded a rosette for their cooking and Hugh Miller, the chef, is striving for a second one. The food is balanced, well presented and simply delicious and the menu is accompanied by a comprehensive wine list. The staff, many of whom are long serving members, are courteous, discreet and efficient. The hotel caters for everyone in that conferences can be arranged for the business traveller, there are all manner of facilities for the sportsman and there is something for every member of the family, whatever the weather. Even the dog is welcome.
The hotel has its own golf course, which was the venue for the British Professional Shortcourse Championship in 1980 and which brought Edward VIII, when Prince of Wales, to Thurlestone on a number of occasions.

Single room including breakfast £45-90.
Double room including breakfast from £90.
Leisure breaks Dinner, b&b from £60 per person per night Nov-March. Others on application.

● 64 en suite bedrooms (inc 8 suites & 21 deluxe), all with colour TV (+Sky), direct-dial telephone + modem, music/radio/alarm clock, hairdryer, laundry/valet service, tea/coffee making facilities, 24-hr room service, trouser press. ● Open all year.
● Table d'hôte dinner £30; à la carte, lunch & special diets available; last orders 2100 hrs.
● Outdoor & indoor swimming pools; continental terrace; billiards/snooker, croquet, fitness centre, 9-hole golf course, indoor games, jacuzzi, massage/sauna, squash, tennis, children's playrooms. Fishing, watersports, riding, sailing/boating nearby.
● Hairdressing/beauty salon. Conferences to 120.
● Mastercard & Visa accepted

Kingsbridge 4, Plymouth 20, Torquay 21, Exeter 36, London 236.

Devon, Nr Okehampton

Collaven Manor Hotel

Sourton, Okehampton,
Devon EX20 4HH
Tel: (01837) 861522; Fax: (01837) 861614
E-mail: collavenmanor@supanet.com
Website: www.collavenmanor.co.uk

Those readers looking to stay in a small country manor house need look no further. Collaven is a picturebook Devon Manor both externally and internally. Dating from the 15th century, it stands in four acres of picturesque gardens and paddocks. It has been sympathetically restored to cater for discerning guests as it would have done in the days of its earlier owners. Notable amongst these are the Hamilton family (of Nelson fame) and the house positively exudes Devon history. On entering the manor via the Baronial Reception Hall, the visitor is greeted by a feeling of warmth and comfort, enhanced by log fires in winter and cooled by medieval thick walls in summer. The Hamilton Restaurant offers a 4-course dinner, changing daily, with the emphasis on the Best of British cuisine, with Continental and Oriental influences. A vegetarian speciality is always on the menu. Here the atmosphere is serene, the setting tranquil but, for the adventurous, the moors are on the doorstep, to delight the walker, naturalist or outdoor sportsman.

*Single: inc. breakfast from £54; **double** from £84.
Leisure Breaks: Oct 4-mid Dec, Jan to end March, for a two nights+ stay, dinner b & b is at 20% discount.*

● 9 en suite bedrooms (inc one family room & 3 four-posters), all with direct dial telephone, colour TV, hairdryer, laundry/valet service, tea/coffee making facilities, trouser press, music/radio/alarm clock.
● Table d'hôte £22.50; vegetarian dishes a speciality; last orders 20.30.
● Croquet, bowls.
● Meeting room to 28. Car parking for 30.
● Open all year.
● Mastercard, Visa, Delta & Switch accepted.

Okehampton 7, Tavistock 11, Crediton 17, Exeter 22, Plymouth 25, London 192.

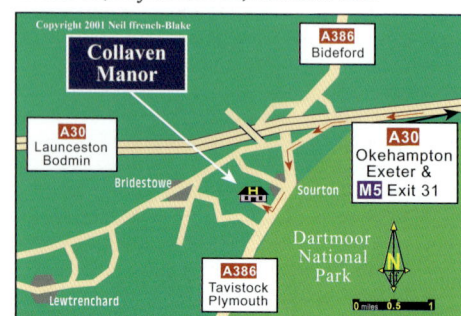

The symbol Ad means the hotel will grant an upgrade or a 10% reduction in the room rate to Signpost Advantage Card holders.

Devon, Nr. Okehampton

THE WEST COUNTRY

Lewtrenchard Manor

Lewdown, Nr. Okehampton,
Devon EX20 4PN
Tel: (01566) 783256; Fax: (01566) 783332
E-mail: s&j@lewtrenchard.co.uk
Website: www.lewtrenchard.co.uk

Our stay at Lewtrenchard was memorable. James and Sue Murray are hands-on hosts and nothing is too much trouble. They know many of their guests personally and are always ready to advise on local attractions. The hotel will even get tickets for the Eden Project. The Manor, whose site is mentioned in the Domesday Book, is a 17th century house situated between Okehampton and Launceston. It overlooks a deeply wooded valley on the edge of Dartmoor. Inside antiques and oil paintings furnish the reception rooms. Panelled ceilings, stained glass windows and ornate plasterwork were installed in the 19th century when hymn writer and novelist Sabine Baring Gould lived at the Manor. Today the house is known for its comfort and seclusion and the restaurant for its award winning cuisine and extensive wine list built up by host James Murray over 13 years. Outside is a beautiful sunken garden and extensive grounds to explore. Riding and golf are available nearby. Trout fishing on the river Lew or clay and rough shooting and hawk walking on the Lewtrenchard Estate can be arranged. An enchanting spot for a break at any time of the year.

Rates: Single with breakfast from £100; double inc breakfast from £130.
Leisure Breaks; Discounts of up to 15% available Nov-March. Please write for details.

● 9 en suite bedrooms, all with direct dial telephone, col TV & radio, modem points, safe, hairdryer, laundry/valet service, 18-hr room service.
● Alc dinner from £35; lunch & diets available. Last orders 9 pm.
● Two meeting rooms, capacity 16 and 50. P 50.
● Croquet, fishing. Golf 6 m, riding 5m, clay shooting by arr't. Helicopter landing pad.
● & major credit cards accepted.
● Open all year.

Launceston 7, Okehampton 10, Tavistock 10, Exeter 25, Plymouth 24, London 195.

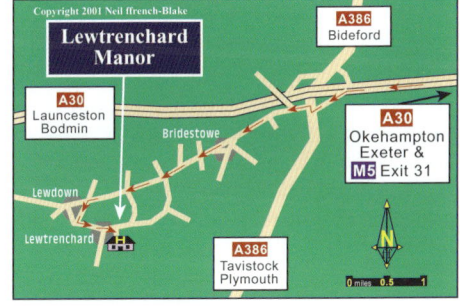

Tides Reach Hotel

South Sands, Salcombe, South Devon
TQ8 8LJ
Tel: (01548) 843466; Fax: (01548) 843954
E-mail: enquire@tidesreach.com
Internet: www.tidesreach.com

The position of Tides Reach is perfect - a beautiful secluded sandy cove. The quiet luxury of the hotel strikes you as you enter the conservatory-style hall with its indoor water garden and the flower garden lounge-hall so full of sunshine and scented blooms. The décor throughout was chosen and supervised by Mrs. Edwards and the colours are wonderfully vibrant and original. The indoor heated swimming pool, around which has been built a bar and coffee shop, is as glamorous as a Hollywood film set - there is an outdoor sun patio and sun deck leading off and a hairdressing and beauty salon, multi gym and exercise suite, sunbed, spa bath, sauna and squash court. In addition to these facilities, the dining room has been extended and the bedrooms and public rooms have been refurnished throughout in a most comfortable and luxurious manner. The food is superb, the daily changing menu being really first class.

Rates: Dinner, room and breakfast from £85.00 to £150.00 per person including VAT according to season and length of stay.
Leisure Breaks available from mid February - end of May (excluding Easter & Bank Holidays) and Oct,Nov,Dec. 2-day breaks £130-£170 for dinner, bed and breakfast. 4-day breaks £240-£400 for dinner, bed and breakfast. Extra days pro rata.

- 35 en suite bedrooms with colour TV, radio, direct dial telephone; some family suites.
- Lift; children over eight welcome; dogs by arrangement; some diets available.
- Games room; snooker room; indoor heated pool; solarium; sauna; spa bath; squash; indoor and outdoor water gardens; drying room; golf, tennis, riding nearby; sea bathing; boating; fishing; windsurfing, water sports from own boathouse.
- Resident proprietor - Roy Edwards FHCI
- AMERICAN EXPRESS & major credit cards accepted.
- Closed Dec-January.

Kingsbridge 7, Totnes 19, Plymouth 26, Exeter 43, London 214

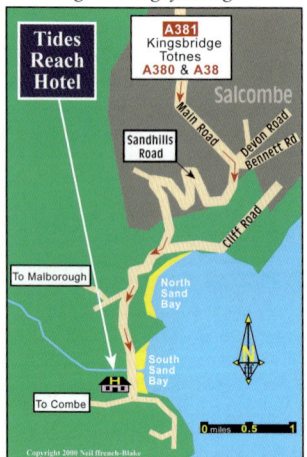

Devon, Woolacombe

THE WEST COUNTRY

Woolacombe Bay Hotel

Woolacombe, Devon EX34 7BN
Tel: (01271) 870388; Fax: (01271) 870613
E-mail: woolacombe.bayhotel@btinternet.com
Website: www.woolacombe-bay-hotel.co.uk

Rugged moors, rocky tors, endless National Trust walks on beach and headland; picturesque villages of "olde worlde" charm are the feel and freedom of Devon. Set amidst six acres of quiet gardens running to three miles of golden sand is the luxurious Woolacombe Bay Hotel, built in the halcyon days of the mid 1800's. It exudes a relaxed air of friendliness, good living, comfort and traditional service. The hotel has been extensively but sensitively modernised, combining discreet old fashioned ambience with modern charm. Dining is simply a delight, the best of English and Continental cooking, using the freshest local produce with special diets catered for. Complementing the menus is an interesting wine list, and you can also enjoy a drink in one of the relaxed bars. Guests have unlimited use of the extensive leisure and sporting amenities (see facilities below), and the hotel's *MV Frolica* boat is available for charter.
A magnificent ballroom and spacious lounges, combined with the outstanding facilities at the Woolacombe Bay Hotel, enables everyone to have the holiday of their choice. Energetic or relaxed - the decision is yours.

Rates: room and breakfast from £50 per person,
Dinner, room and breakfast from £80 per person
including VAT. **Leisure breaks:** *Special seasonal offers available. Please enquire for details. Christmas tariff on application*

● *64 en suite bedrooms, all with telephone and TV, room/night service; baby listening, lift.*
● *Last orders for dinner 9 p.m; bar meals in bistro; special diets; children welcome; conferences max. 200.*
● *Games room; snooker/billiards; short mat bowls; tennis coaching; indoor and outdoor heated swimming pools; the 'Hot House' fitness centre with aerobics studio, fitness room, beautician, masseur, trimtrail; 2 squash courts; 9 hole approach golf course; 2 floodlit all-weather tennis courts; sea bathing (blue flag beach); sailing/boating; own motor yacht; riding, shooting and fishing nearby.*
● *& all credit cards accepted.*
● *Hotel closed Jan.-mid Feb.*

Barnstaple 14, Exeter 56, Taunton 62, Bristol 79, London 203

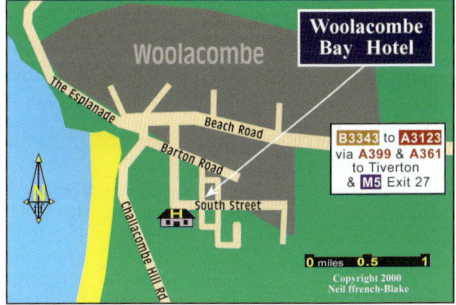

Somerset, Nr. Bath

Hunstrete House

Hunstrete, Chelwood, Nr. Bath BS39 4NS
Tel: (01761) 490490; Fax: (01761) 490732
E-mail: info@hunstretehouse.co.uk
Website: www.hunstretehouse.co.uk

This elegant 18th century country house has been carefully and thoughtfully converted into a very special hotel. The original estate was donated by King Athelstan in AD963 to Glastonbury Abbey. In the early 1600s it passed into the hands of the Popham family, whose home it was for 350 years. Set in classical English countryside on the edge of the Mendip Hills, yet only eight miles from both Bath and Bristol, many rooms have uninterrupted views over undulating fields and woodlands, and deer graze in the park beside the house. Reception rooms are beautifully furnished with antiques, paintings and a profusion of flowers from the lovely gardens. Bedrooms are all individually decorated and furnished to a high standard in the style of an exclusive country house. In 2002 three new ground floor rooms, including a honeymoon suite, were added in a converted garden house. Head chef Phil Hobson and his award-winning 6-man team offer light and interesting dishes in the Terrace dining room, using the best British meat and fish as well as produce from the hotel's own kitchen garden. Haflinger ponies are bred in the grounds. An ideal spot to break the journey from London to the South-West.

Rates: Single inc. breakfast from £135; double/twin from £165; suite from £230.
Leisure Breaks: 2 & 3 night breaks available in off-peak months. Details on application.

- 25 en suite bedrooms (inc 2 family & 5 four-posters), all with colour TV+ satellite, direct dial telephone, hairdryer, laundry service, music/radio/alarm, trouser press.
- Dinner from £35; à la carte from £15.95; special diets available. ✄ ◐◐ restaurant; last orders 9.30 pm.
- Conference room - cap'y 50. Car parking for 50.
- Croquet, tennis, heated outdoor swimming pool.
- Children and pets welcome.
- Open all year.
- & all major credit cards accepted.

Bath 8, Bristol 8, Radstock 8, Yeovil 31, Bridgwater 35, London 120.

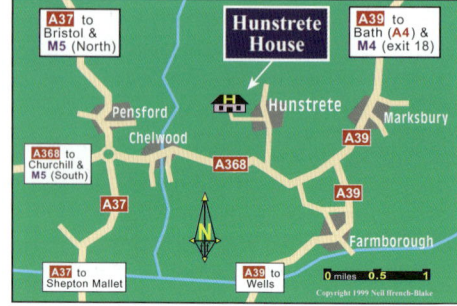

Somerset, Bath

The Windsor Hotel

69 Great Pulteney Street, Bath BA2 4DL
Tel: (01225) 422100; Fax: (01225) 422550
E-mail: sales@bathwindsorhotel.com
Website: www.bathwindsorhotel.com

A Grade I listed building, sympathetically restored into a fine townhouse hotel, entirely in keeping with its location, Gt Pulteney Street, which was built between 1769 and 1794 and is one of the most elegant boulevards in Europe. On arrival at the Windsor, one immediately feels a sense of welcome, the public areas being spacious and bright but retaining a warm, homely feeling. A unique feature of the hotel and unique to Bath is the *Sakura* Japanese Restaurant which overlooks the hotel's garden with its giant pebbles and bamboo trees. The restaurant, open Tuesday to Saturday, is personally supervised by Mrs Sachiko Bush, offers three styles of Japanese cooking, *Shabu Shabu*, *Sukiyaki* and *Seafood nabe*. For those unfamiliar with Japanese cuisine, there are English descriptions and sampling tips. An opportunity not to be missed. Each bedroom is different and decorated with Georgian and traditional English patterns. The Windsor is in the heart of Bath, a World Heritage site, with rooms facing either the Georgian façades of the city inspired by Palladio or the hills to the South. The Windsor is ideally situated for those wishing to explore this historic city on foot or to visit attractions in the area by car.

Rates: Single with breakfast from £85; double inc. breakfast from £135.
Midweek Breaks: Prices on application.

- *14 en suite bedrooms (inc 1 suite and 2 junior suites), all with direct-dial telephone, colour TV+satellite, hairdryer, laundry/valet service, 24-hr room/meal service, fax/modem points.*
- *Japanese table d'hôte dinner £25; lunch available; last orders 9.30 pm.*
- *Business services inc meeting room, capacity 14*
- *Car parking for 8. Open all year.*
- *Entire premises non-smoking.*
- *& all major credit cards accepted.*

Radstock 8, Bristol 13, Chippenham 13, Warminster 16, Wells 19, London 119.

THE WEST COUNTRY

The Walnut Tree Hotel

North Petherton, Bridgwater,
Somerset TA6 6QA
Tel: (01278) 662255; Fax: (01278) 663946

E-Mail: sales@walnuttreehotel.com
Website: www.walnuttreehotel.coms

The Walnut Tree Hotel is a former 18th Century coaching inn, set in the heart of the pretty Somerset village of North Petherton, on the A38. Traditional values have been maintained here over the years. All the rooms are quietly located at the rear of the Inn, and every possible comfort is provided for guests. Each of the thirty two bedrooms offer superb amenities. The décor is tasteful and warming, and the four-poster bed suite is a popular choice for those seeking a special or romantic weekend break. The Walnut Tree also specialises in receptions, meetings and weddings, the public rooms having an abundance of charm and character. The popular bar and *Dukes* Restaurant & Bistro can tempt you with real ales, light bar snacks, succulent steaks and first class international cuisine, with presentation, service and excellent wines making for a memorable repast. The Walnut Tree Hotel is a hostelry of high standards with friendly staff attending to your every need. Well located for touring the South West. Do sample the charm of this hotel, and you are bound to return.

Rates: Single with breakfast from £62; Double inc. breakfast from £72; suite from £125.
Leisure breaks: Special weekend packages available.

- 32 en suite bedrooms (inc. suites) (3 for the disabled), all with direct dial telephone and TV; room service; baby listening; night service.
- Last orders for dinner 10 p.m., bar meals, special diets.
- Children welcome; meetings/conferences to 110.
- Extensive parking facilities.
- Open all year.
- AMERICAN EXPRESS & all major credit cards accepted.

M5 (exit 24) 1,
Bridgwater 1½,
Taunton 8,
Wells 12,
Bristol 35,
Exeter 40,
London 150.

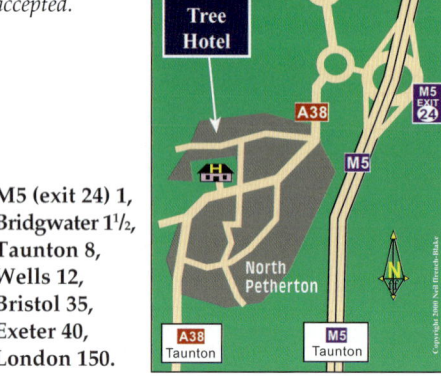

Somerset, Exford

The Crown Hotel

Exford, Somerset TA24 7PP
Tel: (01643) 831554; Fax: (01643) 831665
E-mail: info@crownhotelexmoor.com
Website: www.crownhotelexmoor.com

This famous hotel has been looking after the needs of local inhabitants, holiday makers and sportsmen for many years. It is no wonder that its reputation for comfort and cuisine has continued to grow. It will continue to grow this year as Hugo Jeune, recently of the Rising Sun, Lynmouth is in the process of refurbishing the Crown. He is aiming for a standard above all other accommodation in the district and, knowing his success with the Rising Sun, I am sure he will succeed here too. I look forward to staying next year in this beautiful part of Exmoor. Exford is a centre for fishing (the hotel has its own beat on the river Lyn), walking (Dunkery Beacon - the highest point in Exmoor - is nearby), game shooting and hunting (there are three packs of foxhounds and one of staghounds and the season on Exmoor lasts normally from September until April). Red deer safaris in a Land Rover can be arranged from the hotel and nearby riding stables will provide mounts for all levels of experience. Packed lunches can be arranged. The Crown has a comfortable lounge for residents, a soothing water garden to relax in and a convivial bar in which to meet locals and have a drink whilst choosing from the AA ❀❀ rosette restaurant menu.

Rates: Single with breakfast from £55; double inc. breakfast from £95.
Leisure Breaks: Details on application.

● *17 en suite bedrooms, all with direct-dial telephone + modem pts, colour TV, hairdryer, radio/alarm clock, safety deposit box, ✾ bedrooms available.*
● *Table d'hôte dinner approx. £29.50; à la carte, lunch and spec. diets available; last orders 9.30 pm*
● *Fishing, walking, game shooting, riding. River bathing nearby. Golf, tennis, hunting, red deer safaris by arrangement. Ample* 🅿
● & *all major credit cards accepted.*
● *Open all year.*

Dunster 11, Lynmouth 14, Barnstaple 22, Ilfracombe 24, Taunton 35, London 177.

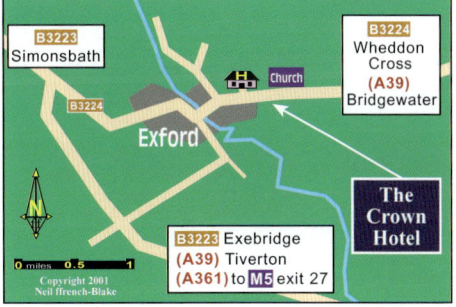

Signpost Guide 2003
Central Southern England

Fact File
Illustrated Guide to
Historic Houses, Gardens & Sites
Diary of Events

Hotels in	PAGE
Dorset	32
Hampshire	40
Isle of Wight	43
Oxfordshire	44
Wiltshire	46

Central Southern England

Historic Houses, Gardens & Parks

Berkshire
Beale Wildlife Gdns, Lower Basildon
Cliveden, Nr. Maidenhead
Dorney Court, Nr. Windsor
Forbury Gardens, Reading
Highclere Castle, Nr. Newbury
Mapledurham House and Watermill, Nr. Reading
Stonor House, Henley-on-Thames
Stratfield Saye House, Nr. Reading

Buckinghamshire
Claydon House, Nr. Winslow
Hughenden Manor, High Wycombe
Stowe Landscape Gdns, Nr. Buckingham
Waddesdon Manor, Nr. Aylesbury
West Wycombe Park, Nr. High Wycombe

Dorset
Athelhampton House & Gardens, Puddletown, Dorchester
Forde Abbey & Gardens, Chard Hardy's Cottage Garden, Higher Bockhampton, Dorchester
Kingston Lacey House, Nr. Wimborne

Hampshire
Breamore House & Museums, Nr. Fordingbridge
Broadlands, Romsey
Exbury Gardens, Nr. Southampton
Furzey Gardens Minstead, Nr. Lyndhurst
Highclere Castle
Lymington Vineyard
Lymore Valley Herb Garden, Nr. Milford-on-Sea
Sir Harold Hillier Gardens & Arboretum, Ampfield, Nr. Romsey
Stratfield Saye House & Wellington Country Park

Oxfordshire
Basildon Park, Nr. Pangbourne
Blenheim Palace, Woodstock
Peoples Park, Banbury
Rousham House & Gardens, Steeple Aston
Waterperry Gardens, Wheatley

Wiltshire
Avebury Stone Circles, Nr. Marlborough
Great Western Railway Museum, Swindon
Longleat House, Warminster
Museum & Art Gallery, Swindon
Old Wardour Castle, Tisbury
Salisbury Cathedral
Stonehenge, Nr. Amesbury

Walks & Nature Trails

Berkshire
Riverside & Country Walk to Speen Moors
Heritage Walk, Reading
Look Out Countryside & Heritage Centre Nr. Bracknell
Reading Town Trails

Dorset
Brit Valley Walk
The Dorset Coastal Path
Hardy's Dorset Walk

Hampshire
Avon Valley Path, Salisbury to Christchurch
Itchin Way, Southampton to Hinton Ampner
Solent Way, Milford on-Sea to Emsworth
Three Castles Path, Windsor to Winchester

Oxfordshire
Guided Walking Tours of Oxford
Oxford Ecology Trail

Wiltshire
Discover the Villages Trail
The Imber Range Perimeter Path

Historical Sites & Museums

Bedfordshire
Bunyan Museum, Bedford
Elstow Moot Hall, Church End
Stockwood Craft Museum & Gdns
Shuttleworth Collection, Biggleswade

Berkshire
Blake's Lock Museum, Reading
Foxhill Collection of Historic Carriages, Nr. Reading
Newbury Museum
Reading Abbey
St. George's Chapel, Windsor Cas.
Windsor Castle

Buckinghamshire
Buckinghamshire County Museum, Aylesbury
Chiltern Brewery, Terrick, Aylesbury

Dorset
Corfe Castle
Dorset County Museum, Dorchester
Maiden Castle, Dorchester
Portland Castle
Sherborne Castle

Hampshire
D Day Museum, Portsmouth
Hurst Castle, Keyhaven
New Forest Museum & Visitor Centre, Ashurst,
Portchester Castle
The Sammy Miller Museum, New Milton

Oxfordshire
Banbury Museum & Art Gallery
Broughton Castle, Banbury
Cogges Manor Farm Museum, Witney
Didcot Railway Museum
The Oxford Story, Oxford

Entertainment Venues

Berkshire
Bucklebury Farm Park Nr. Reading
Crown Jewels of the World Exhibition, Windsor
Holme Grange Craft Centre/Art Gallery, Wokingham Trilakes Country Park & Fishery, Sandhurst
Legoland, Windsor
Wyld Court Rainforest, Nr. Newbury

Buckinghamshire
Flamingo Gardens & Zoological Park, Olney
Glass Craft, Holtspur, Beaconsfield
Gullivers Land, Milton Keynes
West Wycombe Caves

Dorset
Brownsea Island, Poole
Lyme Regis Marine Aquarium
Lodmoor Country Park, Weymouth
Weymouth Sea Life Park

Hampshire
Lepe Country Park, Exbury
Marwell Zoological Pk, Winchester
Swimming & Diving Complex, Southampton
New Forest Buttefly Farm, Ashurst
Paultons Park, Nr. Lyndhurst
Portsmouth Sea Life Centre

Oxfordshire
Cotswold WildIife Park, Burford
CuriOXiTy (Science Gallery) Oxford
The Oxford Story, Oxford
Waterfowl Sanctuary, Hook Norton

Wiltshire
Lions of Longleat Safari Park, Warminster

Central Southern England

DIARY OF EVENTS

January

1. **King Alfred Bus Running Day.** Winchester, Hampshire
25-26. **Calne Model Railway Show.** Calne, Wilts.

February

7-9. **Bournemouth Int'l Holiday Show.** Bournemouth Exhib Ctre, Dorset.
16. **Tank Engine Days.** Ashley Heath, Hampshire.

March

28.2-1.3. **Racing** at Newbury.
4. **Sway Pancake Race.** Sway, Hampshire.
7-16. **Science Week - SET 2003.** Dorchester, Dorset.
15. **Petersfield Music Festival.** Petersfield, Hants.
16. **Newbury Dolls & Miniatures Fair.** Newbury, Berks.
16. **World Poohsticks Championship.** Little Wittenham, Oxfordshire.
30*. **Easter Teddy Bear Fair,** Kingston Mauward, Dorset.
21-22. **Newbury Spring Meeting.** Newbury, Berks.

April

2 & 30. **NH Racing** Ascot, Berks
4-6. **Abingdon Music Festival.** Abingdon, Oxon.
7,14,28. **Racing** at Windsor, Berkshire.
19-21. **Day Out With Thomas.** Wallingford, Oxon.

May

1-10*. **Swindon Festival of Literature.** Shaw, Swindon.
4-5. **War of the Roses by the Levy.** Shaftesbury, Dorset.
3-5. **Hampshire Beautiful Craft & Garden Show.** Exbury, Hants.
3-5. **Country Homes, Gardens & Flower Show.** Highclere, Berks.
4. **Racing** at Salisbury, Wilts.
5-6. **Weymouth Int'l Beach Kite Festival.** The Beach, Weymouth, Dorset.
10-24. **International Newbury Spring Festival.** Various venues, Newbury, Berkshire.
12. **Racing** at Windsor.
14-18. **Royal Windsor Horse Show.** Windsor Home Park, Windsor, Berks.
15. **Racing** at Salisbury.
16-17. **Newbury Spring Meeting,** Newbury Racec'se, Berks
31-1 June. **Racing** at Windsor.

June

7-22. **Isle of Wight Walking Festival.** High St, Newport IOW
11-12. **Racing** at Newbury.
16-23. **Bishops Waltham Festival.** Bs Waltham, Hants.
17-20. **Royal Ascot Race Meeting.** Ascot Racecourse, Berks.
19-20. **Blenheim Palace Flower Show.** Woodstock, Oxon.
21. **Round the Island Race.** Cowes, Isle of Wight.
25-26. **Racing** at Salisbury
27-29. **Youth Afloat Festival** . Poole, Dorset.
28-6 July. **Beaminster Arts Festival.** Beaminster, Dorset.

July

2-6. **Henley Royal Regatta & Festival.** Henley Reach, Henley-on-Thames, Oxfordshire.
3-6. **Winchester Hat Fair.** Winchester, Hampshire.
5-6. **Ocean FM Balloon & Flower Festival.** Southampton
9-13. **Henley Festival.** Henley-on-Thames, Oxon.
13-19*. **Swan Upping.** River thames, Abingdon, Oxfordshire.
18-19. **Racing** at Newbury, Berks.
18-20. **Blenheim Palace Food & Wine Festival.** Woodstock, Oxon
19-20*. **Tolpuddle Martyrs Memorial Rally & Festival.** Tolpuddle, Dorset
21-27*. **Farnborough International Air Show,** Farnborough, Hants.
25-27. **King George VI & Queen Elizabeth Meeting.** Ascot, Berks
26-27. **Lulworth Cntry Fair & Horse Trials.** Lulworth, Dorset.
29-31. **New Forest & Hampshire Cnty Show,** Brockenhurst, Hants

August

2-9. Skandia Life **Cowes Week** , Isle of Wight.
10. **Sandown Bay Regatta Week.** Sandown, Isle of Wight.
3, 15,16. **Racing** at Newbury.
16-24. **Christchurch Regatta & Carnival.** Christchurch, Dorset.
20. **Gillingham & Shaftesbury Agric Show.** Motcombe, Dorset.
24-25. **Festival of Horse & Intl Horse Trials.** Highclere, Berks.

September

4-7. **Blenheim Petplan 3-Day Event.** Woodstock, Oxon.
12-21. **Southampton Intl Boat Show 2003.** Western Esplanade, Southampton, Hants.
13-14. **Beaulieu Int'l Autojumble & Automart.** Beaulieu, Hants.
20-21. **Royal Co Berkshire Show.** Hermitage, Berks.
26-28. **Holiday Caravan 2003 Exhibition.** Beaulieu, Hampshire.
26-28. **Queen Elizabeth II Stakes/Fillies Mile.** Ascot Racecourse, Berkshire.
28. **Walking & Cycling New Forest Experience.** Brockenhurst

For further details contact:
The Southern Tourist Board
40 Chamberlayne Road,
Eastleigh, Hampshire SO5 5JH
Tel: (02380) 625400
Website: www.southerntb.co.uk

(*Denotes provisional date)

Central Southern England

The Solent waterway between Southampton and the Isle of Wight is the sailing playground of southern England. Portsmouth Harbour is home to Nelson's *Victory*, the restored Elizabethan galleon recently brought to the surface The *Mary Rose* and *HMS Warrior*, Britain's first iron-clad warship.

Beaulieu on the west side of the Solent is the site of Lord Montagu's *National Motor Museum*. *Broadlands* at Romsey nearby was the seat of Lord Mountbatten and houses an exhibition from his life of public service.

On the way north from the south coast the visitor passes through Winchester with its 11-13th centruy cathedral and castle remains, where King Arthur's reputed Round Table can be viewed.

North of Winchester on the way to the Midlands, the visitor passes over the chalk Newbury Downs, site of some of the most famous racing stables in England, on his or her way to Oxford. The dreaming spires, echoing quads and cloistered lawns of the colleges have a timeless beauty. The *Ashmolean* Museum is Britain's oldest public museum, opened in 1683. It contains gold and jewellery beleived to have been the property of King Alfred, the lantern carried by Guy Fawkes and riches from ancient Egypt and Greece. The *Bodleian* Library, founded in 1596, is one of six University Libraries in the British Isles which receives a copy of every book published in the UK.

Wiltshire to the west of the region was the cradle of Druidic early English life and Stonehenge must be one of the seven wonders of Britain, a must-see for visitors. Neraby the Avebury stone circle is equally puzzling. Salisbury Cathedral's 404ft spire is the tallest in England.

Southwest of Wiltshire lies Dorset, Thomas Hardy's county, with the ancient cities of Dorchester (Roman remains), Hardy's *Casterbridge* and hilltop Shaftesbury (Hardy's *Shaston*). Cerne Abbas dates form the 10th centur y and has the (in)famous 180-ft Chalk Giant looking down on the village. Elsewhere there are prehistoric earthworks and white chalk horses carved into the hills of Dorset and Wiltshire.

Buckinghamshire, northeast of Oxford, contains Stowe, now a public school, with parks landsacped by Capability Brown, and Waddesdon, seat of the Rothschild Collection.

Neighbouring Berkshire's most visited monument is Windsor Castle, now fully restored after the fire of 1995.

Monkey Island Hotel

Bray-on-Thames, Maidenhead SL6 2EE
Tel: (01628) 623400; Fax: (01628) 784732
E-mail: reservations@monkeyisland.co.uk
Website: www.monkeyisland.co.uk

Unique, romantic, historically elegant, charming, tranquil and beautifully located on a $4\frac{1}{2}$ acre island in the Thames is the Monkey Island Hotel - the name deriving from the medieval *Monk's Eyot*. On your arrival, having parked your car, a footbridge leads you across the water to an island of sweeping lawns and sheltering trees. In ca. 1723 the island was purchased by Charles Spencer, 3rd Duke of Marlborough, who built the fishing lodge and temple, both of which are Grade I listed. The Pavilion's Candles Lounge, overlooking acres of riverside lawn, is an ideal spot for a light lunch, afternoon tea or a relaxing cocktail and the award-winning Pavilion Restaurant, perched on the island's narrowest tip with fine views upstream, boasts fine English cuisine, an award winning cellar and friendly service. The Temple has 26 comfortable bedrooms and suites, all with picturesque garden and river views; also the Wedgwood Room, with its splendid ceiling in high-relief plaster and the octagonal Temple Room. Monkey Island is within easy reach of Maidenhead, Royal Windsor, Eton, Henley and London. It is even possible to arrange exclusive use of the island for that truly special occasion.

Rates: Single with b'fst from £130; double with b'fst from from £190.
Leisure Breaks: £105 pppn, dinner, b & b, Fri/Sat/Sun/Bankhol. Boating weekend break £284 per couple. Windsor Castle weekend break £116.50 pp.

● 26 en suite bedrooms (inc 2 suites), all with direct-dial telephone, colour TV+ satellite, mini-bar, hairdryer, trouser press, laundry service, tea/coffee making, radio/alarm, safe. ✄ rooms avail.
● Tdh dinner £35 (✄); alc, lunch & special diets available; last orders 10 p.m.
● 6 mtg/conf. rooms, cap. 150. ₽ over bridge 50.
● Croquet, boating, clay shooting on island; golf, watersports, indoor pool, tennis, riding, squash nearby. Airport pickup on demand.
● Visa, Switch accepted.
● Open all year.

Maidenhead 2, Windsor 5, Heathrow 15, London 30.

BERKSHIRE, Maidenhead   31

Taplow House Hotel

Berry Hill, Taplow, Maidenhead, Berkshire SL6 0DA
Tel: (01628) 670056; Fax: (01628) 783985
E-mail: taplow@wrensgroup.com
Website: www.wrensgroup.com/taplow

Lovely Taplow House, situated in six acres of beautiful gardens on the outskirts of a beautiful old village in the Thames Valley, offers peaceful quiet for weary travellers. Located near the magnificent forest of Burnham Beeches, Taplow has its own aged trees, including Europe's largest and oldest tulip tree, planted by Queen Elizabeth I. Inside the 32 bedrooms are tastefully and elegantly designed to enhance your visit here. The Louis XIV styled restaurant offers superb cuisine, supported by an extensive wine list. Al fresco dining in the beautiful gardens on a warm summer's evening or the cosy ambience of a roaring log fire in winter, each combined with the attentiveness of friendly staff, will enhance your visit. Sitting in one of the living rooms, you can marvel at the original features and fireplaces of this stunning Georgian home and be cast back in time while enjoying the comforts of the 21st century. On my first visit I was so taken by the tranquility and beauty of the place that I shall return very soon.

Rates: Single with b'fst from £160; double/twin with b'fst from from £170; suite from £225.
Leisure Breaks: Three nights for price of two (rack rate) Please enquire for details.

● 32 en suite bedrooms (inc 4 suites), all AC, colour TV, hairdryer, laundry/valet service, trouser press, tea/coffee making facilities, fax/modem points, radio/alarm clock, 24-hour room service. ✻ bedrooms available.
● Tdh dinner £27.50; alc, lunch & special diets available; last orders 9.30 p.m.
● 7 conf. rooms, capacity 90. Parking for 100+.
● Croquet, jogging track. Fishing, golf, watersports, sailing, shooting, squash, tennis, riding nearby. ● Open all year.
● AMERICAN EXPRESS & all major credit cards acc'd.
Slough 4½, High Wycombe 9, Henley 10, Heathrow 10, London 24.

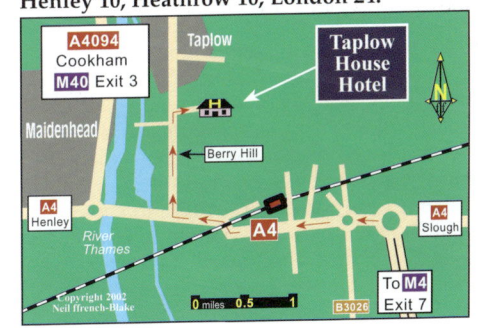

CENTRAL SOUTHERN ENGLAND

Dorset, Bournemouth

The Norfolk Royale Hotel

Richmond Hill, Bournemouth BH2 6EN
Tel: (01202) 551521; Fax: (01202) 299729
E-mail: norfolkroyale@englishrosehotels.co.uk
Website: www.englishrosehotels.co.uk

In the vibrant heart of Bournemouth, you will find the Norfolk Royale. Step inside and you could be in a country house hotel - what a nice surprise! Built in the Edwardian style, but sensitively restored, it gives an inviting feeling of warmth and sophistication. You can stroll in the pretty landscaped gardens, sunbathe on the lawns, take afternoon tea on the terrace or a cocktail on the patio. Bedrooms, mostly in a recently reconstructed wing overlook the gardens. Available meals vary from light snacks to fine dining, *à la carte* or *table d'hôte* in the Orangery Restaurant with unobtrusive service and offering very good value. Indoor leisure facilities include a very attractive domed swimming pool, spa bath, steam room and sauna. Special suites are available to suit a variety of functions - weddings, private dinners, small meetings and conferences. These are thoughtfully located so as not to intrude on leisure guests' activities. The Norfolk Royale makes an ideal oasis of peace, quiet and comfort in the middle of this bustling town.

Rates: Single with b'fst from £105; double with b'fst from £145; suite from £175.
Leisure Breaks: Norfolk Classic Breaks - min. 2 nights, dinner b & b 1.4.01-31.10.01 £75 pppn Sun-Thurs/£75 Fri-Sat; 1.11.00-31.03.01 £57.50 pppn Sun-Thurs/£67.50 Fri-Sat.

- 95 en suite bedrooms (inc 29), all with direct-dial telephone, colour TV+ satellite, minibar, hairdryer, trouser press, tea/coffee making. Lift
- Tdh dinner £22.50; alc, lunch & special diets available; last orders 9.30 p.m.
- 3-room conf. centre with hi-tec presentation suite
- Indoor heated swimming pool, spa bath, steam room, sauna, solarium. Ample car parking.
- & all major credit cards acc'd. Open all year

Ringwood 12, Blandford Forum 17, Dorchester 27, Southampton 34, London 114.

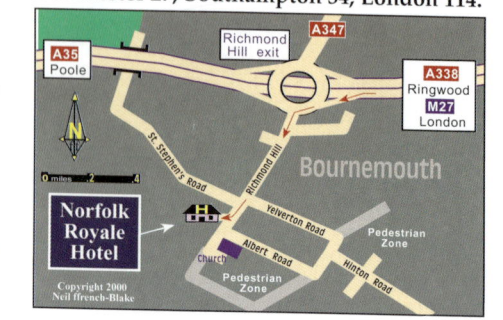

Dorset, Bridport

The Manor Hotel
West Bexington, Dorset DT2 9DF
Tel: (01308) 897616; Fax: (01308) 897035
E-mail: themanorhotel@btconnect.com
Website: themanorhotel.com

The Manor Hotel, located amidst some of the most dramatic scenery on the South Dorset coast, is somewhere very special just waiting to be discovered. This ancient manor house is well mellowed with age, and offers a wonderful combination of flagstone floors, panelled walls, beamed ceilings, yet the en suite bedrooms include every modern comfort and facility. Their décor certainly brings the vibrance of Dorset flowers and countryside through every window. Views are breathtaking. The natural gardens of the hotel are colourful and well established. Beyond is the sweeping geographical landmark of Chesil Bank with the clear seas of Lyme Bay lapping and ebbing over miles of pebbles. A more dramatic and scenic, yet quiet and relaxing situation for an hotel, one could not wish to find. The Cellar Bar provides a varied choice of bar meals through the day and in the evening, the elegant restaurant enjoys a fine reputation for well chosen culinary specialities, with fresh local produce, vegetables and especially seafood being used by the chef to present an excellent menu. A fine wine list satisfies all tastes. New owners, Peter King and Sheree Lynch state that, for their guests *"nothing is too much trouble"*, please discover and pamper yourself with a visit to the Manor Hotel - a real treat!

Rates: Room and breakfast from £52.50 per person; four-poster room from £62.50 per person; dinner, b & b weekly charge from £450 per person
Leisure breaks: Two-day stay - dinner, bed & breakfast from £145 per person; five-day stay - dinner, bed & breakfast from £350 per person.

- 13 en suite bedrooms, all with direct-dial telephone, colour TV, room service, baby listening.
- Last orders for dinner 9.30 pm; bar meals; special diets available.
- Children welcome; conferences max. 60.
- Sea bathing; golf five miles; riding two miles.
- & major credit cards accepted.
- Open all year.

Bridport 7, Dorchester 10, Weymouth 11, Lyme Regis 14, Bournemouth 50, Exeter 50, London 135.

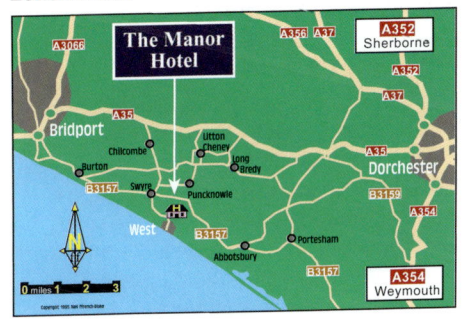

Dorset, Studland Bay

Knoll House Hotel

Studland Bay, Dorset BH19 3AH
Tel: (01929) 450450; Fax: (01929) 450423
E-mail: info@knollhouse.co.uk
Website: www.knollhouse.co.uk

This delightful hotel is situated on the finest stretch of Dorset heritage coastline surrounded by some of the prettiest countryside in the West and it is well worth a visit. It is within a National Trust Reserve and overlooks three miles of golden beach with first class swimming, fishing, boating and windsurfing. Knoll House is an independent country house hotel under the personal management of its family owners and is set in pine trees with the most attractive gardens where you can relax away from the cares of everyday life. The sporting facilities are numerous - tennis courts, a nine-hole par 3 golf course and outdoor heated level deck swimming pool. For relaxation there is a sauna, steam-room, Jacuzzi, plunge-pool and gym set in a marvellous health spa complex with fruit juice and coffee bar. Many of the bedrooms are arranged as suites, ideal for families. Log fires and an attractive cocktail bar add to the unique atmosphere of this extremely efficiently run hotel. The quality,

Dorset, Studland Bay

choice and presentation of the menus is excellent. At lunchtime a superb hors d'oeuvres selection and buffet table laden with cold meats, pies and salads is a speciality, followed by delicious puddings and a good English cheese board. Young children are catered for in their own dining room and there are many and varied facilities to keep them amused all day. Sandbanks and Bournemouth are easily reached via the car ferry. Dorchester, Corfe Castle and the picturesque villages of Dorset are only a short drive away.

Rates: Half board from £99 daily or full board (weekly) from £720 (April) to £825 (August). Generous full board terms for five nights out of season.
Special Breaks: 'Family Five' (two adults, one or two children under 13) - five nights full board in low season £799. Purbeck Five (single or twin rooms without private bathroom) five nights full board in low season £317 per person. September 14th-October 17th, two nights full board £179-£199 per person. Prices include VAT. There is no service charge.

- 79 bedrooms (many ground floor), comprising 30 family suites, 29 single, 20 twin bedded rooms; 57 with private bathrooms.
- Five lounges; children's dining room; self-service laundry, giftshop, colour TV lounge.
- Three games rooms; children's disco in season; 9 acre golf course; two hard tennis courts, playground, outdoor swimming and paddling pools; full leisure centre; adjoins clean sandy beach, safe bathing; Isle of Purbeck Golf Club two miles, two courses. ● Open early Easter to end-October.
- Mastercard and Visa accepted.

Studland 1, Swanage 3, Bournemouth 8, Corfe Castle 6, London 113. (Heathrow two hours)

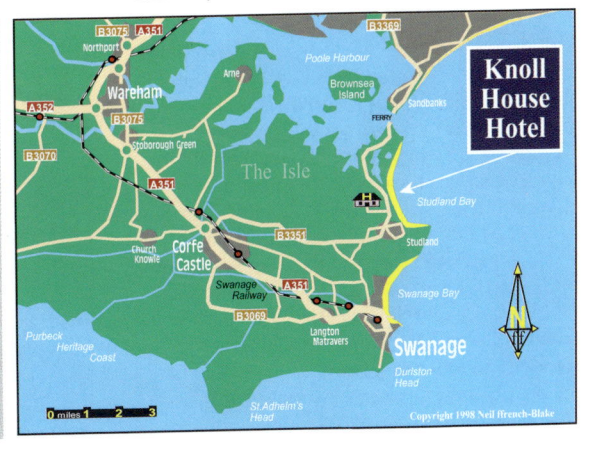

Knoll House Hotel

Manor House Hotel

Studland Bay, Nr. Swanage,
Dorset BH19 3AU
Tel & Fax: (01929) 450288
E-mail: themanorhousehotel@lineone.net
Website: www.themanorhousehotel.com

The site of the Manor House is mentioned in the Domesday Book and parts of the present rambling Gothic house date back to 1750. Set within 20 acres of elevated grounds, the hotel commands beautiful views overlooking the beaches and waters of Studland Bay. History and character are in abundance; the hotel's medieval carvings are said to have come from the residential quarters of Corfe Castle, home of the famous Mary Banks, who defended it so bravely against Cromwell's troops. Most of the en suite bedrooms (four with four-poster beds) have spectacular views over the bay and out to Old Harry Rocks. Wall carvings in the Westminster Bedroom are of particular interest, reputed to have come from the Old Palace of Westminster, circa 1636. A delightful conservatory has extended the dining area, where décor is sophisticated, and the atmosphere and service is most warming. The menu has an excellent choice of fresh local produce and the delicious Studland Lobster is a must! The Manor House is an ideal base from which to explore the beauty, beaches and nature trails of Studland and surrounding Dorset.

*Rates: Dinner, room & breakfast from £60 per person. **Bargain Breaks:** Three or five night specials - 3 nights = 10% off daily rate; 5 nights = 20% off daily rate.*

- 21 en suite bedrooms, all with colour TV, radio, tea/coffee making facilities, telephone, hairdryer.
- Last orders for dinner 9 pm; bar lunches & vegetarian diets available.
- Children over five welcome; dogs allowed.
- Sea bathing with sandy beach, sailing and boating; two hard tennis courts.

Riding & golf within two miles.
- Hotel closed for three weeks in January.
- Mastercard & Visa cards accepted.

Swanage 3, Corfe Castle 6, Bournemouth 8, Dorchester 26, London 113.

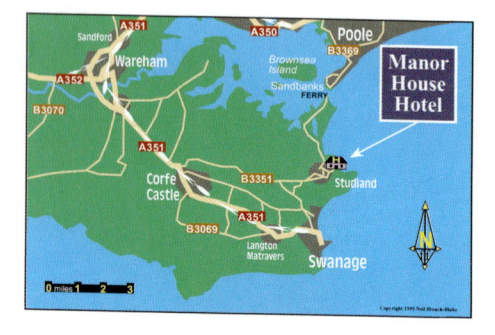

Plumber Manor

Sturminster Newton, Dorset DT10 2AF
Tel: (01258) 472507; Fax: (01258) 473370
E-mail: book@plumbermanor.com
Website: www.plumbermanor.com

This imposing Jacobean manor house is set in idyllic countryside "far from the madding crowd". The Divelish stream weaves its way through delightful grounds, extensive lawns and fine old trees. Dating from the 17th century, the manor has been the home of the Prideaux-Brune family. Since 1973 the careful management of Richard, Alison, Brian (in the kitchen) and now Tim has led to the creation of a first class hotel and restaurant. Richard knows many of his regular diners personally and is always on hand for advice, both about current dishes on the ever changing ◉◉ menu and about what to see in this charming part of Dorset. When we dined there last year we tried the excellent 'medley of seafood' starter, followed by succulent *medallions de boeuf*. Do remember to leave room for one of the excellent Plumber puddings! The wine list is of the same standard, well-chosen and with ever changing freshness. There are six elegant bedrooms within the main house and a further ten in the courtyard and converted barn. Plumber is welcoming, comfortable and has a charming atmosphere in which to relax and savour first class hospitality, cuisine and service.

Rates: *Single room inc. breakfast from £85 ; double/twin room from £100.*
Sensibly priced short breaks: *Min 2-night stay bed & breakfast from £90 per couple per night/3 nights £82 per couple per night. Nov 1st-Mar 31.*

● 16 en suite bedrooms, all with colour TV, direct-dial telephone, trouser press, hairdryer, tea/coffee making facilities.
● 2-cse tdh dinner £20/3-cse £23. Alc, lunch & special diets available; last orders 9.30 pm.
● Conference/meeting room for up to 16. Ample 🅿
● Croquet tennis. Fishing, golf, riding, shooting nearby by arrangement.
● Children & dogs welcome by arrangement.
● Open March 1-January 31.
● AMERICAN EXPRESS & major credit cards accepted.

**Blandford Forum 8,
Shaftesbury 9,
Sherborne 12,
Dorchester 21,
Salisbury 28,
London 125.**

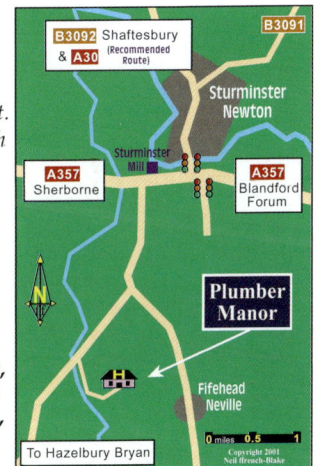

Dorset, Wareham

Springfield Country Hotel & Leisure Club

Grange Road, Stoborough, Wareham, Dorset BH20 5AL
Tel: (01929) 552177; Fax: (01929) 551862
E-mail: enquiries@springfield-country-hotel.co.uk
Website: www.springfield-country-hotel.co.uk

Springfield Country Hotel is a family run hotel set in six acres of beautiful landscaped gardens at the foot of the Purbeck Hills in the scenic Dorset countryside. The hotel is ideally suited for visiting such local attractions as Lulworth Cove, Durdle Door, Corfe Castle, Dorchester (Hardy's *Casterbridge*), the Army Tank Museum at Bovingdon, Poole and Swanage. There is a choice of two dining rooms and excellent facilities for private banquets, conferences and meetings. The Leisure Complex boasts an indoor pool with spa, saunas, steam room, two full size snooker tables, games room and gymnasium with a wide range of exercise machines. Aquafit sessions and swimming lessons are available. Outdoors there is swimming and tennis and watersports and golf are available locally. The 50 smartly furnished bedrooms include family rooms, ground floor rooms and there is a lift. Springfield is an ideal place to while away a few days in summer or in winter.

Rates: Single room inc. breakfast from £75; double/twin room from £115.
Bargain Breaks: Min 2-night stay inc table d'hôte dinner & breakfast from £130 per couple per night

- 50 en suite bedrooms (inc. 3 triple, 2 suites), all with colour TV, direct-dial telephone, trouser press, hairdryer, laundry/valet service, radio/alarm clock, tea/coffee making, lift. ♿ rooms available.
- Grange Restaurant 3 cse tdh £19.50. Alc, lunch & special diets available; last orders 9 pm. (9.30 Sat)
- Business services inc 12 meeting rooms (5-200). Car parking for 150. Beauty salon. ● Open all year.
- Billiards/snooker, gymnasium, indoor & outdoor swimming pools, sauna, massage, squash, tennis, steam room, aerobics theatre. Fishing, golf, sailing & watersports within five miles.
- AMERICAN EXPRESS & major credit cards accepted.

Bournemouth 13, Blandford Forum 14, Dorchester 16, Weymouth 17, Ringwood 21, London 117.

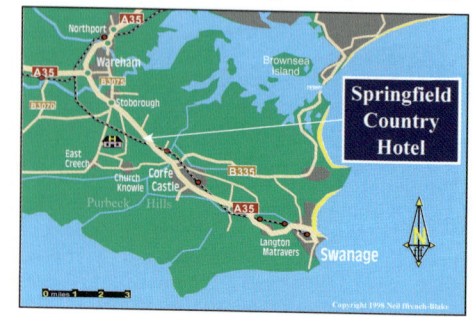

The Eastbury Hotel

Long Street, Sherborne,
Dorset DT9 3BY
Tel: (01935) 813131;
Fax: (01935) 817296
E-mail: reservations@theeastburyhotel.co.uk
Website: www.theeastburyhotel.co.uk

Built in 1715 as a Gentleman's residence, this elegant Georgian townhouse became an hotel in the early 1900s. It has been extended and refurbished over the years with modern facilities added. The hotel's imposing façade is a well known landmark in Old Sherborne. With an acre of walled gardens and lawns, it gives the rare feel of a 'country house hotel in town'. New owners Nicky and Paul King offer a high level of personal service. Meals are served in the AA Conservatory Restaurant, with something for every palate and using fresh local Dorset produce where possible. The bright bedrooms are named after English garden flowers. The Eastbury is the ideal spot for a relaxing break close to the Abbey and Castle and with Dorset's many attractions nearby.

Rates: Single room inc. breakfast from £57.50 ; double/twin room from £95.
Leisure Breaks: Min 2-night stay, dinner, b & b £64 per person per night.
- 14 en suite bedrooms, all with colour TV+ sat, d-dial telephone, trouser press, hairdryer, laundry/valet service, radio/alarm clock, tea/coffee making, fax/modem points, rm service 0730-2200. rooms
- Tdh dinner The Conservatory £22.95; lunch, diets avail. Last orders 9.30 pm. 2 mtg rms - 65.
- Croquet. Fishing, golf, shooting, squash, riding, tennis nearby. Open all yr exc 1st week January
- & all major credit cards accepted. 20.

Shaftesbury 16, Dorchester 18, London 120.

Beachleas Hotel & Restaurant

17 Poole Road, Wimborne
Minster, Dorset BH21 1QA
Tel: (01202) 841684;
Fax: (01202) 849344
E-mail: information@beachleas.com
Website: www.beachleas.com
RAC Blue Ribbon & 3 Dining Awards. AA Good Hotel Guide. Which Hotel Guide.

Anyone looking for a short break, less than a two-hour drive from London or The Midlands, would be well advised to consider Beachleas, a Grade II listed Georgian house on the outskirts of Wimborne. Bedrooms are either in the elegant main house or in the lodge-style Coach House. Dining would be in the conservatory restaurant, al fresco on the patio in summer or by a roaring log fire in winter. Award-winning cuisine is modern English in style with a Mediterranean influence. An excellent base from which to explore Thomas Hardy country, the New Forest and the Purbeck Hills. You could even sail in the hotel's own yacht on the Solent.

Poole 5, Blandford 10, Southampton 30, London 103.

Rates: Single room inc. breakfast from £69; double/twin room from £79.
Leisure Breaks: Two consec. nights Fri/Sat/Sun/Mon, dinner, b & b from £59 per person per night
- 9 en suite bedrooms, all with colour TV, d-dial telephone, hairdryer, laundry/valet service, radio/alarm clock, fax/modem points, early morning tea service. rooms available.
- Tdh dinner £19.95/24.75; lunch, diets avail. Last orders 9.30 pm. Meeting room for 20.
- Tennis, riding, fishing 1/2 mile; golf 2, sailing 6
- Closed Dec 24 for three weeks.
- & all major credit cards accepted.

Hampshire - Andover/Brockenhurst

Esseborne Manor Hotel

Hurstbourne Tarrant, Andover,
Hampshire SP11 0ER
Tel: (01264) 736444;
Fax: (01264) 736725
E-mail: esseborne@aol.com
Website: www.essebornemanor.com

Esseborne is small, unpretentious, yet very stylish. For over 100 years it was a country retreat and it still retains the atmosphere of a well run country house, with efficient yet relaxed service. The hotel is set amidst the splendour of the North Wessex Downs, near the lovely Bourne valley, in an area of outstanding natural beauty. Classic imaginative cooking and individually designed bedrooms ensure a comfortable stay. In the middle of some of Britain's best shooting and fishing country, other activities in the area include country walks, Thruxton motor-racing circuit, hot air ballooning and riding. Salisbury, Winchester, Stonehenge and Highclere Castle are all near at hand. Guests can also take advantage of the hotel's arrangement for membership of Newbury and Salisbury racecourses.

Rates: Single room with breakfast from £100; double room inc. breakfast from £120.
Leisure Breaks: Two day dinner, bed & breakfast for two people from £290.

- 15 en suite bedrooms, all with colour TV+sat, d-dial telephone + modem, radio/alarm, hairdryer, laundry service, tea/coffee making, trouser press.
- Table d'hôte dinner £20; last orders 9.30 pm.
- 2 mtg rooms for up to 50. Ample parking.
- Tennis, croquet. Golf, shooting, fishing, squash, riding nearby. ● Open all year.

& all major credit cards accepted.
Newbury & Andover 8, Southampton 33, London 77

Whitley Ridge Country House Hotel

Beaulieu Road, Brockenhurst,
New Forest, Hampshire SO42 7QL. Tel: (01590) 622354;
Fax: (01590) 622856
E-mail: whitleyridge@brockenhurst.co.uk
Website: www.newforest-hotels.co.uk

Secluded, yet very accessible, this Georgian house was once a hunting lodge near to the centre of the New Forest. The hotel is maintained to a very high standard and owners Rennie and Sue Law's attention to detail and good taste are evident in the choice of decor and furnishings. Renowned for its cuisine, Whitley Ridge has two AA 🌹🌹 and offers both table d'hôte and à la carte menus, together with a good vegetarian choice and an extensive wine list. Pre-dinner drinks can be taken either in the attractive cocktail bar or in the south-facing lounge with its welcoming log fire. Public rooms and the majority of bedrooms have fine views of the Forest, where ponies can be seen grazing. There is an all-weather tennis court and your hosts will be pleased to advise on local walks and excursions in this popular area.

Rates: Single with b'fst from £60; double fm £98.
Leisure Breaks: 3 nights for price of two Nov 10-Apr 3 Sun-Thurs £68 p pers per night, dinner, b & b.

- 14 en suite bedrooms, all with colour TV, direct dial tel, hairdryer, laundry/valet serv, tea/coffee making, radio/alarm; trouser press. ✂ rms available
- 3 cse tdh dinner fm £26; alc, Sun lunch, spec. diets avail. Last orders 9 pm. Meeting room for 20.
- Tennis, forest walks from hotel. Riding nearby.
- & major credit cards acc'd. Open all year.

Directions: From North, left on B3055, signed Beaulieu, past Balmer Lawn Hotel. Under rlwy bridge - hotel on left
Beaulieu 5, Lymington 5, Southampton 15, London 88.

Hampshire, New Milton   41

Chewton Glen
The Hotel, Health & Country Club

New Milton, Hampshire BH25 6QS
Tel: (01425) 275341; Fax: (01425) 272310
E-mail: reservations@chewtonglen.com
Website: www.chewtonglen.com

Look for a great team, a fine building situated close to the sea and on the edge of the New Forest , less than a two-hour drive from southwest London and you have found Chewton Glen. Offering consistently high standards and attention to detail in all areas, it is the only privately owned 5-red star hotel in the UK and has consistently set standards which others hotels aspire to emulate. The high point of your stay will probably be dining in the spacious airy restaurant with views from every table over the immaculate gardens. Preparation, presentation and service are of the highest standard, possibly equalled elsewhere, but certainly not surpassed. The hotel has 60 first class bedrooms including some on the ground floor overlooking the golf course, others a mix of traditional bedrooms and suites with balconies and terraces all with views over the gardens. The spa facilities are top class. If asked to sum up my visit, I would say "Ask and you shall get is the philosophy here."

Rates: Single/double room with breakfast from £280. Junior suite from £380; suite from £480. Rate including tdh dinner from £425 per room.
Leisure Breaks: 12% disc. for stays of 5+ nights; 7% disc. on the inclusive Sun-Thurs night prices.

- *59 en suite bedrooms (inc 22 suites), all with colour TV+ sat. direct-dial telephone, hairdryer, laundry service, trouser press, 24-hr room/meal service, radio/alarm clock, safe. bedrooms avail.*
- *Tdh dinner £55; last orders 9.30 pm; à la carte, lunch & special diets available. Open all year.*
- *6 meeting rms for up to 100. Barber/beauty shop*
- *Snooker, croquet, golf (9hole), spa, steam room, sauna, massage, in/outdoor pools, in/outdoor tennis. Riding, sailing, fishing, shooting nearby.*
- *& all major credit cards accepted. 100.*

Lymington 7, Bournemouth 10, Lyndhurst 12, Southampton 24, London 97.

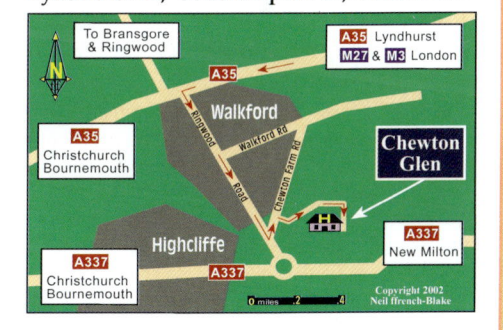

CENTRAL SOUTHERN ENGLAND

The Winchester Royal Hotel

St. Peter Street, Winchester,
Hampshire SO23 8BS
Tel: (01962) 840840; Fax: (01962) 841582
E-mail: royal@marstonhotels.com
Website: www.marstonhotels.com

The Winchester Royal is located in a quiet backwater just a hundred or so yards from the bustle of the pedestrian High Street, close to the famous cathedral, college and most of the historic attractions in Winchester, England's ancient capital. Built as a private residence in the mid 16th century, it has served as a bishop's house, a Benedictine convent and, since 1857, an hotel. In recent years the Winchester Royal has been extended and refurbished. However many of the original features have been retained and the atmosphere is one of warmth and comfort rarely found. As soon as you walk through the door, you know you are somewhere special. The AA rosetted restaurant produces daily changing menus, accompanied by a varied and sensibly priced wine list. In summer afternoon tea can be taken in the tranquillity of the garden. The staff are friendly and welcoming as well as being most knowledgeable about the city and surrounding area.

Rates: Single room with breakfast from £99; double room inc. breakfast from £129.
Getaway Breaks: Min. two nights from £67 per person inc. dinner, b & b. 3 & 4-day breaks available Easter & Xmas; 2-day New Years Breaks. Details on application or check our website (see address at left)

- 75 en suite bedrooms, all with colour TV+ satellite, direct-dial telephone, hairdryer, laundry service, tea/coffee making facilities, trouser press. Non-smoker bedrooms available. Car parking for 80.
- Table d'hôte dinner from £26; last orders 9.30 pm; à la carte, lunch & special diets available.
- Tennis $^{1}/_{2}$ mile; golf & riding three miles.
- & all major credit cards accepted.
- Open all year.

Romsey 10, Southampton 12, Basingstoke 18, Salisbury 23, Newbury 24, London 65.

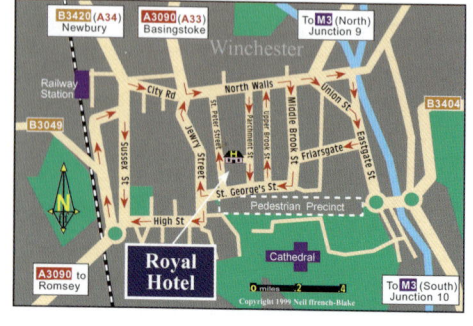

The Priory Bay Hotel

Priory Drive, Seaview,
Isle of Wight PO34 5BU
Tel: (01983) 613146;
Fax: (01983) 616539
E-mail: reception@priorybay.co.uk
Website: www.priorybay.co.uk

This exclusive 70-acre estate was originally built by medieval monks and is now probably the finest hotel on the Isle of Wight. Its mixture of medieval, Tudor and Georgian buildings have been carefully restored into a unique Country House Hotel by the sea. Within the grounds are tennis courts, a 9-hole golf course, a helicopter landing pad and an outdoor swimming pool. On the way to the beach is the Priory Oyster Restaurant where we enjoyed an excellent and romantic seafood supper in the summer, overlooking the sands of Priory Bay. Superior rooms are in the main building, whereas those in the converted barn outbuildings are more suitable for families. Self-catering cottages are also available. A nice touch, especially for the nautically inclined, is the provision, upon retiring, of a weather forecast sheet of paper in bedrooms. Subject to weather conditions, you can arrive in style - the hotel will send its own launch to Portsmouth and land you on its own beach. It also has a civil wedding licence. Dinner in the spacious dining room will be the highlight of the day, local game and seafood as well as produce from the hotel's own garden being used where possible. Cuisine is complemented by an exceptional wine list. To aid digestion, a summer stroll exploring the woodland and beach walks is recommended - an ideal end to a great day in a memorably relaxing setting.

- 18 en suite bedrooms (main hotel), 16 in new cottages & tithe barns. All with colour TV, direct-dial telephone, hairdryer, laundry/valet service.
- Tdh dinner £25. Alc, lunch & diets avail L.o.2115
- Tennis, golf, croquet, fishing, outdoor pool, massage, sailing, riding, clay shooting, beach.
- Children welcome. Dogs in cottages only.
- Two meeting rooms, capacity 90. Open all year.
- Visa, Mastercard, Switch accepted.

Ryde 3, Bembridge 3, Sandown 6, Newport 9, Cowes 12, London 77 (via ferry).

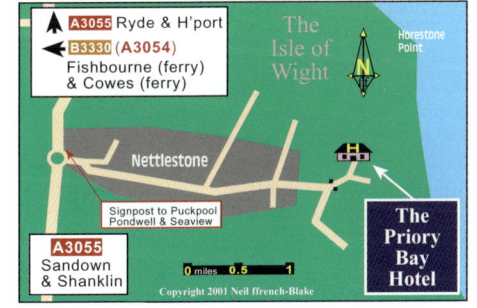

Rates: Single room with breakfast from £49 ; double, b & b from £98. Dinner, bed & breakfast from £69(adult)/£35 (child 4-11) per pers per night. **Bargain Breaks:** Reductions for 3-7 night breaks.

Oxfordshire, Clanfield

The Plough at Clanfield

Bourton Road, Clanfield, Bampton,
Oxfordshire OX18 2RB
Tel: (01367) 810222; Fax: (01367) 810596
E-mail: ploughatclanfield@hotmail.com

The Plough is no ordinary inn, for this fine Cotswold manor house has been painstakingly restored and attractively furnished by John and Rosemary Hodges and their family to provide guests with every modern comfort in an Elizabethan setting. The combined lounge and bar area is invitingly cosy with magnificent fireplace, oak beams and homely armchairs. However guests will wish to savour the delights of the award-winning AA ❀❀ Shires Restaurant, which is famous throughout the Cotswolds. Here in elegant surroundings, guests can enjoy excellent French and English cooking and a wide choice of wines. There is also the smaller Portrait Room for that more private occasion. Bedrooms are traditionally furnished, with nice little extras like a sherry decanter and home-made biscuits; three are ground floor and four are four-posters. Clanfield is near Burford, the 'Gateway to the Cotswolds' and is excellently placed for visiting Oxford and Lechlade. The Plough is a good spot to be pampered for a few days in sleepy English village tranquillity.

Rates: *Single room with breakfast from £90;*
Double *room inc. breakfast from £120.*
Leisure Breaks. *Min. two-night Cotswold Break, £60 pppn, dinner, b & b + aft. tea & a Cotswold gift, available throughout the year.*

- 12 en suite rooms, all with d-dial telephone, colour TV, hairdryer, tea/coffee making, fax/modem points, trouser press, radio/alarm clock. ✗ & ♿ rooms available.
- Tdh 3-cse dinner £23.50, lunch & special diets available; last orders 9 pm.
- Golf and riding nearby.
- Meeting room for 10. Parking for 30.
- Diners, Master-card, Visa, Switch, Delta
- Open all year exc. 24 Dec-4 January.

Faringdon 3, Lechlade 5, Burford 7, Swindon 17, Oxford 20, London 76.

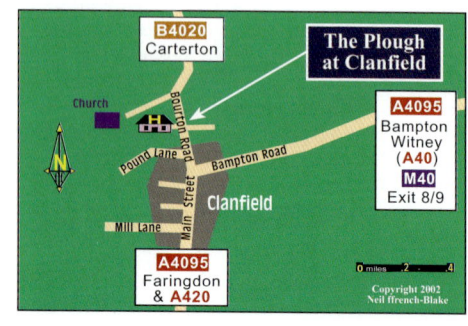

The Cotswold Lodge Hotel

66a Banbury Road, Oxford OX2 6JP
Tel: (01865) 512121; Fax: (01865) 512490
E-mail: sig@cotswoldlodgehotel.co.uk
Website: www.cotswoldlodgehotel.co.uk

The elegant 4-star Cotswold Lodge Hotel is a delightfully peaceful retreat, set in a conservation area only half a mile from the historic dreaming spires of Oxford city centre. Bedrooms are very comfortable - each floor having a different style. The ten deluxe rooms and suites, named after Oxford colleges - the *Pembroke*, the *Merton*, the *Somerville* and so on - are individually designed and resemble those in a country manor. Downstairs the drawing room is smartly furnished with antiques. Current magazines and flowers are in abundance. The Scholars Bar is the perfect meeting place for a light lunch or to relax with a drink in the evening. Fellows Restaurant was redecorated in 2002 and now has large wall frescoes of Georgian scenes. Each table is adorned with fresh flowers and the cuisine, under the supervision of chef Garin Chapman, is international with well thought out dishes to suit every palate. The quality of food is exceptional: freshly baked bread, free-range eggs, specially made sausages, free range local poultry, fresh cod and lobster from Cornwall, wild salmon from Scotland and local lamb and game. Weddings and conferences are a speciality with space for 90 delegates. The new ground floor opens onto the patio and courtyard, ideal for al fresco dining and drinks. The hotel is excellently placed for that leisure break in Oxford or the Cotswolds and is highly recommended for both business or pleasure.

Single room with breakfast from £125; ***Double*** *room inc. breakfast from £175; suite from £245.* ***Leisure Breaks.*** *Fri/Sat/Sun, dinner (to value of £25 per head), b & b £225 per couple per night.*

- *49 en suite rooms (inc 10 suites), all with d-dial telephone, colour TV+SKY, laundry/valet service, hairdryer, tea/coffee making, 24-hr room/meal service, trouser press. E-mail facilities.*
- *Alc 3-cse dinner from £17.50, lunch & special diets available; last orders 10 pm.* 🅿 *45.*
- *Golf, in/out door swimming pool, riding nearby.*
- *Business services inc. meeting rooms to 90.*
- AMERICAN EXPRESS *& all major credit cards acc'd.*
- *Open all year.*

Banbury 23, High Wycombe 26, Aylesbury 22, Cheltenham 43, London 56.

Oxfordshire, Bledington. **Wiltshire**, Salisbury

The King's Head Inn & Restaurant

The Green, Bledington, Oxfordshire OX7 6XQ. Tel: (01608) 658365; Fax: (01608) 658902
E-mail: kingshead@Orr-Ewing.com
Website: www.kingsheadinn.net.
Runner-up *Sunday Times Pub of the Year 2000.*
Good Pub Guide '*Gloucestershire Pub of the Year Award 2001*'

The King's Head occupies a striking position on the village green of this pretty Cotswold village, frequent winner of the Bledisloe Cup *Best Kept Village* Award. Cosy bedrooms are either in the 15th century older part of the inn (access via outside staircases) or in the newer block, approached across a leafy small courtyard. The restaurant, with inglenook fireplace, pews and oak chairs, has earned a high local reputation for creative personal cuisine. Everything is prepared in-house and whether you go for snack in the bar (popular with locals) or eat *à la carte* from the enterprising menu where fresh meat, game and fish all feature, you will be well satisfied. There is a private dining/sitting room and an upstairs quiet 'smoking room'.

Rates: Single room with breakfast from £50; double room inc. b'fast from £70-85; 4-poster £100.

- 12 en suite bedrooms, (one four-poster) all with colour TV, direct-dial telephone, radio/alarm, hairdryer, tea/coffee making facilities.
- Table d'hote 3 cse dinner £9.95; alc 3-cse ca £20. Bar meals, lunch & vegetarian dishes available. Last orders 9 pm. Real ale.
- Walks, garden. Golf, clay pigeon shooting, quad biking, fishing, riding nearby. No dogs. P ample.
- & Mastercard, Visa, Switch accepted. **Stow-on-the-Wold** 3, Chipping Norton 4, Oxford 21, London 81

Howard's House Hotel

Teffont Evias, Nr. Salisbury, Wiltshire SP3 5RJ
Tel: (01722) 716392; Fax: (01722) 716820
E-mail: enquiries@howardshousehotel.co.uk
Website: www.howardshousehotel.co.uk

It would be difficult to find a better setting for a small hotel than Teffont Evias. Tucked away in a fold of the Nadder valley, the village has remained almost unchanged for 300 years. The Grade II listed Howard's House is a little gem. Its Swiss-style roof and gables were inspired by a 19th-century owner. Today it sits in two acres of glorious garden and exudes understated luxury. Spacious bedrooms, each one different, are furnished with top quality fabrics and come with many little extras. A cosy lounge, adorned with fresh flowers and magazines, where a log fire burns in winter, is complemented by a newly refurbished restaurant overlooking the garden. For anyone looking for a quiet break near Salisbury, Wilton and Stonehenge, Howard's House comes highly recommended.

Rates: Single room with breakfast from £75; double room inc. b'fast from £125.

- 9 en suite bedrooms, all with colour TV, direct-dial telephone, radio/alarm, hairdryer, tea/coffee making facilities.
- Table d'hote 3 cse dinner from £25; alc & sp diets available. Last orders 9.30 pm. ● Mtg room for 20.
- Croquet, garden. Golf, shooting, fishing, riding nearby. Dogs welcome. P 10 cars.
- & Mastercard, Visa, Diners accepted. **Wilton** 7, Salisbury 10, Shaftsb'y 11, Stonehenge 13, London 102

Signpost Guide 2003
London & the South

Fact File
Illustrated Guide to
Historic Houses, Gardens & Sites
Diary of Events

Hotels in	PAGE
London	53
East Sussex	62
Kent	67
Surrey	70
West Sussex	75

London & the Southeast

Historic Houses, Gardens & Parks

London
Carlyle's House, Chelsea
Fenton House, Hampstead
Kensington Palace, Kensington Gardens, W8
Osterley Park, Isleworth
Tower of London, Tower Hill, EC3
Westminster Abbey Chapter House, SWI

Kent
Bedgebury National Pinetum, Nr. Goudhurst
Chilham Castle Gardens, Nr Canterbury
Doddington Place Gardens, Nr Sittingboume
Godington House & Gardens, Godington Park, Ashford
Goodnestone Park, Wingham, Nr. Canterbury
Iden Croft Herbs, Staplehurst
Kent Garden Vineyard, Headcorn
Penshurst Place & Gardens, Nr. Tonbndge
Sissinghurst Garden

Surrey
Clandon Park, West Clandon
Claremont Landscape Garden, Esher
Ham House, Richmond
Hampton Court Palace, East Molesey
Hatchlands Park, East Clandon
Kew Gardens (Royal Botanic Gardens), Richmond
Polesden Lacey, Great Bookham, Nr. Dorking
The RHS Garden, Wisley, Nr. Woking
The Savill Garden, Nr. Egham
Winkworth Arboretum, Hascombe, Nr. Godalming

East Sussex
Alfriston Clergy House, Alfriston
Battle Abbey, Battle
Brickwall House & Gardens, Northiam, Nr. Rye
Carr Taylor Vineyards, Hastings
Great Dixter House & Gardens, Northiam, Nr. Rye
Michelham Priory, Upper Dicker, Nr. Hailsham
Merriments Gardens, Hurst Green
Pashley Manor Gardens Ticehurst
Preston Manor, Preston Park, Brighton
Royal Pavilion, Brighton
Sheffield Park Garden, Danehill, Nr. Uckfield

West Sussex
Denmans Garden, Fontwell, Nr. Arundel
GoodwoodHouse,Goodwood
Leonardslee Gardens, Lower Beeding, Horsham
Parham House & Gardens, Parham Park, Pulborough
Petworth House & Park
St. Mary's House,Bramber, Nr. Steyning
Standen, East Grinstead
Wakehurst Place Gardens, Ardingly, Nr.Haywards Heath

Walks & Nature Trails

Kent
Bewl Water Walks and Rides, Nr. Lamberhurst
Cobtree Manor Park Nature Trail
The Ecological Park, Elms Vale
Hastings Country Park, Hastings
Haysden Country Park Nature Trail
The Western Heights, Dover
White Cliffs Country Trail (various walks), around Kent

West Sussex
Burton Pond Nature Trail
Worth Way Walk, from Worth Way to East Grinstead

Historic Sites & Museums

London
Bntish Museum Great Russell Street, WC1
Guinness World of Records, The Trocadero Centre
The London Dungeon, 28 -34 Tooley Street, SE1
Mall Galleries The Mall, SWl
National Portrait Gallery, St. Martin's Place, WC2
Natural History Museurn, Cromwell Road, SW7
The Queen's Gallery, Buckingham Palace
Royal Mews, Buckingham Palace Road, SWI
Science Museums, Exhibihon Road, SW7
The Tate Gallery, Millbank, SWl
Tower Bridge SEl
Victoria & Albert Museum, Cromwell Road, SW7

East Sussex
Anne of Cleves House Museum, Lewes
Bodiam Castle, Bodiam
Brighton Museum & Art Gallery
Filching Manor Motor Museum, Polegate
Hastings Castle and 1066 Story, West Hill, Hastings Hove Museum & Art Gallery
Quarry Farm Rural Experience, Robertsbridge

West Sussex
Arundel Castle, Arundel

Kent
Canterbury Cathedral
The Canterbury Tales, Canterbury
The Dickens Centre, Rochester
Dover Castle & Hellfire Comer
Eurotunnel Exhibition Centre, Folkestone
Guildhall Museum, Rochester
Leeds Castle, Nr. Maidstone
Lympne Castle, Nr. Hythe
Rochester Castle

Surrey
Brooklands Museum, Weybndge

Entertainment Venues

London
Madame Tussaud's & The London Planetarium, NWl
London Zoo, Regent's Park, NWl

East Sussex
The Bluebell Railway - Living Museum, Shenfield Park
Hastings Sea Life Centre

West Sussex
Butlins Southcoast World, Bognor
Coombes Farm Tours, Lancing
Pulborough Brooks RSPB Nature Reserve

Kent
The Buttefly Centre, Swingfield Dover
Kent & East Sussex Steam Railway, Tenterden
Port Lympne Wild Annmal Park, Mansion & Gardens
Toy & Model Museum, Lamberhurst

Surrey
Birdworld, Nr. Farnham
Gatwick Zoo, Charlwood
Thorpe Park, Chertsey

DIARY OF EVENTS

January

1. **New Years Day Parade.** Trafalgar Square, London SW1.
9-19. **49th London Internat'l Boat Show**, Earls Court, London SW5.
4-12. **Embassy World Professional Darts Championship.** Lakeside Cntry Club, Frimley Surrey.
10-26. **London Int'l Mime Festival.** Various venues, London.
16-20. **Art 2002.** the London Contemporary Art Fair. Business Design Centre, 52 Upper Street, N1.
14-19. **Decorative Antiques & Textiles Fair.** Battersea Park, London SW11.
17-20. **The Knit, Stitch & creative Crafts Show** - Southeast. Sandown Park Exhibition Centre, Esher, Surrey.

February

2. **Chinese New Year Celebrations.** Centred on Gerrard St & Leicester Sq, London W1
2-9*. **Snooker: Benson & Hedges Masters Tournament.** Wembley Conference Centre.
6. **Gun Salute.** Accession Day. Hyde Park & Tower of London.
14-16. **Brighton Intl Modelworld.** Brighton Centre, E Sussex
15-16*. **Motorsport Day.** Brooklands Museum, Weybridge, Sur'y
15. **England v France.** Lloyds 6-Nation Rugby Cup, Twickenham.
21-23. **13th Sussex Beer & Cider Festival**, Hove, Sussex.
23. **Winter Bearfest.** Festival of Bears. Kensington Town Hall, W8.
25-2.3*. **Fine Art & Antiques Fair.** Olympia, Hammersmith Rd, W14.
27-1.3. **Philatex.** London Int'l Stamp Show. Royal Hort Soc Halls, Vincent Sq, Lon SW1.

March

1-3*. **National Wedding Show.** Olympia, London W14.
8-9*. **London Classic Motor Show.** Alexandra Palace, N22.
9. **England v Italy.** 6-nations cup, Twickenham.
12-6.4. **Daily Mail Ideal Home Show.** Earls Court, London SW5
15-16. **RHS London Orchid Show.** RHS Halls, Vincent Sq, London SW1.
16-18. **London International Book Fair.** Olympia, SW5
19-23. **Country Living Fair.** Business Design Centre, Lon N1
19-25. **BADA Antiques & Fine Art Fair,** Duke of York's HQ, Kings Road, London SW3.
29. **Head of the River Race** - Mortlake to Putney, London.
22. **England v Scotland.** Lloyds 6-Nation Cup, Twickenham.
23. **Daily Mail Schools Rugby Day.** Under 15s/Under 18s &c, Twickenham, Middlesex.

April

1-30*. **London Int'l String Quartet Competition.** Goldsmiths Hall, London EC2
5. **Oxford v Cambridge University Boat Race,** Putney to Mortlake, London
6. **MG Day.** Brooklands Museum, Weybridge, Surrey.
6. **Vintage Car Show.** Amberley Museum, Arundel, W Ssx.
8-9*. **RHS Daffodil Show.** RHS Halls, Greycoat Pl, LondonSW1
13. **Flora London Marathon.**
18-20. **Goodwood House Elegant Homes & Gardens Show,** Goodwood, W Sussex.
24-27*. **Chelsea Art Fair.** Chelsea Town Hall, Kings Rd, SW3
25-26. **Whitbread Gold Cup.** Sandown Park, Esher, Surrey.

May

1-31.8. **Glyndebourne Festival Opera.** Nr. Lewes, East Sussex
1-5. **Tulip Festival.** Pashley Manor Gardens, Ticehurst, E. Ssx.
3-25. **Brighton International Festival.** Various venues,
3-5. **Weald of Kent Craft Fair.** Penshurst Pl, Tonbridge, Kent
5-6. **Dover Pageant.** Dover College Grounds, Dover, Kent
9*. **Beating the Bounds.** Tower of London, London EC3
10-11* **Festival of English Food & Wine.** Leeds Castle, Kent.
16-20. **England v Sri Lanka.** 1st Test, Lords, London NW1.
17-18. **Christopher Awdry Weekend.** Eastbourne min. Steam Railway Park, E Sussex. Thomas the Tank Engine author.
20-23. **Chelsea Flower Show** Royal Hospital, London SW3.
22-26. **England v Zimbabwe.** Test Match, Lords, London NW1

June

1. **RFU County Championship Shield Final**, Twickenham, Mx
1-31.8. **Royal Academy Summer Exhibition**. Burlington House, Piccadilly, W1.
5-6. **Beating the Retreat.** Horse Guards Parade, London SW1.
6-7. **Vodafone Oaks/Derby Days.** Epsom Racec'se, Surrey
14. **Trooping the Colour.** Horse Guards, London SW1
5-11*. **Stella Artois Tennis Champ'ps.** Queen's C1ub.W14
11-17. **Grosvenor House Art & Antiques Fair.** London W1.
14-22. **Broadstairs Dickens Festival.** Broadstairs, Kent.
17-20. **Royal Ascot.** (Ladies Day = 19th), Ascot, Berks.
23-July 6. **Wimbledon Lawn Tennis Championships.** All England Club, London SW19.
20. **England v Pakistan.** Natwest One-Day Int'l. The Oval.
22. **England v Pakistan.** Natwest One Day Int'l. Lords NW1
28. **England v South Africa.** Natwest AMP. The Oval, SE1.
29. **Zimbabwe v South Africa.** Natwest. Canterbury, Kent

For further details, contact: The South East England Tourist Board. The Old Brew Hse, Warwick Park, Tunbridge Wells, Kent TN2 5TU. Tel: (01892) 540766. Website: www. southeastengland.uk.com or....

London & the Southeast 49

LONDON & THE SOUTHEAST

London & the Southeast

July

1-31*. **Goodwood Festival of Speed.** Chichster, W Sussex.
4-5. **Coral-Eclipse Race Meeting.** Sandown Park, Surrey.
12. **Natwest One-Day Final.** Lords, London NW1.
13-20. **Golf. the Open Championships.** Sandwich, Kent.
18 -Sept 13. **BBC Henry Wood Promenade Concerts.** Royal Albert Hall, London SW7.
21-27*. **Farnborough Air Show** Farnboro' Nr Guildford, Surrey.
29-2 Aug. **Glorious Goodwood.** Goodwood, W Sussex.
31-4.8.**England v South Africa.** 2nd npower Test. Lords NW1

August

2*. **Cranleigh Show.** Surrey
3-26*. **Arundel Art & Craft 2002.** Norfolk Centre, Arundel
24-25. **Notting Hill Carnival.** Ladbroke Grove, London W14

September

1*. **Medieval Country Fayre.** Arundel Town Centre, W Ssx.
26-28. **Ascot Festival Autumn Meeting.** Ascot, Berks.
12-21. **Chelsea Antiques Fair** Town Hall, London SW3.
23-18.10. **London Festival of Chamber Music.**

October

11-25. **Canterbury Festival.** Canterbury, Kent
12*. **Autumn Vintage Vehicle Show.**Amberley Museum,W Ssx
20. **Trafalgar Day Parade.** The Sea Cadet Corps. Traf Sq, SW1
24-2.11. **Festival of Animated Theatre. Visions 2002.** Var. venues, Brighton, East Sussex.

November

2. **London to Brighton RAC Veteran Car Run.** Hyde Park.

Sunday 11. **Remembrance Sunday Ceremony.** London SW1.
8. **Lord Mayor's Show**.City.
10-13. **World Travel Market.** Excel Exhib Ctre, Canary Whrf
24-27.**Royal Smithfield Show** Earls Court Exhib Centre, SW5

December

13-17*. **Olympia Int'l Show-jumping Championship.** Olympia, London W14

Bank & Public Holidays in the British Isles 2003
1 January. *New Year's Day*
1 March. *St David's Day (W)*
17 March. *St Patrick's Day (RI,NI)*
18 April. *Good Friday*
21 April. *Easter Monday*
5 May. *Early May Bank Holiday*
26 May.*Spring Bank Holiday (UK)*
2 June. *June Holiday (RI)*
12 July. *Bank Holdiay (NI)*
4 August. *Bank Holiday (RI,S)*
25 August.*Bank Holiday (E,NI,W)*
27 October. *October Holiday (RI)*
30 November. *St Andrew's Day (S)*
25 December. *Christmas Day*
26 December. *Boxing Day*
E = England; NI = Northern Ireland; RI = Irish Republic; S = Scotland; W = Wales.

London Tourist Board & Convention Bureau. 26, Grosvenor Gardens Victoria. London SW1W 0DU.Tel: 020 7932 2000. Website: www.londontown.com

The South-East

Kent is the garden of England - and its oldest city Canterbury, with its cathedral, is the centre of the Anglicanfaith. The impressive Knole Park, near Sevenoaks, was built in the 15th century by an Archbishop of Canterbury. Near Maidstone is the impeccable Leeds Castle, founded in 857 and later improved by Henry VIII. In East Sussex lies the peaceful Bodlam Castle (below), surounded by its moat and never breached by an enemy.

Over the South Downs lies Brighton, Regency summer capital of Britain with the eccentric Pavilion and to the west of Brighton is the impressive Arundel Castle, Norman stronghold, now inhabited by the Duke of Norfolk (above). Chichester, west of Arundel, has an 11th century cathedral, narrow streets of timber-clad houses and an annual drama festival.

Ashdown Forest, now more heath than forest in East Sussex covers some 6000 acres and is home to badgers and fallow deer.

On the outskirts of London, near Bromley, Kent, Chislehurst Caves have long been a favourite with children. Further East Chatham's 400-year old dock-yard provides a history of Britain's fighting ships. Ashford in southeast Kent is the mouth of the Channel Tunnel, Gateway to Europe. Dover Castle houses the White Cliffs Experience and Churchill's War Rooms - nerve centre for the Dunkirk evacuation and the Battle of Britain of 1940.

**SIGNPOST'S RECOMMENDED AGENT
FOR HOTEL SALES & VALUATIONS**

ROBERT BARRY
& Co
HOTEL, LEISURE & LICENSED PROPERTY SPECIALISTS

We now have seven offices, enabling us to offer an even better service
national marketing...local knowledge

Please contact your nearest office:

LONDON	CIRENCESTER	PLYMOUTH	SOUTHAMPTON
0207 344 6666	01285 641642	01752 664499	023 8063 6333
@robertbarry.co.uk	c@robertbarry.co.uk	p@robertbarry.co.uk	s@robertbarry.co.uk

MANCHESTER	HARROGATE	EDINBURGH
0161 233 7030	01423 566362	0131 225 2944
m@robertbarry.co.uk	h@robertbarry.co.uk	e@robertbarry.co.uk

www.robertbarry.co.uk

London

London's treasures are well chronicled. Most visitors prefer to stay in the west / central Knightsbridge/Kensington areas which are handy for shopping and allow quick access into the West End for theatres and other functions. London's main museums - the Natural History, Science and Victoria and Albert are also in this area.

In the Central/West End area most visited sights are the (now) public rooms of Buckingham Palace, the National Gallery in Trafalgar Square, Westminster Abbey and the Houses of Parliament, the Cabinet War Rooms by Admiralty Arch, whence Churchill directed the second world war when bombing made the rest of the capital unsafe (the 70 rooms, of which 19 are open to the public, cover a subterranean warren of three acres), the Tate Gallery on the Embankment, containing mainly 20th century masterpieces.

Westminster Abbey, nearly a thousand years old, has tombs of many English kings queens, statesmen and writers. The British Museum in Bloomsbury houses one of the world's largest collections of antiquities, including the *Magna Carta,* the Elgin Marbles and the first edition of Alice in Wonderland.

Further east in the city of London is St Paul's Cathedral, designed by Sir Christoher Wren after the original was destroyed in the Great Fire of London (1666), whose epitaph is below the dome *"if you seek hi monument, look around you".* Other notable buildings of the city are the Guildhall, the Mansion House, official residence of the Lord Mayor of London and further East, the Tower of London, a medieval fortress dominated by the White Tower and dating from 1097. The Crown Jewels are housed in the tower, which is policed by the famous Beefeaters.

In North Central London (Baker St - home of the fictitious Sherlock Holmes) are the Planetarium and Madame Tussauds, although the London Dungeon, near London Bridge Station, has recently overtaken Tussauds' *Chamber of Horrors* as childrens' favourite collection of gruesome displays.

London's parks are its 'lungs' and a pleasant place to relax on a summer's afternoon. St James, the oldest one, was founded by Henry VIII in 1532, is the most central and covers 90 acres. Hyde Park, bordering Kensington, Mayfair and Marylebone is the largest at 630 acres and includes the famous Serpentine artificial lake where the hardy still swim on Christmas Day. Regents Park, lies north of Oxford Circus, and was given to the nation by the Prince Regent. Further out are Richmond Park in the southwest, where deer still abound, and Kew Gardens, with its famous tropical greenhouses and plants.

In the south-east of the capital, land to the East of the Tower of London has been reclaimed and Canary Wharf and the Docklands area provide an interesting study of urban renewal. On the south bank opposite Docklands is Greenwich Observatory, the National Maritime Museum and the Millennium dome.

The Ascott Mayfair

49 Hill Street, London
W1J 5NB
Tel: (020) 7499 6868;
Fax: (020) 7499 0705
Reservations tel: 020 7659 4321
Reservations fax: 020 7659 4322
E-mail: enquiry.london@the-ascott.com
Website: www.the-ascott.com

Situated in the heart of prestigious Mayfair, the Ascott is a superb compliment to its elegant surroundings and combines all the services of an hotel within the privacy and spaciousness offered by self-styled 'residences'. These luxurious apartments have every modern facility, including fax and computer modem points and the Business Service can provide the use of a boardroom with secretarial and executive support functions. Yet the central location and home comforts make it ideal for the leisure visitor too: the one, two or three-room air-conditioned apartments each have lounge, dining and study areas, whole stylish design themes reflect the sophisticated art deco period of the building. Wide sofas and cosy chairs make for easy relaxation with satellite television, video players and music system providing in-house entertainment. Bathrooms are luxurious, whilst personal maid and 24-hour concierge ensure that all needs are met. The club offers a comfortable lounge and bar exclusively for residents and the Hothouse a health club. Guests seeking to be shamelessly pampered will be pleased to discover that this is the Ascott's primary objective as well!

- 56 apartments, all with air-conditioning, radio, colour TV+ satellite, direct-dial telephone with voicemail, hairdryer, laundry/valet service, tea/coffee making, CD player, fax machine in rooms, modem point, honesty bar, safety deposit box, fully equipped kitchen, washers/dryers, iron + board.
- Terrace Room with free continental breakfast.
- Business services inc 2 meeting rooms, capacity 40, secretarial help.
- Fitness centre/gym, sauna, steam room, solarium.
- 24-hour concierge, landscaped garden, maid service.
- The Club - lounge and bar.
- & major credit cards accepted.
- Open all year.

Rates: Studio apartments: daily £205; weekly £1360; monthly £5620.
One-bedroom apartments: daily £260; weekly £1725; monthly £7100.
Two-bedroom apartments: daily £435; weekly £2895; monthly £11,100.
Three-bedroom apartments: daily £595; weekly £3955; monthly £16,300.
Longer term rates - on request.
All rates + VAT @ $17\frac{1}{2}$%.

The Leonard

15 Seymour Street, London W1H 7JW
Tel: (020) 7935 2010; Fax: (020) 7935 6700
E-mail: the.leonard@dial.pipex.com
Website: www.theleonard.com

Behind Oxford Street, four Georgian townhouses have been converted into a smart hotel, whose fine antiques & pictures and state of the art technology make it equally attractive to business and leisure traveller alike. The bar/café serves breakfast and light meals all day from gleaming silver and Wedgwood china. Service is attentive but not intrusive. Rooms vary in size, from spacious suites to compact doubles. All are decorated to a high standard with individual objets d'art, hi-fi, dedicated fax/modem lines, power showers, *Frette* bedlinen, bathrobes and air-conditioning. A refurbishment has brought more rooms and a roof terrace. There is also a small exercise room and a private meeting/dining room. The Leonard is a most complete hotel with welcoming, easy going staff.

Rates: *Single/double/twin, room only, fm £200.*
Leisure Breaks: *Dbl/twin from £115 pppn, min 2 nights, inc. ½ bottle champagne & box of fudge.*

- 44 AC en suite bedrooms, all with radio, colour TV+ sat, d-dial telephone + fax/modem pts, safe, hairdryer, laundry service, 24-hr rm/meal service.
- Meeting rm for 15. Compact exercise room
- & major cards accepted. Open all year.

10 Manchester Street

10 Manchester Street, London W1U 4DG
Tel: (020) 7486 6669; Fax: (020) 7224 0348
E-mail: stay@10manchesterstreet.fsnet.co.uk
Website: www.10manchesterstreet.com

Close to tree-lined Manchester Square and the Wallace Collection, this 1919 townhouse is also convenient for visiting Madame Tussauds and the London Planetarium. Number 10 stands out in a redbrick terrace on a quietish residential street. Its entrance is framed by climbing plants and colourful window boxes. The ground floor lounge is welcoming with coffee, daily newspapers and even an Internet facility tucked away by a corner sofa. This relaxing style continues in the soft-green basement breakfast room where a varied continental buffet is served. There is a mix of rooms and suites, all newly decorated, simply furnished but spotless and comfortable. For a classic boutique hotel at the heart of the West End, No 10 offers exceptionally good value.

Rates: *Single room with b'fst fm £120; double fm £150.* **Weekend Rates:** *£50 per pers. per night, two people sharing Fri/Sat/Sun nights.*

- 46 en suite bedrooms (inc 9 suites), all with radio/CD player, colour TV+sat, d-dial telephone + fax/modem pts, safe, hairdryer, laundry service, tea/coffee making, trouser press. ✂ rms available.
- Visa, Mastercard accepted. Open all year.

The Beaufort

33 Beaufort Gardens,
Knightsbridge, London SW3 1PP
Tel: (020) 7584 5252; Fax: (020) 7589 2834
E-mail: reservations@thebeaufort.co.uk
Website: www.thebeaufort.co.uk

For visitors to London, the Beaufort cannot be better placed - being 100 yards from Harrods in a quiet tree lined square. The many accolades the hotel has received (including *Best of the Best* - Courvoisier and *Best Hotel in London for Service* - US Zagat Guide) made it an interesting visit for your inspector. I was greeted by a smiling member of staff and seated in comfortable country house furniture. Bright colours abound and immediately lift the spirit. 28 rooms of differing size - from singles, doubles/twins to suites, all with their own smart bathrooms and decorated in cheerful pastel shades are fully air-conditioned. The hotel's walls are adorned with over 400 original English water colours. Complimentary breakfast in rooms is served on Wedgwood china with silver cutlery and consists of croissants, home made jam, fresh orange juice and excellent coffee. A pleasant touch is that all visitors are greeted with chocolates, biscuits and refreshing drinks in their rooms on arrival. Afternoon cream teas with home-made scones are served daily in the drawing room free of charge to hotel guests. Complimentary membership of a local health club is also included in the room price. Junior suite prices include a one way airport transfer (3 -night min. stay). There is 24-hour porterage and all guests have a key to the front door for late entry.

- *28 en suite rooms with air-conditioning, colour TV + satellite, direct-dial telephone; hairdryer, laundry/valet service, bedrooms, internet access, radio/alarm, trouser press (on request).*
- *Complimentary residents' bar open for guests 3pm-11 pm.*
- *Gymnasium and indoor pool nearby. (Free usage)*
- *Airport transfer on request. No restaurant.*
- *AMERICAN EXPRESS & all major credit cards accepted.*
- *Open all year.*

Rates: Single room incl. breakfast & service from £185; double from £195-£275; suite from £325.

London, SW3

LONDON & THE SOUTHEAST

Parkes Hotel

41 Beaufort Gardens, Knightsbridge,
London SW3 1PW
Tel: (020) 7581 9944; Fax: (020) 7581 1999
E-mail: reception@parkeshotel.com
Website: www.parkeshotel.com

Parkes is a small, fully air conditioned privately owned townhouse hotel in a quiet tree-lined cul de sac only 100 metres from Harrods. Now totally refurbished and with an oak-panelled ground floor from the reception area to the comfortable lounge this warm, discreet place coveys a relaxed atmosphere with friendly staff on hand 24 hours a day. No two bedrooms or suites are the same in decor or size, although the use of sumptuous fabrics and rich colours is common throughout. Some have patios, others balconies, many come with fully equipped kitchens, all have minibars offering 81 different types of refreshment. The new luxury is understated, traditional, but with modern facilities ranging from personal climate control to heated floors and power showers in the green marble bathrooms. State of the art services include 28 digital TV channels, UK/US modem ports, sockets and voicemail. The suites are ideal for small business meetings or social gatherings.

Full English breakfast is on offer in the attractive dining room - Knightsbridge's fine restaurants take care of the rest of the day.

Rates: *Single room incl. breakfast & service from £235; double from £294; junior suite from £332.*

- 33 en suite AC rooms (inc 14 suites), all with colour TV + satellite, direct-dial telephone, fax/modem points, hairdryer, laundry/valet service, radio/alarm, minibar, trouser press, safe.
- Gymnasium and riding in Hyde Park nearby.
- Airport transfer on request. No restaurant.
- & all major credit cards accepted.
- Open all year.

The De Vere Cavendish St James's

81 Jermyn Street, London SW1Y 6JF
Tel: (020) 7930 2111; Fax: (020) 7839 2125

E-mail: tracey.grehan@devere-hotels.com
Website: www.devere-hotels.com/cavendish

The historic De Vere Cavendish, St James's has remained at the forefront of London hotels for the past 200 years and was run nearly a century ago by Rosa Lewis, the "Duchess of Duke Street", whose influence on an earlier Cavendish made it so much a part of the social scene that Edward VII preferred entertaining here to nearby Buckingham Palace. It is situated in one of London's most prestigious locations, just minutes' walk from theatres, restaurants, clubs and London's fabulous nightlife. The hotel itself offers two bars, a relaxing lounge and an award winning first floor restaurant - *Leyton's Brasserie*. The building has recently undergone a major refurbishment resulting in stylishly redesigned bedrooms, most with magnificent views, furnished to the highest standard and with air-conditioning and modem points. The soothing ambience of the hotel will guarantee guests a restful stay whilst enjoying the benefits of a central location. This makes the hotel a perfect choice for leisure and business traveller alike. Unsurprisingly, the Cavendish has won many top awards for quality, comfort and service.

Rates: Single room incl. breakfast & service from £162; double from £184. All prices VAT inclusive.
Leisure Breaks: Midweek and weekend leisure breaks available from £98 per person sharing twin or double, b & b; from £118 pp dinner, b & b.

● 230 AC en suite rooms with col TV + sat, safe, d-dial telephone + ISDN/modem pts; hairdryer, trouser press, laundry service, minibar, 24-hour room service. Iron & board on request. ✁ rms avail.
● 2-cse table d'hôte dinner from £18.50. A la carte, lunch & special diets available. Last orders 10.30 pm. Ring anytime for current special offers.
● Business services inc. 4 meeting rooms, capacity 100. Car parking. Gymnasium and pool nearby.
● Master-card, Visa, JCB, Diners Club, credit cards accepted.
● Open all year.

Basil Street Hotel

Basil Street, Knightsbridge,
London SW3 1AH
Tel: (020) 7581 3311; Fax: (020) 7581 3693
E-Mail: info@TheBasil.com
Website: www.TheBasil.com

A rare example of a major London hotel still in private ownership, the Basil Street Hotel is a reminder of a more gracious age. It is a treasure trove of fine paintings, antiques and objets d'art, now discreetly adapted to provide contemporary comforts in the heart of fashionable Knightsbridge. A country house hotel in the middle of London, each of the bedrooms is individually furnished and the longstanding staff are reminiscent of family retainers who recognise regular guests. The country house atmosphere is further preserved by the Afternoon Tea tradition in the lounge. In the evening piano playing adds to the pleasure of eating in *one of the loveliest dining rooms in London* where menus offer a choice from a light lunch to a sumptuous dinner. Meeting rooms can cater for up to 30 people and the Parrot Club, recently profiled on BBC television, offers lady guests a soothing retreat. The Hotel is within easy walking distance of Harrods, Harvey Nichols and Peter Jones, convenient for museums and, via Knightsbridge Underground Station, has excellent connections to the West End.

Single room only from £145.00 + VAT.
Double/twin room only from £205.00 + VAT.
Special Breaks: Weekend, Xmas/New Year, August and Long Stay rates available on request.

- 80 en suite rooms inc. 4 family rooms all with satellite TV, radio, direct-dial telephone; hairdryer, 24-hour room/meal service, safety deposit box (at reception). Non-smoker bedrooms available.
- A la carte restaurant; lunch & special diets available; last orders 10 pm.
- Business services inc 3 meeting rooms, cap'y 30.
- AMERICAN EXPRESS & all major credit cards accepted.
- Open all year.

Five Sumner Place

5 Sumner Place, South Kensington, London SW7 3EE
Tel: (020) 7584 7586; Fax: (020) 7823 9962
E-mail: reservations@sumnerplace.com
Website: www.sumnerplace.com

A former award winner for the Best Small Hotel in London, this privately owned property is part of an impressive white 19th century terrace on the border of Knightsbridge, and two minutes from South Kensington tube. The building is grade II listed, being of special architectural merit, and the hotel itself has been sensitively refurbished bringing elegance and warmth to the reception area and good standards of comfort to the accommodation. A bonus to our stay here was breakfast amongst the flowers and shrubs in a fine Victorian-style conservatory, with a complimentary newspaper. All eleven bedrooms have been individually designed and decorated with the emphasis on traditional period furnishings. Five Sumner Place is a quiet small hotel of much charm.

Rates: Single with b'fst from £88; double from £129. **Winter Breaks:** *15% disc Jan/Feb min 5 nts*

- 13 en suite bedrooms, all with colour TV, d-dial tel, radio/alarm, fax/modem points, trouser press, safe, hairdryer, laundry service, minibar. No ✘
- Visa & Mastercard accepted.
- Open all year.

The Montcalm

Great Cumberland Place,
London W1H 7TW

Tel: (020) 7402 4288; Fax: (020) 7724 9180
E-mail: montcalm@montcalm.co.uk
Website: www.montcalm.co.uk

Located on a delightful, tree-lined street behind Marble Arch, this sometime Georgian town house lives up to the dignity and style of the 18th century general, the Marquis de Montcalm. The emphasis is on discreet service to each guest. This begins with the welcome at the imposing entrance, continues in the club-like atmosphere of the foyer and extends to the cosy bar and adjoining area where a relaxing pianola plays classical music. The ❀❀ AA *Crescent* restaurant is dominated by an idyllic country garden mural and offers a variety of good value menus as well as private dining and conference facilities and a special supper service for theatre-goers. The 120 air-conditioned bedrooms (including 12 duplex suites) exude comfort, reinforced by luxury furnishings and marble tiled bathrooms.

Single room inc bfst from £286; **Double** *fm £310.* **Bargain breaks:** *Montcalm Interlude - Fri to Mon & Bank Holidays from £176.25 b & b for two people per night (min. two nights) inc. VAT.*

- 120 en suite bedrooms (15 double, 47 twin, 44 single, 14 suites) with AC, satellite TV, radio, d-d tel, hairdryer, laundry service, voice mail, modem & fax, 24 hour room/meal service, safe, trouser press
- Table d'hôte dinner or lunch 3-courses £25 inc; last orders 10.30 pm; lunch & special diets available
- Three meeting rooms - capacity 80. 🅿 £25-24hrs
- Mastercard, Visa, Diners & JCB credit cards accepted. ● Open all year.

Twenty Nevern Square

20 Nevern Square,
London SW5 9PD
Tel: (020) 7565 9555;
Fax: (020) 7565 9444

E-mail:
hotel@twentynevernsquare.co.uk
Website:
www.twentynevernsquare.co.uk

Overlooking a quiet, tree-lined garden square, this is one of London's newest and, at the same time, most original and discreet boutique hotels. The mosaic patterned steps of the late 19th century mansion give a hint of the Eastern influences within, which are also apparent in the decor of the cosy lounge on the ground floor. European style takes over in the bar area leading to the Café Twenty Restaurant, a light relaxing place, popular locally, where breakfast and dinners with a Mediterranean flavour are served. The bedrooms revert to the Asian style, with unusual handicraft furnishing and rich fabrics of which the Grand Pasha Suite and the Chinese Room are prime examples. Each room is individually designed but they all share the same high standards of comfort via the use of natural materials such as cotton, linen and silk throughout. Bathrooms are fully marbled and luxurious with toiletries and bathrobes. The hotel is close to Earls Court and Olympia Exhibition Centres and has easy access to the West End. To stay in this distinctive townhouse hotel is an experience not to be missed.

- *19 en suite bedrooms (inc 1 suite), all with colour TV, direct-dial telephone, hairdryer, laundry service, 24-hr room service, fax/modem points, safety deposit box, trouser press.*
- *Cafe Twenty providing complimentary tea & coffee 24 hours.*
- *Fitness centre/gym nearby. Airport pickup on request. Private car parking (charged).*
- *& major credit cards accepted.*

Rates: *Single room with breakfast from £110; Double inc. breakfast from £140. Open all year.*

The Clarendon Hotel

Montpelier Row, Blackheath,
London SE3 0RW
Tel: (0208) 318 4321;
Fax: (0208) 318 4378
E-mail: relax@clarendonhotel.com
Website: www.clarendonhotel.com

The location of the Clarendon, on the edge of the beautiful Blackheath common and close to the many attractions of historic Greenwich makes it an alternative to staying in the centre when visiting London. It is a short walk to the railway station and a 20-minute journey to Central London. Stone from the old London Bridge is reputed to have been used in the construction of the hotel, which was later home to rich Georgian merchants and shipbuilders. The nautical background is reflected in the bar which has many maritime artefacts including sea charts. Home comfort is a feature of the bedrooms and the Meridian Restaurant, overlooking the gardens, serves a good choice of cuisine. Otherwise modest in appearance and price, the Clarendon also caters for wedding receptions and has conference facilities for 120 in 5 well-equipped suites.

Rates: *Single inc. breakfast from £70; double/twin inc. breakfast from £80.*

- 182 bedrooms, 3 suites, all en suite, all with cable TV, radio, direct-dial telephone, hairdryer, tea/coffee making facilities.
- Table d'hôte £20; à la carte, lunch & special diets available; last orders 9.45 pm.
- Conference room, capacity 120. Car parking 80.
- & all major credit cards accepted.
- Open all year.

Greenwich 1, Central London 6, Rochester 30, Canterbury 55, Dover 72.

The Langorf Hotel

20 Frognal, Hampstead,
London NW3 6AG
Tel: (0207) 794 4483;
Fax: (0207) 435 9055
E-mail: langorf@aol.com
Website: www.langorfhotel.com

Comprised of three Edwardian houses, the delightful Langorf offers good value with the personal touch. It is quietly situated in a residential street 15 minutes by public transport from the West End and ten minutes' walk from Hampstead Village, with its fashionable shops and restaurants and the open spaces of the Heath. Kenwood House, renowned for open air concerts, is nearby. The attractively furnished and pleasantly decorated bedrooms are a fair size, some large enough for three guests. There are also five fully equipped, spacious apartments ideal for families or long stay guests. The reception area doubles as a comfortable lounge and the adjacent room, overlooking the walled rear garden, serves an excellent buffet breakfast and is also the licensed bar area. A deserved holder of 'commended' and 'highly commended' awards, the Langorf offers some of the best value in town.

Rates: *Single room with breakfast from £82; double from £98; apartment from £130.*
Bargain Breaks: *Special weekend and seasonal rates available - details on request.*

- 36 en suite bedrooms (inc 5 suites), all with colour TV, d-dial telephone, hairdryer, laundry service, 24-hr snack service, safe, radio/alarm clock, fax/modem points.
- Horse riding nearby. Open all year.
- and all major credit cards accepted.

Lansdowne Hotel

King Edward's Parade, Eastbourne,
East Sussex BN21 4EE
Tel: (01323) 725174; Fax: (01323) 739721
E-mail: reception@lansdowne-hotel.co.uk
Website: www. lansdowne-hotel.co.uk
AA 'Courtesy & Care' Award 1992.
RAC Merit Awards for Hospitality, Service & Comfort 1995/6/7/8/2000.

The Lansdowne Hotel commands a fine view over Eastbourne's beach to the sea beyond. Owned by the same family since 1912, this hotel has the true hallmark of hospitality and comfort. Bedrooms are gracefully furnished with many overlooking the sea-front. Last year saw the opening of nine superior seafront rooms, each formed by combining two former smaller rooms. These have been refurbished in great style. There is a choice of elegant lounges, all looking across the Western Lawns, as well as several refreshment places, from the attractive Regency Bar to the stylish Devonshire Restaurant serving fixed price menus of traditional English cuisine. A comprehensive bar and lounge menu is available at lunch and supper time. Traditional Sunday lunch is served and a 4-course dinner every evening in the restaurant. Conferences and seminars are well provided for in a selection of rooms.
Two snooker rooms, table tennis, darts and a pool table provide every opportunity for relaxation. A good centre from which to tour Eastbourne's attractions and the South Coast.

Single room rate including breakfast from £43-74 *Double/twin* room with breakfast from £74. *Leisure Breaks* weekend/weekday from 17th January -30th April (exc. Easter) & 1st November -31 March. Prices from £49 pppn d,b&b. High season June 1-30 Sept fm £63 pppn, d,b&b. Social bridge weekends Feb, Apr, Oct & Nov, prices pp fm £112 (2 nights) or £152 (3 nights). Duplicate bridge w/ ends (3 nights only) from £163 Jan, March, May Sept & Nov. 2-day Golf Breaks all yr fm £150 ppers

● 110 en suite bedrooms with satellite TV, radio, direct-dial telephone, hairdryer, laundry service, tea/coffee making facilities, 24-hour room service, trouser press. ● *Last dinner orders 20.30. Evening bar menu 1830-2130.* ● *Snooker, indoor games room. Special arrange ments for golf with 7 local clubs .* Sky Sports TV in Public Room.
● Complete business service. Five fully equipped conference rooms with capacity of 330.
● P 22 lock-ups
● Hotel closed 1-16 January.
● & all major credit cards accd.

Newhaven 12, Hastings 20, Brighton 25, Tunbridge Wells 29, Dover 61, London 63

East Sussex, Hastings 63

Beauport Park Hotel

Battle Road, Hastings,
East Sussex TN38 8EA
Tel: (01424) 851222; Fax: (01424) 852465
E-mail: reservations@beauportprkhotel.demon.co.uk
Website: www.beauportparkhotel.co.uk

This fine house was built in 1719 and remodelled by a former Governor of Quebec who named it Beauport after his summer home in Canada. It is unspoiled by its transition from residence to first class hotel and guests will particularly enjoy the three most attractive features - seclusion, the stylish elegance of the interior and the extensive range of leisure facilities. Set at the end of a winding drive in 33 acres of tranquil parkland, it is a perfect example of a Georgian country house. The tastefully modernised lounge and bar areas are warmed by open log fires, and the candlelit restaurant, renowned for its cuisine, overlooks the formal Italian and sunken gardens. In 1999 a Victorian conservatory was added and a new Brasserie opened in 2000. The bedrooms too are furnished to a high standard. Beauport is close to the Channel ports and the many attractions of this beautiful part of Britain. Yet in these historic surroundings anyone seeking either peace and quiet or a more active holiday need look no further than this lovely hotel, whose rating of Highly Commended and awards for comfort we found to be fully justified.

Rates: Single room inc. breakfast from £90. Double room inc. breakfast from £120.
Leisure Breaks: Minimum two night short breaks available all year. A four poster room, dinner & breakfast starts at £80 per night.

● 25 bedrooms (7 four-poster rms, 7 double, 7 twin, 3 single, 1 suite), all with colour TV + satellite, direct-dial telephone, hairdryer, laundry/valet service, tea/coffee making facilities, trouser press. Non-smoker bedrooms available.
● Table d'hôte dinner £25. A la carte, lunch & special diets available. Last orders 9.30 pm
● Golf, riding, outdoor swimming pool, tennis. 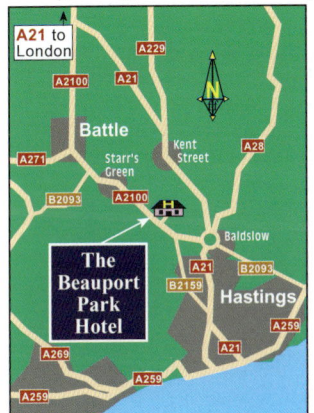
● Full business services inc, 3 meeting rooms - capacity 70. Car parking for 60.
● Open all year.
● AMERICAN EXPRESS & major credit cards accepted.

Rye 11,
Lewes 29,
Brighton 37,
Folkestone 37,
London 65..

Hotels whose prices are followed by ⓐ *accept the Signpost Advantage card, which entitles holders either to a 10% discount from the room (only) rate or to an upgrade, according to availability. See back of this book for an application form.*

Flackley Ash Hotel

Peasmarsh, Near Rye,
East Sussex TN31 6YH
Tel: (01797) 230651; Fax: (01797) 230510
E-mail: enquiries@flackleyashhotel.co.uk
Website: www.flackleyashhotel.co.uk   AA★★★RAC

This is one of Sussex' most charming small country house hotels. Rye is only a few miles away with its many historic buildings including the 15th century church, the Ypres Tower, the famous Landgate and Henry James' Georgian residence, Lamb House. Local activities are many and varied, with antique shops, potteries, local crafts and boutiques and a market on Thursdays. The fellow *Cinque Port*, Winchelsea, is nearby and Camber Sands, with its beautiful beaches and safe bathing, is only a few miles further on. Of course there are castles, abbeys, a cathedral and many gardens in the locality to be visited. The hotel has an indoor swimming pool and leisure complex, with whirlpool spa, gymnasium, steam room, aromatherapy and beautician, sun terrace and croquet lawn. This Georgian house offers its visitors a warm and friendly atmosphere and comfortable en suite bedrooms. The restaurant serves good food and offers an extensive wine list. Dishes are interesting with an emphasis on fresh local fish and seafood. Staff are friendly, helpful and willing.

Rates: Room and breakfast from £57 sharing twin/double per person per night.
Getaway Breaks from £59-£94 pppn - min. 2 nights, dinner, bed & breakfast. Perfect Choice - 7 nights, dinner, bed & breakfast £375-£475 per pers.

● 45 en suite bedrooms, all with direct dial telephone and TV.
● Last orders 9.30 p.m.; bar meals available.
● Children welcome; dogs accepted; conferences/receptions to 120 max.
● Indoor heated swimming pool; leisure centre; sauna; spa pool; steam room; gymnasium; putting; croquet; health & beauty centre. Golf arranged.
● & all major credit cards accepted.
● Open all year;

Rye 3, Hastings 11, Folkestone 29, Dover 36, London 60.

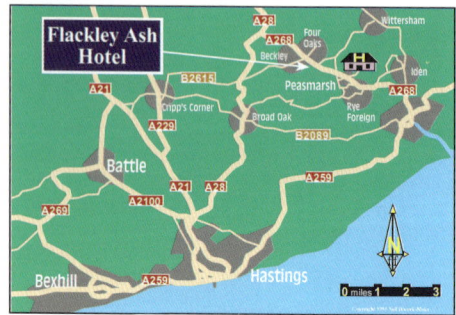

East Sussex, Rye

Rye Lodge Hotel

Hilder's Cliff, Rye, East Sussex TN31 7LD
Tel: (01797) 223838; Fax: (01797) 223585
E-mail: info@ryelodge.co.uk
Website: www.ryelodge.co.uk
AA★★★ RAC. ETC ★★★ Silver Award. Runner-up in Hotel of the Year "under 50 bedrooms" category - SEETB Millennium Awards.

Rye - Ancient Town of the Cinque Ports. No town in England evokes the atmosphere of medieval times better than Rye with the charm and character of its cobbled streets, picturesque period houses, historic buildings and ancient fortifications. Situated on the East Cliff overlooking the estuary and Romney Marshes, yet within yards of the High Street of this beautifully preserved ancient town, stands Rye Lodge, acclaimed and acknowledged as one of the finest small luxury hotels in Southeast England. Much thought has gone into the décor, furnishing and equipping of the bedrooms and public rooms, creating an oasis of tranquillity and comfort for guests. The Terrace Restaurant is elegant, candlelit and its fine cellar houses some rare vintages. The hotel is centrally located, so that all antique shops, art galleries etc are within walking distance. This delightful privately owned hotel is run by the de Courcy family. It offers a degree of comfort and personal service rarely found in hotels these days and only achieved by experienced hoteliers through hard work and dedication to their art.

Rates: Single room with breakfast from £55-£105; double room with breakfast £90-£170.
Short Breaks: Midweek Short Breaks - any 2 nights dinner room & breakfast from £65-£100 pppn. Mini Holidays - 3 nights+ from £60-£95 pppn dinner b&b.

● *20 en suite bedrooms with radio, satellite TV, direct-dial telephone; hairdryer, laundry service, tea/coffee making facilities; de luxe rooms with video, minibar, trouser press & room safe.*
● *A la carte and table d'hôte (£25) dinner - last orders 21.00. Special diets available.* 20.
● *Indoor swimming pool, sauna, spa bath & aromatherapy steam cabinet.*
● *Diners, Mastercard, Visa, Switch & Delta cards accepted.* ● *Open all year.*

Hastings 11, Ashford 20, Folkestone 25, Maidstone 33, Dover 32, Brighton 49, London 63.

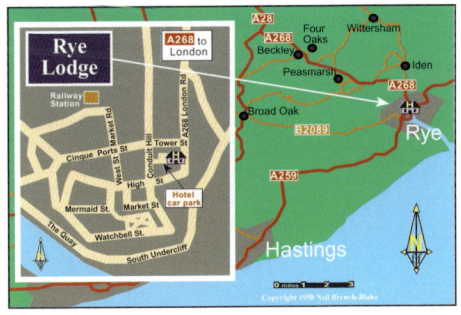

Little Hemingfold Hotel

Telham, Battle, East Sussex
TN33 0TT
Tel: (01424) 774338;
Fax: (01424) 775351
E-mail: littlehemingfoldhote@tiscali.co.uk

An attractively positioned farmhouse hotel, Little Hemingfold is the home of Allison and Paul Slater. It is a part 17th century and part Victorian building is situated 'far from the madding crowd' down a half mile track in a world of its own, comprising 40 acres of farm and woodland with a two-acre spring-fed trout lake. Comfortably and cheerfully furnished throughout, the hotel offers simple accommodation, including one four-poster and some ground floor rooms. The beamed candlelit dining-room serves an ample farmhouse breakfast as well as a freshly prepared 4-course dinner using home grown fruits and vegetables in a daily changing menu. In these peaceful surroundings, you could remain happily undisturbed for many weeks.

Directions: Off North side of A2100 Battle-Hastings road in Telham

Rates: *Single room inc breakfast from £54;double from £88. Weekly terms from £58 pppn, dinner b&b*
Leisure Breaks: *2 nights dinner, b&b £62-64 pppn.*

- 12 en suite bedrooms, all with colour TV, [V] direct dial telephone, laundry/valet service, tea/coffee making facilities.
- Table d'hôte 4 courses £24.50; last orders 7.00 pm.
- Fishing, boating, swimming in the lake, grass tennis court, boules. Squash, riding & golf nearby.
- Closed Jan 2nd-Feb 27th. ● Dogs welcome.
- Visa, & Mastercard accepted.

Hastings 6½, Maidstone 30, Brighton 34, Folkestone 43, London 56.

The Brickwall Hotel

Sedlescombe, Battle,
East Sussex TN33 0QA
Tel: (01424) 870253;
Fax: (01424) 870785
E-mail: brickwallhotel@hotmail.com

The Brickwall Hotel stands overlooking the village green of the pretty East Sussex village of Sedlescombe. Originally built in 1597 for the local ironmaster, the hotel combines a touch of Tudor times with all modern amenities. A feature of the hotel is the large number of ground floor rooms, many looking out onto a sheltered walled garden; also the heated outdoor swimming pool. There is a spacious residents' lounge, an oak panelled lounge bar and a large beamed dining room. Golf is available at the nearby Aldershaw Golf Course at special rates to guests of the Brickwall Hotel and tennis courts are available for hire in the village. The cinque ports of Rye and Winchelsea are within an easy drive as are such Sussex Weald landmarks as Battle Abbey, Bodlam Castle and Pevensey Castle.

Rates: *Single room inc. breakfast from £55;double from £88. Dinner b&b fm £75 (single)/£130 (dble).*
Leisure Breaks: *2 nights din, b&b fm £53 pppn.*

- 26 en suite bedrooms (15 grd fl), with col TV + sat, d-d telephone, tea/coffee making, radio/alarm clock.
- Tdh 3-cse dinner £23.50; last orders 9.00 pm.
- Swimming pool. Tennis, golf, beach, riding nearby.
- Open all year. ● Children & dogs (£4) welcome.
- Visa, & Mastercard accepted.

Battle 3, Hastings 7, Rye 10, Eastbourne 20, Brighton 37, Dover 47, London 55.

Eastwell Manor

Eastwell Park, Boughton Lees,
Ashford, Kent TN25 4HR
Tel: (01233) 213000; Fax: (01233) 635530
E-mail: eastwell@btinternet.com
Website: www.eastwellmanor.co.uk

To stay here was to be treated like the royalty and nobility who have stayed at or been associated with the house during its 1000-year history and after whom rooms are named: The Countess of Midleton, the Duke of Edinburgh, Queen Marie of Romania to name a few. Bedrooms are sumptuous with king size beds, wide-screen TVs, bathrobes, a good selection of books and reading matter, sewing kit, and a view to die for over well tended lawns and hedges right down to the South coast! Dinner was another pleasure in the formal yet intimate Manor Restaurant - excellent food and service serenaded by quiet Beethoven sonatas and Scott Joplin 'rags' on the piano. Eastwell is one of the finest hotels in the South of England - yet it is now more than a hotel. *Eastwell Mews* was opened four years ago and is a converted Victorian stable-block providing 19 self-contained Courtyard Apartments or Country Cottages. The *Pavilion* leisure complex has an indoor pool, 'techno-gym' and sauna. *Dreams*, a state-of-the-art beauty complex offers 14 treatment rooms and a comprehensive range of therapies. Be sure to stay several days to 'tone-up', explore the park and surrounding North Downs countryside and savour the full Eastwell experience.

***Rates:** Single room, inc. breakfast from £170; double room inc. breakfast from £200;* ***Leisure breaks**: Sunday night stay £60 per person b&b.* Ad

● *62 en suite bedrooms (23 in main house; 39 in cottages) all with colour TV+sat, direct-dial telephone, hairdryer, laundry/valet service, tea/coffee making facilities, 24-hr room service, radio/ alarm clock, safety deposit box, trouser press, fax/modem points, ⚡ & ♿ rooms available.*

● *Tdh dinner £35 Manor Restaurant; alc & diets avail; last orders 2130; Pavilion Brasserie open all day.*

● *Croquet, fitness centre/gym, tennis, in-& out-door swimming pools, jacuzzi, sauna, massage, health & beauty salon, pétanque. Golf 2 miles.*

● *7 meeting rooms, cap'y 7-180. Open all yr*

● AMERICAN EXPRESS *& major credit cards accepted.*

Ashford 3, Canterbury 12, Maidstone 19, Dover 24, Hastings 30, London 56.

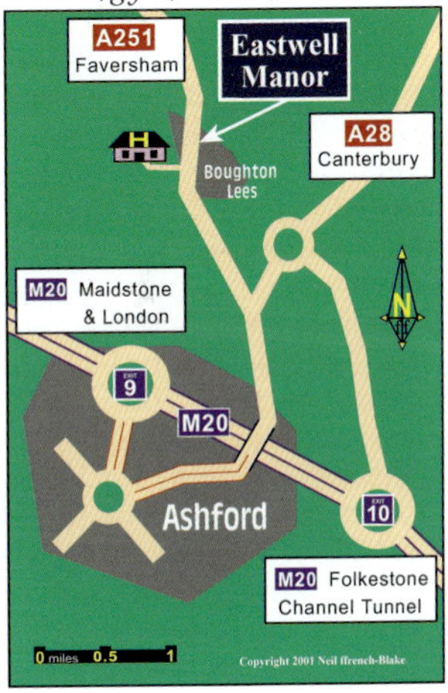

Walletts' Court Country House Hotel, Restaurant & Spa

Westcliffe, St Margaret's Bay, Dover, Kent CT15 6EW
Tel: (01304) 852424; Fax: (01304) 853430
E-mail: wc@wallettscourt.com
Website: www.wallettscourt.com

This lovely old country manor house set in beautiful grounds is located just outside St. Margaret's, opposite a Norman church and both sites date back to the Domesday Book. Most of the present Manor is Elizabethan, and today Walletts'Court testifies to the Oakley Family philosophy of making a home of the place they discovered 26 years ago. The Conservatory is a breakfast room with views across the North Downs. The 17th century beamed, candlelit restaurant is an award-winning gourmets' paradise, which offers deliciously robust and hearty cuisine with menus changing regularly to incorporate fresh seasonal ingredients. The bedrooms are divided between the main house and converted barns whose comfortably furnished rooms are named according to original usage such as *Dairy* or *Stable*. There are four luxury bedrooms: the *William Pitt*, the *Sir Edward de Burgh*, the *Lord Aylmer* rooms and *Crèvecoeur's* Tower. The Spa consists of the *Body & Soul Treatment Suite*, where aromatherapy, holistic and head massage are on offer, the cardiovascular *Oxide Studio* and a Romanesque indoor pool, sauna, hydrotherapy spa and steam room. Walletts today is popular equally with business travellers, London couples looking for a weekend break and as a stopover point for those crossing the Channel.

Single room, inc. breakfast from £75; double room inc. breakfast from £90; Leisure breaks: 2 nights inc. dinner for two £280 October-April.

- 16 en suite bedrooms with colour TV, direct-dial telephone, hairdryer, laundry/valet service, tea/coffee making facilities, radio alarm clock.
- Table d'hôte & à la carte dinner in AA restaurant; last orders 2030 hrs; special diets avail.
- Croquet, fishing, tennis, indoor pool, jacuzzi, sauna, spa, beauty/fitness studio. Golf 6 m, sea 1 m.
- Visa, Mastercard, Switch accepted.
- Open all year. ● 2 mtg rms for up to 55

Folkestone 7, Canterbury 15, Margate 20, London 74.

Stade Court Hotel

West Parade, Hythe, Kent CT21 6DT
Tel: (01303) 268263; Fax: (01303) 261803
E-mail: stadecourt@marstonhotels.com
Website: www.marstonhotels.com

Standing proudly on the seafront of the picturesque Cinque Port of Hythe stands Stade Court, which has been welcoming both business and leisure guests to this historic corner of Kent since 1938 and is thus nearly as old as *Signpost* itself! It provides a quieter and pleasing alternative to its big sister, the Hythe Imperial, just 600 metres away, for those who prefer smaller hotels and the personal service they provide. Many of the 42 beautifully furnished en suite bedrooms, including five family rooms, have lounges with views directly overlooking the Channel. Stade Court's charming location features a promenade along the beach and is a popular fisherman's haunt. Fresh local seafood is regularly featured on the menu in the award-winning Lukin Restaurant where a wide selection of quality wines at favourable prices are also available. Guests of Stade Court have access to the excellent leisure facilities at the nearby Hythe Imperial, including a 9-hole golf course and a beauty parlour. The hotel is well situated for visits to Dover Castle and the White Cliffs Experience, the Romney, Hythe and Dymchurch Light Railway; also Howletts and Port Lympne wild animal parks.

Rates: Single room and breakfast from £63.00; double room inc. breakfast from £83.00.
Leisure breaks: Marston breaks - 2 nights dinner, b&b per person per night sharing from £65 per night; Romantic Breaks from £84; Golfing Breaks from £82.50.

- 42 en suite bedrooms with colour TV + satellite, direct-dial telephone, hairdryer, laundry service, tea/coffee making facilities, 24 hr room/meal service, music/radio/alarm clock, trouser press. Safe at reception.
- Table d'hôte dinner £24.00; à la carte, lunch & special diets available; last orders 9 pm.
- Business services inc 4 meeting rooms, capacity 40
- Billiards, croquet, gymnasium, golf, indoor games, jacuzzi, massage, sauna, squash, indoor swimming pool & tennis all available 600 metres at Hythe Imperial Hotel. Car parking for 12.
- Open all year.
- Visa, Diners & Mastercard, accepted.

Folkestone 5,
Ashford 11,
Canterbury 17,
Rye 21,
London 66.

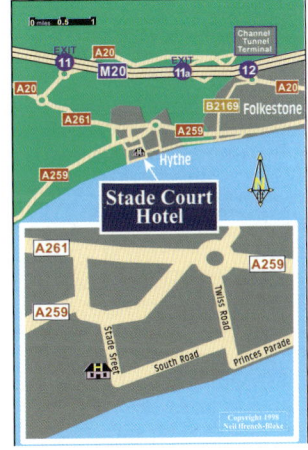

Coulsdon Manor

Coulsdon Court Road, Old Coulsdon.
Nr. Croydon, Surrey CR5 2LL
Tel: (020) 8668 0414; Fax: (020) 8668 3118
E-mail: coulsdonmanor@marstonhotels.com
Website: www.marstonhotels.com

Set in 140 acres of beautiful Surrey parkland, a large part of it laid down as a challenging 18-hole golf course, yet just 15 miles from both central London and Gatwick and easily accessible to the motorway network. Built for Thomas Byron in the 1850s and sympathetically restored, inside you will discover a country house flavour reflected in beautiful woodwork and chandeliers. Relax in the lounge or bars and soak up the atmosphere as it is now and imagine how life was at Coulsdon Manor over 100 years ago. Dine in the award winning Manor House restaurant or choose lighter fare in the popular Terrace Bar. Many of the 35 bedrooms have views over the golf course. Coulsdon Manor is an ideal base from which to explore many places of interest. Children of all ages will enjoy Thorpe Park and Chessington World of Adventures. Croydon Palace, Wisley RHS Gardens, Wakehurst Place and Hever Castle are also near at hand. As well as golf, many other activities are available at Coulsdon and there are five conference rooms which can cater for up to 180 delegates.

Single room with breakfast from £108; Double room including breakfast from £130. Leisure Breaks: Marston Breaks, dinner b&b £85 pppn, min 2-night stay. Romantic Break £102 per head; Golfing Break inc 2 rounds from £116 per person per night.

- 35 en suite bedrooms with colour TV+ satellite, direct-dial telephone, hairdryer, laundry service, tea/coffee making facilities, 24-hr room/meal service, radio, trouser press. Non-smoker bedrooms available. Safe at reception.
- Table d'hote dinner from £29. A la carte, lunch & special diets available. Last orders 21.30.
- Fitness centre, golf, sauna/solarium, squash, tennis. Riding, dry ski slope, water park nearby.
- Business services inc 9 meeting rooms - cap. 175.
- Open all year.
- American Express & major credit cards accepted.

Croydon 6, M25 Motorway 6, Gatwick Airport 15, Central London 15

Surrey, Kingston-upon-Thames 71

Chase Lodge Hotel

10 Park Road, Hampton Wick, Kingston-upon-Thames, Surrey KT1 4AS
Tel: (020) 8943 1862; Fax:(020) 8943 9363
E-mail: info@chaselodgehotel.com
Website: www.chaselodgehotel.com

The Stafford Haworths own and personally run this extremely popular little gem of an hotel, situated just 20 minutes from the heart of London and the same distance from Heathrow. Chase Lodge has been cleverly amalgamated from two old cottages dating from 1870 and is situated in a quiet street adjacent to Bushy Park and very near Hampton Court Palace. Each bedroom is different (one has a four-poster) and decorated with charm and homely colours, which puts the guest immediately at ease. Wickers Village Restaurant offers imaginative English and French dishes - avocado with crab, langoustine and pernod to start, followed by roast barbary duck or venison casserole in a port and redcurrant sauce being just some examples. Meals are served in the conservatory, which is bordered by the prettiest little floodlit courtyard garden. Light bar snacks can be enjoyed in the adjoining sitting room. Chase Lodge is becoming increasingly popular with business people and overseas visitors who do not wish to stay in Central London. I too can thoroughly recommend it to anyone who is looking for good food and the comfort and personal service of a small family-run hotel.

Single room and breakfast from £65 inc.VAT.
Double room with breakfast from £71 (inc VAT).
Leisure breaks: Discounts available for stays of three nights or more. Also Xmas/New Year programmes.

● 12 en suite (with shower) bedrooms, all with d-dial telephone, TV + satellite; tea/coffee making facilities; room service; baby listening; night service.
● Dinner from £16 per head (inc VAT); last orders 10.00 p.m; bar meals; lunch & special diets avail.

● Children welcome; dogs accepted.
● Gymnasium 500 yds; tennis $^1/_2$ mile; indoor heated swimming pool, leisure centre, squash, golf and riding 1 $^1/_2$ miles; ample parking.
● & all major credit cards accepted.
AA ★ ★ ★ ● Open all year.
Hampton Court 1$^1/_2$, Kew Gardens 4, London 7, Wimbledon 7, Heathrow 8.

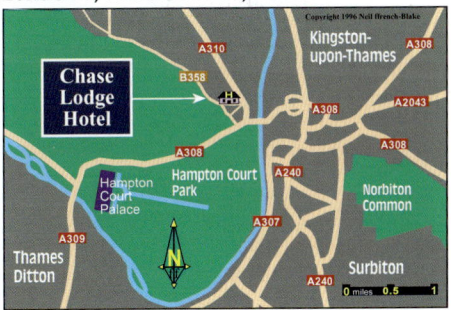

Surrey, Richmond-upon-Thames

The Bingham Hotel

61-63 Petersham Road, Richmond-upon-Thames, Surrey TW10 6UP
Tel: (020) 8940 0902;
Fax: (020) 8948 8737
E-mail: reservations@binghamhotel.co.uk
Website: www.binghamhotel.co.uk

Purchased by the Trinder family in 1984 and restored lovingly to its former glory, the Bingham Hotel, dates in part from 1740. On entering, the visitor is drawn through high-ceilinged rooms with ornate cornices, typical of a Grade II Listed Georgian building, and into the gracious Walpole Restaurant with its glorious views across gardens down to the Thames. Under the direction of chef Pierre Denoyer, whose exquisite recipes have already been featured in *Eden* magazine, the Walpole is considered a charming, undiscovered gem by local residents. In the 1800s Lady Anne Bingham, a relative of the Earl of Lucan and the second Earl Spencer by marriage, lived here as did two lady poets - Katherine Harris Bradley and Edith Emma Cooper, who wrote under the pseudonym Michael Field. In June 1902, the Irish poet W B Yeats was a dinner guest. Now the hotel comprises 23 individually decorated bedrooms, some with four-posters, most with views of the Thames.

The Garden Suite and Bingham Room are both licensed for civil weddings and used as banqueting and conference areas. I lingered over tea on one the balconies, vowing to stay longer next time in this peaceful oasis.

Rates: Single with breakfast from £90; double from £120.
Special Breaks: Min 2 nights b & b £45 pppn.

● 23 en suite bedrooms (inc 4 suites), all with AC, d-dial telephone + modem pts, hairdryer, laundry service, minibar, tea/coffee making, radio/alarm, safe, trouser press. ✂ rms available. Internet access.
● Walpole's Restaurant 3-cse tdh £20+; alc, lunch & diets avail; last orders 10 pm. 2 mtg rms up to 40
● Gym, golf, jogging track, watersports, tennis, swimming pools, riding nearby. ⓟ 12.
● & all credit cards acc'd. ● Open all year.

Surrey, Richmond-upon-Thames

The Richmond Gate Hotel

Richmond Hill, Richmond-upon-Thames, Surrey TW10 6RP
Tel: (020) 8940 0061;
Fax: (020) 8332 0354
E-mail: richmondgate@corushotels.com
Website: www.corushotels.co.uk/richmondgate

High atop Richmond Hill in four elegant 18th-century buildings, stands the Richmond Gate Hotel with magnificent views across the Thames Valley. Antiques, classic décor and open fires create a country house atmosphere, enhanced by its 68 en suite bedrooms, luxury *Gates Cottage* and award-winning *Gates on the Park Restaurant*. Its two rosettes ensure that guests will enjoy fine international dining, after which they can relax in one of the stylish, traditional sitting rooms. The more energetic can visit the *Cedars Health & Leisure Club's* ozone pool, gym, sauna and steam room, or wander through the 2500-acre Richmond Royal Park, home to red and fallow deer, into charming Richmond town.

Single room with breakfast from £120;
Double room with breakfast from £150;

- 68 en suite bedrooms + sep. cottage for 4, all with colour TV + satellite, d-dial tel + modem, hairdryer, laundry service, tea/coffee-making facilities, 24 hour room service, radio/alarm clock, safe, minibar, trouser press. Open all year.
- Tdh dinner £31; last orders 2115; alc, lunch & sp. diets avail. ● Two meeting rooms for up to 50.
- Gym, indoor pool, sauna, aerobics studio.
- & all major credit cards accepted.

The Richmond Hill Hotel

Richmond Hill, Richmond-upon-Thames, Surrey TW10 6RW
Tel: (020) 8940 2247;
Fax:(020) 8940 5424
E-mail: richmondhill@corushotels.com
Website: www.corushotels.co.uk/richmondhill

After climbing Richmond Hill, past the 2500-acre Royal Park with its deer and paths down to the Thames, I arrived at the Richmond Hill Hotel, created out of a Georgian manor. With the oldest part dating back to 1726, its grand past blends with modern comforts in the 138 en suite bedrooms, some with four-posters. The Cedars Health & Leisure Club features an 8 x 20m ozone pool and the Pembrokes Restaurant offers excellent fare....I had a delicious lunch of freshly baked bread, warm duck salad and house wine. The friendly and helpful staff make this ideal for both leisure and business travellers looking for relaxation in a traditional setting. Richmond Hill is a popular venue for weddings and conferences and is convenient for visiting Kew Gardens and Hampton Court.

Single room with breakfast from £55;
Double room with breakfast from £110;

- 138 en suite bedrooms, all with colour TV + satellite, d-dial tel + modem, hairdryer, laundry service, tea/coffee-making facilities, 24 hr room service, radio/alarm clock, safe, trouser press.
- Alc dinner from £23.40; last orders 2130; alc, lunch & sp. diets avail. ● Open all year.
- 16 meeting rooms for up to 220.
- Gym, indoor pool, sauna, aerobics studio.
- & all major credit cards accepted.

Oatlands Park Hotel

Oatlands Drive, Weybridge, KT13 9HB
Tel: (01932) 847242; Fax: (01932) 842252
E-mail: info@oatlandsparkhotel.com
Website: www.oatlandsparkhotel.com

This majestic hotel is set in acres of parkland overlooking Broadwater Lake in the heart of the Surrey countryside, yet is only a 25-minute train journey to central London. Henry VIII built a palace on the estate for his fourth wife Anne of Cleves and it was used by many subsequent monarchs before being rebuilt as a country residence for the Duke and Duchess of York in 1795. It became an hotel in 1856, patronised by many famous writers such as Zola, Lear and Trollope, and today the historic character remains very apparent. You pass through the porticoed entrance into the splendid galleried lounge, with marble columns and tapestries under a large glass dome. Here refreshments and light meals are served throughout the day. The lounge bar and Broadwater Restaurant are equally stylish offering table d'hôte and à la carte menus, and a particularly popular traditional Sunday lunch. The bedrooms are designed to high standards of comfort, with wide doors and plenty of space. The hotel has everything for the leisure guest and is also popular as a conference venue. Oatlands' logo is a cedar tree, planted in commemoration of Charles 1st's eighth child and still standing. Also in the grounds stands an oak which is reputed to be the 'oldest recorded' oak tree in the world.

Single room with breakfast from £152.50;
Double room with breakfast from £212.00;
Leisure Breaks: *Weekend rates available from £50 per person per night, bed & full Eng. b'fast*

● *144 en suite bedrooms (69 double, 50 twin, 22 single, 3 suites), all with colour TV + satellite, direct-dial telephone with modem point & voicemail, hairdryer, laundry/valet service, tea/coffee-making facilities, 24 hour room/meal service, music/radio/alarm clock, safety deposit box, trouser press; non-smoker bedrooms available.*
● *Broadwater Restaurant table d'hôte £29; last orders 9.30 pm; à la carte, lunch & special diets available.*
● *Conference facilities for up to 300 persons.*
● *Croquet, gym, 9-hole golf course.* 🅿 *for 100.*
● *& all major credit cards accepted.*
● *Open all year.*

Woking 7, Kingston-upon Thames 8, Bagshot 11, Epsom 12, London 18.

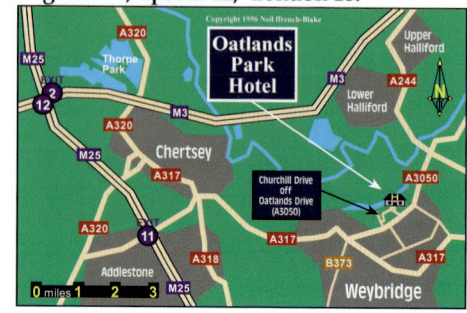

The Cedar House Hotel

Mill Road, Cobham, Surrey
KT11 3AL
Tel: (01932) 863424; Fax: (01932 862023.
E-mail: info@cedarhousehotel.com
Website: www.cedarhousehotel.com

Cedar House was a great discovery! As we drove into its pebbled courtyard and parked by the forsythia-covered old kitchen garden wall, we knew this would be a pleasant home-from-home for a few nights. Inside the new owners are carefully restoring the 1450s house which has many original features. Built during the reign of Henry VI, it is situated on the banks of the river Mole with views across to the North Downs. All eight bedrooms have already been renovated in great style with queen size beds, duvets and antiques in every room. The Gallery Restaurant has a magnificent timbered ceiling, inglenook fireplace and minstrels' gallery. The superb food provides yet another reason for visiting this delightful family-run hotel. Nearby attractions include Cobham Mill, Epsom Racecourse, Chessington World of Adventures and the Claremont Landscape Garden.

Rates: Single room with b'fast £65; double/twin £117.50. & all major credit cards acc'd.

- 8 en suite bedrooms, all with col TV, d-dial telephone, safe, tea/coffee making facilities. 16-hr room service. rms available. ● Open all year.
- Gallery Restaurant alc, last orders 10 pm.
- Mtg room 20. ● Garden, Riding 2 miles. 10.

Directions: On A 245 Cobham-Stoke d'Abernon Road. Cobham 1, Stoke d'A 1, Epsom 5, Central London 18 m.

Burpham Country House Hotel

Burpham, Nr. Arundel, West Sussex BN18 9RJ. Tel: (01903) 882160; Fax: (01903) 884627
E-mail: burphamchh@ukonline

Paul Michalski and Anne McCawley took over Burpham in August 2001. It is a charming small hotel, tucked away at the end of a country lane three miles from Arundel. It is reputed to have started life as a Victorian hunting lodge for the Duke of Norfolk. Most of its ten bedrooms look over the delightful gardens and beyond, the stunning Sussex countryside. The hamlet has an historic Norman church, pub and cricket ground. There is croquet in the garden. Award winning chef Stephen Piggott's dinner menus use local English produce where possible and the dishes have a Swiss influence. Arundel Castle and Wildfowl Sanctuary is nearby, the coast is only six miles away and horse racing takes place locally at Goodwood, Fontwell and Brighton. An excellent spot for a *Stress Remedy Break*.

Rates: Single room with breakfast from £45; double with breakfast from £120. Open all year.
Bargain Breaks: Min. 2 night breaks avail all year (exc Gooodwood events & Xmas) dinner, b & b from £64 per person per night.

- 10 en suite bedrooms (inc. 1 single), all with col TV, d-dial tel, tea/coffee-making, radio/alarm, safe, trouser press, fax/modem points. rms available.
- 3-cse tdh dinner £25 Tues-Sat; last orders 9 pm; special diets available.● Croquet in garden.
- Golf, sea bathing, riding, fishing nearby.
- & Mastercard, Visa accepted. Arundel 3, Chichester 13, Brighton 21, London 61.

Signpost Guide 2003

East of England

Fact File
Illustrated Guide to
Historic Houses, Gardens & Sites
Diary of Events

Hotels in	PAGE
Cambridgeshire	80
Hertfordshire	81
Norfolk	82
Suffolk	86

East of England

Historic Houses, Gardens & Parks

Bedfordshire
Luton Hoo, Luton
The Swiss Garden, Old Warden
Woburn Abbey, Woburn
Wrest Park House & Garden, Silsoe

Cambridgeshire
Anglesey Abbey Nr. Cambndge
Chilford Hundred Vineyard, Linton
Docwra's Manor Garden, Shepreth
Elton Hall, Elton, Peterborough
Hinchingbrooke House, Huntingdon
Kimbolton Castle
Peckover House, Wisbech
University of Cambridge Botanic Garden

Essex
Audley End House & Park, Saffron Walden
BBC Essex Garden, Abridge
Bridge End Gardens, Saffron Walden
Felsted Vineyard
New Hall Vineyards, Purleigh
Ingatestone Hall
Layer Marney Tower
Priory Vineyards, Little Dunmow
RHS Garden, Rettendon, Chelmsford

Hertfordshire
Ashridge Estate, Nr. Berkhampstead
Cedars Park Waltham Cross
The Gardens of the Rose, Chiswell Green, St Albans
Hatfield House
Knebworth House

The National Trust Wimpole Hall, Arrington, Nr. Royston
Priory Gardens, Royston
Verulamium Park, St Albans

Norfolk
Beeston Hall, Beeston St Lawrence
Bickling Hall
Fairhaven Garden Trust, South Walsham
Felbrigg Hall Fritton Lake Countryworld
Holkham Hall, Wells-next-the-Sea
Sandringham
Hoveton Hall Gardens, Wroxham
Mannington Gardens, Norwich
Norfolk Lavender Ltd, Heacham
Rainham Hall and Gardens, Tasburgh

Suffolk
Blakenham Woodland Garden, Nr Ipswich
Bruisyard Vineyard and Herb Centre
Euston Hall, Thetford
Haughley Park
Helmingham Hall Gardens
Kentwell Hall, Long Melford
Melford Hall, Long Melford
Somerleyton Hall & Gardens

Walks & Nature Trails

Bedfordshire
Greensand Ridge Walk from Leighton Buzzard to Gamlingay
Upper Lea Valley Walk, from Leagrave Common to E Hyde

Cambridgsehire
Bishops Way, north of Ely
Devil's Dyke, from north of Feach to south of Stechworth
Grafham Water Circular

Hertfordshire
The Lea Valley Walk, from Ware to Stanborough Lakes
Tring Reservoirs

Lincolnshire
Chambers Farm Wood Forest Nature Reserve, Aply, Lincoln

Hartwholme Country Park, Lincoln
Tattershall Park Country Club, Tattershall, Lincoln

Norfolk
Peddars Way & Norfolk Coast Path with Weavers Way
Marriott's Way, between Norwich & Aylsham

Suffolk
Constable Trail
Painters Way from Sudbury to Manningtree
Suffolk Coastal Path, from Bawdsey to Kessingland
Suffolk Way, from Flatford to Lavenham

Historical Sites & Museums

Bedfordshire
Bunyan Museum, Bedford
Elstow Moot Hall, Church End
Stockwood Craft Museum & Gardens
Shuttleworth Collection, Biggleswade

Cambridgeshire
Ely Cathedral
Imperial War Museum, Duxford
Fitzwilliam Museum, Cambridge
Oliver Cromwell's House, Ely
Cromwell Museum, Huntingdon

Essex
Central Museum and Planetarium, Southend-on-Sea
Colchester Castle
Hedingham Castle, Castle Hedingham
Maritime Museum, Harwich
National Motorboat Museum, Pitsea
Working Silk Museum, Braintree

Hertfordshire
Berkhamsted Castle
Hertford Castle
Roman Baths, Welwyn Garden City
Roman Theatre, St Albans
Verulamium Museum, St Albans

Lincolnshire
Bishop's Palace, Lincoln
Bolingbroke Castle, Spilsby
Lincoln Castle
Lincoln Guildhall
Woolsthorpe Manor, Nr. Grantham
The Incredibly Fantastic Old Toy Show, Lincoln

Norfolk
100th Bomb Group Memorial Museum, Dickleburgh
Alby Lace Museum and Study Centre
Ancient House Museum, Thetford
Bygones Collection, Holkham Hall, Wells-next-the-Sea Bygone Heritage Villa, Burgh St Margaret
Charles Burrell Museum, Thetford
City of Norwich Aviation Museum, Horsham St Faith
Maritime Museum, Great Yarmouth
Muckleburgh Collection, Weybourne
Shrine of our Lady of Walsingham, Walsingham
Wolverton Station Museum
Tales of the Old Gaol House, King's Lynn

Suffolk
Bridge Cottage, Flatford
Dunwich Underwater Exploration Exhibition, Orford

East of England

Framlingham Castle
Gainsborough's House, Sudbury
Guildhall of Corpus Christi, Lavenham
Moot Hall & Museum, Aldeburgh
National Horse Racing Museum, Newmarket
Sizewell Visitors Centre, Sizewell B Power Station
Sue Ryder Foundation Museum, Cavendish
Tolly Cobbold Brewery, Ipswich
Woodbndge Museum

Entertainment Venues

Bedfordshire
Stagsden Bird Gardens
Whipsnade Wild Animal Park, Dunstable
Woburn Safari Park, Woburn

Cambridgeshire
Grays Honey Farm, Warboys
Hamerton Wildlife Centre
Linton Zoo
Peakirk Waterfowl Gardens Trust, Peterborough
Sacrewell Farm & Country Centre, Thornhaugh

Essex
Colchester Zoo
Dedham Rare Breed Farm
Layer Marney Tower
Mole Hall Wildlife Park, Widdington
Southend Sea Life Centre

Hertfordshire
Maltings Centre, St Albans
Paradise Wildlife Farm, Broxbourne
Water Hall Farm & Craft Centre, Nr. Hitchin

Lincolnshire
Brandy Wharf Cider Centre, Gainsborough
Battle of Britain Memorial Flight, RAF Coningsby, Lincoln
The Butterfly & Falconry Park, Long Sutton
Skegness Natureland Sea Sanctuary, Skegness
Cobb Hall Craft Centre, Lincoln

Norfolk
Banham Zoo
Kingdom of the Sea, Great Yarmouth
Norfolk Wildlife Centre & Country Park, Great Witchingham
Otter Trust, Earsham
Park Farm & Norfolk Farmyard Crafts Centre, Snettisham
Pensthorpe Waterfowl Park
Thrigby Hall Wildlife Gardens, Filby

Suffolk
East of England Birds of Prey and Conservation Centre, Laxfield
Suffolk Wildlife Park, Kessingland

DIARY OF EVENTS

January

8-12*. **Whittlesey Straw Bear Festival.** Cambridgeshire.
24-26*. **Woburn Elegant Homes & Gardens Show.** Woburn Abbey, Bedfordshire.

February

1-28. **Walsingham Abbey Snowdrop Walks.** Little Walsingham, Norfolk.
16-23*. **Lambing Sunday & Spring Bulb Day.** Kentwall Hall, Long Melford, Suffolk.

March

12. **NH Racing** at Huntingdon.
1-8*. **Bedfordshire Festival of Speech & Drama.** Corn Exchange, Bedford.
15-16*. **National Shire Horse Show.** East of England Showground, Alwalton, Cambs.
28-31*. **Blickling Craft Show.** NT Blickling Hall, Suffolk.
28-31*. **Southend-on-Sea Chess Congress**, Civic Centre.
30-31. **Gamekeeper & Countryman's Fair** .Herts Agricultural Society, Redbourn, Herts.

April

21. **Morris Dancing** on Easter Monday, Hunstanton, Norfolk.
1. **Racing** at Huntingdon, Fakenham & Market Rasen.
5-6* **Belton Horse Trials**,Lincs
15-17. **Newmarket Craven Stakes.** Newmarket, Cambs.
21-26. **Hertford Theatre Week** Castle Hall, Hertford, Herts.
25-27*. National Motorhome Show. E of Eng Showgrd, Alwalton, Cambs.

May

2-4. **Craven Festival.** The Racecourse, Newmarket.
4-5*. **Truckfest 2002.** E of Eng Showgr'd, Alwalton, Cambs.
5*. **Woodbridge Horse Show.** Suffolk Showground, Ipswich
8-11***Living Crafts Exhibition** Hatfield House, Hertfordshire
9-25*. **Bury St Edmunds Festival.** Various venues in Bury St. Edmunds, Suffolk.
11*. **South Suffolk Show.** Ampton Park Pt-to-Pt Cse, Ingham, Suffolk.
17-18*. **BMF Bike Show.** E of Eng Showgrd, Alwalton, Cbs
24-25*. **Herts County Show.** Redbourn, Herts.
28-29. **Suffolk Show.** Ipswich Shgrd, Suffolk.

June

1-8. **Downham Market Festival.** Town Hall, Downham Market, Norfolk.
1-8. **Felixstowe Drama Festival.** Spa Pavilion, Felixstowe, Suffolk.
3. **Luton International Carnival**, Luton, Beds.
6-24. **56th Aldeburgh Festival of Music & Arts.** Snape Maltings (and var. venues), Aldeburgh, Suffolk.
13-15*. **Pearl East of England Show.** East of England Showground, Alwalton, Cambs.
14-16. **Woburn Abbey Flower & Garden Show**.Woburn, Beds
18-29. **16th Ampthill Music Festival.** St Andrews Church. Ampthill, Beds.
25-26*. **Royal Norfolk Show 2003.** The Showg'd, Dereham Rd, New Costessey,Norwich
27-July 6*. **Harwich Festival.** Harwich, Essex.
28-13.7*. **Peterborough Festival.** Peterborough, Cambs

July

2-6*. Wisbech Rose Fair. St Peters Ch, Wisbech, Cambs.
6*. Ipswich Music Day. Christchurch Park, Ipswich.
6-18* Southend-on-Sea Men's Open Bowling Tournament. Southend-on-Sea, Essex.
8-10. Newmarkety July Meeting. Newmarket Racecourse, Newmarket, Suffolk
6-12*. Ashton Graham E of England Tennis Championships. Felixstowe, Suffolk
10-12*. Lord Mayor's Celebrations 2003. Norwich.
24.7-2.8*. Kings Lynn Festival Various venues, Kings Lynn, Norfolk.
20*. Gt Eastern Classic car Rally. Ingatestone, Essex.
30*. Sandringham Flower Show. Sandringham, Norfolk.

August

1-3. Crowning Glory Flower Festival. Bury St Edmunds, Sk
1,2,8,9,15,16,22,23. Racing at Newmarket, Suffolk.
12-17*. Ponies Association (UK) 2002 Summer Championship Show. East of Eng Showgr'd, Alwalton, Cambs.
23-25*. Chelmsford Spectacular. Hylands Park,Chelmsford

September

7-10*. Burghley Horse Trials. Burghley Park, Stamford, Lincs
19-21*. Woodhall Spa Festival of Flowers. Var. venues, Woodhall Spa, Lincs.

October/November

1-15*. Norfolk & Norwich Festival 2002. Various- Norwich
2-4. Newmarket Tote Cambridgeshire Meeting. Suffolk
16-18. Newmarket Dubai Champions Meeting.
8.11. Cambridge Music Fest

East of England Tourist Board area encompasses the predominantly agricultural counties of Bedfordshire, Hertfordshire, Norfolk, Suffolk, Cambridgeshire and Essex. Norfolk is thickly afforested in the west around Thetford, whereas the east is crisscrossed by waterways and Lakes known as *The Broads* - the remains of medieval man's peat diggings.

The county town of Norfolk and informal capital of East Anglia is the university city of Norwich, whose fine cathedral with walls decorated with biblical scenes dates from 1046. There are 30 medieval churches in central Norwich dominated by Norwich Castle Museum. Brideswell Museum and Church Museum should also not be missed.

Near King's Lynn in the northwest of the county is Sandringham, royal palace bought for King Edward VII while prince of Wales by Queen Victoria in 1862. Rising above the fens south of Kings Lynn is the magnificent 11th century Ely Cathedral, built on the site of a 7th century Benedictine Abbey.

East Suffolk's coast with its inlets and estuaries is popular with yachtsmen. Framlingham Castle, near Aldeburgh, stands intact since the 13th century. The hills and river valleys surrounding the Suffolk-Essex border open up to magnificent skies, captured in paintings by Constable and Gainsborough. Heart of Constable country is Nayland and Dedham Vale. Fine woollen towns are exemplified by Lavenham, Long Melford and Sudbury, among others.

Cultural capital of East Anglia is the tranquil city of Cambridge whose colleges, dating from the 13th century, were mostly founded as acts of piety. Most are open during daylight hours. Evensong at Kings College Chapel on Sundays is memorable. Rubens' *Adoration of the Magi* hangs there. The Fitzwilliam Museum is one of Europe's treasure houses, housing antiquities from Egypt, Greece and Rome as well as English and Chinese porcelain. Also worth a visit is the University Museum of Archaeology and Anthropology, with emphasis on prehistoric artefacts from the Cambridge area. Cambridge is also a centre for shopping and theatre.

Bedfordshire has the palace and theme park of Woburn to visit and Luton Hoo. Whipsnade open air zoo will appeal particularly to children.

St Albans in Hertfordshire has Verulamium Roman remains and Hatfield House was the home of Elisabeth I. Tewin Hoo is an example of a small Elizabethan Manor.

* = Provisional Date. For further information contact:
East of England Tourist Board. Toppesfield Road, Hadleigh, Suffolk, Suffolk IP7 5DN. Tel: 01473 822922 Website: www.visitbritain.com/east

Mill House Hotel & Restaurant

Mill Road, Sharnbrook, Bedford
MK44 1NP
Tel: (01234) 781678;
Fax: (01234) 783921
E-mail: andyatmillhouse@aol.com
Website: www.themillhousehotelandreastaurant.co.uk

Between the M1 and the A1, on the banks of the Great Ouse, lies the Mill House, a newly opened restaurant with rooms, which is carving itself quite a reputation in the Bedford area. Chef-patron Andy Judge offers table d'hote or à la carte menus in either the River View Conservatory or the Fine Dining area, with local fish, lamb and steak and the freshest ingredients on both menus. On certain Sundays, lunch is accompanied by a live jazz trio. Bedrooms are bright and cheerful with ISDN lines and luxury en suite facilities. Three new rooms were added in 2002. The hotel is next to the thriving amateur Mill Theatre, three miles from the Thurleigh Corporate race track and an ideal spot for a relaxing break on the river.

Rates: Single room with breakfast from £70.50. Double room inc. breakfast from £100. **Leisure Breaks** available weekdays. Weekends stay Fri & Sat and get 50% off Thurs or Sun accommodation
- 11 en suite bedrooms, all with colour TV, d-dial telephone, hairdryer, 24-hr room/meal service, trouser press, modem points, ✄ and ♿rooms avail.
- 3-cse tdh dinner £25; lunch (£17.50) & alc avail; Sun lunch 2-cse £15.50/3-cse £19.50; last orders 2145. ● 2 mtg rms up to 40. ● Open all year.
- Fishing. Golf, clay shooting, riding nearby. 🅿 30
- & all major credit cards accepted.

Bedford 7, Wellingboro' 9, Northampton 14, London 57

The Inn at Woburn

George Street, Woburn
MK17 9PX
Tel: (01525) 290441;
Fax: (01525) 290432
E-mail: hotel@woburn.fsbusiness.co.uk

We are pleased to welcome The Inn at Woburn, (formerly *The Bedford Arms*) back into Signpost after its considerable refurbishment. Outbuildings have been converted to provide seven smart new *cottage*s including three suites. The reception area has been extended and there are now three dining areas. The Tavistock Bar has been upgraded with newly commissioned murals but retains its local appeal. The result is one of the best hotels in the area, appealing both to visitors to Woburn Abbey and to business travellers alike. The attractive village, with its antique and craft shops, retains its quiet character but is convenient for Milton Keynes, Dunstable and Luton. The Inn can book tee-times on Woburn Golf Course, just up the road, and obtain entrance tickets for the Abbey and Safari Park.

Rates: Single room with breakfast from £105. Double room inc. breakfast from £120.
Weekend Breaks: rates on application.

- 59 en suite bedrooms, all with colour TV+ Sat/Sky, d-dial telephone, hairdryer, laundry/valet service, 24-hr room/meal service, tea/coffee making trouser press, modem points, minibar, safe, radio/alarm clock. ✄ and ♿rooms available.
- Three meeting rooms, capacity up to 90. ● 🅿 80
- Golf one mile; squash, swimming, riding, leisure centre 5m; sailing, shooting 10m. ● Open all year.
- & all major credit cards accepted.

M1 Junc 13 4m, Milton Keynes 6, Bedford 13, London 43

Arundel House Hotel

Chesterton Road, Cambridge CB4 3AN
Tel: (01223) 367701; Fax: (01223) 367721)
E-mail: info@arundelhousehotels.co.uk
Website: www.arundelhousehotels.co.uk

The Arundel House Hotel occupies one of the finest sites in the City of Cambridge, overlooking the River Cam and open parkland. It is only a short walk across the park known as Jesus Green to the city centre with its wealth of historic buildings. The hotel is well known for its bar, restaurant and conservatory. The bright, cheerful colours in the bar, coupled with its comfortable sofas and armchairs, leather bound books, beautiful fireplaces and its magnificent Victorian-style bar, carved out of solid American red oak, combine to create a warm and refreshing atmosphere, ideal for a pre-lunch or -dinner drink, or just to relax in. The restaurant, which is equally sumptuous, having been completely refurbished at the end of 2001, has a reputation for providing some of the best food in the area. All tastes are catered for, thanks to the several different menus on offer, all featuring a wide range of imaginative dishes, freshly prepared in the hotel's award winning kitchen. As an alternative to the restaurant, there is a Victorian style conservatory, providing a luscious green environment. The Conservatory is open all day and offers a wide range of different options from cooked meals to cream teas, all of which can also be served in the hotel's secluded garden (weather permitting).

Rates: single with breakfast from £72.50; dble fm £85
Leisure Breaks: £130 per person sharing for 2 nights, dinner, b & b. Singles £120 for 2 nts.

● 105 bedrooms, 102 en suite with colour TV, direct-dial telephone, hairdryer, tea-coffee making facilities, radio/alarm clock.
● Table d'hôte £19.75. Table d'hôte lunch, à la carte, special vegetarian and children's menu also available. Last orders 9.30 pm restaurant; 10 pm conservatory.
● Car parking for 70. ● Open all year.
● Three meeting rooms, maximum capacity 50.
● AMERICAN EXPRESS & Visa, Mastercard, Diners accepted.

Newmarket 13, Ely 16, Stansted 26, Ipswich 54, Norwich 61, London 55.

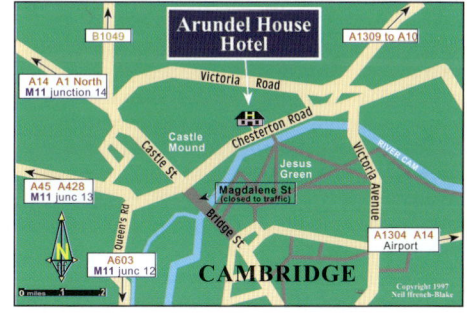

Redcoats Farmhouse Hotel

Redcoats Green, Nr. Hitchin,
Hertfordshire SG4 7JR
Tel: (01438) 729500; Fax: (01438) 723322
E-mail: sales@redcoats.co.uk Web: www.redcoats.co.uk

Near Little Wymondley village, set amidst rolling Hertfordshire countryside, yet only a few minutes from the A1, lies the 15th century Redcoats Farmhouse. It has been in the Butterfield family for generations and in 1971 Peter and his sister Jackie Gainsford converted the building into an hotel. Today it retains its relaxed and easy going country atmosphere. The bedrooms in the main house, some with crooked floors and all with exposed beams, have great character, whereas those in the adjacent converted stables are more functional. Three intimate dining rooms and the conservatory serve outstanding cuisine, recently recognised by the award of an AA rosette. Menus are changed every two weeks and include a good choice of dishes such as Danish herring with dill sauce, half a Gressingham duckling with peach and ginger sauce or a Fillet Steak Carpetbagger. Breakfast, which has also just won a special AA award, is equally memorable with devilled kidneys and Fynon haddock on the menu. Redcoats is ideal for visiting Knebworth or Woburn, Hatfield House or the Shuttleworth Aircraft Collection.

Rates: *Single room with breakfast from £80. Double room inc breakfast from £90.*
Bargain Weekend Breaks *from £120 per person for two nights, b & b.*

- 12 en suite bedrooms, 9 ground floor; all with colour TV, direct-dial telephone + modem link.
- Last dinner orders 9-9.30 pm; two intimate dining rooms; children welcome; conferences max. 20; garden suitable for wedding (civil ceremony) and other marquee receptions.
- Tennis one mile; golf 1½ miles.
- Closed Dec 24-Jan 3 except Christmas lunch.
- & Visa, Mastercard, Switch accepted.

A1(M) 1.5 miles, Hitchin 3, Hatfield 10, Woburn 15, Cambridge 20, London 32.

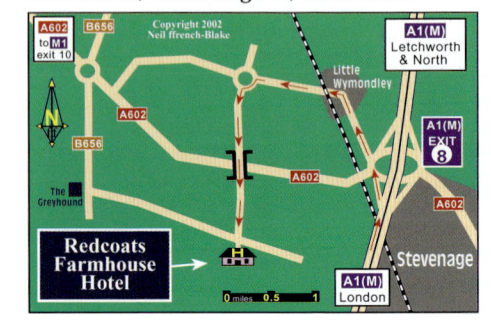

The Blakeney Hotel

Blakeney, Nr. Holt, Norfolk
NR25 7NE
Tel: (01263) 740797;
Fax: (01263) 740795
E-mail: reception@blakeney-hotel.co.uk
Website: www.blakeney-hotel.co.uk

The Blakeney Hotel is a traditional privately owned, friendly hotel which overlooks the National Trust Harbour to Blakeney Point in an area of outstanding natural beauty. The area is ideal for walking, cycling, bird-watching, sailing, fishing, tennis and golf. Close by are many stately homes such as Sandringham, pretty villages, market towns and sandy beaches. The lovely city of Norwich and the port of King's Lynn are each within an hour's drive. The Blakeney offers a wide choice of accommodation and all rooms have private bathroom, colour TV and tea/coffee making facilities. The restaurant, which serves a choice of good, fresh food and the cocktail bar both overlook the estuary. There are comfortable lounges and fine, south-facing gardens in which to relax.

Rates: Single room with breakfast from £64.
Double room inc. breakfast £128.
Leisure Breaks: Dinner, b&b min. two nights from £74 per ppn; 7-day holidays from £462 pp.
- 60 en suite bedrooms (10 grd fl) all with TV, direct-dial telephone, night service. Lift . ♿ access.
- A la carte dinner fm £25; lunch & special diets available; last orders 9.15 pm. Car parking for 60.
- Business services inc 7 meeting rooms for 45.
- Indoor heated swimming pool, spa bath, mini-gym. Beach, golf, tennis, sailing nearby.
- & major credit cards accepted. Open all yr

Brancaster & Cromer 15, Norwich 25, London 127

Gissing Hall

Gissing, Diss, Norfolk IP22 5UN
Tel: (01379) 677291; Fax: (01379 674117
E-mail: gisshall@keme.co.uk
Website: www.gissinghall.co.uk

Gissing Hall is an historic family owned mansion, with Elizabethan origins and later additions, providing country house peace and comfort with full 21st century facilities. Bedrooms, which vary in size, are on two floors, and all have great character. Public rooms include the Library (for meetings) the Blue Room Restaurant with an excellent local reputation and, for less formal meals, the Gallery. Gissing Arts, a local co-operative of artists and craftspeople, frequently hold exhibitions as well as musical events here. The Hall is also geared for weddings, and what a romantic spot from which to start married life or spend a quiet weekend or midweek break. It is 20 miles from the historic city of Norwich. Closer attractions include Blooms Garden Centre & Steam Museum, the Otter Trust and Banham Zoo.

Rates: Single room with breakfast from £50.
Double room inc. breakfast from £65.
Leisure Breaks: Dinner, b&b min. two nights from £40 per pppn.
- 18 en suite bedrooms all with TV, tea/coffee making facilities.
- 3-cse tdh dinner fm £25; lunch & special diets available; last orders 9 pm. Car parking for 60.
- Business services inc meeting room for up to 120.
- Grass tennis court, croquet, gardens. Golf, riding swimming pool, gliding, fishing nearby.
- & major credit cards accepted. Open all yr

Diss 5, Attleborough 10, Norwich 20, London 103

Petersfield House Hotel

Lower Street, Horning, Nr. Norwich,
Norfolk NR12 8PE
Tel: (01692) 630741; Fax: (01692) 630745
E-mail: reception@petersfieldhotel.co.uk
Website: www.petersfieldhotel.co.uk

Colin and Susan Pratt bought Petersfield in 2001 and are busy putting their stamp on it. It is a comfortable 18-bedroom hotel tucked away in two acres of landscaped garden in the centre of the picturesque village of Horning, at the heart of the Norfolk Broads. The hotel has its own mooring on the river Bure and boat and a trip out in it is included in the room rate for those staying seven nights! Otherwise day launches can be booked through the hotel. There is also great fishing in the area with 20lb pike and large bream regularly caught locally. Bedrooms are bright and welcoming and most overlook the landscaped gardens which feature an ornamental pond, a putting green and a flintstone moon gate. Saturday night dinner dances are a feature here and the hotel is a popular wedding venue. Well placed for visiting historic Norwich and nearby attractions and stately homes such as Beeston Hall, Blickling Hall, Aylsham Old Hall and the Bure Valley Railway.

Rates: Single room with breakfast from £64. Double room inc. breakfast £85.
Leisure Breaks: dinner, b&b min. two nights £55 per ppn; stay seven nights and enjoy a free Norfolk Broads trip + coffee after dinner.

- 18 en suite bedrooms (inc. one family room) all with wide-screen TV, direct-dial telephone, tea/coffee making facilities, radio/alarm clock.
- 3-course tdh dinner £19.95; lunch & special diets available; last orders 9.30 pm.
- Two meeting rooms for up to 100. Parking for 40
- Fishing, boating, sailing. Golf nearby.
- AMERICAN EXPRESS & major credit cards accepted.
- Open all year.

Hoveton 2, Norwich 10, Gt Yarmouth 17, Cromer 19, London 122.

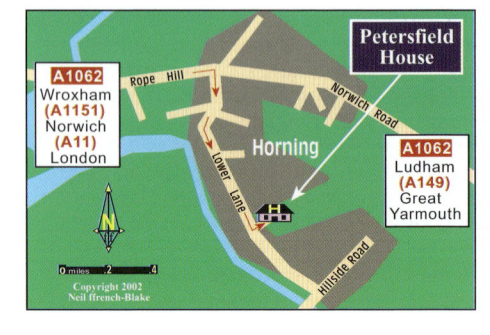

Norfolk, Norwich/Thorpe Market 85

EAST OF ENGLAND

The Georgian House Hotel

32-34 Unthank Road, Norwich NR2 2RB. Tel: (01603) 615655; Fax: (01603) 765689
E-mail: reception@georgian-hotel.co.uk
Website: www.georgian-hotel.co.uk   AA★★★ETC

Only a few minutes' walk from Norwich City Centre with its cathedral, state of the art shopping mall and colourful open market and with easy access to the ring road, two turn-of-the century townhouses comprise the family owned Georgian House Hotel. The rear of the hotel and the dining room look onto an attractive and well tended garden. Inside one is greeted by a young, efficient and enthusiastic staff. We had booked dinner and we were shown into a dining-room with beautiful linen and delightful decor. The meal was well presented and imaginative, with nouvelle cuisine overtones. The wine list is extensive and the hotel also has a variety of specialist beers. En suite bedrooms, which are of varying size, all have desks and seating and are again well decorated. We can recommend Georgian House to anyone visiting the city.

Rates: Single room with breakfast from £65. Double room inc. breakfast from £85. **Leisure Breaks:** Weekend breaks available from October to May (exc. Bank Holidays); min. stay 2 nights.
- 28 en suite bedrooms, all with digital TV, d-dial telephone + Internet connection, hairdryer, laundry service, 24-hr room/meal service, tea/coffee making, radio/alarm clock. ✄ rooms available. 🅿 30.
- 3-cse tdh £19.95; diets available; last orders 2100.
- Meeting room for 30. Hotel closed 24/25 Dec.
- Fishing, fitness centre, golf within two miles.
- & all major credit cards accepted.

E Dereham 16, Gt Yarmouth 18, Cromer 23, London 111

Elderton Lodge

Gunton Park, Thorpe Market, North Walsham NR11 8TZ
Tel: (01263) 833547; Fax: (01263) 834673
E-mail: enquiries@eldertonlodge.co.uk
Website: www.eldertonlodge.co.uk

Set in the heart of beautiful unspoiled North Norfolk countryside, Elderton Lodge was once the shooting lodge and Dower House to adjacent Gunton Park estate, much favoured by Edward, Prince of Wales and Lillie Langtry. Pheasant and deer still roam in the neighbouring parkland. There are eleven comfortable individually decorated bedrooms, each with its own character, numbers 6, 8, 9 & 12 being our favourites. Public rooms include the Lounge Bar with views across the park, the conservatory and the elegant, candle-lit Restaurant, which has an AA ❀. The emphasis is on fresh local produce with fish, lobster and crab from the nearby coast and game in season. New owners Michael Parsey and Pat Roofe and their friendly staff show genuine concern for every guest and will make your stay most comfortable.

Rates: Single room with breakfast £60. Double room inc. breakfast from £95. **Bargain Breaks:** From £55 per person per night.
- 11 en suite bedrooms all with colour TV, direct-dial telephone, hairdryer, tea/coffee making. Non-smoking rooms available.
- A la carte dinner from £23; lunch & bar snacks available; last orders 9 pm. 🅿 for 50.
- Business services inc two meeting rooms for 30.
- Fishing, golf, riding, shooting nearby. Dogs welcome
- & major credit cards accepted.
- Open all year.

North Walsham 3, Cromer 5, Norwich 15, London 123.

Broom Hall Country Hotel

Richmond Road, Saham Toney,
Thetford, Norfolk IP25 7EX
Tel/Fax: 01953 882125
E-mail: enquiries@broomhallhotel.co.uk
Website: broomhallhotel.co.uk

Broom Hall is a family-run Victorian country house set in 15 acres of garden and parkland in the peaceful West Norfolk countryside. The traditional English gardens are laid out with mixed and herbaceous borders and mature trees to provide a welcome oasis of colour and fragrance in which guests can relax. Inside a feature of the public rooms are the ornate ceilings. Bedrooms are spacious and airy with pretty bedspreads (but no telephones to spoil the peace!) and most have views over the grounds. Traditional home cooked food is prepared by chef Stephen Wright using fresh local produce, including vegetables from the garden when in season. They pride themselves also on their mouth-watering home made desserts. Home made cream teas are another treat. There is an indoor heated swimming pool to burn off those extra calories and within easy driving distance are Sandringham and Blickling Hall. Thetford Forest Park and the trans-Norfolk Peddars Way are near at hand for the more energetic.

Rates: *Single room with breakfast from £68. Double room inc. breakfast from £90.*
Leisure Breaks: *winter breaks available Oct-mid March 2 days dinner, b & b £195 per room/3 days £305. Weekly rates available on request.*

● 10 en suite bedrooms all with colour TV, tea/coffee making facilities. [+ 5 ground flr rooms from Spring 2003, of which two suitable for guests].
● 3-course tdh dinner £16.50-22; lunch & bar snacks available; last orders 8.30 pm.
● Meeting room for 20. P for 50.
● Indoor swimming pool. Fishing, golf, riding, shooting nearby. Dogs welcome
● Major credit cards accepted.
● Open all year except 25 Dec - 2 Jan.

Watton 1, Swaffham 6, East Dereham 8, Thetford 12, Norwich 23, London 93.

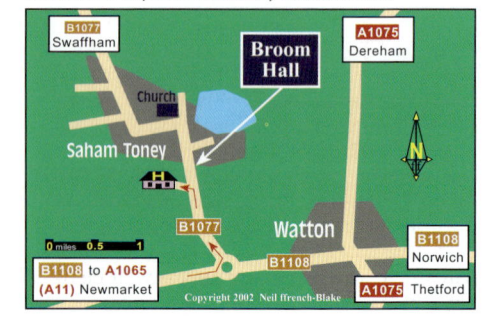

Wentworth Hotel

Wentworth Road, Aldeburgh IP15 5BD
Tel: (01728) 452312; Fax: (01728) 454343
E-mail: stay@wentworth-aldeburgh.co.uk
Website: www.wentworth-aldeburgh.com

The Pritt family have been the owners of this charming Victorian hotel for over 80 years and they are continually upgrading and refurbishing it. The Wentworth Hotel is ideally situated on the sea front in the historic town of Aldeburgh, a centre for music lovers worldwide. The atmosphere is very much of a country house. The lounge is beautifully furnished with antiques and decorated in restful yellows and russets, picking out the colours of the elegant Crown Derby china. The walls are hung with a large collection of Russell Flint prints. The cuisine is excellent, offering local produce such as shellfish (the famous Aldeburgh sprats), fresh fish and asparagus. Bedrooms are individually decorated, many overlooking the sea. Each contains a copy of *Orlando the Marmalade Cat*, the childrens story set in Owlbarrow (Aldeburgh). Superior rooms have king size beds and there is one lovely pine-panelled suite on the ground floor. This is a truly special hotel, with Michael Pritt always on hand to ensure the well-being of guests, many of whom return year after year.

Rates: Single room with breakfast from £60. Double room inc. breakfast from £93.
Leisure Breaks *available throughout the year with special value breaks Jan-March and Nov/Dec.*

- *37 bedrooms, 35 en suite, all with colour TV, radio, direct-dial telephone, tea/coffee making facilities; bedrooms available.*
- *Restaurant, bar & 2 lounges; table d'hôte from £13.50; lunch and special diets available; last orders 9 pm. Car parking for 30. Meeting room for 14.*
- *Sea adjacent; golf, sailing, tennis nearby. Squash 4m, riding 15m, shooting 10 miles.*
- *& all major credit cards accepted.*
- *Closed Dec 27-Jan 10 2003.*

<u>Directions:</u> *From A1094 (A12) head into centre of town, left at T junction, narrow one way street to back of hotel & car park.*
Saxmundham 7, Ipswich 25, Lowestoft 27, Norwich 41, London 103.

Suffolk, Southwold

The Swan

Market Place, Southwold, Suffolk IP18 6EG
Tel: (01502) 722186; Fax: (01502) 724800
E-mail: swan.hotel@adnams.co.uk

The Swan has occupied its present site since the 14th century. Following the Great Fire of 1659, it was rebuilt in time to provide refreshments for bell-ringers pealing out the restoration of Charles II in 1660. In 1880 the owner at the time substantially remodelled the hotel and built himself a fine house next door, now the Town Hall. Subsequent alterations of great character were made in 1938 and in more recent times the Swan has been fully restored and refurbished in a most comfortable and attractive style. There are 26 bedrooms in the main building and a further 17 clustered round the old bowling green in the garden. The public rooms have the traditional character of an English country house, enhanced by fine furniture, carved 18thC doorframes and mantelpieces, prints, paintings and photographs connected with the history of Southwold. The dining room has a daily changing table d'hôte menu and a seasonal à la carte menu, and is complemented by a fine wine list. Britain's first new pier for 50 years was opened at Southwold in August 2001. The relaxed atmosphere and friendly service at the Swan will ensure that your stay will be a memorable one.

Rates: single room with breakfast from £65; double from £105. **Midweek breaks** (Sun-Fri inc.) available annually Oct-April from £65 pppn inc. breakfast, 3-course dinner, newspaper, early morning tea, VAT.

- 43 en suite bedrooms with colour TV, direct-dial telephone, hairdryer, music/radio/alarm clock.
- *Table d'hôte dinner £25. Last orders 2130. Special diets catered for.*
- *Business services inc meeting room for 20.*
- *Croquet. Fishing, golf, riding, sailing/boating, tennis nearby. Car parking for 40.*
- *& Diners, Switch, Visa, Mastercard accepted.* ● *Open all year.*

Darsham Station 9, Lowestoft 12, Norwich 34, Ipswich 34, Gt Yarmouth 24, London 108.

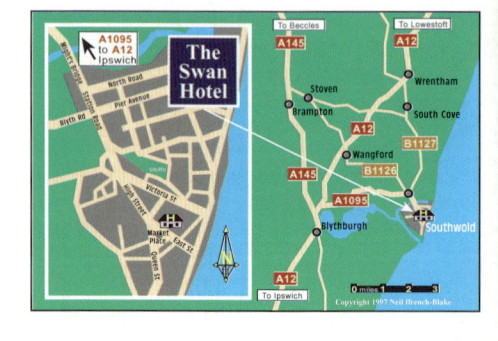

Signpost Guide 2003
Heart of England

Fact File
Illustrated Guide to
Historic Houses, Gardens & Sites
Diary of Events

Hotels in	PAGE
Derbyshire	95
Gloucestershire	103
Herefordshire	108
Leicestershire	109
Lincolnshire	109
Northamptonshire	111
Nottinghamshire	113
Shropshire	115
Warwickshire	119
Worcestershire	121

Historic Houses, Gardens & Parks

Derbyshire
Calke Abbey Park & Gardens, Ticknall
Chatsworth House & Gardens, Bakewell
Eyam Hall, Eyam
Haddon Hall, Bakewell
Kedleston Hall, Derby
Lea Gardens, Matlock
Melbourne Hall, Gardens & Craft Centre
Sudbury Hall & Museum of Child Care, Sudbury

Gloucestershire
Berkeley Castle
Barnsley House Garden
Buscot House, Nr. Lechlade
Hidcote Manor Garden, Hidcote Bartrim
Painswick Rococo Garden
Snowshill Manor, Nr. Broadway
Stanway House, Nr. Winchcombe
Sudeley Castle & Gardens

Herefordshire
Abbey Dore Court Gardens
Berrington Hall, Nr. Leominster
Burford House Gardens, Burford
Eastnor Castle, Nr. Ledbury
Eastgrove Cottage Garden Nursery, Nr. Shrawley
Hergest Cloft Gardens, Kington
Hill Court Gardens, Nr. Ross-on-Wye
How Caple Court Gardens
Moccas Court, Moccas
Queenswood Country Park, Nr. Leominster

Leicestershire
Belgrave Hall, Belgrave
Stanford Hall, Lutterworth
Whatton Gardens, Loughborough

Northamptonshire
Althorp, Nr Northampton
Castle Ashby House & Gardens
Canons Ashby House, Nr Daventry
Coton Manor, Nr Guilsborough
Cottesbroke Hall, Cottesbroke
Elton Park, Peterborough
Deene Park, Nr Corby
Holdenby House Gardens, Nr Northampton
Lamport Hall, Lamport
Rockingham Castle, Market Harborough

Nottinghamshire
Naturescape Wildflower Farm, Langar
Newstead Abbey, Linby
Wollaton Hall Natural History Museum

Shropshire
Attingham Park, Nr. Shrewsbury
Benthall Hall, Broseley
Boscobel House, Nr. Albrighton
Goldstone Hall Garden, Market Drayton
Hawkstone Hall, Weston
Weston Park

Staffordshire
Biddulph Grange Garden & Coun try Park,Biddulph
Chillington Hall, Codsall Wood
Greanway Bank Country Park, Nr. Biddulph
Hanch Hall, Lichfield
Shugborough, Milton
Trentham Gardens

Warwickshire
Arbusy Hall, Nr. Nuneaton
Baddesley Clinton House
Charlecote Park, Nr. Wellesboume
Coughton Court
Harthill Hayes Country Park, Nr. Nuneaton
Jephson Gardens, Leamington Spa
Kingsbury Water Park
Middleston Hall
Packwood House, Nr. Hockley Heath
Ragley Hall, Nr. Alcester
Ryton Organic Gardens, Coventry

West Midlands
Aston Hall, Birmingham
Birminghar n Botanical Gardans
Clent Hills Country Park, Nr. Stourbridge
Coombe Abbey Country Park, Nr. Coventry
Moseley Old Hall, Fordhouses
Selly Manor & Minworth Greaves, Bourneville
Sutton Park, Sutton Coldfield
Wightwick Manor, Wolverhampton

Worcestershire
Hagley Hall, Nr. Stourbridge,Worcs
H anbury Hall, Nr.Droitwich,Worcs
Spetchley Park, Nr. Worcester
The Picton Gardens at Old Coust Nurseries, Colwall Village

Walks & Nature Trails

Derbyshire
Carsington Water, Ashbourne
Gulliver's Kingdom, Matlock Edge
Longshaw Estate, Hathersage

Gloucestershire
Cotswold Water Park, South of Cirencester
Crickley Hill Country Park. Nr. Great Witcombe
Dean Heritage Centre, Nr. Cinderford
Great Western Railway Museum, Coleford
Forest of Dean Trails, starts at Cannop Ponds
Gloucester Guided Walks

Herefordfshire
City of Hereford Guided Walks
Croft Garden Centre, Nr. Leominster
Kingsford Country Park, Wolverley
Symonds Yat Forest Trail, SW of Ross-on-Wye

Leicestershire
Beacon Hill Country Park, Woodhouse Eaves
Bradgate Park, Newtown Linford
Burbage Common Visitors Centre
Melton Mowbray Country Park
Watermead Country Park, Syston
Rutland Water, Oakham

Northamptonshire
Barnwell Country Park, Oundle
Brigstock Country Park, Kettering
Daventry Country Park, Daventry
Pitsford Water, Brixworth
Sywell Country Park, Northampton

Nottinghamshire
Burnstump Country Park, Arnold
C lumber Park, Worksop
Colwick Park, Colwick
Portland Park & Visitor Centre, Kirkby-in-Ashfield
Rufford Country Park & Craft Centre
Rushcliffe Country Park, Ruddington
S herwood Pines Country Park, Edmonstowe

Shropshire
Broadway Tower Country Park
Cardingmill Valley, Long Mynd
Clee Hills, Cleobury Mortimer
Offa's Dyke, Clun Forest
Historic Hawkstone Park & Follies, Weston-under-Redcastle

Staffordshire
Cannock Chase Country Park
Codsall Nature Trail
Deep Hayes Country Park, Nr. Longsdon
Manifold Valley, Nr. Waterhouses
The Wildlife Sanctuary, Nr. Cheadle

Warwickshire
Crackley Wood, Kenilworth
Edge Hill, Nr. Kineton
Hatton Locks, Nr. Warwick
Ufton Fields Nature Reserve

West Midlands
Birmingham City Centre Canal Walk
Longmore Nature Trail
Wren's Nest National Nature Reserve, Dudley

Worcestershire
Malvern Hills Walks & Trails
The North Worcestershire Path
The Worcestershire Way

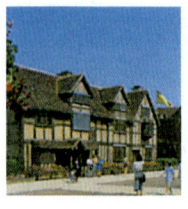

The Heart of England

Historical Sites & Museums

Derbyshire
Arkwrights's Cromford Mill, Matlock
Bolsover Castle, Bolsover
Blue John Museum, Ollernshaw Collection, Castleton
Hardwick Old Hall, Doe Lea
National Trust Museum of Childhood, Sudbury Hall
National Tramway Museum, Crich
Peveril Castle, Castleton

Gloucestershire
Chedworth Roman Villa, Nr. Cheltenham
Clearwell Caves, Nr. Coleford
Corinium Museum, Cirencester
Cotswold Motor Museum & Toy Collection, Bourton-on-the-Water
Gloucester Cathedral
Gloucester City Museum & Art Gall.
Gloucester Folk Museum
Holst Birthplace Museum, Cheltenham
Tewkesbury Abbey

Herefordshire
Goodrich Castle, Nr. Ross-on-Wye
Hereford Cathedral

Leicestershire
Ashby-de-la-Zouche Castle
Bradgate House, Newtown Linford
Stanford Hall, Lutterworth
Bosworth Battlefield Visitor Centre & Country Park
Donington Collection of Grand Prix Racing Cars, Castle Donington

Northamptonshire
Althorp House, Nr Northampton
Boughton House, Nr Kettering
The Canal Museum, Stoke Bruerne
Chichele College, Higham Ferrers
Lyveden New Bield, Oundle
Rushton Triangular Lodge, Rushton

Nottinghamshire
Holme Pierrepoint Hall, Nottingham
Newark Castle, Notts
Newstead Abbey, Linby
Brewhouse Yard Museum of Social History, Nottingham
DH Lawrence Birthplace Museum, Eastwood, Nottingham
Nottingham Castle Museum & Art Gallery

Shropshire
Acton Scott Historic Working Farm
Aerospace Museum, Cosford
Blists Hill Open Air Museum, Ironbridge
The Childhood & Costume Museum, Bridgnorth
Coalbrookdale Furnace & Museum of Iron
Ludlow Castle
Midland Motor Museum, Nr. Bridgnorth
Wroxeter Roman City, Nr. Shrewsbury

Staffordshire
Bass Museum, Visitor Centre & Shire Horse Stables, Burton-on-Trent
The Brindley Mill & Museum, Leek
Gladstone Pottery Museum, Longton
Lichfield Cathedral
Samuel Johnson Birthplace Museum, Lichfield
Stafford Castle
Wall (Letocetum) Roman Site, Nr. Lichfield

Warwickshire
Anne Hathaway's Cottage, Shottery
James Gilbert's Rugby Football Museum, Rugby
Kenilworth Castle
Shakespeare's Birthplace, Stratford-upon-Avon
The Shakespeare Countryside Museum & Mary Arden's House, Wilmcote
Warwick Castle

West Midlands
Bantock House Museum, Wolverhampton
Birmingham Cathedral
Birmingham Museum & Art Gallery
Birmingham Museum of Science & Industry
Black Country Museum, Dudley
Broadfield House Glass Museum, Kingswinford
Coventry Cathedral
Jerome K Jerome's Birthplace Museum, Nr Walsall
The Lock Museum, Willenhall
Midland Air Museum, Coventry
Museum of British Road Transport, Coventry
National Motor Cycle Museum, Bickenhill
Walsall Leather Museum

Worcestershire
Avoncroft Museum of Buildings, Nr. Bromsgrove
Cotswold Teddy Bear Museum, Broadway
Elgar's Birthplace, Lower Broadheath
Hartlebury Castle State Rooms, Nr. Kidderminster
The Droitwich Spa Brine Baths
Worcester Cathedral
Worcester Royal Porcelain Dyson Perrins Museum

Entertainment Venues

Derbyshire
American Adventure, Ilkeston
Cauldwell's Mill & Craft Centre, Rowsley
Bentley Fields Open Farm, Longford
Denby Pottery Visitors Centre, Denby
Lathkill Dale Craft Centre, Bakewell
Royal Crown Derby Museum & Factory, Derby

Gloucestershire
Bibury Trout Farm
Birdland, Bourton-on-the Water
Cheltenham Hall of Fame, Racecourse
Cotswold Woollen Weavers, Nr. Lechlade
Gloucester Docks
House of Tailor of Gloucester
Model Village, Bourton-on-the-Water
National Birds of Prey Centre, Newent
The Wildfowl & Wetland Trust Centre, Slimbridge

Herefordshire
Cider Museum & King Offa Distillery
The Hop Pocket Farm, Bishop's Frome
The Jubilee Park, Symonds Yat West

Northamptonshire
Billing Aquadrome, Northampton
Wickstead Park, Kettering

Nottinghamshire
The Lace Centre, Nottingham
The Tales of Robin Hood, Nottingham
Newark Air Museum
Nottingham Industrial Museum
Patchings Farm Art Centre, Calverton
Sherwood Forest Visitor Centre & Country Park, Edwinstowe

Shropshire
Dinham House Exhibition Centre
The Domestic Fowl Tr't, Honeybourne
Lickey Hill Country Park
The Shrewsbury Quest, Shrewsbury
Twyford Country Centre, Nr. Evesham

Staffordshire
Alton Towers, Alton
Drayton Manor Family Theme Park & Zoo, Nr. Tamworth
Stoke-on-Trent - china factory tours

Warwickshire
Ashorne Hall Nicklodeon, Ashorne Hill
Heritage Motor Centre, Gaydon
Royal Shakespeare Theatre, Stratford
Stratford open-top Bus Tours
Swan Theatre, Stratford
Twycross Zoo, Atherstone

West Midlands
Birmingham Jewellery Quarter Discovery Centre
Cadbury World, Bourneville, Birmingham
Cannon Hill Park, Edgbaston, Birmingham
Royal Doulton Crystal, Amblecote

Worcestershire
Severn Valley Railway, Bewdley to Bridgnorth
West Midlands Safari Park, Nr. Bewdley

DIARY OF EVENTS

January

5. **The Great British Autojumble 2003 & Classic Car Show.** NEC, Birmingham.
18-19. **Motorbike 2003.** Spalding, Lincs.

February

12-16. **Tonex All-England Badminton Championships.** Nat Indoor Arena, Birmingham
15-23. **National Boat, Caravan & Leisure Show.** National Exhibition Centre, Birmg'm
15-23. **Childrens Week.** Ripley, Derbyshire.

March

1,3,8,22,24. **Racing at Wolverhampton** (all weather)
2. **Ludlow Stamp & Postcard Fair.** Ludlow, Shropshire.
6-9. **Crufts Dog Show.** National Exhib Centre, Birmingham
11 & 13. **Racing** at Southwell.
11-13. **Gold Cup National Hunt Week.** Cheltenham,Glos
12-13. **British Travel Trade Fair.** NEC Birmingham.
14-16. **The Outdoors Show.** Birmingham NEC.
14-16. **IAAF World Indoor Champ's.** Nat Indoor Arena.
28-30. **Go Fishing.** NEC, Birmingham, West Mids

April

1 & 21. **Racing** at Nottingham
19,21,28. **Racing** at Towcester.
4-6*.**Spring Festival of Literature.** Var venues, Cheltenham
8-9*. **Newark Int'l Antiques & Collectors Fair,** Notts.
21-25. **Skegness Stage Dance Festival 2003.** Skegness, Lincs

May

1-5*. **Cheltenham Int'l Jazz Festival.** Var. venues, Cheltenhamn, Glos.
1-4*.**Badminton Horse Trials.** Badminton House Grounds, Badminton, Gloucestershire.
2.-5. **Childrens Bookfest.** Shrewsbury, Shropshire.
3-5*. **Spalding Flower Festival/ Springfields Cntry Fair,** Lincs
4-6*. **Malvern Spring Gardening Show.** 3 Counties Showground, Malvern, Worcs
5-12*. **38th Buxton Antiques Fair,** Buxton, Derbs
10-11*. **NEC Sports Car Show.** Nat Exhib Ctre, Birmingham.
16-17. **Racing** at Nottingham.
17-18*. **Chatsworth Angling Fair.** Chatsworth House & Gardens, Bakewell, Derbs.
18*.**Derbyshire County Show** The Showground, Elvaston, Thulston, Derby.
30-31. **Racing** at Stratford-u-A
30-8.6*. **Leominster Festival of the Arts.** Var venues, Le'mster

June

3* **Midland Counties Show** Uttoxeter Racecourse, Staffs
3-6*. **Blenheim Palace Flower Show.** Blenheim Palace, Oxon
9-13*. **DFS Classic Tennis Tournament,** Edgbaston.
10-12*.**Three Counties Show.** 3 Counties Showground, Malvern, Worcs.
26-July 4*. **Ludlow Festival.** Ludlow Castle, Shropshire.
28-July 9*. **Warwick & Leamington Festival.** Warwicks.
30-3.7. **Royal Show.** NAC. Stoneleigh, Warwickshire.

July

1-9*. **HMV Birmingham Int'l Jazz Festival.** Various venues.
4-20. **Cheltenham International Festival of Music & Fringe.** Cheltenham Town Hall, Cheltenham, Glos.
6. **England v Zimbabwe.** Natwest 1 day series, Bristol.
8. **England v South Africa** Nat-west 1-day series, Edgbaston
14-24*.**Buxton International Festival,** Buxton, Derbs.
18-20. **British Grand Prix.** Silverstone Racing Circuit, Northamptonshire
20-21. **The Royal Int'l Air Tattoo.** RAF Fairford, Glos
24-28. **Npower 1st Test England v South Africa.** Edgbaston
25-27. **Warwick Folk Festival**

August

1-31*. **Malvern Festival.** Malvern Theatres, Worcs
1-2*. **172nd Bakewell Show.** Bakewell, Derbyshire.
15-17*. **Hot Air Balloon Festval,** Northampton.
11-21* **Ross-on-Wye Int'l Festival,** Ross, Herefordshire.
18-23*.**Three Choirs Festival.** Gloucester Cathedral.

September

8-9* .**18th Buxton Country Music Festival.** Octagon Pavilion Gardens, Buxton, Derbs
9*. **Heart of England Judo Association Championships.** National Indoor Arena, Birm'.
14-18. **Npower 3rd Test England v South Africa.** Trent Bridge, Nottingham.

October

4*. **Nottingham Goose Fair.** Forest Recreation Ground, Nottingham.
11-19. **Cheltenham Festival of Literature.** Cheltenham Town Hall, Glos.
7*. **Pearl World Conker Championships,** The Village Green, Ashton, Northants
17-29*. **Int'l British Motor Show.** NEC Birmingham

*Denotes provisional date

For further information contact **The Heart of England Tourist Board**, *Larkhill Road, Worcester WR5 2EF. Tel: (01905) 761100 Website:www.visitbritain.com/ heart-of-england*

The Heart of England

The Heart of England: a name that defines this lovely part of the world so much better than its geographical name: *The Midlands*. It is certainly at the very centre of England, with the advantage of fast motorway access from all parts of the UK, but, once off the major roads - whether you strike out north, south, east or west - you will quickly be deep into countryside of huge variety, from stark and dramatic moorlands in the north, to the gentler landscapes of the Cotswolds, dotted with dozens of picturesque tiny villages with "twinned" names such as Lower and Upper Slaughter, Little and Great Rissington, Temple Guiting and Guiting Power; the magnificent churches at Fairford, Cirencester and Chipping Campden, built by prosperous wool merchants of earlier days; and the relics of Roman settlements of even earlier days - all slumber in a timeless beauty. Some of Britain's best country house hotels are in this area and it is was the birthplace of SIGNPOST.

If you really want to escape to unknown places, head west to Herefordshire and the lovely Wye Valley, or to Shropshire - both counties are bordered by the Welsh Marches where England meets Wales - the scene of many past conflicts. But today all is peaceful - you can drive for miles without meeting another car, though undoubtedly the best way to experience the lovely views and fresh air is at a more leisurely pace, by cycle. You will pass through countryside that changes quickly from rich pastureland and small villages to wild hill land dotted with ancient castles and fortified manor houses. Here you will find few large hotels but any amount of country inns - often old black and white timbered buildings that have provided simple accommodation and food for centuries.

The Welsh border lands are perfect for walkers whether you want to tramp along Offa's Dyke, climb the mountains of Long Mynd or wander the wooded lanes of the Wrekin; Staffordshire too, in the northern part of the region, offers superb walking and cycling in the moorlands of the southern Peak district.

In Warwickshire Stratford-upon-Avon attracts huge numbers of visitors but retains the charm of a riverside market town. Experience a performance by the Royal Shakespeare Company at one of the three theatres in season (April-November) and visit the old timbered houses of Shakespeare's time.

The Heart of England has always played an important part in England's history: from the early border conflicts with the Welsh to the series of battles in the Civil War. This has left a heritage of great fortifications: the castles at Warwick, Kenilworth, Goodrich and Berkeley are especially worth a visit - and inevitably many homes of the aristocracy which display art and architecture of special interest.

Bibury

Boscobel House, Shropshire

The Wye Valley

Ragley Hall

Ragley, near Stratford, and the home of the Marquess of Hertford, has a magnificent Great Hall decorated with some of the finest baroque plasterwork in England. Weston Park, the home of the Earls of Bradford, on the Staffordshire/Shropshire borders, is a superb Restoration house with a noted art collection; Hagley Hall, home of Lord Cobham, is another beautiful Palladian house with fine Italian plasterwork; and Sudeley Castle was the last home and burial place of Katherine Parr, the only one of Henry VIII's queens to outlive him.

These houses are all surrounded by acres of landscaped parkland and beautifully kept gardens. Garden enthusiasts should visit Hidcote and Kiftsgate in the Cotswolds, both of which are famous for their rose gardens; and also Hodnet Hall and Hergest Croft high up on the Hergest ridge looking towards Wales. Many of these gardens provide wonderfully atmospheric settings for out-of-doors performances of plays and music, notably at Sudeley and Ludlow, but also at several National Trust properties. There is also a great variety of festivals throughout the summer months (*see previous pages*), many of international repute: The Malvern Festival, the Cheltenham International Festivals of Music and Literature, the Ludlow Festival, the Buxton Festival, the Stratford Festival, the Lichfield Festival and the oldest musical festival of them all: the Three Choirs, held in 1998 in Gloucester, but rotating on a 3-year cycle to the cathedral cities of Hereford and Worcester.

The area holds many reminders of England's industrial history. In Staffordshire, the manufacturers of Stoke on Trent, centre of the world's ceramic industry, demonstrate the traditional skills still used in china making, and the Gladstone Pottery Museum in Longton tells the story of British ceramics. At the Chatterley Whitfield Mining Museum, visitors can tour the coalface 700 feet underground. Shropshire's Ironbridge Gorge holds a complex of fascinating museums centred around the iron bridge over the river Severn, and the whole area at the Heart of England is criss-crossed by waterways. The canal system in Birmingham's city centre can be explored on a trip by long boat.

Birmingham also offers important museum collections of fine and applied arts, historic buildings to study and explore, Botanical Gardens covering 10 acres as well as theatres, the new Indoor Arena and Symphony Hall with its resident symphony orchestra, and nearby the National Exhibition Centre. In the northeast of the area the most touristic county is Derbyshire, with its celebrated Peak District, recently portrayed to good advantage in the BBC's *Pride and Prejudice* serialisation. The 17th-century palladian Chatsworth, home of the Duke & Duchess of Devonshire, is one of the country's finest palaces. Nottingham is famous for its Museum of Costume and Castle Museum, whereas our home county of Northamptonshire boasts several stately homes and castles including Fotheringhay and Althorp, where there is now an exhibition, open July & August only, dedicated to the late Diana, Princess of Wales.

So the contrasts in the Heart of England are many, the choice is wide. Whatever your interest, there will be something to entertain and inspire you: walks in the Cotswolds, Malvern Hills or Derbyshire Dales, Shakespeare Country, Shropshire's Uplands, gardens, music or theatre and some of England's grandest stately homes and castles. All within one hour's drive of an area which was the powerhouse of the Industrial Revolution.

The Izaak Walton Hotel

Dovedale, Ashbourne,
Derbyshire DE6 2AY
Tel: (01335) 350555; Fax: (01335) 350539
E-mail: reception@izaakwaltonhotel.com
Website: www.izaakwaltonhotel.com

The Izaak Walton Hotel is situated just above the river Dove in the idyllic hills of Dovedale. Originally built as a farmhouse in the 17th century, the hotel retains much of its original charm. There are magnificent views of Thorpe Cloud and the surrounding scenery from all the public rooms and from many bedrooms. The Dovedale Bar, whose walls are adorned with fishing memorabilia, is a most welcoming place with an open stone fireplace. Generous salads and snacks are served here at lunchtime. The AA rosetted Haddon Restaurant serves both traditional and modern dishes in a candle-lit atmosphere in the evenings, adding to the romance of the spot. High peaks swoop down dramatically to the river Dove below the hotel and gently rolling fields surround it. There are four rods (four miles) on the river available to residents. The Izaak Walton is the perfect location for a restful holiday and is well placed for visiting Haddon Hall, Chatsworth and the many attractions of Derbyshire.

Rates: *Single room and breakfast from £89.00; double room inc. breakfast from £115.00.*
Weekend breaks: *(Summer period 1.5-31.10.03) 2-night min. stay (Fri & Sat), dinner, b & b, from £76 pppn + enjoy Sunday bonus - £40 per pers*
Midweek Breaks: *(Summer period) 2 night min. stay (Sun-Thurs), dinner, b & b from £66 pppn.* **Winter Warmer Breaks:** *From £68 pppn, dinner, b & b 2 sharing. (exc Xmas/New Year/Easter)*

- 30 en suite bedrooms, all with colour TV+ SKY, direct-dial telephone, hairdryer, laundry service, radio/alarm, tea/coffee making facilities, safety deposit box, trouser press. rms available.
- 3-course tdh dinner £26; lunch & special diets available; last orders 9 pm. ● Open all year.
- Business services inc. meeting room for 40.
- & all major credit cards accepted.
- Croquet, fishing, walks. Squash nearby

Ashbourne 5, Leek 10, Derby 14, M1 24, London 144

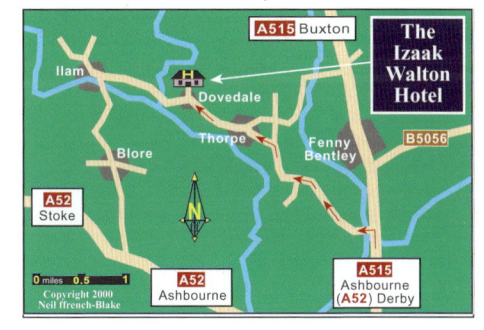

Riverside House Hotel

Ashford-in-the Water, Nr. Bakewell, Derbyshire DE45 1QF
Tel: (01629) 814275; Fax: (01629) 812873
E-mail: riversidehouse@enta.net
Website: www.riversidehousehotel.co.uk

The owners of the Riverside, the Thornton family (whose excellent chocolates are in each bedroom), have refurbished bedrooms and public areas to make this gem even more attractive. It nestles by the river Wye in a quiet cul-de-sac with the beauties of the Peak District National Park on all sides and several classic stately homes: Chatsworth, Haddon Hall and Hardwick Hall near at hand. The country house, Georgian in origin, stands in mature gardens in this quaint unspoiled village of stone houses between Bakewell and Buxton, a wonderful spot for those seeking peace and quiet. Oak panelling and crackling log fires in cooler weather welcome the visitor who is then shown to one of the individually decorated and named bedrooms, some of which have four-posters. The two AA restaurant has an excellent local reputation for seasonally available game and fish from the neighbouring river. There is a separate meeting/dining room for that important private party and the hotel has a civil wedding licence. An excellent centre for touring the Peak District or for relaxing in 'home-from-home' comfort

Rates: Single room and breakfast from £95.00; double room inc. breakfast from £115.00.
Leisure Breaks - 2-day inclusive break (dinner, b & b) from £150 per person.

- 15 en suite bedrooms (10 double, 5 twin) all with direct-dial telephone, hairdryer, laundry service, colour TV, tea/coffee making facilities, music/radio/alarm clock, trouser press. All bedrooms
- 4-course dinner £39.95; lunch & special diets available. Last orders 9.30 pm. ● Open all year.
- Facilities for the disabled. Car parking for 30.
- Business services inc meeting room for 20.
- Fishing, riding, walking, shooting in the area.
- & all major credit cards accepted.
- Open all year.

Matlock 9, Buxton 10, Chesterfield 12, Ashbourne 17, Sheffield 18, London 186.

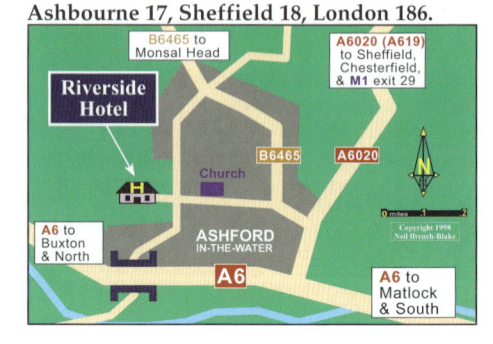

The Croft Country House Hotel

Great Longstone, Bakewell,
Derbyshire DE45 1TF
Tel: (01629) 640278;
Fax: (01629) 640369
E-mail: jthursby@ukonline.co.uk
Website: www.croftcountryhouse.co.uk
Which Hotel Guide Derbyshire Hotel of the Year 1996. ETC Silver Award. Central England Les Routiers Hotel of the Year 2001

The Croft was bought by John and Pat Thursby in 2000 and they have an ongoing programme of redecoration. The cosy small hotel nestles between Ashford and Hassop, in its own grounds of three acres. A spectacular feature is the Main Hall, where drinks are taken before dinner. It has a lantern ceiling and galleried landing, from which lead the nine very different, comfortable bedrooms. Fresh flowers and a sherry decanter greet you. The intimate AA ❀ restaurant offers a table d'hôte menu with outstanding home made soups and desserts. Nearby attractions include Bakewell (of pudding fame), Haddon Hall, Chatsworth and, for walkers, Calver and Monsal Head.

Rates: Single room and breakfast from £63; double from £88.50. Dinner, b&b from £89.50 (single)/£141 double. Major credit cards accepted.
Leisure Breaks: 5 day+ mini-breaks available from £157 per room per night.

- 9 en suite bedrooms, all with colour TV, hair-dryer, tea/coffee making facilities. All bedrooms ♿. Ample parking. Lift.
- 3-course tdh dinner £26.50 at 1930h; special diets available. ● Open 14 February-January 2nd.
- Meeting room for 15. Walking, fishing nearby.

Bakewell 3, Buxton 10, Matlock 9, Sheffield 16, London 185

Dannah Farm Country Guest House

Bowmans Lane, Shottle, Nr. Belper, Derbyshire DE56 2DR
Tel: (01773) 550273;
Fax: (01773) 550590
E-mail: reservations@dannah.demon.co.uk
Website: www.dannah.co.uk

Dannah Farm was a great find, an 18th century farmhouse situated high within the Chatsworth estates between Belper and Wirkworth. Bedrooms are very appealing, furnished with antiques and old pine. Unusual touches include first aid kits and communal umbrellas in the hall. Hopefully neither will be needed! One unit is The Cottage with separate entrance and consisting of two double rooms. The *Mixing Place* Restaurant has been awarded the coveted *Derbyshire Life Golden Goblet* and has an enviable local reputation for good food and wine. Breakfast is also a special treat, with free range eggs, Dannah's own organic sausages and home made bread. An outstanding spot for a short break and a great centre for touring Derbyshire's Peak District and many stately homes.

Rates: Single room and breakfast from £54; double from £79.50. Major credit cards accepted. [Ad]

- 8 en suite bedrooms (3 suites) all with colour TV, direct-dial telephone, hairdryer, tea/coffee making facilities, radio/alarm clock. All bedrooms ♿. Parking for 12. ● 3-course tdh dinner (by arr't) £19.50; special diets available. Last orders 6.30 pm.
- Open all year exc. Xmas.
- Meeting rm for 15. Fired Earth shop on premises.
- *Directions:* Take turning for Shottle off A517 Ashbourne-Belper road, straight on through village northbound, branch right down Bowmans Lane.

Belper 2½, Ashbourne 10, Matlock 9, Derby 10, London 144.

Biggin Hall

Biggin-by-Hartington, Buxton,
Derbyshire SK17 0DH
Tel: (01298) 84451;
Fax: (01298) 84681

E-mail: enquiries@bigginhall.co.uk
Website: www.bigginhall.co.uk

Biggin Hall is an historic manor house of 17th century origin, situated 1000 ft above sea level in the Peak District National Park. The Hall is Grade II* listed and stands in its own grounds of some eight acres. There are eight bedrooms furnished with antiques in the main house (inc. one suite) and a further 11 studio apartments in a bothy and barn in the grounds. Dinner is a daily changing menu of traditional home cooking with the emphasis on local ingredients and free range wholefoods. Guests will feel very much at home in this exceptionally welcoming, comfortable house. A superb centre for walking or touring in Derbyshire, with many historic houses within a 20 mile radius. Packed lunches can be arranged. There is even stabling for those who wish to bring their own horse or pony.

Rates: Double/twin room and breakfast from £60 (apartments); £72 (main house & bothy). Dinner, bed & breakfast from £43 pppn midweek (low) to £65pppn weekend (high). **Leisure Breaks:** Ice-breaker specials - 2 nights midweek, from £86 pp dinner b & b, packed lunch and Glühwein.

- 19 en suite bedrooms all with colour TV, hair-dryer, telephone, tea/coffee making, fridge. 'Silent' dogs allowed in bothy/annex. ● Tdh dinner £15.50 @ 7 pm. ● P 20. Open all year ● 2 mtg rms 10/20.
- Visa, Mastercard, Switch accepted.

Ashbourne 9, Buxton 10, Leek 15, Derby 22, London 153

Santo's Higham Farm

Main Road, Higham, Nr.
Alfreton, Derbyshire DE55 6EH
Tel: (01773) 833812; Fax: (01773) 520525

E-mail: reception@santoshighamfarm.demon.co.uk
Website: www.santoshighamfarm.demon.co.uk

The core of Santo's is a 15th century farmhouse which has been extended to provide 28 bedrooms. Eight of these are 'Italian' themed with names like *Donatello, Botticelli* etc, two have 4-posters, three have waterbeds and two jacuzzi air baths. Most unusual are the seven themed bedrooms: *Mandela's*, with African furniture, *Bradman's* with cricketing memorabilia, *Camelot, Maharaja* and so on. *Guiseppe's* Restaurant serves excellent table d'hôte and à la carte menus, specialising in seafood, thanks to its state-of-the-art Seafood Holding Station. There is also an Italian restaurant and a Sports Bar for snacks. The Crystal Room is available for weddings, banquets and celebrations. Santos overlooks the spectacular Amber Valley, and is easily reached from Sheffield, Derby and the motorway network.

Rates: Single room inc. breakfast from £65; double room with breakfast from £95.
Weekend breaks: 2-night stay to include room, breakfast & dinner from £62.50 per person per nt.

- 28 en suite bedrooms with d-d tel, radio & TV +sat, hairdryer, tea/coffee making, laundry, trouser press, 24-hr room service. ✗ & ♿ rooms avail.
- Tdh 3-course dinner + coffee £23.30; alc, lunch & special diets available. Last orders 9.30 pm.
- 2 mtg rms, capacity 100. Ample P ● Tennis, riding, shooting, fishing, golf, squash nearby.
- ● & major credit cards acc'd. ● Open all yr.

Chesterfield 4, Derby 15, M1 (ex 28) 5, London 136.

Derbyshire - Hope/Matlock

Underleigh House
off Edale Road, Hope, Hope Valley, Derbyshire S33 6RF
Tel: (01433) 621372;
Fax: (01433) 621324
E-mail: underleigh.house@btinternet.com
Website: www.underleighhouse.co.uk
ETC/AA ◊◊◊◊◊ Silver Award/Premier Collection

Philip and Vivienne Taylor acquired Underleigh three years ago and have extended its reputation as an upmarket b & b . The house is tucked away up a *cul de sac* off the Edale road out of Hope, 800 ft up in the Peak District at the head of its own valley. Stunning views of peaceful green fields stretch over the valley to the hills beyond. Bedrooms are individually styled with names like *Shatton, Brough* and *Derwent* and a teddy bear greets you on each bed! Underleigh no longer provides dinner but sumptuous breakfasts are taken at a communal table. For the bird watcher, cyclist , walker or for anyone simply wanting to recharge the batteries in the peace of the Derbyshire countryside and who likes the informality of a private house, Underleigh is paradise indeed.

Rates: Single room inc. breakfast from £40; double room with breakfast from £69.
Leisure breaks: 3-night stay £62 per room per night.

● 6 en suite bedrooms (inc one suite) with d-d telephone, radio/ TV, hairdryer, tea/coffee making.
● Sorry, no children under 12; no pets. Ample P
● Walking, climbing. Fishing, golf three miles; riding three miles.
● Visa, Mastercard, Switch accepted. Open all year

Hope Railway Station 2, Hathersage 4, Buxton 15, Sheffield 15, Derby 50, London 180.

The Red House Country Hotel
Old Road, Darley Dale, Matlock, Derbyshire DE4 2ER
Tel: (01629) 734854;
Fax: (01629) 734885
E-mail: enquiries@theredhousecountryhotel.co.uk
Website: www.theredhousecountryhotel.co.uk

David and Kate Gardiner came down from Scotland to take over the Red House some three years ago and, in that time, have enhanced its reputation for personal service, hospitality and good food. It commands superb views over its own lawned garden to the Derwent Valley. Three of the ten bedrooms are on the ground floor of the adjacent 19th century coach house, two being family rooms. Two of the house bedrooms have four posters and one an antique French bed. Menus in the candle-lit dining room are changed regularly with the emphasis being on fresh herbs and seasonal vegetables. Next to the hotel is the Red House Carriage Museum, whose carriages can be hired. The Derbyshire Dales, Chatsworth, Haddon Hall and Eyam Hall are all also near at hand.

Rates: Single room inc. breakfast from £57.50; double room with breakfast from £85.
Leisure breaks: 2-night 'minibreak' stay, dinner, b & b, 2 people sharing, £230 per room.

● 10 en suite bedrooms, all with direct dial telephone, colour TV, fax/modem points, hairdryer, tea/coffee making facilities, radio/alarm clock.
● Table d'hôte 3-course dinner £20.50; Sunday lunch & special diets available. Last orders 8.30 pm
● Meeting room, capacity 30. Car parking for 15.
● Riding, walking nearby. ● Open all year.
● Visa, Mastercard, Switch accepted.

M1 13m, Matlock 3, Bakewell 5, Buxton 17, Derby 24, London 155

DERBYSHIRE, Matlock

Riber Hall

Riber, Nr Matlock, Derbyshire DE4 5JU
Tel: (01629) 582795; Fax: (01629) 580475
E-mail: info@riber-hall.co.uk Website: www.riber-hall.co.uk
AA ★★★ 76% RAC 2 blue ribbons. ETC Silver Award.
AA wine award Finalist UK Top 25 2002 & 2003.

This historic manor house with 15th century origins was established as an hotel by proprietor Alex Biggin in 1972 and has been welcoming discerning travellers ever since. It is set high in the Derbyshire Hills, on the edge of the Peak National Park and with uninterrupted views over the Amber valley. Surrounded by its own walled garden and orchard, it is truly a spot where one can forget the cares of the world. When I stayed, a birthday dinner in a private room was being enjoyed by guests from all over the North of England. My own dinner was excellent with a *trio of fish* starter, fillet of local beef and a selection of Riber desserts to finish. Alex is a wine specialist and takes great pride in his house choices. My room was spacious, with a four-poster and whirlpool bath, furnished with antiques and with many extras. Riber Hall is just 20 minutes from the M1 yet convenient for visiting Chatsworth, Haddon Hall, Kedleston and other historic houses and sites of Derbyshire. Sailing and watersports are available on nearby Carsington Water and there are splendid walks from the hotel.

Rates: Single room inc. breakfast from £97; double room with breakfast from £127.
Hideaway breaks: 2-night stay to include room, breakfast & dinner from £185 per person (winter) to £196 (summer).

- 14 en suite bedrooms all with direct dial telephone, colour TV, hairdryer, tea/coffee making facilities, minibar, trouser press, room service.
- Table d'hôte 2-course dinner £29.75; lunch & special diets available. Last orders 9.30 pm. AA
- Meeting room, capacity 20. Ample car parking.
- Tennis, clay shooting. Fishing, golf nearby.
- & all major credit cards accepted.
- Open all year.

Directions: From the East, turn off A615 at Tansley, 2 m before Matlock, opp. Royal Oak PH, signed 'Riber Hall'.

Derby 20, Nottingham 26, M1 (exit 28) 11, Chesterfield 11, Sheffield 25, London 150.

Derbyshire, Rowsley

East Lodge Country House Hotel & Restaurant

Rowsley, Matlock, Derbyshire DE4 2EF
Tel: (01629) 734474; Fax: (01629) 733949
E-mail: info@eastlodge.com
Website: www.eastlodge.com   AA★★★ 74%

The Hardman family took over East Lodge three years ago and have enhanced its small country house hotel comfort. Set in 10 acres of picturesque Derbyshire countryside, it was originally the East Lodge to Haddon Hall, seat of the Duke of Rutland. Today it has a high reputation for comfort, service and style with a warm and friendly ambience. Many guests come a long way to sample the AA ❀ restaurant. I had calves liver and asparagus salad to start with, followed by pan fried breast of duck and a delicious frozen toffee and banana cheesecake dessert. With an excellent house wine, an *amuse-gueule* and an 'intermediate' if one wanted one, coffee and *petit fours*, this was very good value and was served promptly and unobtrusively, even when the hotel was busy. Sunday lunches, light weekday lunches and Derbyshire cream teas are also available. My room was spacious and comfortable and I did not see the benign ghost who is reputed to appear occasionally! The hotel is well situated for weddings (civil licence) and business meetings. Unsurprisingly the AA has nominated it *'one of the most romantic hotels in Britain'*.

Rates: Single room with breakfast from £75; double inc. breakfast from £95.
Bargain breaks: Two-day leisure breaks available to include dinner, bed & breakfast.

- 15 en suite bedrooms all with colour TV, direct-dial telephone, hairdryer, laundry service, tea/coffee making, radio/alarm, trouser press. ♿ rms avail
- Table d'hôte dinner £23.95; lunch & special diets available; last orders 9 pm.
- Business services inc 3 meeting rooms - cap 60.
- Croquet on premises. Fishing nearby. P 40.
- Visa, Mastercard accepted.
- Open all year.

Bakewell 3, Matlock 5, Chesterfield 10, Sheffield 16, M1 South 17, M1 North 12, Nottingham 30, Birmingham 60, London 140.

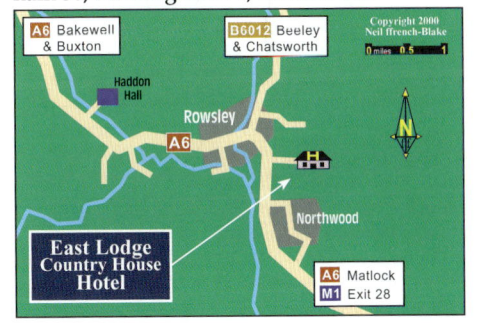

HEART OF ENGLAND

The Peacock Hotel

Rowsley, Nr Matlock, Derbyshire DE4 2EB
Tel: (01629) 733518; Fax: (01629) 732671
E-mail: jpeacock.gm@jarvis.co.uk
Website: www.jarvis.co.uk/peacock

At the Peacock, now owned by the Manners family and managed by Jarvis, the welcome is warm and the unwinding process begins as soon as you walk in. This 17th-century house, set on the banks of the river Derwent, is furnished with antiques and many original features are preserved. The Peacock Bar with its oak beams and rough stone walls is a fine example and an excellent place to enjoy a pre-dinner drink after a busy day visiting the sights of Derbyshire. The restaurants provide a perfect setting for a delicious dinner or lunch, where the menus focus on traditional British cooking using a variety of fresh, local ingredients. Some of the individual bedrooms have four-posters or half-testers and most are grouped around central landings, lending a country house atmosphere. Bathrooms were refurbished in 1999. The many attractions in the neighbourhood include historic houses such as Haddon Hall, Chatsworth and the Heights of Abraham; yet understandably the hotel's speciality is fishing and packages are available which include tuition. The hotel has 14 rods on the river Wye (for trout) and two on the river Derwent.

Rates: Single room inc. breakfast from £80; double room with breakfast from £100.
Leisure breaks: Min 2-night stay to include room, breakfast & dinner £140 per room per night; VIP Break - 2 nights £300 for two persons.

● 16 en suite bedrooms all with direct dial telephone, colour TV, hairdryer, laundry/valet service, tea/coffee making facilities, room service.
● Table d'hôte 3-course dinner £24.50/lunch £16.95; special diets available. Last orders 9.30 pm
● Two meeting rooms, capacity 30 theatre-style or 12 & 8 board meeting. Car parking for 35 cars.
● Walking. Fishing. Golf, shooting available nearby
● & all major credit cards accepted.
● Open all year.

Chesterfield 11, Sheffield 16, Derby 23, Nottingham 30, M1 (exit 28 south, 29 north) 20 minutes, London 148.

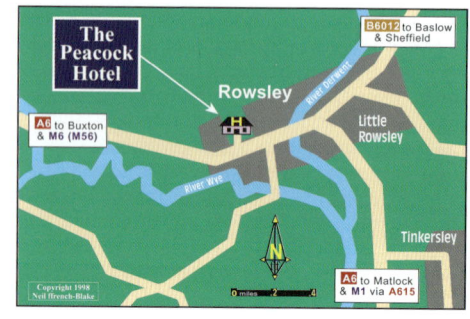

The Swan Hotel

Bibury, Gloucestershire GL7 5NW
Tel: (01285) 740695; Fax: (01285) 740473
E-mail: swanhot1@swanhotel-cotswolds.co.uk
Website: www.swanhotel.co.uk

William Morris called Bibury the prettiest village in England. The Swan hotel is proud to be at its heart. Summer or Winter the village has so much charm with the river Coln running past the front of the hotel and through the village. Indeed the hotel has its own beat on the river. The Swan Hotel is enchanting - privately owned, efficiently run and managed by very friendly staff. It has elegance yet the feeling of being welcomed into a private home. A choice of formal or informal dining is on offer - I actually sat outside in glorious sunshine on the terrace full of flowers and sampled the Bibury-reared trout which is to be heartily recommended. The bedrooms are wonderful - all individually decorated in luxurious style with good sized bathrooms. For that extra special occasion, check out the two wonderful cottage bedrooms, with their private lounge, dining area and kitchen. The Swan is a marvellous retreat for relaxation and perfectly placed for visiting all the interesting towns and villages of the Cotswolds - the Roman Villa at Chedworth, for example, is ten miles away.

Rates: Double/twin room inc. breakfast from £180; family room from £275. **Midweek:** *Room only, doubles from £99. Please 'phone for details.* **Cotswold Breaks:** *Min 2-night stay, 4-course dinner, b & b, VAT from £220 per room per night*

- 20 en suite bedrooms, all with direct dial telephone + modem pts, colour TV, hairdryer, laundry/valet service, trouser press.
- *Signet Dining Room tdh dinner £28.50; alc approx £40; 3-cse Sunday luncheon £19.85. Last orders 9.30 pm. Special diets catered for. Jankowski's Brasserie for informal dining open lunch & dinner. Main courses from £7.85.*
- *Two Conference rooms. Car parking for 20.*
- *Private trout fishing on the river Coln. 'Le Spa' Health & Leisure Club, Cirencester 7 miles. Golf, shooting, riding nearby.* ● *Open all year.*
- Diners, Visa, Mastercard, JCB, Delta, Switch cards accepted.

Cirencester 7, Burford 10, Kemble 10, Stow-on-the-Wold 14, Cheltenham 17, London 96.

The Dial House Hotel

The Chestnuts, High Street, Bourton-on-the-Water, Gloucestershire GL54 2AN
Tel: (01451) 822244; Fax: (01451) 810126
E-mail: info@dialhousehotel.com
Website: www.dialhousehotel.com
'Best Hotel in Gloucestershire 2002' - *West Country Cooking*

Bourton-on-the-Water is one of the prettiest Cotswold villages, with the river Windrush running through it, a perfect Model Village made from local stone to walk around, exotic birds at Birdland Zoo Gardens, the Village Life exhibition in the Old Mill and the Cotswold Motor Museum. In its heart is the Dial House, a 17th century mellow stone small country house hotel. Adrian and Jane Campbell-Howard took over the hotel in 2000 and are bringing their youthful enthusiasm and good taste to the establishment. The cosy, beamed two AA restaurant enjoys an excellent local reputation. In winter log fires burn in the public rooms. In summer, guests can relax in the 1½ acre garden. The Dial House is the perfect place for a relaxing break all year round. Three of the country-style bedrooms have four-poster beds and one has a half-tester. Sherry decanters greet guests in these rooms and flowers, chocolates and champagne can be arranged too for that special occasion. Bourton is well placed for touring the Cotswolds and is handy for Stow-on-the-Wold, Cheltenham, Stratford & Oxford.

Rates: *Double/twin/single room inc. breakfast £57 per person; deluxe 4-poster £69 per person.*
Bargain Breaks: *Dinner, bed & breakfast from £75 per person per night (min. two nights' stay)*
Winter Breaks *(November-February, Mon-Thurs only): dinner, b & b £57.50 per person per night (min. two night stay). Christmas & New Year Programme. Details on request.*

- 13 en suite bedrooms, all with direct dial telephone, colour TV+satellite, hairdryer, trouser press, radio/alarm clock. ✂ bedrooms available.
- Tdh dinner £14.95; alc, lunch, special diets available. Last orders 9.30 pm.
- Fishing, golf, riding nearby.
- Airport pickup on request. Ample car parking.
- Visa, Mastercard, JCB, Switch cards accepted. ● Open all year.

Stow-on-the-Wold 4, Burford 10, Cirencester 16, Cheltenham 16, London 84.

Gloucestershire, Chipping Campden

Charingworth Manor

Charingworth, Nr. Chipping Campden, Gloucestershire GL55 6NS
Tel: (01386) 593555; Fax: (01386) 593353
E-mail: charingworthmanor@englishrosehotels.co.uk
Website: www.englishrosehotels.co.uk/charingworth

The ancient Manor of Charingworth lies in the beautiful, gently rolling Cotswold countryside, and is approached by a winding drive through its own 54-acre parkland estate. The present building dates from the 14th century and has later Jacobean additions. Chevrons painted on the drawing room beams date from about 1316. The characterful bedrooms are named after past owners of the Manor - John Barnsley, Richard Stafford and so on. All have welcoming sherry decanters and most have stunning views over the Cotswolds. Further Courtyard and Cottage bedrooms have been created from former stables. The low-ceilinged 👹👹 John Greville Restaurant is divided by alcoves, giving privacy. The recent addition of a Leisure Spa - indoor pool, sauna and gym, together with two meeting rooms, have made Charingworth a 'Hotel for All Seasons' - a memorable spot for a romantic break or business meeting. The famous Hidcote Gardens are two miles away.

Rates: Single, inc. breakfast from £115. Double/twin room inc. breakfast from £150.
Bargain Breaks: Midweek and weekend breaks available - details on request.

- 26 en suite bedrooms, all with direct dial telephone, colour TV, hairdryer, laundry/valet service, room service, trouser press, room safe.
- Table d'hôte dinner £38.50; lunch, special diets available. Last orders 9.30 pm.
- Two Conference rooms (12 and 24 cap'y). Car parking for 20.
- Leisure Spa - indoor swimming pool, gym, sauna, steam room & solarium. Tennis court.
- AMERICAN EXPRESS & major credit cards accepted.
- Open all year.

Chipping Campden 3, Stratford-u-Avon 12, Moreton-in-Marsh 6, Cheltenham 24, London 80

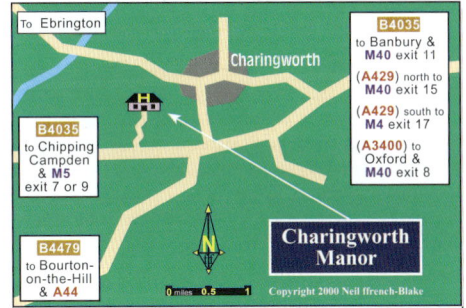

Gloucestershire, Chipping Campden

The Malt House

Broad Campden, Nr. Chipping Campden, Gloucestershire GL55 6UU
Tel: (01386) 840295; Fax: (01386) 841334
E-mail: info@the-malt-house.freeserve.co.uk
Website: www.malt-house.co.uk

Judi Wilkes took over the Malt House in 2002 and continues to run it like a private house. The award-winning cuisine is modern British in style, with many fresh vegetables, herbs and fruit from the hotel's own kitchen garden in season and local produce predominating. The mellow stone building dates from the 16th century when it was used as a malting house. It sits in 4^1/$_2$ acres of immaculate, mature gardens with lawns sweeping down to the brook. To one side a summer house makes an attractive hideaway for tea or a drink before dinner. Public rooms are attractively decorated and furnished with antiques. One sitting room has rare gold flake wallpaper. Each bedroom is different. There is one four-poster and one ground floor suite with direct access to the garden - perfect family accommodation. Broad Campden is one of the prettiest tucked-away hamlets in the North Cotswolds. Stow on the Wold and Stratford are nearby and the public gardens of Hidcote, Kifsgate, Snowshill and Sudeley are within easy reach.

Rates: Single, inc. breakfast from £89.50. Double/twin room inc. breakfast from £112.50.
Leisure Breaks: Two-night, dinner, bed & breakfast offers available.

● 7 en suite bedrooms (inc one suite), all with TV, radio, hairdryer, tea/coffee making facilities.
● Table d'hôte 3-cse dinner £32.50 Thursday through Monday; AA ❀❀; special diets available. Last orders 8.15 pm
● Car parking for 10. Payphone in hotel.
● Croquet, gardens.
● Open all year (exc. Xmas).
● Visa, Mastercard, Switch, JCB accepted.

Chipping Campden 1, Stratford-u-Avon 10, Moreton-in-Marsh 6, Cheltenham 24, London 75.

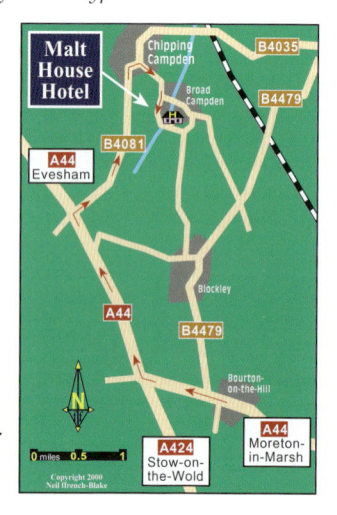

Gloucestershire, Cheltenham (Southam), Tetbury

Hotel de la Bere
Southam, nr. Cheltenham GL52 3NH
Tel: (01242) 545454;
Fax: (01242) 236016
E-mail: delabere@corushotels.com
Website: www.regalhotels.co.uk/delabere

Commanding views over Cheltenham Racecourse, the Delabere has been welcoming guests since the late 15th century. The fine Tudor manor house stands in its own grounds, approached down a tree lined driveway between sweeping lawns. Recently refurbished bedrooms are named after Kings and Queens of England and other prominent families. Some have four-posters and others are in the quieter Courtyard wing. Intricate oak panelling, ornate plasterwork and original fireplaces are very much in evidence throughout the house and the Beaufort Restaurant has fine stained glass windows. There are extensive leisure facilities and function rooms.

Rates: Single room with b'fst from £100; double/twin from £110.
Leisure Breaks: 2 nights+ inc. dinner, b & b from £62 (Mon-Thurs); £55 (weekends) pppnight.

- 57 en suite bedrooms, all with colour TV, radio, hairdryer, direct dial telephone, trouser press, tea/coffee making.
- Beaufort Restaurant tdh dinner £19.95; lunch avail; last orders 2130.
- 4 meeting rooms for up to 80 persons. P 100.
- Outdoor pool (May-Sept), badminton, squash, gym, sauna, solarium. Golf one mile.
- & major credit cards accepted.
- Open all year. Cheltenham 5, Gloucester 11, Stow-on-the-Wold 11, Birmingham Airpt 45, London 100.

The Hare & Hounds Hotel
Westonbirt, nr. Tetbury, Glos GL8 8QL
Tel: (01666) 880233; Fax: (01666) 880241
E-mail: hareandhoundswbt@aol.com
Website: www.hareandhoundshotel.com

This most attractive Cotswold stone Country House has been owned by the Price family for nearly fifty years, and has appeared in Signpost for 68 years! The house is welcoming, with plenty of fresh flowers around and the spacious, comfortable lounges have views of the garden and log fires in winter. Many of the bedrooms have recently been refurbished to the highest of standards. The extremely pleasant Coach House rooms are located on ground floor level at the side of the hotel with one particularly suitable for disabled visitors. You can dine either in the elegant Westonbirt Restaurant overlooking the garden or informally in Jack Hare's bar where there are also outdoor tables in the warmer months. Westonbirt is the site of the famous Arboretum and the well known girls' school.

Rates: Single room with b'fst from £80; double/twin from £99.
Leisure Breaks: 2 nights+ inc. dinner, b & b throughout the year £55-£70 per person per night

- 31 en suite bedrooms, all with colour TV, radio, hairdryer, d-dial telephone, tea/coffee making.
- Tennis, squash, half-size snooker, croquet in summer, table tennis. Golf one mile.
- Children & dogs welcome; conference rms (200); large garden.
- Open All Year. Member of Best Western Hotels.
- & major credit cards accepted. Bath 21, Gloucester 22, Cheltenham 26, London 105.

The Feathers Hotel

High Street, Ledbury,
Herefordshire HR8 1DS
Tel: (01531) 635236;
Fax: (01531) 638955
E-mail: mary@feathers-ledbury.co.uk
Website: www.feathers-ledbury.co.uk

The Feathers is a quintessential English coaching inn right in the centre of Ledbury. Its origins are Tudor, some of its floors and walls may be crooked, but it is the ideal spot from which to explore Herefordshire, the Malvern Hills and Powys. Public areas are relaxing with deep sofas and chairs. Dining is either in Quills Restaurant or in the popular Fuggles Brasserie - named after a variety of hop which has made Herefordshire famous. Both the original and the newer bedrooms are spacious and done up with bright fabrics. Fruit bowl, fresh flowers and magazines are provided. There are private dining or meeting rooms and, for that special function, The Courtyard Room is available. The Leisure Spa offers a pleasant environment in which to unwind and burn off some of those calories gained in the AA ⬥ Restaurant.
Ledbury is proud of its 17th century Market House and retains its old world fascination with narrow lanes and cobbled streets.

Rates: Single room inc. breakfast from £71.50; double/twin from £95; 4-poster/family rooms £135.
Leisure Breaks: Dinner (allowance of £19.50 towards), b & b, two people sharing from £130 per room per night.

Malvern 8, Ross-on-Wye 12, Tewkesbury 14, Hereford 14, Gloucester 16, London 119.

- 19 en suite bedrooms, all with colour TV+ sat, direct-dial telephone, hairdryer, tea/coffee making facilities, radio/alarm clock, trouser press. Some with ISDN lines.
- Top Bar, Fuggles Brasserie, Quills Restaurant a/c available; Special diets & lunch available. Last orders 9.30 pm.
- Fitness centre/gym, jacuzzi, sauna/ solarium, indoor swimming pool.
- Meeting/function room for 120. Parking for 50.
- & all major credit cards accepted.
- Open all year.

Leicestershire (Rutland), Uppingham. **Lincolnshire,** Lincoln

The Lake Isle
Restaurant & Town House Hotel
High Street East, Uppingham,
Rutland LE15 9PZ.
Tel: (01572) 822951;
Fax: (01572) 824400
E-mail: info@lakeislehotel.com Web: lakeislehotel.com

The Lake Isle changed hands in 2001 and Richard and Janine Burton are determined to build on the success of the previous owners. The restaurant used to be Sweeney Todds barber shop and old Uppinghamians may remember having their hair cut in what is now the bar. Today it has won many awards, the cuisine specialising in local game and fish and the desserts and soups to die for! The 12 delightful bedrooms, on different levels, are named after famous wine growing regions: *Dom Perignon* (which also has a whirlpool bath), *Champagne, Bordeaux* and so on. Over the courtyard are three cottage suites with bedrooms upstairs and sitting rooms downstairs. All bedrooms come with thoughtful extras: a sherry decanter, bowl of fresh fruit and home made biscuits. Upstairs there is a comfortable lounge and private dining room for up to 12.

Uppingham is a friendly small town with easy parking, craft, antique and book shops and Rutland Water nearby.

Rates: *Single with b'fst fm £55; double fm £70; family rm fm £125. Major credit cards accepted*
● *12 en suite bedrooms with colour TV; direct-dial telephone; hairdryer, trouser press, tea/coffee making, radio/alarm.*
● *Meeting room for 12. Garden terrace.* **P** *at rear*
● *Tdh dinner £19.50 2 cse/£23.50 3 cse. L.o.21.30. Lunch & spec. diets avail.*● *Open all year.*
Leicester 19, Northampton 28, Nottingham 35, London 101.

Branston Hall Hotel
Branston, Nr. Lincoln
Lincolnshire LN4 1PD
Tel: (01522) 793305
Fax: (01522) 790549
E-mail: info@branstonhall.com
Website: www.branstonhall.com

We were pleased to have been able to include Branston Hall in Signpost, in an area where country house hotels are few and far between. The Old Hall was built in 1735 although the present building dates from 1885. It sits in 88 acres of its own parkland and woodland and has been the subject of considerable refurbishment in recent years to make it a leading light in the area. The hotel retains the high ceilings and spacious feel of the Victorian era. Dining is either in the Lakeside Restaurant or in the less formal Melville Bar area. Most bedrooms overlook the lake and grounds and reflect the architecture of the original building. The leisure centre has an indoor pool with impressive murals, sauna and fitness suite. Branston Hall is ideal for those visiting Lincoln on business or pleasure who do not wish to stay in the city.

Rates: *Single room with breakfast from £68.50; double/twin from £115.* **Leisure Breaks:** *2 nights dinner, b & b from £120 per night for a double rm*
● *48 en suite bedrooms with colour TV & radio, d-dial telephone; fax/modem points, hairdryer, laundry service, tea/coffee making, 24-hr room service.* ✄ *rooms available. Lift. 5 mtg rms to 150.*
● *3-cse tdh dinner £18.95; alc, diets avail. L.o. 9pm*
● *Fitness centre/gym, indoor pool, sauna, jacuzzi. Fishing, golf, watersports, tennis, riding nearby.*
● *& all major credit cards acc'd. Open all year.*
Lincoln 3, Sleaford 15, Newark 16, London 140.

HEART OF ENGLAND

The Olde Barn Hotel

Toll Bar Road, Marston, Nr. Grantham, Lincolnshire NG32 2HT
Tel: (01400) 250909; Fax: (01400) 250130
E-mail: enquiry@theoldebarnhotel.co.uk
Website: www.olde-barn-hotel.co.uk

This authentic rustic hotel has been imaginatively refurbished and modernised to provide every facility for today's discerning business and leisure guest, whilst retaining much of its original rural farmstead character. Situated deep in the Lincolnshire countryside, The Olde Barn is a charming and stylish hideaway offering tranquillity and an excellent environment for any business event. All suites are equipped with dedicated conference furniture and open onto private gardens. Guests can dine in the lofty Barn Restaurant which is adorned with fresh flowers and memorabilia. It has an excellent reputation for expertly prepared traditional English and Fusion cuisine. Less formal meals can be taken in the bar which has a welcoming and hospitable ambience. A state-of-the-art Health & Fitness Suite provides ideal relaxation after a day's touring or business in the area. Marston is a fine base from which to explore the rich countryside and historic houses and castles of the area. Sir Isaac Newton was born nearby at Woolsthorpe Manor and Belton House and Belvoir Castle are but a short drive away.

Rates: Single room with breakfast from £65. double/twin room inc b'fst from £75.
Leisure Breaks: 2 nights, dinner, b & b £50 pppn

● 57 en suite bedrooms (inc 5 four-posters & family rooms), all with colour TV, d-dial telephone + modem pts; hairdryer, trouser press, tea/coffee making, laundry service, radio/alarm, safe, writing desk, 24-hr room service. ✂ & ♿ rooms available.
● Tdh & alc available lunch & dinner. Sp. diets catered for. Last orders 9.30 pm.
● 6 meeting/function rooms, cap.140. Parking 130
● Fitness centre/gym, indoor pool, steam & sauna, jacuzzi, spa, massage. Golf, riding, fishing nearby.
● Visa, Mastercard, Switch acc'd. Open all yr
Directions: Hotel is halfway between Newark & Grantham 3m off the A1. From the south, turn across carriageway (with care) signed 'Marston' by a Texaco garage

Grantham 4, Newark 5, Sleaford 6, Nottingham 28, London 115.

Northamptonshire, Badby/Castle Ashby

The Windmill at Badby

Main Street, Badby, Nr. Daventry, Northamptonshire NN11 6AN.Tel: (01327) 702363; Fax: (01327) 311521
E-mail: windmill-badby@fsmail.net
Website: www.windmillinn.info

The Windmill is a homely village inn with a popular and imaginative restaurant. Specialities include king prawns and Gressingham duck with a berry sauce. There is always a selection of 'Fresh Specials', Grills and a sensible childrens' menu. The bar serves cask-conditioned ales. There are some excellent new world wines on the list. Décor is bright and cheerful; bedrooms have individual names like the *Fawsley Room* and there is one family or honeymoon room - *The Windmill Room*. This year two bedrooms have been added in a neighbouring cottage. Badby is in excellent walking and cycling country (both The Knightley Way and The Nene Way start here) and local places to visit include Althorp, Sulgrave Manor, Silverstone Circuit, Warwick and Stratford-upon-Avon.

Rates: Single inc. breakfast from £57.50; double from £69.50. **Leisure Breaks:** *Summer Weekend Breaks from £120 per room for two nights/£175 for three nights, b & b. Dinner to be taken in hotel.*
● *10 rooms, all with colour TV + satellite, direct-dial telephone, hairdryer, laundry service, tea/coffee making, trouser press, music/radio/alarm clock.*
● *A la carte restaurant open lunch & dinner. Special diets avail. Last orders 9.30 pm. Parking 25.*
● *New conference/meeting room for up to 16.*
● *& Visa, Mastercard, Diners cards accepted.* ● *Open all year.*

Daventry 3, N'ton 10, Banbury 13, Stratford 30, London 86.

The Falcon Hotel

Castle Ashby, Northampton NN7 1LF.Tel: (01604) 696200; Fax: (01604) 696673

E-mail: falcon.castleashby@oldenglishinns.co.uk

This traditional 16th century country cottage is made for relaxation. The Falcon is cosy, warm and comfortable. The pretty restaurant, serves modern English cuisine using produce from the hotel's own vegetable garden, where possible. The oak-beamed cellar bar offers a fine selection of real ales to accompany the excellent value bar meals. Michael and Jennifer Eastick are 'hands-on' hosts who will make you feel very much at home. Each of the 16 bedrooms, 5 in the main old house and 11 in a cottage across the car park, is individually decorated, with scrubbed or painted pine wardrobes and restful lighting. Bathrooms have power showers, complimentary toiletries and bathrobes. The hotel can also cater for business meetings and wedding receptions. The Falcon is minutes from Castle Ashby House and well placed for Silverstone, Stratford, Woburn and Althorp.

Rates: Single inc. breakfast from £89.50; double/ twin from £109.50. Premier rooms fm £129.
Leisure Breaks: *Min 2 nts d,b&b £69.50 pppn.*
● *16 en suite bedrooms, all with colour TV+ satellite, direct-dial telephone, radio, tea/coffee making, hairdryer, bathrobe, trouser press.*
● *Table d'hôte 3 cse dinner £23.95/lunch £18.95; alc & bar meals available. Last orders 10 pm. AA*
● *Two meeting rooms to 40* 🅿 *50.* ● *Open all year*
● *Golf, riding, clay pigeon shooting, fishing nearby*
● *& all major credit cards accepted.*
Directions: Off A428 Northampton-Bedford Rd

Olney 5, Northampton 8, Wellingboro' 10, Bedford 16, London 76.

HEART OF ENGLAND

Fawsley Hall

Fawsley, Nr. Daventry,
Northamptonshire NN11 3BA
Tel: (01327) 892000 Fax: (01327) 892001
E-mail: info@fawsleyhall.com Website: www.fawsleyhall.com

Fawsley Hall opened as an hotel in 1998 and has rapidly established itself as one of the finest hotels in the Midlands. It stands in 2000 acres of quiet parkland where sheep graze beside the 14th century ironstone church, beyond which stretch lakes landscaped by Capability Brown. The Hall has three distictive styles of architecture: the original Tudor rooms form the core of the house and include the wonderful panelled Great Hall and eight authentically furnished bedrooms. This part of the house includes the Queen Elizabeth Chamber, where the Tudor monarch is reputed to have stayed. There are then 14 Georgian rooms with large windows and high ceilings and eight Victorian rooms. In 2002 13 modern classic rooms were added, individually furnished and many overlooking the lakes. All have de luxe touches like dataports and digital television, power showers and telephone extensions in the bathroom. The Knightley Restaurant is under the supervision of chef Philip Dixon. Fawsley is well placed for visits to Althorp, Sulgrave Manor and Silverstone. The perfect place to be pampered for that promised short break.

Rates: *Single room and cont. breakfast from £125; double room from £180.*
Leisure Breaks: *- tdh dinner, b & b, 2-night + stay for 2 people from £99 per person per night (de luxe room) to £160 pppn (suite).*

- 43 en suite bedrooms, including three suites & six four-posters, all with direct dial telephone, TV + satellite, laundry/valet service, 24-hr room service, radio/alarm clock, safety deposit box, minibar, fax/modem points. rooms available.
- 3-cse table d'hôte dinner menu £31; à la carte, lunch & special diets avail; last orders 9.30 p.m.
- Croquet, tennis, health & beauty treatment rooms, fitness studio on site. Golf & swimming pools within 5 miles. Car parking for 100.
- 7 mtg rooms, up to 100 capacity. Open all yr
- & all major credit cards accepted.

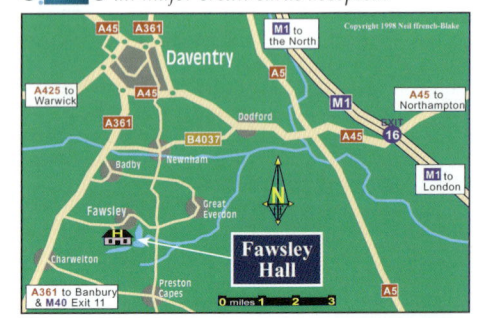

Northampton 10, Banbury 13, Stratford 30, Oxford 36, London 86

Langar Hall

Langar, Nottinghamshire
NG13 9HG
Tel: (01949) 860559;
Fax: (01949) 861045
E-mail: langarhall-hotel@ndirect.co.uk
Website: www.langarhall.com
César Award for 'the most highly enjoyable hotel of the Year 2000' - Good Hotel Guide

I always love my visits to Langar Hall. Although close to Nottingham, it is beautifully situated overlooking the Vale of Belvoir - a lovely country house, built in 1837, standing beside an early English church, with glorious views over the gardens, moat and parkland. The Hall is the family home of Imogen Skirving, where her father used to entertain famous cricketers of the 1930's. Nowadays the Test Match Special team stay here during Trent Bridge test matches! The public rooms are delightful. The charming proprietor and her excellent team make every effort for their guests' happiness. Together with her chef Toby Garratt, Imogen works to produce excellent, reasonably priced à la carte menus of French and English food which include such dishes as local lamb, turbot, steak and chips with bernaise sauce or lobster. The restaurant now has two AA. This year Imogen has extended the 'library' and created a bar area with high 'billiard stools', where she serves her celebrated fruit juice mixes. All the bedrooms are charming and uniquely furnished; one has been redecorated in pink as the *Barbara Cartland Room*, as the novelist used to stay at Langar on her way down from Scotland. This is a truly lovely spot, with a peaceful and relaxing atmosphere.

Rates: Single room and breakfast from £75; double room and breakfast from £100; suite from £175. **Weekend breaks** - room and breakfast 2-night stay for 2 people from £175.

● 10 en suite bedrooms, all with direct dial telephones, TV; room service; baby listening.
● Weekday tdh dinner menu £25; àlc menus from £30; lunch from £12.50; last orders 9.30 p.m.
● Children welcome; dogs by arrangement. (£10)
● Own coarse fishing - bring your own rod; golf four miles. Hunting and shooting can be arranged.
● Licensed to hold marriages; exclusive house party booking; conferences 20 max. Open all year.
● American Express & Mastercard, Visa Cards accepted.

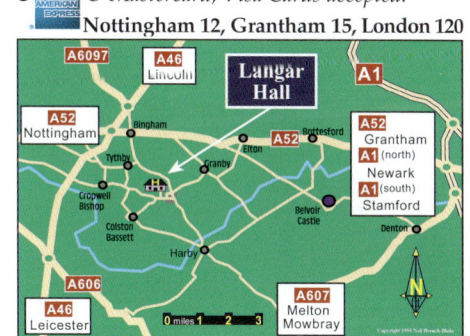

Nottingham 12, Grantham 15, London 120

HEART OF ENGLAND

Cockliffe Country House Hotel

Burnt Stump Country Park, Burnt Stump Hill, Arnold, Nottingham NG5 8PQ.
Tel: (0115) 968 0179;
Fax: (0115) 968 0623
E-mail: enquiries@cockliffehouse.co.uk
Website: www.cockliffehouse.co.uk

Cockliffe was an intriguing find six miles north of Nottingham. Dane and Jane Clarke acquired the property seven years ago and converted the 17th century manor house into a luxurious, contemporary furnished country house hotel. Jane is an interior decorator and colours in the bedrooms are bold and striking; pictures would be superfluous. The shapes of the rooms are also unusual, reflecting the contours of the original building. Most baths have jacuzzis; some are restored 'lions' feet' tubs. We chose our dinner in the relaxed atmosphere of the bar, then adjourned to the attractive *Sherwood* dining room. The imaginative cuisine is under the supervision of chef/patron Dane Clarke. . There is a barn extension which has been turned into a beamed conference suite or private dining room. The whole effect provides a relaxing alternative to staying in central Nottingham, and, for leisure guests, Burnt Stump Country Park is adjacent and Newstead Abbey nearby.

Rates: Single room and breakfast from £95; double room with breakfast £105-150.

- 10 en suite bedrooms, all with TV+sat&CD, d-d tel with fax-modem points, radio/alarm clock, hair-dryer, tea/coffee making, trouser press. Open all yr
- Meeting room for up to 25 with A/V mat'l.
- 3-cse alc dinner £35; last orders 9.00.pm. 80.
- Fishing, golf, riding, fitness centre nearby.
- & M/card, Visa, Diners acc'd.

Nottingham 6, Mansfield 8, Leicester 32, Derby 20, London 182

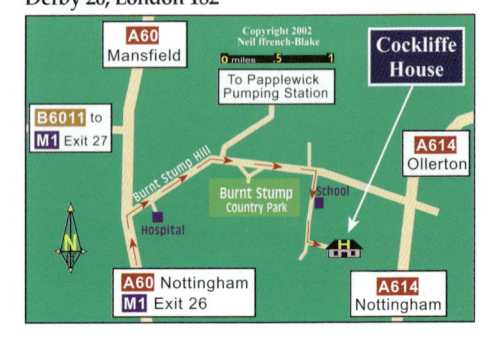

The Old Vicarage

Worfield, Nr. Bridgnorth, Shropshire
WV15 5JZ
Tel: (01746) 716497; Fax: (01746) 716552
E-mail: admin@the-old-vicarage.demon.co.uk
Website: www.oldvicarageworfield.com

Situated in the pretty conservation village of Worfield, the Old Vicarage Hotel is a peaceful retreat for travellers, whether on business or pleasure. The original style has been preserved with subtle refurbishment in keeping with modern comfort, and pretty watercolours add an intimate and homely touch. The small restaurant is renowned for its first class cuisine, award-winning wine list and efficient service. People travel from far afield just to enjoy a superb dinner. My bedroom was in the main house. It had great Victorian charm with a huge antique bed and wardrobe, and a marvellous view over the tranquil Shropshire countryside. Further large bedrooms have been converted from former stables and all are exquisitely decorated. There is a ground floor suite for disabled guests. The hotel is close to Ironbridge Gorge Museum and Severn Valley Railway. David & Sarah Blakstad, the resident proprietors, are attentive and welcoming hosts who will do their best to make your stay memorable.

Rates: Single with breakfast from £80; double from £130. **Leisure Breaks:** *Any two days (or longer) from £150 per room per night.*
Sunday night saver: *£99 per room, b & b.*

● 14 en suite rooms (inc. 4 suites), all with colour TV, d-dial telephone, hairdryer, laundry/valet service, minibar, radio/alarm clock, safe, trouser press. ♿ rooms available.
● Tdh dinner £24.50; alc, lunch & sp. diets available, last orders 9 pm. dining room.
● 2 meeting rooms, cap'y up to 30. Parking for 40.
● Croquet, jacuzzi. Tennis 1/2 m; fitness centre, golf, squash, in/outdoor swimming pools nearby.
● Children welcome; dogs accepted.
● AMERICAN EXPRESS & major credit cards accepted.
● Open all year

Bridgnorth 4, Telford 8, Kidderminster 12, Birmingham 25, London 150.

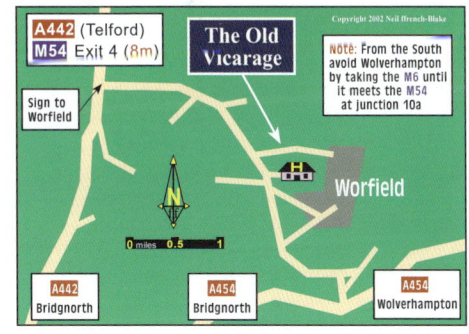

The Feathers Hotel

Shropshire, Ludlow

The Bullring,, Ludlow,
Shropshire SY8 1AA
Tel: (01584) 875261;
Fax: (01584) 876030
E-mail: Feathers.Ludlow@btconnect.com

The Feathers is a town centre hotel with forty very different bedrooms, including four posters and luxury four poster junior suites. One even has a jacuzzi for two! At the heart of the hotel is the early 17th century building. It has been described as *'that prodigy of timber framed houses'* by Pevsner and *'the most handsome inn in the world'* by Ian Morris in the New York Times. The hotel is conveniently located in the centre of town with antique shops, the castle and the open-air market all within walking distance. Ludlow has recently also become something of a gastronomic centre with several Michelin-rosette eateries in the town. Another glory of the Feathers is the Housman Restaurant which offers both traditional and contemporary dishes. Homemade cakes and scones are there to tempt the palate at tea-time. There are several smaller dining and meeting rooms, including the James I lounge with its historic ceiling and fireplace panelling, the Writing Room and Tanners Room. In the summer, the enclosed courtyard garden is available as a restaurant extension. Ludlow is an excellent centre from which to explore the Welsh March country, Clee Hill and Offa's Dyke; Stokesay Castle, the Stretton Hills and Secret Hills Discovery Centre also being near at hand.

- 40 en suite rooms, all with colour TV + sat, d-dial telephone, fax/modem points, hairdryer, laundry/valet service, tea/coffee making, radio/alarm clock, trouser press. ✍ rooms available.
- Tdh 3-cse dinner £21.95 in AA ❀ Housman Restaurant; alc, lunch & sp. diets available. Last orders 2130. ● Billiard Room.
- 3 meeting rooms, capacity 120. Car parking 30.
- Switch, Visa, Mastercard accepted.
- Open all year.

Rates: Single, room only from £60; double, room only from £85; four-poster from £110.
Leisure Breaks: Two days or more, dinner, b & b from £55 pppn (Winter); £65 May-Sept.

Leominster 11, Knighton 15, Shrewsbury 27, Worcester 29, London 143

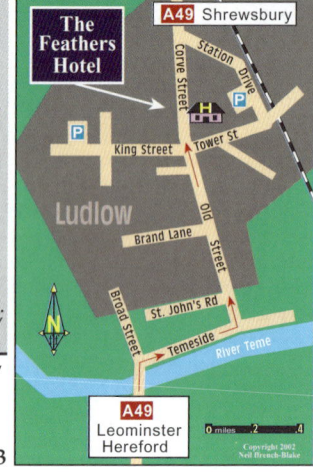

Overton Grange Hotel

Old Hereford Road, Ludlow,
Shropshire SY8 4AD
Tel: (01584) 873500;
Fax: (01584) 873524
E-mail: overton@choblet.fsnet.co.uk
Website: overtongrangehotel.co.uk

Situated on a rise at the end of a private driveway and overlooking the glorious Shropshire countryside, you will find Overton Grange, just a mile from Ludlow on the B4365. Ludlow has a rich programme of events throughout the year, including the famous food festival. Overton's 14 sumptuous bedrooms and suites have period-style furniture and the views from most rooms are simply stunning. The AA ❀❀❀ Restaurant 'O' is widely recognised for its excellent cuisine and service. The extensive wine list offers over 200 fine vintages and New World wines and the bar is well stocked. The public rooms have log fires are and are filled with fresh flowers. An application has been made for a Civil Wedding Licence. Overton is the perfect venue for weekend or mid-week breaks, weddings and conferences.

Rates: *Single room and breakfast from £70; double from £95.* **Leisure Breaks:** *2-day stay Sun-Thurs dinner, b & b from £150 per room p nt*
- 14 en suite bedrooms, all with TV, d-dial tel + modem pts, laundry/valet service, radio/alarm, safe, hairdryer, tea/coffee making, ✄ rms available, trouser press ● 3 meeting rooms, capacity 20-120.
- Dinner, lunch & special diets available. Last orders 9.30.pm. 🅿 50+. ● Open all year.
- Croquet, fishing from hotel. Gym, swimming pool, golf, clay shooting, tennis and riding nearby.
- Visa & Mastercard accepted. ● Open all year.

Ludlow 1, Leominster 10, Shrewsbury 27, London 143.

Wynnstay Hotel

Church Street, Oswestry,
Shropshire SY11 2SZ
Tel: (01691) 655261;
Fax: (01691) 670606
E-mail: info@wynnstayhotel.com
Website: www.wynnstayhotel.com

The Wynnstay was once a well known posting house on the Liverpool to Cardiff road. Situated opposite the parish church, it was renovated in 1988/89 in the style of a Georgian country house. A unique feature of the hotel is its 200-yr old walled Crown Bowling Green. Equally unusual in a town centre hotel is its health, fitness and beauty suite, opened in 1995 and popular with visitors and locals alike. The AA ❀ Restaurant is the Georgian heart of the hotel. The Pavilion Lounge, where lighter meals are available, features an impressive American walnut bar. Executive (larger) bedrooms feature sofas and coffee tables; suites have whirlpool baths and many other extras. The hotel can cater for weddings and conferences for up to 200.

Rates: *Single room and breakfast from £74.45; double from £83.90.* **Leisure Breaks:** *2-day stay dinner, b & b £116 per person sharing twin room.*
- 29 en suite bedrooms, all with TV, direct-dial telephone, laundry/valet service, radio/alarm, hairdryer, tea/coffee making, ✄ rms available, trouser press ● 3 meeting rooms for up to 200.
- Tdh dinner £18.50; lunch & special diets avail. Last orders 9.30.pm. 🅿 80. ● Open all year.
- Fitness centre/gym, whirlpool, massage, sauna, steamroom, indoor swimming pool, bowling green. Fishing, golf, tennis, riding nearby; shooting 10 m.
- AMERICAN EXPRESS & M/card, Visa, Diners acc'd. **Shrewsbury** 18, Llangollen 18, Chester 28, London 182.

Soulton Hall

Wem, Nr. Shrewsbury,
Shropshire SY4 5RS
Tel: (01939) 232786;
Fax: (01939) 234097

E-mail: j.a.ashton@soultonhall.fsbusiness.co.uk
Website: www.soultonhall.fsbusiness.co.uk

John and Ann Ashton turned their Elizabethan manor house into a small hotel in 1988 and the result is one of the best kept secrets of Shropshire! The Manor of Soulton featured in the Domesday Book and the site of the original moated manor house may be seen nearby. Rowland Hill, first protestant Lord Mayor of London, bought the present house in 1556 and a descendant, Thomas Hill, has his coat of arms above the front door to this day. Guests here are treated like members of the family. Drinks are taken in the cosy drawing room, well stocked with games and magazines, before moving into the dining room for a leisurely four course dinner, which might start with home made cream of celery and Stilton soup or a terrine of salmon in leek leaves and whose main course might be roast Shropshire lamb or wild mushroom pie with sherry gravy. Four of the bedrooms are in the main house, while the Coach House outside has two further ground floor bedrooms, one with a sitting room. Alternatively Cedar Lodge has a suite and garden rooms. Soulton is a working farm, and guests are welcome to explore it. In all, Soulton is a peaceful spot in which to just relax or from which to explore the beauties of North Shropshire, including Wem itself, Hawkstone Park, Shrewsbury, Hodnet Hall's gardens, Grinshill and Nescliffe Hill. The Welsh hills and border castles are also within easy reach.

- 10 en suite bedrooms, all with TV, direct-dial telephone, laundry/valet service, radio/alarm, hairdryer, tea/coffee making, trouser press.
- 4-cse tdh dinner £23.50; special diets available. Last orders 8.30. pm. Car parking for 20.
- Working farm, walks, rough fishing. Clay shooting, golf, archery nearby/by arrangement.
- & all major credit cards accepted.
- Open all year.

Wem 2, Whitchurch 10, Telford 15, Chester 28, Shrewsbury 14, London 158.

Rates: Single room and breakfast from £42.50; double from £75.

Leisure Breaks Winter breaks available 2-3 nights, dinner b & b for 2 sharing from £51 per person per night. 7 nights from £43 per person per night.

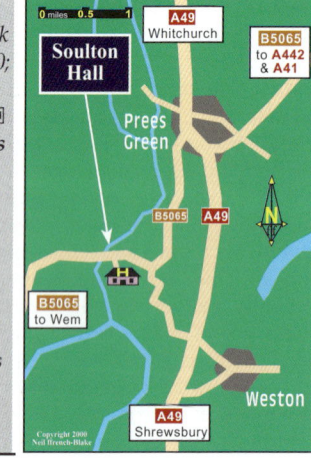

Warwickshire, Stratford-upon-Avon (Charlecote) 119

The Charlecote Pheasant

Charlecote, Nr. Stratford-upon-Avon,
Warwicks CV35 9EW
Tel: (01789) 279954;
Fax: (01789) 470222
E-mail: charlecotepheasant@corushotels.com
Website: www.regalhotels.co.uk/charlecote

Situated in the peaceful village of Charlecote and facing Charlecote Manor and Park, where Shakespeare is said to have poached deer, beside the river Avon, nestles The Pheasant. The reception area frequently has (buyable) print exhibitions. 20 stylish bedrooms are in the Farmhouse wing; others being in the more modern extensions, many at ground floor level. In summer families are made particularly welcome, with a heated swimming pool, childrens' play area and tennis court. The award-winning restaurant offers a wide selection of classic dishes, including a traditional carvery. There are nine meeting rooms and a 4-acre field for driving events or family fun days. The hotel has discounted tickets for Charlecote Park and Warwick Castle and is well placed for visiting Stratford-upon-Avon and the North Cotswolds. It also runs Golf, Shopping, Murder/Mystery and Classic Car two-day breaks.

Rates: Single room and breakfast from £99; twin/double from £115; suite from £140
Leisure Breaks: Dinner, b&b, min. two day breaks, sharing, from £57 per person per night.

● 70 en suite bedrooms, all with TV, direct-dial telephone, radio/alarm, hairdryer, tea/coffee making, 18-hr room service. ✁ rooms available.
● 3-cse Carvery dinner £18.50; alc, lunch & special diets available. Last orders 9.30.pm. Ⓟ 100.
● 9 meeting rooms, up to 250. Open all year.
● Swimming pool, tennis, play area. Golf nearby.
● AMERICAN EXPRESS & major credit cards accepted.

Stratford 5,
Warwick 5,
Coventry 13,
Oxford 40,
London 94.

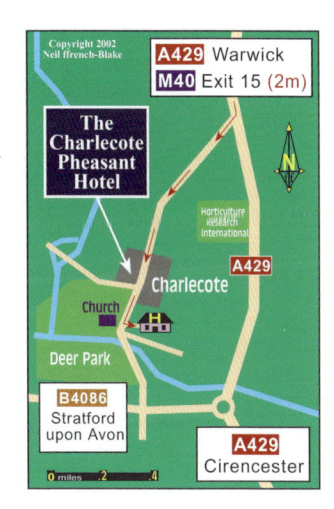

HEART OF ENGLAND

Stratford Victoria

Arden Street, Stratford-upon-Avon,
Warwickshire CV37 6QQ
Tel: (01789) 271000; Fax: (01789) 271001
E-mail: stratfordvictoria@marstonhotels.com
Website: www.marstonhotels.com

I highly recommend this luxurious hotel in the centre of Stratford. Opened in 1996, it is a welcome addition to the room stock in the town and gives excellent value for money. Now owned by Marston Hotels, the loyal staff are highly motivated and this rubs off to give the visitor a warm and personal welcome. The Victoria Restaurant and Bar will tempt you with snacks throughout the day or main meals from the carvery and grill menus. Purpose-built conference suites and board rooms seating up to 140 have all modern facilities and full back-up from the hotel's conference office. There is a mini-gym to work off those extra calories gained in the restaurants! Bedrooms are generously proportioned and, for special occasions, there are Executive Rooms, a four-poster room or the luxury suite. There are also family rooms, interconnecting rooms and rooms for the disabled. The hotel is very well run and a great centre for visiting the heart of Shakespeare country. It is within walking distance of the Royal Shakespeare Theatre and the Town Centre and adjacent to the Railway Station.

Rates: Single room and breakfast from £110; double inc. breakfast from £147.00
Leisure Breaks: Two nights, dinner b & b from £75 per pers per night, (2 nts min.) based on 2 sharing. 4-poster rooms/suites avail. at a suppl't.

- 102 en suite bedrooms, all with colour TV + satellite, direct-dial telephone, hairdryer, laundry service, tea/coffee making facilities, trouser press. Non-smoking and rooms for disabled available. Car parking for 102 cars.
- Table d'hote £26; à la carte, lunch & special diets available. Last orders for dinner 9.30 p.m.
- Business services inc 6 mtg rooms, cap'y to 140.
- Guests have access to fitness centre/gym, jacuzzi & beauty salon at sister hotel 3 miles away.
- & all major credit cards accepted
- Open all year.

Warwick 8, Banbury 20, Birmingham 23, Oxford 39, London 93.

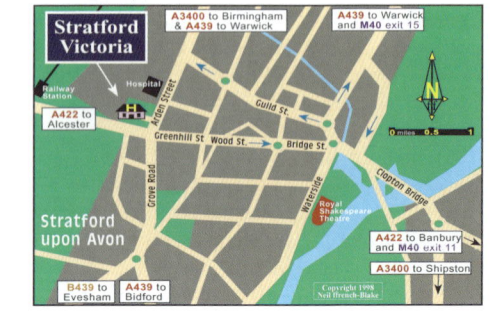

Worcestershire, Broadway

Dormy House Hotel

Willersey Hill, Broadway,
Worcestershire WR12 7LF
Tel: (01386) 852711; Fax: (01386) 858636
E-mail: reservations@dormyhouse.co.uk
Website: www.dormyhouse.co.uk

It has always been a great joy for me to visit the Dormy House Hotel. The standards are high, yet the hotel is so welcoming and friendly. The hotel is under the personal management of Ingrid Philip-Sorensen, whose style and taste are impeccable and who cares for her staff as much as for her guests. All 49 bedrooms are beautifully and individually decorated with all modern luxuries and the public lounges are comfortable and inviting - one has a large inglenook with a roaring log fire. Flowers are arranged beautifully throughout the hotel. In *Tapestries* restaurant you can enjoy Chef Cutler's wonderfully varied menus and in the *Barn Owl* Bar less formal lunches and evening meals are available throughout the week. The building is a beautifully converted 17th century farmhouse with spectacular views over the Cotswold escarpment and is adjacent to Broadway golf course. Guests who stay at Dormy House receive the hotel's newsletter *Dormy Days* which details special events throughout the year: New Year's Eve, Opera Evening, Jazz Brunch, Easter, Summer Ball, Special August Breaks and Tapestries Champagne Dinners.

Rates: Single room with breakfast from £108. Double room including breakfast from £156.
Classic Dormy break: *Two or more consecutive nights including full English breakfast and table d'hôte dinner - please enquire for prices.*

● 49 en suite bedrooms with radio & TV, direct-dial telephone, hairdryer, trouser press, laundry service; tea/coffee making facilities, safety deposit box.
● Last orders for dinner 21.30 hrs. Special diets.
● 8 meeting rooms - capacity 170. Car parking 80.
● Billiards, croquet, putting, gym, sauna/steam, indoor games on site. Jogging trail, riding, boating, shooting, tennis & fishing by arrangement.
● & all major credit cards accepted.
● Open all year exc. Xmas/Boxing Day.

Broadway 2, Cheltenham 17, Stratford-upon-Avon 15, Birmingham Airport 40, London 95.

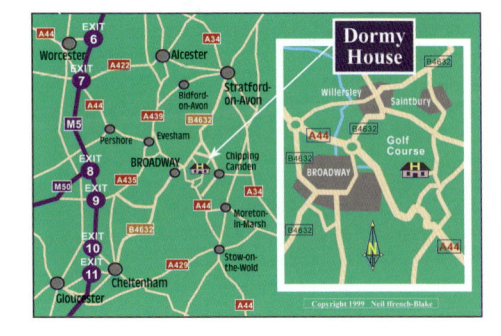

Worcestershire, Little Malvern

Holdfast Cottage Hotel

Marlbank Road, Little Malvern,
Worcestershire WR13 6NA
Tel: (01684) 310288; Fax: (01684) 311117
E-mail: enquiries@holdfast-cottage.co.uk
Website: www.holdfastcottage.co.uk

This friendly and intimate hotel was bought by Martyn and Elizabeth Bishop early in 2002. Holdfast Cottage dates from the 17th century and was enlarged in Victorian times. The public rooms are comfortable and welcoming, with pretty fabrics and antique furniture. The emphasis is on friendly and unobtrusive service. There are just eight bedrooms. All are individually decorated and each is named after one of the surrounding hills. The Dining Room serves an award-winning menu, constantly changing and making use of the finest seasonal produce. Special touches include home baked rolls, home made ice cream & chocolates and herbs from the hotel's own garden. Set in its own high wooded grounds surrounded by orchards and open farmland, it is secluded and quiet - an ideal place to relax after a day at the Malvern Showground or walking in the Malvern Hills. The Wye Valley, Forest of Dean, the Cotswolds, Worcester, Hereford and Gloucester are all within easy driving distance.

Rates: Single room with breakfast from £60. Double room including breakfast from £88.
Away Breaks: Two or more nights dinner, b & b £68 per person per night, sharing; 3rd & subs nts £64 pppn. 7 nights for 6 accommodation only.

- 8 en suite bedrooms with radio & TV, direct-dial telephone, hairdryer, laundry service; tea/coffee making facilities, 24-hr room service, fax/modem pts. ✂ rooms available.
- 3-cse tdh dinner £25; lunch & diets avail. Last orders 9 pm. ● Meeting room for 25. 🅿 20.
- Croquet, walks. Golf & riding nearby.
- Mastercard, Visa, Solo, Switch accepted.
- Open all year. ● 🐾 by arrangement.

Gt Malvern 3, Worcester 12, Cheltenham 23, Stratford-upon-Avon 34, London 119.

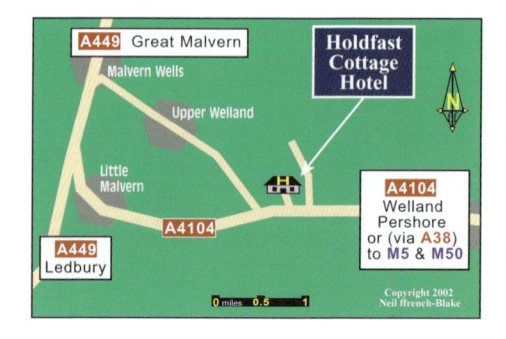

Worcestershire, Malvern Wells

The Cottage in the Wood Hotel

**Holywell Road, Malvern Wells
Worcestershire WR14 4LG
Tel: (01684) 575859; Fax: (01684) 560662**
E-mail: reservations@cottageinthewood.co.uk
Website: www.cottageinthewood.co.uk

High above the village of Malvern Wells, half hidden amongst hillside trees, you will find this former Georgian dower house, now an hotel of charm and character owned and run by John and Sue Pattin and family. Within the 7-acre grounds are the Coach House and Beech Cottage. Secluded and peaceful, they have been converted to provide 12 further delightful, if smaller, bedrooms. They share with the main house the unique qualities that make it so special - the wonderful 30-mile view and the friendliness of the Pattin family and their team. In the Dower House, the spacious partially book-lined sitting room can be enjoyed in every season of the year. There are log fires in winter and, in the summer months, the windows are thrown open onto the terrace and garden. The elegant dining room serves a menu essentially modern English in style, with a first class wine list completing a superb dining experience. If you can be persuaded to leave the seductive comfort of the house, you can walk directly from the grounds onto the Malvern Hills. By car the area from the Welsh Marches to Shakespeare's Stratford awaits you, whilst all around is Elgar country, from where the great composer drew much of his inspiration.

Rates: Single room with breakfast from £79. Double room including breakfast from £98.
Leisure Breaks: 2 day breaks available any time. Prices range fm £68-£98 pppn Dec/Jan to £78-£108 pppn in peak season.

- 20 en suite bedrooms with radio & TV+video, direct-dial telephone, hairdryer, trouser press (some), laundry service; tea/coffee making facilities.
- A la carte dinner ca £30; lunch & special diets available; last orders 21.00 hrs (20.30 Sundays)
- Meeting rooms - capacity 14. Car parking for 40
- Golf one mile, clay shooting 3 miles, squash ½ mile, riding 2 miles.
- Open all year.
- Visa & Mastercard accepted.

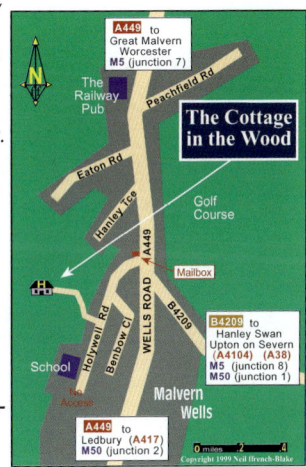

Gt Malvern 3, Worcester 11, Cheltenham 24, Stratford-upon-Avon 35, London 120.

HEART OF ENGLAND

Signpost Guide 2003

North West

Fact File
Illustrated Guide to
Historic Houses, Gardens & Sites
Diary of Events

Hotels in	PAGE
Cheshire	128
Cumbria	130
Greater Manchester	147
Lancashire	148

Cumbria - English Lakeland

In this beautiful corner of England, there is beauty in breathtaking variety - in the famous Lake District, loved by so many who come back again and again to its inspirational magic, brilliant blue lakes and craggy mountain tops.

There are other kinds of beauty to be enjoyed too. The central Lake District with its mountains, lakes and woods is so well known and loved that there is a tendency to forget that the rest of Cumbria contains some of the most varied and attractive landscape in Britain. In the east of the county, the lovely peaceful Eden Valley is sheltered by the towering hills of the Pennines, and everywhere are dotted charming little red sandstone villages. Further north, the border lands are flatter, with forests and lush green fields patterned by the typically English hedges and lanes. Cumbria's long coastline is itself full of variety. There are rocky cliffs with myriad sea birds, sandy estuaries, miles of sun-trapping sand dunes and friendly harbours, and everywhere something interesting to see, from reminders of our Roman occupation to the Flookburgh shrimp fishermen who go fishing, not in boats, but on tractors!

Wherever you choose to stay in Cumbria, you will not be far away from beautiful scenery: and whatever kind of accommodation you would like, Cumbria has it, from gracious country house hotels to country inns and bed-and-breakfasts. Don't think that summer is the only time when Cumbria is beautiful. In autumn the deciduous woodlands and bracken-covered hillsides glow with colour. In winter, the mountain tops stand in dazzling magnificence against blue skies. In spring, you can discover the delights of the magical, constantly changing light and joy of finding carpets of wild flowers. This is really the best time of the year to go walking or climbing - spending each day in the crisp fresh air to return in the evening with a healthy appetite to enjoy a delicious Cumbrian meal by the fireside in a cosy pub or friendly hotel.

There are many holidays in Lakeland which offer both activity and instruction in a range of sports - walking, climbing, orienteering, potholing, cycling, riding, golf, sailing, sailboarding, water-ski-ing, canoeing and fishing. A good way to absorb the beauty of this unique area is to plan your own personal route on foot or on cycle. *The Cumbria Cycle Way*, designed to avoid all the cyclist's problems like main roads and precipitate hills takes a circular route 250 miles (400 kms) long around this beautiful county. There are also good, cheap public transport services, and, where the big coaches cannot go, *Mountain Goat* minibuses run, even over the steepest mountain passes.

For a change from the great outdoors, there is a wealth of historic houses to visit, including a uniquely constructed thatched farmhouse, stately homes that have seen centuries of gracious living and the small cottages where famous writers have lived. Other houses are important because of their architecture, like the round house on Belle Isle, or majestic Hutton-in-the-Forest, which has a central tower dating from the 14th century, surrounded by later additions. The Cumbrian climate is ideal for gardens and the area is famous for the rhododendrons and azaleas which grow in abundance.

You will find out more about the secrets of this ancient kingdom by watching, or even joining in, some of its old customs, some of which are unique to Cumbria. There are many traditional agricultural shows displaying the essence of the English countryside - spiced in Cumbria with local specialities like *hound trailing*, which is like hunting but without the fox, and *fell races* - crazy lung-bursting ascents of the nearest hill, followed by a bone-bruising descent!

Above: Rydal Water. Below: Chester town centre

The North West

Historic Houses, Gardens & Parks

Cheshire
Arley Hall & Gardens, Nr. Great Budworth
Bridgemere Garden World, Nr. Nantwich
Brookside Garden Centre, Poynton
Cholmondeley Castle Gardens
Dunham Massey, Nr. Altrincham
Gawsworth Hall Nr. Macclesfield
Little Moreton Hall, Nr. Nantwich
Ness Gardens Neston
Stapeley Water Gardens, Nantwich
Tatton Park, Knutsford

Cumbria
Acorn Bank Garden, Nr. Temple Sowerby
Brantwood House, Coniston
Dalemain Historic House & Gardens, Nr. Pooley Bridge
Graythwaite Hall Gardens, Newby Bridge
Holker Hall & Gardens, Cark-in-Cartmel
Hutton-in-the-Forest, 6 miles from Penrith
Larch Cottage Nurseries, Melkinthorpe
Levens Hall & Topiary Garden, Nr. Kendal
Lingholme Gardens, Linghholme, Keswick
Mirehouse, Underskiddaw
Sizergh Castle, Nr. Kendal

Lancashire
All in One Garden Centre, Middleston
Astley Hall & Park, Nr. Chorley
Catforth Gardens & Nursery, Nr Preston
Gawthorpe Hall, Burley
Leighton Hall, Carnforth
Rufford Old Hall, Ormskirk
Williamson Park, Lancaster

Merseyside
Croxteth Hall & Country Park, Nr. Liverpool
Speke Hall, Liverpool

Walks & Nature Trails

Cheshire
Jodrell Bank Science Ctre & Arboretum, Nr. Holmes Chapel
Styal Country Park
Walk the Walls, Chester
Wirral Peninsula

Cumbria
Cark to Cartmel Village
Dodd Wood
Dunnerdale Forest Nature Trail
Grange-over-Sands to Hampsfell
Grizedale Forest Park Visitor Centre Hawkshead
Numerous fell walks and trails throughout Cumbria
Ulverston Town Trail

Tatton Park

Lancashire
Carnforth Canal Circuit, from Carnforth Railway to Bolton-le-Sands
Pendle Way Walk at Pendle Heritage Centre, Nelson
The Weaver's Shuttle, around Pendle

Historical Sites & Museums

Cheshire
The Boat Museum, Ellesmere Port
Chester Cathedral
Experience Catalyst, Widnes
Macclesfield Silk Museum
Peckforton Castle, Nr. Tarporley
Quarry Bank Mill, Styal

Cumbria
Abbot Hall Art Gallery, Kendal
Appleby Castle, Appleby-in-Westmoreland
Birdoswald Roman Fort, Brampton
Brough Castle, Kirkby Stephen
Brougham Castle, Nr. Penrith
Carlisle Castle
Cartmel Priory
The Cumberland Pencil Museum & Exhibition Centre, Keswick
Dove Cottage, Grasmere
Furness Abbey, Barrow-in-Furness
Heron Corn Mill & Museum of Papermaking,
Milnthorpe Laurel & Hardy Museum, Ulverston
Museum of Natural History, Kendal
Penrith Museum
Rydal Mount, Nr. Ambleside
Stott Park Bobbin Mill, Newby Lake
Wordsworth Museum, Grasmere

Greater Manchester
Castlefield Urban Heritage Park, Manchester
Manchester Cathedral
Manchester United Football Museum

Newton, Forest of Bowland

Museum of Science & Industry, Manchester

Lancashire
Lancaster Castle, Lancaster

Merseyside
Liverpool Museum
Merseyside Maritime Museum, Albert Dock, Liverpool Museum of Liverpool Life, Pier Head
Pilkington Glass Museum, St Helens

Entertainment Venues

Cheshire
Cheshire Candle Workshops, Burwardsley
Chester Zoo, Upton-by-Chester
Gulliver's World, Warrington
Port Sunlight Visitor Centre, Wirral
Wetlands & Wildfowl Trust Centre, Martin Mere

Cumbria
Cumbria Crystal, Ulverston
Fell Foot Park, Newby Bridge
Lake District National Park Visitor Centre, Windermere Lakeland Bird of Prey Centre, Lowther
Ravenglass & Eskdale Railway, Ravenglass
Sellafield Visitors' Centre
South Lakes Wild Animal Park, Dalton-in-Furness
Ullswater Cruises
Webb's Garden Centre, Kendal
Windermere Lake Cruises
World of Beatrix Potter, Bowness-on-Windermere

Greater Manchester/Lancashire
Alexandra Craft Centre, Saddleworth
Blackpool Tower & Pleasure Beach
Butterfly World, Bolton
Camelot Theme Park, Chorley
Frontierland, Morecambe Bay
Granada Studio Tours, Manchester
Lakeland Wildlife Oasis, Nr. Carnforth
Life Centre, Blackpool
Noel Edmonds' World of Crinkley Bottom, Morecambe Sea

Merseyside
The Beatles Story, Albert Dock, Liverpool
Knowsley Safari Park, Prescot
Pleasureland Amusement Park, Southport
The Tate Gallery at the Albert Dock, Liverpool

DIARY OF EVENTS

February

7-9. Manchester Championship Dog Show. G-Mex Centre, Manchester M2 3GX
9. Youth Brass Band Entertainment Festival of Great Britain. Blackpool, Lancs.
21-23. 51st Blackpool Magicians Club Annual Convention. Winter Gdns, Blackpool.

March

7-9. Blackpool Chess Conference. Blackpool, Lancs.
9. Boosey & Hawkes Brass Band Championships. Blackpool, Lancashire.
15-16. Ambleside Daffodil & Spring Flower Festival. Ambleside, Cumbria.
15-22. Mary Wakefield Westmoreland Festival. Kendal, Cumbria.
23-24. Int'l Hair & Beauty Festival, Blackpool, Lancs.

April

3-5. Martell Grand National Race, Aintree Racecourse, Merseyside.
11-14. Easter Festival of Sport. Douglas, Isle of Man
19. Racing at Haydock Park.
17-21. Nantwich Jazz & Blues Festival. Nantwich, Cheshire.
18-21. Maritime Festival. Lancaster.
26-2.5. Manx Competitive festival of Music, Speech & Drama. Douglas, Isle o Man

May

6-8. Chester May Meeting. Chester Racecourse, Chester
19-21. Jennings Keswick Jazz Festival. Keswick, Cumbria.
24-28. Cartmel Steeplechases.
23-24.Tote Credit Silver Bowl Haydock Park, Merseyside.
24-26. British Cactus & Succulent Society Show. Festival. Liverpool.
24-6.6. Isle of Man TT Motorcycle Festival. Douglas, I oM.

June

June.**The Mersey River Festival.** Liverpool, M'side
5-7. John of Gaunt Stakes. Haydock Park Racecourse, Merseyside.
6-7. Keswick Beer Festival. Keswick, Cumbria.
17. England v Pakistan. Natwest 1-day. Old Trafford.
17-18. Cheshire County Show. The Showground, Tabley, Cheshire.
21. Todmorden Agricultural Show. Todmorden, Lancs.
25-26. Carlisle Races.
28. Chester Races. Chester.
28. Barrow Carnival. Barrow-in-Furness, Cumbria
30-19.7.Chester Mystery Plays

July

July. **Merseyside Int'l Street Festival.** Liverpool.
3. England v South Africa. Natwest 1-Day series. Old Trafford, Manchester.
3-5.Letherby & Christopher Lancashire Oaks. Haydock Park, Merseyside.
6. Liverpool-Chester-Liverpool Bike Ride. Liverpool.
12. Lakeland Rose Show. Crooklands, Cumbria.
13. Country Fair. Liverpool.
13. Race Meeting. Haydock Prk
19. Street Theatre Festival. Morecambe, Lancashire.
19-26. Yn Chruinnaght Inter-Celtic Festival. Ramsey, IoM.
29. Royal Lancashire Show. Chorley, Lancashire.
31. Ambleside Traditional Lakeland Sports. Rydal, Cum

August

2. Coast to Coast Classic Tour. Blackpool, Lancs.
2-3. Festival of Light & Water Morecambe, Lancashire.
8-10. Lowther Horse Driving Trials & Country Fair. Lowther Castle, Penrith, Cumbria
7-9. Racing at Haydock Park
17. Macclesfield West Patk Family Fun Day. Macclesfield
20-25. International Beatles Festival. Liverpool, Merseyside
23 & 25. Cartmel Steeplechases. Cartmel, Cumbria.
24. Grasmere Lakeland Sports & Show. Grasmere, Cumbria.
25. Keswick Agricultural Show Keswick Showgr'd, Cumbria.
29. Fylde Folk Festival. Fleetwood, Lancs.
29-Nov 2. Blackpool Illuminations. Talbot Sq, Blackpool.

September

5-6. Historical Fayre. Preston.
6.Barrow & District Horticult'l Society Annual Fruit & Veg Show. Barrow-in-Furness, Cum
5-6. Haydock Sprint Cup Meeting. Haydock Park, Merseyside
14. Vintage Vehicle Run & Red Arrows Display. Morecambe, Lancs.
27-5.10. Int'l Open Chess Tournament, Port Erin, IoM

October-November

17-19.10.Blackburn Model Railway Exhibition. Blackburn
25-26. Kirkby Stephen Charter Fair. K Stephen, Cum Lake Windermere, Cumbria.
Nov. **Liverpool Biennial 2003** Int'l Exhibition, Liverpool.
13.11*. Biggest Liar in the World Competition. Bridge Inn, Santon Bridge, Cumbria.
14-23. Int'l Guitar Festival of Great Britain. Wirral, M'yside.
22. Lancaster Jacobite Day. Lancaster, Lancashire

*Denotes provisional date.

For further information, contact: The Cumbria Tourist Board, Ashleigh, Holly Road, Windermere, Cumbria LA23 2AQ. Tel: (015394) 44444. Website: www.gocumbria.co.uk. OR **The North West Tourist Board**, Swan House, Swan Meadow Road, Wigan Pier, Wigan, Lancashire WN3 5BB. Tel: (01942) 821222 Website: www.visitnorthwest.com

Cheshire, Nr. Chester

Broxton Hall Hotel & Restaurant

Whitchurch Road, Broxton, Chester, Cheshire CH3 9JS
Tel: (01829) 782321; Fax: (01829) 782330
E-mail: reservations@broxtonhall.co.uk
Website: www.broxtonhall.co.uk

The tone for this super hotel is set as soon as you enter the front door. Whilst you are receiving a warm welcome from new owners Angela and John Ireland or one of their helpful staff, you will almost be able to touch the historical atmosphere. Throughout this fine example of a Tudor half timbered country house, there are fascinating antiques and artefacts, superb fireplaces and staircase, oak-panelled walls and elegant furniture. The ten en suite bedrooms are beautifully furnished but have every modern convenience. The award-winning restaurant serves international cuisine, including game in season and freshly caught fish, with a lightness of touch and delicacy of flavour. Breakfast is served in the hotel's sunny garden room, overlooking pretty borders, lawns and five acres of grounds. The hotel is an ideal venue for small business meetings or for special occasions and is well placed for exploring Cheshire and North Wales.

Rates: Single with breakfast from £75; double inc. breakfast from £80.
Leisure Breaks: Dinner, b & b two nights £280 per room, two sharing.

- 10 en suite bedrooms (inc 1 suite), all with colour TV, direct dial telephone, hairdryer, radio/alarm, trouser press, tea/coffee making; ✂ rooms available.
- 3-cse tdh dinner £32.50; lunch & special diets available; last orders 9.30 pm.
- Meeting room for 40; Car parking 36.
- Civil marriage licence. ● Open all year.
- AMERICAN EXPRESS & all major credit cards accepted.

M6 (J16) 20, Whitchurch 8, Chester 12, Nantwich 12, Stoke-on-Trent 29, Manchester 44, London 197.

Sutton Hall

Bullocks Lane, Sutton, Nr.
Macclesfield, Cheshire SK11 0HE
Tel: (01260) 253211; Fax: (01260) 252538

As befits the former 16th century baronial residence of the Sutton family, the Hall is full of immense character and old world charm. A wealth of beams, log fires and four poster beds are all in evidence, and the ales, conditioned in cask, are matched by the choice of food from an excellent menu. As with the inns of old, there is an atmosphere of warmth, hospitality and good cheer. This, married to such modern conveniences as en suite bathrooms and colour TV, makes a very happy amalgam of past and present. To travel, even from afar, is well worth while and this is made easy by the fact that the M6 and Manchester Airport are less than half an hour away. Also in the area are many other famous old houses as well as the scenic beauty of the Peak District. The hotel is personally run by Robert and Phyllida Bradshaw, who, along with their friendly staff, will provide a warm welcome and ensure that your stay in this unique "inn of distinction" is enjoyed to the full.

Rates: Room and breakfast from £75.00 single, £45.00 double, per person, inclusive of VAT.

- 10 en suite bedrooms, all with four poster beds, colour TV, direct dial telephones, tea/coffee maker; trouser press.
- Late meals to 10 p.m.; diets available.
- Dogs welcome; conferences up to 20.
- Golf, tennis, riding nearby; Peak National Park adjacent. Civil wedding licence.
- & major credit cards accepted.
- Open all year.

Macclesfield 1, M6 (J18/19) ½ hour, Manchester Airport ½ hour, London 240.

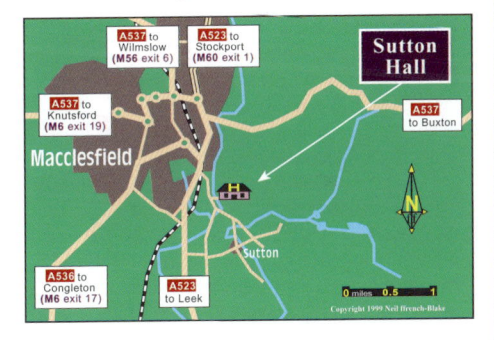

Cumbria, Nr. Alston

Lovelady Shield Country House Hotel

Nenthead Road, Nr. Alston, Cumbria CA9 3LF
Tel: (01434) 381203; Fax: (01434) 381515

E-mail: enquiries@lovelady.co.uk
Website: www.lovelady.co.uk

Lovelady Shield. The name conjures up an image of the peace and tranquillity that you will certainly find in this gracious country house hotel. Set beside a river in a wooded valley high in the Pennines, just $2^{1}/_{4}$ miles from Alston (England's highest market town), this quiet retreat is an ideal situation for exploring the border country, the Lake District, Hadrian's Wall and the Yorkshire Dales. Only 35 minutes from the Penrith exit of the M6, via the dramatic A686 - one of the world's top drives - it is a very pleasant stopover. The new owners, Mr & Mrs Haynes, together with their friendly staff, are maintaining the hotel's tradition of warm hospitality and service. Chef Barrie Garton produces imaginative and beautifully presented meals and has been awarded two AA rosettes for his cooking. Service in the pretty dining room is discreet and attentive. The hotel is well furnished and welcoming, with log fires. A very peaceful spot.

Rates: Room with breakfast from £60 per person; dinner, bed & breakfast from £80.
Bargain breaks November-March, midweek, dinner, room & breakfast from £160 per night for 2 people; weekend to come to come to come.

● 12 en suite bedrooms all with direct dial telephone and TV, room service; hairdryer.
● Tdh ◉◉ dinner £32; bar lunches & special diets available; last orders 8.30 p.m.
● Croquet, fishing, tennis. Shooting, fishing, golf, riding nearby. Children welcome. Dogs accepted.
● & all major credit cards accepted.

Alston $2^{1}/_{4}$, Penrith 20, Hadrian's Wall 20, Carlisle 31, Newcastle 43, London 300.

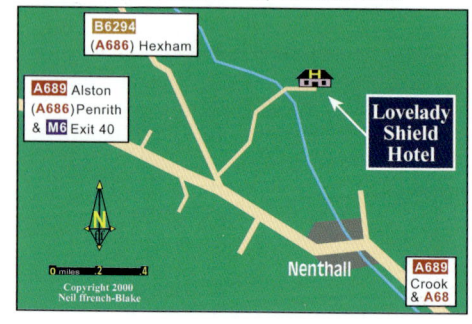

Cumbria, Ambleside   131

Rothay Manor Hotel

Rothay Bridge, Ambleside, Cumbria
LA22 OEH
Tel: (015394) 33605; Fax: (015394) 33607
E-mail: hotel@rothaymanor.co.uk
Website: www.rothaymanor.co.uk

If you believe, as I do, that one of the main ingredients of civilised life is good food and wine taken in comfortable surroundings, then Rothay Manor is, without a doubt, one of the finest venues in which to enjoy that life. The hotel has been voted top of the list by a publication on hotel breakfasts, and the excellence of the lunches and dinners complements the sumptuous surroundings. Antiques and fresh flowers are abundant, and the feeling of warmth and well-being are everywhere. The whole ambience is orchestrated by Nigel and Stephen Nixon and their wives, and the reputation that they have gained for all round excellence is more than justifiably deserved. These impressions were echoed by many of the other guests to whom I spoke. It seems unnecessary to add that the surrounding mountains, lakes and the air of the Lake District, make a superb backdrop in which to indulge these pleasures. In Winter the hotel can organise holidays on such thems as antiques, heritage, bridge and music.

Rates: *Double room and breakfast from £122.00 for 2 people; dinner, room and breakfast from £165.00 for 2 people.*
Leisure breaks *available all year, e.g. November-March, midweek, dinner, room & breakfast from £160 per night for 2 people; weekend break from £175 per night.*

- 17 en suite bedrooms (2 for the disabled) all with direct dial telephone and TV, room service; baby listening.
- Last orders for dinner 9.00 p.m.; special diets.
- Children welcome; conferences max. 20.
- Free use of nearby leisure centre; tennis and fishing 1/4 mile (free permits); sailing/boating 1/2 m.
- & all major credit cards accepted.
- Open all year.

Kendal 13, Manchester 80, London 280.

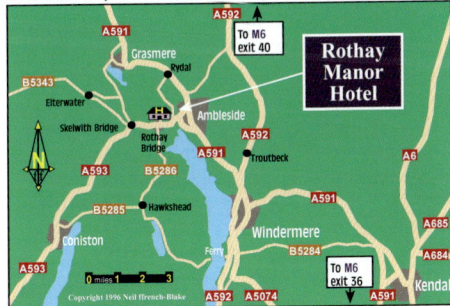

Cumbria, Ambleside

Waterhead Hotel

Waterhead Bay, Ambleside, Cumbria
LA22 0UR
Tel: (015394) 32566; Fax: (015394) 31255
E-mail: waterhead@elhmail.co.uk
Website: www.elh.co.uk/hotels/water

The Waterhead, on the shores of Lake Windermere, is at the very heart of the Lake District and presents a delightful world of contrasts, far and away from the hustle and bustle of everyday cares and problems. Accommodations is comfortable, service is friendly and cuisine is excellent - three essentials for a break in The Lakes. The elegant Waterfront Restaurant has picture windows on to the lake and to the hills beyond. There is also the relaxed Mediterranean-style Cafe del Lago bar and bistro to savour. Here pizzas and pasta are served. Or guests can soak up the traditional atmosphere of Mc Ginty's Irish fun pub, which has weekly live entertainment. Guests of the waterhead receive and English Lakes Privilege Card enabling them to take advantage of the superb leisure facilities at sister hotel Low Wood (see page 137) with swimming pool, fitness centre, aromatherapy and other facilities. All guests also have the option of free boat launching and mooring from the Low Wood Watersport Centre.

Rates: Single with breakfast £44-£102; double inc. breakfast £88-£134.
Leisure Breaks: Long Weekend - stay Friday & Saturday and add Sunday night at half price.

● 28 en suite bedrooms, all with d-dial telephone, hairdryer, colour TV+ satellite and video, laundry service, tea/coffee making facilities, radio/alarm clock, trouser press, rooms available.
● 3-cse tdh dinner £18.95; lunch avail; last orders 9.30 p.m. ● Meeting room for up to 40. 50.
● Leisure centre, gym, indoor pool, squash, sailing, water-sports one mile; golf 8 miles.
● & all major credit cards accepted.
● Open all year.

Kendal 13,
Keswick 18,
Penrith 30,
Carlisle 47,
London 272.

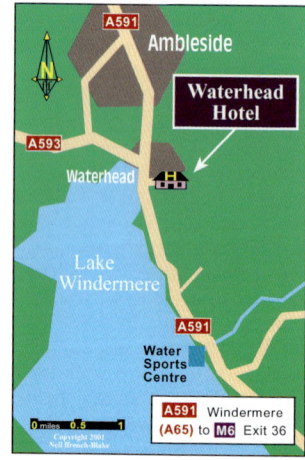

Cumbria, Appleby-in-Westmorland

Appleby Manor Country House Hotel & Leisure Club

Roman Road, Appleby-in-Westmorland, Cumbria CA16 6JB
Tel: (017683) 51571; Fax: (017683) 52888
E-mail: reception@applebymanor.co.uk
Website: www.applebymanor.co.uk

Appleby Manor stands high, commanding views of the historic little town, its romantic castle and the sweeping countryside and fells beyond. Within you will find relaxing and friendly courtesy, and most attractive and spacious public rooms. Facing south, the house gives shelter to its sunny gardens onto which some of the delightful rooms in the new wing have direct access. The spotlessly clean bedrooms are comfortable and furnished in keeping with the period of the house. The popular award-winning restaurant offers an international and imaginative selection of tasty dishes. The wine list offers a selection of wines from 20 countries and the bar stocks over seventy single-malt whiskies. There is plenty to see and do locally, with walks to suit all abilities. Appleby is ideally situated for touring the scenic Lake District, and the Borders Hadrian's Wall, the Roman Camps, the high Pennines and the Yorkshire Dales are all within easy motoring distance.

Rates per person start at £55 for bed and breakfast, £75 for dinner, bed and breakfast; weekly rates from £432, including dinner, bed and breakfast.
Leisure Breaks: *min. 2 nights from £65 pppn; also "Flying Falcon" breaks, 2 nights from £189 and the "Cloud Nine Experience" from £155 and "Hangover Breaks" from £157 - all inc. dinner, b & b & VAT.*

- *30 en suite bedrooms (10 ground floor; 5 four-posters), all with telephone, hairdryer, colour TV, satellite and video film channels.*
- *Last orders 9. 00 p.m; diets available.*
- *Children welcome; baby listening; dogs in coachhouse bedrooms only; conferences 30 max.*
- *Games room; snooker and pool; indoor heated swimming pool; jacuzzi; sauna, solarium, leisure centre, squash 1/2 mile, fishing locally; riding 13 miles; golf 2 miles.*
- *Hotel closed 3 days at Xmas.*
- *& all major credit cards accepted.*

M6 (junctions 38 & 40) 13, Penrith 13, Ullswater 15, Kendal 25, Keswick 31, London 272.

Armathwaite Hall Hotel

Bassenthwaite Lake, Keswick,
Cumbria CA12 4RE
Tel: (017687) 76551; Fax: (017687) 76220
E-mail: reservations@armathwaite-hall.com
Website: www.armathwaite-hall.com

Few hotels are as beautifully situated as Armathwaite Hall - one of the original stately homes of England, set magnificently in 400 acres of deerpark and woodland, bordered by the beauty of Bassenthwaite Lake and framed by the dramatic vista of Skiddaw Mountain and the surrounding fells. The Graves family, who have owned and run Armathwaite Hall for twenty-five years, know exactly how to pamper their guests. Cuisine is under the supervision of Masterchef Kevin Dowling. Style is traditional English, with Cumbrian specialities and using local produce, and classical French, but with a light touch. This is just a prelude to all the activities available. Discreetly hidden is the magnificent 'Spa' Leisure Club with indoor pool, gymnasium, holistic beauty salon and in the grounds is a farm park with exotic and rare animals. Fishing and boating are on the doorstep. Armathwaite Hall is the perfect base from which to enjoy the Northern lakes area.

Rates: single with breakfast from £69; double with breakfast from £138. **Breaks**: Easter, Christmas/New Year, Bank Holiday and other packages available. Details on request.

- 43 en suite bedrooms with colour TV + satellite, telephone, hairdryer, laundry/valet service, tea/coffee making facilities, 24-hr room/meal service, radio/alarm clock, safety deposit box at reception, trouser press.
- 6-course table d'hôte dinner £38.95. Last orders 9.15 p.m; lunch & special diets available.
- Business services inc. 3 conference rooms to 100
- Billiards/snooker, croquet, fishing, indoor heated swimming pool; jacuzzi; sauna, solarium, steam room, fitness centre, clay shooting, beauty therapy, tennis, falconry, farm park, quad bikes; golf $1\frac{1}{2}$ m.
- Diners, Visa & Mastercard accepted.
- Open all year.

Cockermouth 5, Keswick 5, Carlisle 25, London 295

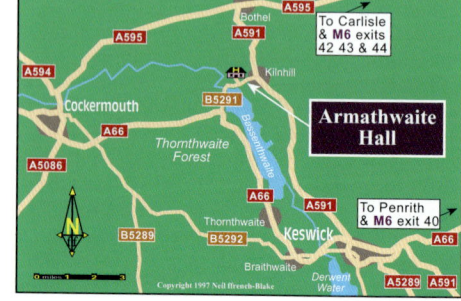

Cumbria, Bassenthwaite Lake

The Pheasant Inn

Bassenthwaite Lake, Nr. Cockermouth, Cumbria CA13 9YE
Tel: (017687) 76234; Fax: (017687) 76002
E-mail: info@the-pheasant.co.uk
Website: www.the-pheasant.co.uk

The history of the Pheasant Inn stretches back over 500 years. Orinally a farmhouse, it was converted in 1778 to a popular alehouse. One of its 19th century regulars was the huntsman John Peel. Today guests can enjoy bar snacks and real ale in the original bar, and there are a further three lounges in which to relax, all tastefuly decorated and furnished. The bedrooms likewise are comfortable, each with its own character and décor. It is heart-warming to return from any of the activities which may have brought you to this beautiful Northen part of the Lake District and to relax in front of a welcoming log fire. Non-residents too come from far and wide to dine here - testament to the fact that the food is prepared from the freshest ingredients and cooked to the highest standards. With pretty gardens and its own 60 acres of additional grounds and woodlands at the foot of Thornthwaite Forest, and Bassenthwaite Lake only a few minutes' walk away, The Pheasant is a little step back into history - a nature lover's paradise and a gourmet's delight.

Rates: single inc. breakfast & 5-course dinner from £80; double, dinner, b & B from £130.
Leisure Breaks: 3 nights, Sunday-Thursday £220 per person, dinner, b & b.

- 13 en suite bedrooms with direct-dial telephone, hairdryer, laundry service, tea/coffee making facilities, fax/modem points. TV on request
- 3-cse tdh dinner £25. Alc, lunch & spec. diets available. Last orders 8.45 p.m.
- Fishing, golf nearby. Car parking for 80.
- Visa & Mastercard accepted.
- Open all year exc. Xmas Day.

Cockermouth 5, Keswick 8, Carlisle 25, London 295.

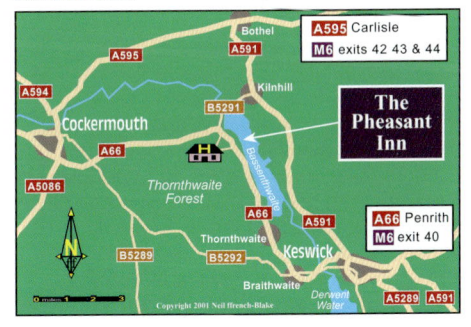

Aynsome Manor Hotel

Cartmel, Nr. Grange-over-Sands,
Cumbria LA11 6HH
Tel: (015395) 36653; Fax: (015395) 36016
E-mail: info@aynsomemanorhotel.co.uk
Website: www.aynsomemanorhotel.co.uk

This beautiful old manor house, parts of which date back to 1510, was once the residence of the Earl of Pembroke, founder of the historic 12th century Cartmel Priory. It is now run by two generations of the Varley family. The elegant and comfortable atmosphere is expressed by the tasteful furnishings and decor throughout the hotel. The superb candle-lit dining room, with its views of the Norman Priory, is an ideal setting in which to enjoy the imaginative and carefully chosen menu. This might start with pressed terrine of Cartmel valley game with apricots and pistachios and continue with Aynsome lemon sole and prawn fish-cakes or roast saddle of saltmarsh lamb. Home made soups, bread rolls and sumptuous desserts are specialities of the house. The bedrooms, mainly built around a courtyard, are quite charming in their individuality. Two are in Aynsome Cottage, an adjoining converted stable. Local places of interest include Holker Hall (Beatrix Potter's home), Sizergh Castle, Brockhole Visitor Centre and Levens Hall, as well as the Priory.

Rates: single inc. breakfast & 5-course dinner from £76; double, dinner, b & B from £130.
Leisure Breaks: Seasonal breaks avail. through out the year. 4 days from only £52 pppn; 2 day breaks from £55 per pers per night inc 5-cse dinner.

- 12 en suite bedrooms with colour TV, telephone, hairdryer, laundry service (limited), tea/coffee making facilities, radio/alarm clock.
- 3-cse tdh dinner £20. Last orders 8.30 p.m; Sunday lunch available. (No under 5s in res't eve's).
- Fishing, golf, watersports, sailing, shooting, riding nearby. Car parking for 20.
- Visa & Mastercard accepted.
- Open February-December.

Newby Bridge 5, Bowness 12, Coniston 15, M6 (J36) 16, Kendal 16, London 263.

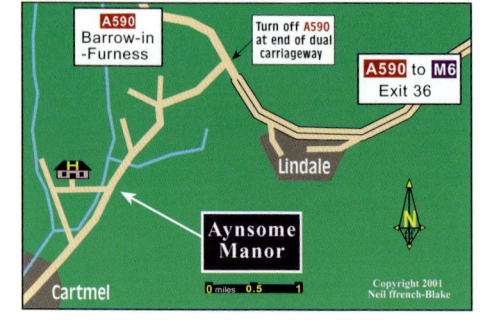

Cumbria, Grasmere

The Wordsworth Hotel

Grasmere, Ambleside,
Cumbria LA22 9SW
Tel: (015394) 35592; Fax: (015394) 35765
E-mail: enquiry@wordsworth-grasmere.co.uk
Website: www.grasmere-hotels.co.uk

Set in the centre of Grasmere, in $1^1/_2$ acres of landscaped gardens, this hotel offers all that is best for a holiday in the Lakes. It is spacious, airy and has all the modern amenities to be expected by today's discerning traveller. The bedrooms are well equipped, one retaining its original Victorian bathroom. There are also three romantic four-poster rooms, one of which is a suite. The public rooms are tastefully furnished in keeping with the period of the buildings. The swimming pool opens onto a patio and makes an excellent place in which to relax after a few days' walking, climbing or sightseeing. There is also a small gym and sauna. The hotel is owned by Reg Gifford, of Michael's Nook Country House Hotel fame, and the AA ◉◉ cuisine is presided over by chef Bernard Warne. As well as the acclaimed Prelude Restaurant, there is the private Coleridge Suite and the hotel's own pub *The Dove and Olive Branch*. What could be better than a day in the fresh air of the Lake District, followed by a relaxed evening at the Wordsworth?

Rates: Single with breakfast from £70; double inc breakfast from £140.
Leisure Breaks: 2+ nights midweek from £79.50 per person per night, dinner, b & b, two sharing.

● 37 en suite bedrooms (inc 2 suites), all with colour TV + sat, d-dial telephone, fax/modem points, hairdryer, laundry/valet service, radio/alarm clock, trouser press. ♿ rooms available.
● Tdh & alc dinner; last orders 9.00 p.m.; lunch & special diets available. ● 2 meeting rooms to 100.
● Croquet, fishing, fitness centre/gym, indoor games, jacuzzi, jogging track, indoor pool; golf, sailing, tennis, riding, watersports nearby.
● AMERICAN EXPRESS & major credit cards accepted.
● Open all year

Ambleside 4,
Keswick 13,
Kendal 17,
London 271.

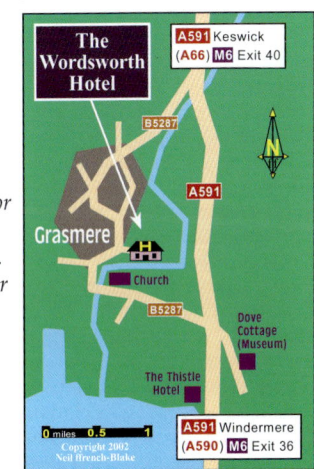

THE NORTH WEST

Cumbria, Keswick

Dale Head Hall Lakeside Hotel

Thirlmere, Keswick, Cumbria CA12 4TN
Tel: (017687) 72478; Fax: (017687) 71070
E-Mail: onthelakeside@daleheadhall.info
Website: www.daleheadhall.info

At the northern end of Thirlmere, you will find an hotel situated in one of the most idyllic positions in the Lake District. Set in a clearing on the shores of the lake, with Helvellyn rising majestically behind. A small, yet luxurious hotel, this 16th century Hall is beautifully decorated in keeping with the age of the building. It exudes that intimate atmosphere of a true family home. The untiring enthusiasm, skill and innate sense of hospitality of the resident proprietors, Alan and Shirley Lowe, Hans and Caroline Bonkenburg, combine to make it a very special place. As the sun set over the lake and fell, I joined fellow guests in the lounge for an aperitif, all in eager anticipation of yet another wonderful meal. The award-winning cuisine is truly superb. They even grow their own vegetables, fruit, herbs and flowers in the Victorian kitchen garden. Dale Head Hall is in an ideal position for exploring the Lake District, with all the major attractions not far away. Which Hotel Guide has named Dale Head Hall *Hotel of the Year* for 2003. It comes highly recommended and represents some of the best value in Cumbria.

Rates: Room and breakfast from £45; dinner, room & breakfast from £82.50. Cumbria Tourist Board 3 Star Gold Award.
Leisure Breaks: Logfire Winter Breaks available from 07.02.03-17.04.2003 & 10.11.03-22.12.03 book two nights dinner, room & bfst and get 3rd night FREE. Spring & Summer Breaks available from 22.04.03-10.11.03 any three nights from £72.50 dinner, bed & breakfast per pers per night.

● 12 en suite bedrooms, all with direct dial telephone room service.
● Last orders for dinner 8.00 p.m.; special diets
● Sailing, boating, shooting, fishing, tennis, spa pool gymnasium, squash courts nearby. Golf five miles, riding seven miles.
● Visa and Mastercard accepted.
● Open all year.

Keswick 4, Grasmere 5, Penrith 16, London 285..

Cumbria, Nr. Keswick

Derwentwater Hotel

Portinscale, Nr. Keswick, Cumbria
CA12 5RE
Tel: (017687) 72538; Fax: (017687) 71002
E-mail: info@derwentwater-hotel.co.uk
Website: www.derwentwater-hotel.co.uk

The epitome of a Lakeland Country House hotel, the Derwentwater has undergone, since the mid-1980s, a substantial programme of upgrading and refurbishment. Still privately owned, it now offers guests a comfortable, though unpretentious, standard of accommodation. Guestrooms have every modern convenience, some having a separate sitting area and others with four-poster beds. Many enjoy stunning views of the lake. The Deers Leap Restaurant serves a good selection of dishes, locally sourced where possible. The hotel sits in 16 acres of grounds, much of which is dedicated to the preservation of local wildlife. The owners have worked alongside English Nature to enhance a protected area of wetland, a natural habitat for birds, mammals and deer. In the same grounds is Derwent Manor, a selection of one and two-bedroomed self-catering apartments; also Glaramara Cottage. Both hotel and manor guests can take advantage of the new Oxley's Heath Spa at Underscar, some two miles away.

Rates: Single with breakfast from £80; Double inc. breakfast from £130.
Leisure Breaks: Stays of two nights+ avail. from £55 per person per night, inc cream tea on arrival and a liqueur with coffee after each dinner.

- 48 en suite bedrooms, all with colour TV, d-dial telephone, hairdryer, tea/coffee making, 24-hr room service, radio/alarm, trouser press. ✗ & ♿ rms avail
- 4-cse tdh dinner £22.50; Sunday lunch & spec. diets avail; last orders 9 pm. ● 2 mtg rooms to 20.
- Fishing from hotel. Fitness centre, indoor pool, massage, sauna, jacuzzi two miles away.
- & all major credit cards accepted.
- Open all year.

Keswick 1, Cockermouth 13, Ambleside 18, Carlisle 30, Penrith (M6) 17, London 285.

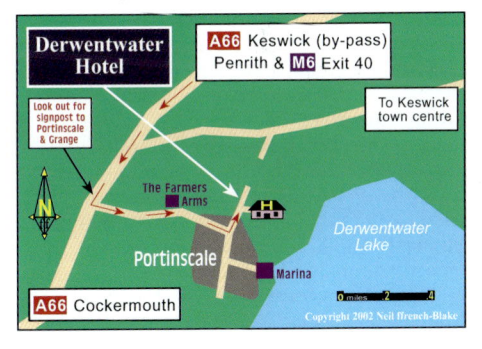

Cumbria, Nr. Keswick

Scafell Hotel

Borrowdale, Nr. Keswick, Cumbria
CA12 5XB
Tel: (017687) 77208; Fax: (017687) 77280
E-mail: info@scafell.co.uk
Website: www.scafell.co.uk

It is not surprising that the Scafell is becoming one of Lakeland's leading hotels following its recent improvements and the consistent efforts of its management. Situated almost at the head of the beautiful Borrowdale Valley, its position is as outstanding as the service and comfort which it provides for all its guests. There is an excellent table d'hôte menu and for those wishing to dine later, a comprehensive à la carte supper menu. Both menus are accompanied by a well balanced wine list. Year after year guests return to walk and climb for they know that they are going to be comfortable and well looked after. For the less energetic, there are cosy and homely lounges. The bedrooms are comfortable and attractively furnished, all of them having their own private bathroom. Pleasant views are to be had of the sheltered garden ringed by mighty mountains on which internationally famous climbers have learned their craft. Yes, this is a home for the visitor seeking peace or exercise and wishing to 'get away from it all'.

Rates: Room and breakfast from £44; dinner, room & breakfast from £66.50 inc. VAT.
Bargain breaks *available spring/summer and winter, min. two nights. Rates on application.*

- 24 en suite bedrooms (8 ground floor), all with direct-dial telephone, tea/coffee making facilities, TV; full central heating.
- Children welcome and dogs accepted; bar meals.
- Drying room; river bathing; boating; fishing; pony trekking; tennis six miles; golf ten miles.
- Visa, Mastercard accepted.
- Hotel open all year.

Keswick 6, Penrith 24, Carlisle 36, Kendal 36, London 291.

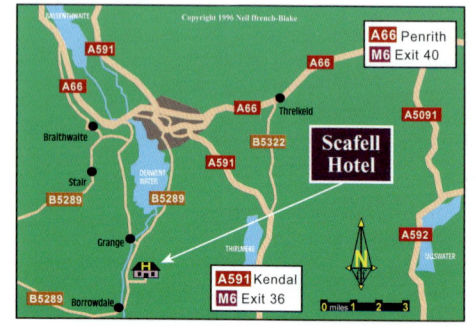

Cumbria, Ullswater

Sharrow Bay Country House Hotel

Ullswater, Howtown, Nr. Penrith, Cumbria CA10 2LZ
Tel: (017684) 86301/86483;
Fax: (017684) 86349
E-mail:enquiries@sharrow-bay.com
Website: www.sharrow-bay.com

In 1948 the young Francis Coulson had a dream,. This was to create the very first Country House Hotel. This dream became a reality when in 1952 Brian Sack, a young man with the same philosophy, joined Francis and so began one of the most celebrated partnerships within the hotel industry. Over the past 55 years, Sharrow has striven to set and maintain standards for others to follow and has been the inspiration for many present day country house hotels. Sadly both Francis and Brian have now passed away. Their dream was for the hotel to continue and to this aim they have left Sharrow to Nigel Lightburn, who has himself been involved at the hotel for the past 29 years, more recently holding the position of Managing Director. In 2000 Sharrow once again set new standards by opening the new Garden rooms. These consist of three luxury suites and two king size doubles, 100 metres from the hotel and all enjoying magnificent views of the gardens and lake.

2001 saw the completion of the refurbishment programme for the rooms in the main building. This involved creating two beautiful suites from 4 smaller rooms. This now gives the building 6 extremely well appointed bedrooms, 3 of which at the front enjoy the magnificent view of Ullswater and Striding Edge. In 2002 Sharrow created a magnificent new building which has enlarged the lounge area of the hotel, enhancing the pre-lunch and dinner experience. Add to all this the beauty of the lake and mountains and you have total perfection.

- *26 bedrooms, all with private bath and/or shower, including 6 cottage suites, TV, radio, antiques, peace. Small conference facilities. Tariff on application.*
- *Golf locally, lake bathing, boating, riding, fishing.*
- *Closed end-Nov to end-Feb.*
- *Licensed for small civil weddings (20).*
- *Visa & Mastercard accepted.* **Penrith 7, Keswick 20, Kendal 33, London 289.**

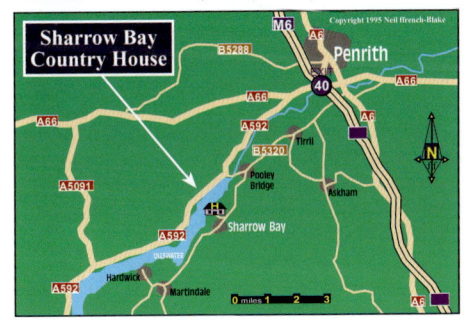

Cumbria, Windermere

Gilpin Lodge Country House Hotel

Crook Road, Nr. Windermere, Cumbria LA23 3NE
Tel: (015394) 88818; Fax: (015394) 88058
E-mail: hotel@gilpin-lodge.co.uk
Website: www.gilpin-lodge.co.uk

Troutbeck and *Patterdale*, *Kentmore* and *Crook* are just some of the names of the 14 romantic bedrooms at Gilpin Lodge, reflecting the profusion of beauty spots close to this charming small hotel by Lake Windermere. With such a wealth of natural attractions virtually on the doorstep, owners John and Christine Cunliffe have little need to recommend excursions and activities to their guests, for a gentle car tour or slightly more energetic walk brings them to some of England's finest scenery, with the promise of extreme luxury and comfort awaiting them at the end of each day's exploration. There is fine and challenging golf at the nearby Windermere course and bargain hunters will be tempted by the local antique shops. Gilpin Lodge is meticulously run by the Cunliffes, with a dedicated, long serving staff. Their experience is evident in every corner of this pretty hotel, where the main aim is to pamper guests in the matchless surroundings of the Lake District.

Kendal 8, Penrith 26, Lancaster 28, London 246

Rates: Single room including breakfast from £55. Double room with breakfast from £110. **Leisure Breaks:** Rates inc. breakfast & dinner available all year round from £65 per person per night. Special 3-night 'Great Little Escapes' from £195 per pers dinner, bed & breakfast. **Golf Breaks**, inc.$^{1}/_{2}$ board and 2 games of golf at Windermere fm £260 per pers. **Golf tuition courses** (4,5,6 or 7 nts at Gilpin Lodge) fm £455. Xmas/NYear arrts.

● 14 en suite bedrooms with radio & colour TV+ satellite, direct dial telephone, hairdryer, laundry service, tea/coffee making, trouser press, safe.
● Table d'hôte dinner ●●● £38.50; last orders 9 pm. Alc & tdh lunch Mon-Sat; tdh Sunday luncheon £19.50; special diets catered for. Open all year.
● Croquet, jogging track. Fitness centre/gym, fishing, golf, jacuzzi, watersports, sauna, sailing, indoor pool, tennis, riding all nearby. ℗ 40.
● & major credit cards accepted.

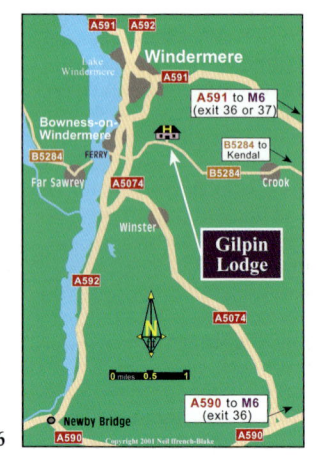

Cumbria, Windermere   143

THE NORTH WEST

Linthwaite House Hotel & Restaurant

Crook Road, Windermere, The Lake District, Cumbria LA23 3JA
Tel: (015394) 88600; Fax: (015394) 88601
E-mail: admin@linthwaite.com
Website: www.linthwaite.com

This hotel, situated on the B5284 Bowness to Kendal road, only a mile or so from Bowness, is surely the epitome of what every Sign-poster would like to find. It is set in 14 acres of superbly kept grounds with magnificent views of Lake Windermere and of every major peak in the Lake District. There is a well stocked tarn (in which 5 lb trout have been caught) and where one can while away the day with a picnic. The golf practice area is surrounded by lovely woodland walks. Naturally, within a very short distance are all the other amenities that one expects in the area, such as swimming, yachting and tennis. Inside, the hotel is immaculate, tastefully interior designed. A feature is the use of old trunks and suitcases. The food is superb and many of the guests return to Linthwaite again and again. Surely this speaks more eloquently than any words? Any Signposter who visits here for the first time will, like others, keep coming back to the atmosphere of peace and tranquillity.

Rates: Room and breakfast £99-£286
Romantic breaks (minimum 2 nights) - including champagne in room on arrival, box of hand made chocolates, canopied king size double bed with lake view, breakfast and candlelit dinner.

● 26 en suite bedrooms (7 ground floor), all with direct dial telephone and satellite TV; room service
● Last orders for dinner 8.45 p.m., light lounge lunches; special diets. No under 7s in restaurant.
● Children welcome (special menu 6-7pm in rest't).
● Sauna, solarium, spa pool, gymnasium and golf one mile; mountain walking and riding three miles; sailing/ boating and water-skiing one mile; golf practice hole par 3; own tarn brown trout. Mountain bikes to hire at hotel. Conferences to 30.
● AMERICAN EXPRESS & all major credit cards accepted.
● Open all year;
Bowness 1, Kendal 7, Manchester 76, London 280.

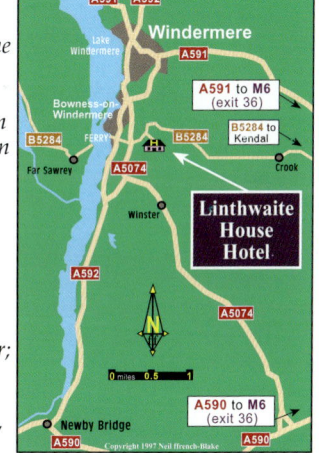

Low Wood

Windermere, Cumbria LA23 1LP
Tel: (015394) 33338; Fax: (015394) 34072
E-Mail: lowwood@elhmail.co.uk
Website: http://www.elh.co.uk/hotels/lowwood

Beautifully situated on the shores of Lake Windermere, Low Wood commands views from many of its public and bedrooms across the lake to the magnificent Langdale Pikes. Its setting in the heart of the southern Lake District makes it one of the best bases from which to explore the wealth of attractions and spectacular scenery in this part of Cumbria. The Low Wood Club and the Watersports and Activity Centre offer some of the best leisure facilities in the region: waterski-ing, sailing, windsurfing, canoeing and even an archery range. Low Wood is one of the premier conference and banqueting venues in the Northwest, with capacity for 350. The hotel has three food outlets: the Windermere Restaurant, specialising in traditional English cuisine; Penny Lane's 60s Brasserie, evoking the decor and atmosphere of the swining sixties and the light hearted Sullivan's Australian Fun Pub. In all and throughout the hotel, guests will experience English Lakes Hotels' high standards of service and care which will make their stay an enjoyable one.

Rates: Single with breakfast £68-£128; double inc. breakfast £146-£186.
Leisure breaks: Fifth night free. Stay any 4 nights at published terms and enjoy the 5th free!

- 110 en suite bedrooms (100 double/twin; 10 suites) all with d-dial telephone, colour TV+ sat, hairdryer, minibar, tea/coffee making, trouser press, 24-hr room service. ✄ & ♿ rooms available.
- 3-cse tdh inner £18; alc, lunch & diets avail; last orders 9.30 pm. ● 9 meeting rooms, cap'y 350
- Snooker, fishing, fitness centre/gym, indoor games room, jacuzzi, massage, sauna, sailing, watersports, squash, indoor swimming pool, hairdresser, beauty salon. Car parking for 200.
- AMERICAN EXPRESS & major credit cards accepted.

Ambleside 2,
Windermere 2,
Kendal 11,
Junc 37 M6 -17,
Lancaster 30,
London 248.

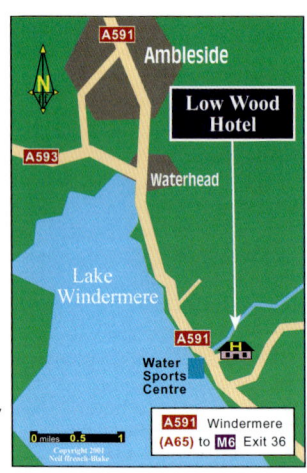

Cumbria, Windermere

The Samling

Ambleside Road, Windermere, Cumbria LA23 1LR
Tel: (015394) 31922; Fax: (015394) 30400
E-mail: info@thesamling.com
Website: www.thesamling.com

In ancient Cumbria, a *samling* meant a gathering of people (from the Saxon/German *Sammlung*), and for some years The Samling has provided a luxurious base for all kinds of small gatherings - be they celebratory or business - for up to 20 people. In 2001, however, under the new ownership of Tom and Jocelyn Maxfield and with managing director Simon Rhatigan, the Samling has been developed as a luxury hotel. A hotel in the country, NOT a Country House Hotel, as the owners emphasise. Built in the late 1700s, the Samling sits in 67 acres of wild flowers, woodland, garden and fields with a commanding view of Lake Windermere. It has ten beautiful and individually designed suites either in the main house or on the Estate, each enjoying a level of comfort befitting the discerning guest of the 21st century. There is a cosy drawing room in which to relax, and the dining room offers light cuisine, full of ideas, accompanied by a first class wine list. The Samling has a magical ambience, with few equals in the Lake District.

PRIDE OF BRITAIN HOTELS

Rates: Single /double/twin from £130.
Leisure breaks: Two nights min. dinner, b & b breaks avail. from £215 per night for two people.

- 10 en suite bedrooms (inc 2 suites) all with d-dial telephone, colour TV+ sat, hairdryer, laundry service, radio/alarm clock, ✂ rooms available.
- 3-cse tdh dinner £40; Sunday lunch & diets avail; last orders 9.30 pm.
- Meeting room, capacity 16. 🅿 20.
- Snooker, croquet, hill walking, river bathing. Watersports, squash, sailing nearby.
- Open all year.
- Visa, Mastercard accepted.

**Kendal 8,
Penrith 26,
Lancaster 28,
London 246.**

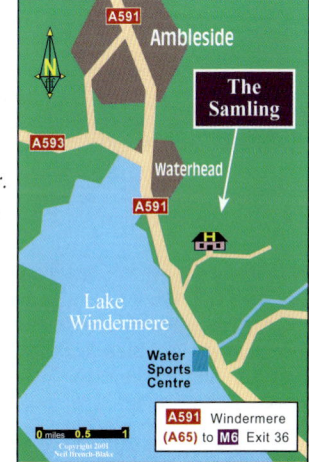

THE NORTH WEST

The Wild Boar Hotel

Crook Road, Nr. Windermere,
Cumbria LA23 3NF
Tel: (015394) 45225; Fax: (015394) 42498
E-mail: wildboar@elhmail.co.uk
Website: www.elh.co.uk/hotels/boar

The Wild Boar is a former coaching inn, situated in the beauty of the Gilpin valley. It is said that Sir Richard Gilpin slew the last wild boar in England outside its doors. Today it makes a very comfortable retreat from the stresses of everyday living. On entering you will find public rooms with low beams, open log fires and chintzy furnishings. The bedrooms are all warm and comfortable, beautifully decorated and with every modern facility. In the attractive candle-lit dining room, you can choose from the award winning menu, which even includes fresh wild boar, and complement it with a select vintage from the cellar. If you like the wine, you can buy further bottles from the Wine Shop by the Reception area! Windermere Golf Course is virtually next door and the many attractions of Lake Windermere and Bowness are less than three miles away. Guests are also entitled to use the Leisure Centre at English Lakes' sister hotel, Low Wood, nearby. A romantic spot for a short break and a good centre for touring the Lake District.

Rates: Single with breakfast £58-95; double inc. breakfast £116-150
Leisure Breaks: Long weekend. Stay Friday & Saturday and add Sunday night at half price. (exc Bank Hols.)

- 36 en suite bedrooms (inc 5 suites) all with d-dial telephone, colour TV+ sat, hairdryer, radio/alarm clock, trouser press, fax/modem points, ✄ rooms available.
- 3-cse tdh dinner £20; alc, lunch & diets available, last orders 9.30 pm.
- Meeting room (with a/c), capacity 40. 🅿 80.
- Golf ½ mile. Watersports, sailing, squash, leisure centre, indoor swimming pool seven miles.
- Visa, Mastercard & Diners accepted.
- Open all year.

Bowness 3,
Kendal 6,
Ambleside 7,
Grasmere 11,
Blackpool 50,
Manchester 75, London 275.

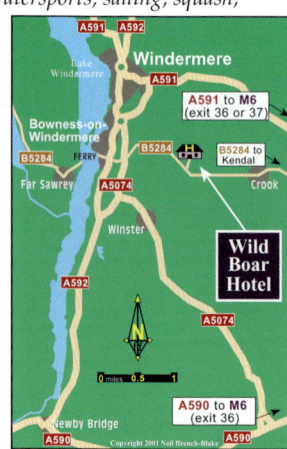

… Greater Manchester, Manchester Airport

Etrop Grange Hotel

Thorley Lane, Manchester Airport M90 4EG
Tel: (0161) 499 0500;
Fax: (0161) 499 0790
E-Mail: etropgrange@corushotels.com
Website: www.corushotels.co.uk

It is my experience that hotels situated near airports are somewhat functional in nature - not so Etrop Grange. This gracious Georgian mansion built in 1780 is not just a luxurious base for those visiting the airport, but it is an attractive country house hotel and restaurant in its own right, hidden away and offering leisure and business guests excellent service. The hotel enjoys a fine reputation locally for its accommodation and food; general manager Kevin Pearson and his staff make every effort to meet guests' needs and to maintain that reputation. There are 64 individually furnished en suite bedrooms, the majority of which have brass or four-poster beds. Each is named after a Cheshire village. Who said that in group-owned hotels guests are simply a number? The ◎◎ Coach House Restaurant is an elegant environment in which to enjoy fine dining on traditional and modern English cuisine complemented by an extensive wine list. The hotel offers 24-hour room service which is particularly useful for those arriving very late, and just in case you need the airport, a complimentary chauffeur driven Jaguar will ferry you there and back. Etrop Grange is of course a wonderful base from which to visit Manchester with its excellent shopping, culture, entertainment, sporting and leisure opportunities and from which to explore the super Cheshire countryside with its historic houses and stately homes. So don't think of Etrop Grange as just another airport hotel. It is a country house hotel, near which they later built an airport!

Rates: Single with breakfast from £70; double inc. breakfast from £95.
Car Parking Packages available from £99 per room.

● 64 en suite bedrooms, all with telephone, col TV + sat, hairdryer, laundry/valet service, 24-hr room/meal service, tea/coffee making, trouser press, fax/modem points, radio/alarm clock, ✗ rms available.
● A/c dinner fm £25.50. Lunch & special diets available. Last orders 10 pm.
● Complimentary airport pickup.
● Business services inc. 10 meeting rms, cap'y 90.
● & all major credit cards accepted.
● Open all year.

M56 Junction 5 - ½ m, M6 Jn 19 - 5, Knutsford 5, Manchester 9, Macclesfield 9, London 194.

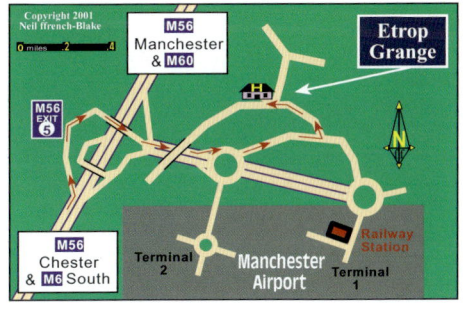

The Pines Hotel

Preston Road, Clayton-le-Woods,
Chorley, Lancashire BB3 2QB
Tel: (01772) 338551; Fax: (01772) 269002
E-Mail: mail@thepines-Hotel.co.uk
Website: www.thePines-Hotel.co.uk

One of the pleasures of visiting this part of Lancashire is to stay at The Pines. It has always impressed me that Mrs Duffin, the owner, has every year been able to add some new facility or to improve the hotel. With superbly comfortable public rooms, beautiful bedrooms with all the 'extras', there is surely nothing more a discerning guest could want? The food is delicious, the wine list long and well chosen and Lancastrians from all over the county gather here to dine. Various suites are available for conferences and small meetings and one of them, *The Dixon Suite*, is in great demand for wedding receptions. An acre of beautiful garden provides a fitting backdrop for ensuing photographs! The hotel is ideally situated for the business traveller, being only minutes from the M6 and M61. For the holidaymaker and North-South traveller, Blackpool and Lytham St Annes (for golf) are near at hand; the Pennines and South Lake District only an hour away and the entertainment and academic centre of Manchester 30 minutes down the motorway.

Rates: *Single room with breakfast from £80; double rom inc. breakfast from £90.*
Leisure Breaks: *One night's accom, dinner, b & b + cabaret & dancing £60 per pers, 2 sharing. Or Weekend Break £290 for two nights in a suite.*

● 37 en suite bedrooms (inc 2 suites) all with telephone, colour TV, hairdryer, tea/coffee making, trouser press, laundry service, fax/modem points, radio/alarm, ✄ & ♿ rooms available.
● Tdh dinner £18.50. Alc, lunch & special diets available. Last orders 9.45 pm (Mon-Sat); 9 pm Sun
● Open all year.
● & all major credit cards accepted

M6 Junction 8 - 1mile,
Blackburn 10,
Bolton 10,
Southport 19,
Manchester 22
London 203.

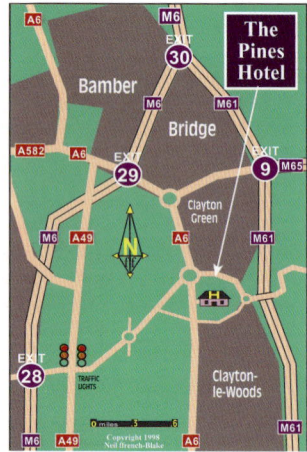

Lancaster House Hotel

Green Lane, Ellel, Lancaster L1 4AJ
Tel: (01524) 844822; Fax: (01524) 844766
E-mail: lancaster@elhmail.co.uk
Website: www.elh.co.uk/hotels/lancs

When first impressions count, you can rely on Lancaster House to impress. From the balconied Reception Lounge, you instinctively know that this is a place to savour the good things of life, such as excellent cuisine from the Gressingham Restaurant or a drink in the courtyard of the Sandeman's Bar. This relaxed elegance is also reflected in each of the 80 bedrooms. The hotel's Sandpiper Leisure Club lets you take life at your own pace - whether you want to work out or simply relax and unwind. From Lancaster House you can explore the superb Lancashire coastline or the historic city of Lancaster itself. With the Trough of Bowland, Lune Valley and Lake District on your doorstep, the possibilities are endless. Lancaster House is the discerning choice for a memorable weekend break, special occasion or as a convenient base for touring this magical region. Williamson Park, Lancaster Castle, Lancaster Leisure Park, the Maritime Museum and Crook O'Lune are on the doorstep. The hotel has extensive conference and reception facilities as well as the Sandpiper Club health and leisure centre.

Rates: Double/twin room and breakfast from £82 (weekends); £99 midweek. **Connoisseur Breaks.** 2 nights+, dinner, b & b from £71.50 per pers. per nt.

● 80 en suite bedrooms (inc one suite) all with d-dial telephone, colour TV + sat, hairdryer, tea/coffee making, radio/alarm clock, laundry service, trouser press, safety deposit box, radio, fax/modem points, 24-hr room service. ✯ & ♿ rms available.
● Alc & tdh dinner in Gressingham Restaurant; last orders 9.30 pm. Lunch & special diets avail.
● Fitness centre/gym, jacuzzi, sauna, indoor swimming pool, barber shop/beauty salon. Fishing, golf, clay shooting, tennis & riding nearby. 🅿 90.
● Business services inc 16 meeting rooms, up to 120.
● AMERICAN EXPRESS & major credit cards accepted.
● Open all year
M6 (Junc 34)
4½m, Kirkby
Lonsdale 16,
Preston 22,
Blackpool 24,
London 238.

Chadwick Hotel

South Promenade, Lytham St Annes, Lancashire FY8 1NP
Tel: (01253) 720061;
Fax: (01253) 714455

Best Small Hotel of the Year Award

E-mail: sales@thechadwickhotel.com
Website: www.thechadwickhotel.com

The Chadwick Hotel has been owned and run by the Corbett family since 1947 and is now with the third generation. In a wonderful sea front position overlooking the Ribble Estuary, the hotel offers ideal facilities for those looking for a leisure break, family holiday or business stopover. The lounges are bright, comfortable and have panoramic sea views; the cosy Bugatti Bar features over 100 malt whiskies; the Four Seasons Restaurant serves excellent food and wine and the en suite bedrooms have very good amenities including individual temperature control. Add to this the Atlantis Health Centre and excellent service throughout from friendly and helpful staff, and you have a very well-run operation - a hotel for all seasons.
Blackpool 7, Preston 14, Lancaster 30, Manchester 47.

Rates: Double/twin room and breakfast from £32 per person, including VAT. Open all year.
Leisure breaks. *Midwinter breaks with two per - sons sharing £39.95 for dinner, bed & breakfast. Weekend breaks inc. dance & banquet 2 nts £90 pp*
- 75 en suite bedrooms (2) all with telephone and TV; room service; baby listening; night service; 24-hour food service; lift. ● Children welcome
- Indoor heated pool; leisure centre/gym; sauna; solarium; spa pool; sea fishing; golf ½ mile; sailing/boating, tennis & squash courts 1 m; riding 3 m. & all major credit cards accepted.

Singleton Lodge Country House Hotel

Lodge Lane, Singleton, Nr. Poulton-Le-Fylde, Lancs FY6 8LT
Tel: (01253) 883854; Fax: + 894432

E-mail: enquiries@singletonlodgehotel.co.uk
Website: www.singletonlodgehotel.co.uk

Set in five acres of tranquil parkland and surrounded by an attractive garden, Singleton Lodge is a charming former Georgian vicarage offering peace and relaxation. It is owned and personally run by Alan and Ann Smith, who, along with their friendly staff, will provide you with a warm welcome and do all they can to make your stay enjoyable. They will also provide a relaxed atmosphere in which to enjoy the log-fired lounges, comfortable bedrooms, cosy well-stocked bar and elegant dining room, where traditional home cooked meals and a wine list to suit all tastes and pockets are available. Located only five miles from the Fylde coast and the facilities of Blackpool and Lytham St Annes, and with a wealth of golf courses and other attractions nearby, Singleton Lodge is an ideal base for that relaxing country house break.
M6 J32 10m, Preston 12, Lytham 5, Blackpool 6, London 240.

Rates: Single room and breakfast from £48; double., inc. breakfast from £70. ***Leisure Breaks:*** *Dinner, bed & breakfast @ £99 per couple.*
- 13 en suite bedrooms (inc one suite) all with telephone, colour TV, hairdryer, tea/coffee making, radio/alarm, trouser press. & rms available.
- Alc dinner, last orders 9 pm. Special diets avail.
- Croquet, gardens. Fishing, golf, sailing/boating, tennis, shooting, squash & riding one mile. P 25.
- Business services inc 3 meeting rooms 50/20/10. *Directions: Leave M55 at J3, follow A585 signs to Fleetwood for 3m; at fst traffic lights turn lft, next trfc lts lft again; Lodge 400m, 3rd entrance on left.*
- & major credit cards accepted.
- Closed 25 December-2nd January;

Lancashire, Lytham St Anne's

THE NORTH WEST

The Grand Hotel

South Promenade, Lytham St Annes,
Lancashire FY8 1NB
Tel: (01253) 721288; Fax: (01253) 714459
E-mail: book@the-grand.co.uk
Website: www.the-grand.co.uk

The Grand is an imposing Victorian hotel right on the seafront of Lytham St Anne's. Inside, the reception area, the lounges and other public rooms have that warm, country house atmosphere that makes a hotel stay so welcoming. Again, the bedrooms are spacious and airy. Overall the atmosphere is one of tranquillity. This is enhanced by the friendliness of the staff and the unhurried service in the dining-room. The food here is excellent, vouched for by the many local residents who dine here. There are also conference facilities. For the leisure visitor, Blackpool and its illuminations are near at hand, as is the Trough of Bowland and some of the best golf courses in England - Royal Lytham, The Old Links and the Fairhaven. This year a Leisure Centre was added, with techno-gym, indoor swimming pool, jacuzzi and Sanarium; also a further fifteen superior bedrooms and three luxury penthouse suites, confirming The Grand as the premier choice for a relaxing break on the Fylde coast.

Rates: Single room with breakfast from £84; double room inc. breakfast from £88.
Special Breaks available throughout the year - min. 2 nights. Contact Reception or visit our website for details. When booking mention SIGNPOST for a free upgrade!

● 53 en suite bedrooms (inc 3 Turret Rooms & 3 penthouses), all with d-dial telephone, col TV+ sat, hairdryer, laundry service, tea/coffee making, 24-hr room service, DVD, fax/modem points, radio/alarm, trouser press. ♿ rooms available.
● Bay Restaurant 3-cse tdh dinner £21.50; alc, lunch (wine bar) & diets available; last orders 9.30
● 6 meeting rooms, cap. 200.
● Closed 23-27 December.
● Croquet, fitness centre/gym, jacuzzi, sanarium, indoor swimming pool. Golf nearby
● [American Express] & major credit cards exc. Diners accepted
**Blackpool 5,
Preston 14,
Lancaster 30,
Manchester 47,
London 224.**

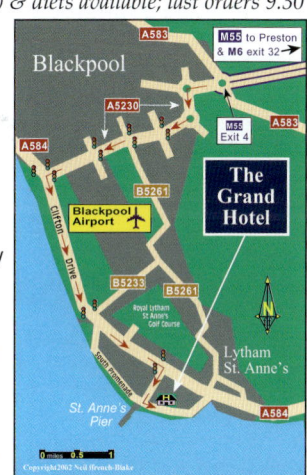

Signpost Guide 2003

Yorkshire/North East

Fact File
Illustrated Guide to
Historic Houses, Gardens & Sites
Diary of Events

Hotels in	PAGE
Cleveland	158
Durham	159
Northumberland	162
North Yorkshire	164

Yorkshire & The North East

Historic Houses, Gardens & Parks

Cleveland
Burn Valley Gardens, Hartlepool
Fairy Dell, Middlesbrough
Ormesby Hall, Ormesby, Middlesbrough
Ward Jackson Park, Hartlepool

County Durham
Eggleston Hall Gardens, Eggleston
Hardwick Hall Country Park, Stockton-on-Tees
Houghall Gardens, Durham

East Riding of Yorkshire
Burton Agnes Hall, Driffield
Burton Constable Hall & Country Park, Nr. Hull
Sledmere House, Driffield

Northumberland
Alnwick Castle
Belsay Hall, Castle & Gardens, Belsay
Cragside House & Country Park, Rothbury
Hexham Herbs, Chollerford
Howick Hall Gardens, Alnwick
Hulne Park, Alnwick
Lady Waterford Hall, Berwick on-Tweed
Meldon Park, Morpeth
Otterburn Hall
Paxton House, Berwick on-Tweed
Seaton Delaval Hall, Blyth
Shaw Garden Centre Cramlington
Wallington House Walled Garden & Grounds, Morpeth

Tyne & Wear
Bessie Surtees House, Newcastle-upon-Tyne
Bolam Lake Country Park, Newcastle-upon-Tyne
Kirkley Hall Gardens, Ponteland
Rising Sun Country Park & Countryside Centre, Benton
Saltwell Park, Gateshead

Yorkshire - North, West & South
Allerton Park, Knaresborough
Beningbrough Hall, York
Bramham Park, Wetherby
Burnby Hall Gardens, Pocklington
Castle Howard, Coneysthorpe
Constable Burton Hall Gardens, Leyburn
Duncombe Park, Helmsley
East Riddlesden Hall, Keighley
Epworth Old Rectory, Doncaster
Fairfax House, York
Golden Acre Park, Bramhope
Harewood House, Leeds
Harlow Carr Botanical Gardens, Harrogate
Japanese Garden, Horsforth
Kiplin Hall Richmond
Land Farm Garden, Hebden Bridge
Lotherton Hall, Leeds
Margaret Waudby Oriental Garden, Upper Poppleton Newburgh Priory, York
Newby Hall Gardens, Ripon
Normanby Hall, Scunthorpe
Nostell Priory, Wakefield
Nunnington Hall, York
Parceval Hall Gardens, Skipton
Ripley Castle, Harrogate
St Nicholas Gardens, Richmond
Sheffield Botanical Gardens
Sheriff Hutton Park, Nr. York
Stockfield Park, Wetherby
Sutton Park, Nr. York
Temple Newsam House, Leeds
Thorp Perrow Arboretum, Bedale

Walks & Nature Trails

Cleveland
Bilingham Beck Valley Country Park

County Durham
Allensford Park, Consett
Blackton Nature Reserve, Teesdale
Derwent Walk, Consett
Durham Coast, Peterlee
Hamsterley Forest, Bishop Auckland

East Riding of Yorkshire
Elsham Hall Country & Wildlife Park, Brigg
Humber Bridge Country Park, Hessle
Normanby Hall Country Park, Scunthorpe

Northumberland
Allen Banks Woods, Hexham
Bedlington Country Park
Carlisle Park & Castle Wood, Morpeth
Fontburn Nature Reserve
Hareshaw Dene, Bellingham, Hexham
Ingram National Park Visitor Centre
Northumberland Coast, Newton-by-the-Sea, Alnwick
Plessey Woods Country Park
Scotch Gill Wood Local Nature Reserve, Morpeth

Tyne & Wear
Derwent Walk Country Park, Rowlands Gill
The Leas & Marsden Rock, S.Shields
Thornley Woodlands Centre, Rowlands Gill

Yorkshire - North, West & South
Anglers Country Park, Wintersett
Barlow Common Nature Reserve, Selby
Bretton Country Park, Wakefield
Bridestones Moor, Pickering
Brimham Rocks, Harrogate
Cannon Hall Country Park, Barnsley
Chevin Forest Park, Otley
Dalby Forest Drive & Visitor Centre, Pickering
Hardcastle Crags, Hebden Bridge
Howstean Gorge, Pateley Bridge
Malham Tarn, Settle
Millington Wood Local Nature Reserve
Marston Moor, Huddersfield
Newmillerdam Country Park, Wakefield
Ogden Water, Halifax
Ravenscar Coastline, Scarborough
Rother Valley Country Park, Sheffield
Sutton Bank Nature Trail - between Helmsley & Thirsk
Ulley Country Park, Sheffield
Worsbrough Country Park, Barnsley

Historical Sites & Museums

Cleveland
Guisborough Priory, Guisborough
Gray Art Gallery & Museum, Hartlepool
Guisborough Museum, York
Saltburn Smugglers Heritage Centre
PSS Wingfield Castle, Hartlepool

County Durham
Barnard Castle
Beamish - The North of England Open Air Museum
Durham Cathedral
Durham Castle
Raby Castle, Staindrop

East Riding of Yorkshire
Burton Agnes Manor House, Driffield
Maister House, Hull
Wilberforce House, Hull

Northumberland
Aydon Castle
Bamburgh Castle
Berwick Castle, Berwick on-Tweed
Brinkburn Priory, Longframlington
Chesters Roman Fort, Hexham
Chillingham Castle
Dunstanburgh Castle
Edlingham Castle
Etal Castle, Etal, Cornhill-on-Tweed
Grace Darling's Museum, Bamburgh
Hadrian's Wall
Hexham Abbey
House of Hardy Museum & Country Store, Alnwick
Lindisfarne Castle, Holy Island, Berwick-on-Tweed
Marine Life Centre & Fishing Museum, Seahouses
Norham Castle, Berwick-on-Tweed
Prudhoe Castle
Warkworth Castle
Wine & Spirit Museum & Victorian Chemist Shop, Berwick-on-Tweed

Tyne & Wear
Castle Keep, Newcastle-upon-Tyne
Hatton Gallery, Newcastle-u-Tyne
The Laing Art Gallery, Newcastle-upon-Tyne
Newbum Hall Motor Museum, Newcastle-upon-Tyne
The Shipley Art Gallery, Gateshead
South Shields Museum, South Shields

Yorkshire & The North East

Yorkshire North, West & South
Aldborough Roman Town, Nr. Boroughbridge
Assembly Rooms, York
BardenTower, Bolton Abhey
Barley Hall, York
Beverley Minster, Beverley
Bishops House, Sheffield
Bolling Hall, Bradford
Bolton Castle, Leyburn
Borthwick Institute of Historical Research, York
Bronte Parsonage Museum, Haworth
Captain Cook Memorial Museum, Whitby
Clifford's Tower, York
Dales Countryside Museum, Hawes
Eureka! The Museum for Children, Halifax
Fountains Abbey a Studley Royal, Ripon
Fulneck Moravian Settlement & Museum, Nr. Pudsey
Gainsthorpe Deserted Medieval Village
Georgian Theatre Royal & Museum, Richmond
Jervaulx Abbey, Ripon
Jorvik Viking Centre & Brass Rubbing Centre, York
Kirstall Abbey, Leeds
King's Manor, York
Marmion Tower, Ripon
Mount Grace Priory, Northallerton
National Museum of Photography, Film & Television, Bradford
National Railway Museum, York
Red House, Gomerad
Rievalulx Abbey, Rievaulx
Sion Hill Hall & Birds of Prey Centre, Kirkby Wiske
Skipton Castle, Skipton
The Old Smithy & Heritage Centre, Owston Ferry
Tetleys Brewery Wharf, Leeds
Treasurer's House, York
York Castle Museum, York
York Story, York
York Minster, York

Entertainment Venues

Cleveland
Botanic Centre, Middlesbrough
Cleveland Craft Centre, Middlesbrough
Margrove South Cleveland Heritage Centre, Boosbeck, Saltburn-by-Sea
Stewart Park, Middlesbrough

County Durham
Bowlees Visitor Centre, Middleton-in-Teesdale

East Riding of Yorkshire
Bondville Miniature Village, Sewerby
Fosse Hill Jet Ski Centre, Driffield
Humberside Ice Arena, Hull
Sewerby Hall, Park & Zoo, Bridlington

Northumberland
Belford Craft Gallery
Tower Knowe Visitor Centre, Kielder Water, Hexham

Tyne & Wear
Bowes Railway Centre, Gateshead
Predator Paintball, Newcastle-upon-Tyne

Yorkshire North, South & West
Catterick Indoor Ski Centre, Catterick Garrison
Flamingo Land Family Funpark & Zoo, Malton
Harrogate Ski Centre, Yorkshire Showground
Hemsworth Water Park & Playworld
Hornsea Pottery Leisure Park & Freeport Shopping Village
Kinderland, Scarborough
Lighwater Valley Theme Park, North Stainley
North of England Clay Target Centre, Rufforth
Piece Hall, Halifax
Sheffield Ski Village, Sheffield
The Alan Ayckbourn Theatre in the Round, Scarborough
Tockwith (Multi-Drive)Activity Centre, Tockwith Thybergh Country Park
Turkish Baths, Harrogate
Watersplash World, Scarborough
The World of Holograms, Scarborough

DIARY OF EVENTS

January

1. **Newcastle to Morpeth Road Race.** Morpeth, Northumberland.
6. **Old Custom: Haxey Hood Game.** Haxey, South Yorks.
30-7.2. **Wakefield Rhubarb Trail & Festival.** Var. venues, Wakefield.

February

1-4*. **33rd Harrogate Winter Antiques Fair.** Harrogate Pavilions, Gt Yorks Showgr'd
8-9. **Festival of British Railway Modelling.** Doncaster, South Yorks.
8 & 25. **NH Racing.** Catterick.
15-23. **Jorvik Viking Festival - Jolablot 2003.** Var venues, Coppergate, York.
15 & 24. **NH Racing.** Newcastle

March

2*. **National Classic Bike Show.** Flower Hall, Gt Yorks Showground, Harrogate.
7-22*. **Bradford Film Festival** National Museum of Photography, Pictureville, Bradford.
10-15. **Eskdale Festival of the Arts.** Whitby. N Yorks.
8-16*. **British Society of Painters Art Exhibition.** Ilkley, West Yorkshire.
20-22. **Racing** at Doncaster.
29-1.4 **Easter in Hull.** Var venues, Kingston-u-Hull.
28-30. **The Motorhome and US RV Show.** Harrogate, North Yorkshire.
29. **Leeds Doll & Teddy Fair** Civic Centre, Pudsey, W Yks
30. **Motorcycle Motocross Fair.** Wrelton, North Yorks.

April

8 & 21. **Racing** at Pontefract.
12-13. **Gateshead Spring Flower Show.** Gateshead, Tyne & Wear.
14-16*. **Ripley Castle Antiques Fair.** Ripley Castle, North Yorks.
19-23. **Harrogate Int'l Youth Music Festival.** Harrogate, North Yorkshire.
19-21. **Selby Game Fair.** Carlton, East Yorkshire.
21. **Old Custom: World Coal Carrying Championship.** Ossett, West Yorkshire.
21. **Danby Antique & Collectors Fair.** Danby, N Yorks.
24-27. **Harrogate Spring Flower Show.** Great Yorkshire Showground, Harrogate.
25-27. **Morpeth Northumbrian Gathering.** Northumberland.
25-5.5*. **Bridlington Arts Festival**, Bridlington, E Riding.

Yorkshire & The North East

May

3-27.7. **Jewellery Showcase, Exhibition: Drawing from Childhood, Ceramic Showcase.** Leeds, West Yorks
3-4. **Newcastle Community Green Festival.** Newcastle-upon-Tyne.
3-5. **Raby Castle Orchid Show.** Staindrop, Co. Durham.
5. **Allerdean Charity Country Fair.** Berwick-u-Tweed, N'umb
5. **Danby Antique & Collectors Fair.** Danby, North Yorks.
10-17. **Wharfdale Festival.** Rural Arts. Ilkley, West Yorks
13-15. **Race Meeting.** York RC
17-18. **Settle Flag Festival & Sheep Shambles.** Settle, North Yorks.
21. **Otley 10-mile Road Race.** Otley, West Yorkshire.
24-27*. **7th Harrogate Int'l Antiques & Fine Art Fair.** Pavilions, Gt Yorks Shwgrd, Harrogate, North Yorks.
25. **Amble Community Carnival.** Amble, Northumbs.

June

June. **Holy Island Jazz and Blues Festival.** Holy Island, Northumberland.
3-29.8. **Cookson Country Festival.** South Shields. T&W
5-9. **Npower Test. England v Zimbabwe.** Durham.
9. **Miniature Steam Railway Public Open Day.** Keighley, West Yorks.
20-6.7. **Nidderdale Festival 2003.** Harrogate. N Yorks.
20-21. **Racing** at Redcar.
21. **Ovingham Goose Fair.** Ovingham, Northumberland.
21. **Otley Carnival.** W Yorks.
27-28. **Newcastle Plate Meeting.** Newcastle Race Course.
28-29. **Darlington Community Carnival.** Darlington, Durham
28-29. **Preston Hall Fire Engine & Historic Vehicle Rally.** Stockton-on-Tees, Cleveland
29-5.7. **Alnwick Fair.** Alnwick, Northumberland.

July

1. **England v Zimbabwe.** Natwest 1-Day Series, Headingley.
4-13*.**York Early Music Festival.** Various venues, York, North Yorkshire.
5. **Breeze Festival of Music & Arts.**Wooler, Northumberland
5. **Summer Music Festival.** Durham.
5-6. **Sunderland Int'l Festival of Kites, Music & Dance.** Washington, Tyne & Wear.
8-10. **Great Yorkshire Show.** Gt Yorks Showground, Harrogate, N Yorks
11-13. **Whitley Bay Jazz Festival.** Newcastle-u-Tyne.
19-24. **Teesside Int'l Eisteddfod.** Middlesbrough.
19-20. **Otterburn Festival.** Otterburn, Tyne & Wear.
25-26. **York Stamp & Coin Fair.** York.
26. **Cleveland Show.** Middlesbrough, Cleveland.
26-27. **Sunderland Int'l Air Show.** Sunderland, T & Wear

August

August. **Sheepdog Trials & Powburn Show.** Powburn, Northumberland.
Aug. **Slaley Show.** Slaley, Northumbs.
1-3. **Car Show MOG 003**. Newcastle-upon-Tyne.T & W
2-9. **Alnwick Int'l Music Festival.** Northumberland.
6-10. **Saltburn Int'l Festival of Folk Music, Dance & Song.**
15-17.**Alnwick Castle Horse Driving Trials & Country Fair.** Alnwick, Northumbs.
16-22. **Whitby Folk Week.** Var venues, Whitby, N Yorks.
19-21. **York August Meeting.** York Racecourse.
21-25.**England v South Africa** 4th Test. Headingley, Leeds.
23-25.**Stockton Summer Show**

September

3-20. **Leeds International Piano Competition.** Leeds.
6. **Alnwick Show.** Alnwick, Northumberland.
10-13. **Rothmans Royals St Leger Meeting.** Doncaster.
13. **Stanhope & Bowes Agric. Shows.** Co Durham.
13. **Bradford Centenary Square Historic Vehicle Display** . Bradford, W Yorks
18-26. **Hexham Abbey Festival.** Hexham,Northumbs.

October

4-19. **Northumberland Traditional Music Festival.**
6. **Leeds Doll & Teddy Fair.** Leeds, W Yorkshire.
6-2.11. **Wetherby Festival.** Wetherby, West Yorks.
24-25. **Racing Post Trophy Meeting.** Doncaster,S Yorks

November

Nov. **Newcastle Comedy Festival.** Necastle-u-Tyne.
1-2.**Complementary Medecine Festival.** Ilkley, WYorks
5. **Firework Displays.** Peterlee, Stockton & Gateshead.
7-8. **Racing** at Doncaster.
21-23*. **43rd Annual Wakefield Model RailwayExhibition.**Thornes Park Athletics Stadium, Wakefield.
28-30.**City of Durham Christmas Festival.** Durham.

* = denotes provisional date. For further information Contact

TOURIST BOARDS

Yorkshire Tourist Board
312 Tadcaster Road
York YO2 2HF.
Tel: (01904) 707961
Website: yorkshirevisitor.com

Northumbria Tourist Board
Aykley Heads, Durham DH1 5UX.
Tel: (0191) 375 3000
Website: ntb.org.uk

Northumbria

Northumbria is an undiscovered holiday paradise, where the scenery is wild and beautiful, the beaches golden and unspoiled, and the natives friendly. The region is edged by the North Sea, four national parks and the vast Border Forest Park. Its eastern boundary with the sea is a stunning coastline - stretching 100 miles from Staithes on the border of Cleveland and North Yorkshire to Berwick-on-Tweed, England's most northerly town. In between you'll find as many holiday opportunities here as changes of scenery. There's a wonderful variety of seascapes, from Cleveland's towering cliffs to the shimmering white sands of Northumberland, where you can lose yourself in the dunes. Inland you will find the remarkable Hadrian's Wall, the National Park, hills, forests, waterfalls, castles, splendid churches and quaint towns and villages. Northumbria combines the fun of a seaside holiday with the relaxation of a break in the country.

History books come alive in Northumberland and exploring its heritage could take a lifetime. In the far north, Berwick-on-Tweed (fought over by the English and Scots for centuries) is steeped in history and has the finest preserved example of Elizabethan town walls in the country. The town is an ideal gateway to the Borders. Visitors can trace man's occupation of the region from prehistoric times to the Victorian age of invention. Prehistoric rock carvings, ancient hill forts, Roman remains, Saxon churches, Norman priories, medieval castles and a wealth of industrial archaeology can all be discovered here.

The region has a rich maritime heritage too. Imposing ruins, such as the gaunt remains of Dunstanburgh or fairy-tale Lindisfarne, are relics of a turbulent era when hordes of invaders landed on Northumberland's shores. Of course you don't have to explore castles and museums to capture the maritime flavour. Instead laze on a beach, fish from the end of the pier or take a trip from the fishing village of Seahouses, Northumberland, to the Farne Islands - a marvellous bird sanctuary and breeding ground of the Atlantic Grey Seal.

Lovers of the great outdoors will find Northumbria a paradise. In the National Park, where sheep outnumber people, the views will take your breath away. It is possible to enjoy the splendours of this area by car, but the remote hills are for the walker. Some of the wildest, highest and most beautiful scenery in England can be seen in the North Pennines. The noisiest thing in this peaceful refuge is the dramatic waterfall High Force! You'll pass through pretty villages such as Cotherstone in Teesdale, St John's Chapel in Weardale and Blanchland in Northumberland.

Holy Island. Photo - Northumbria Tourist Board

Searchers for activity will find the perfect base here also. Hike it, bike it, watch it - whatever your sport, you can do it in Northumbria. The countryside is ideal for pony trekking, walking, climbing, ballooning, orienteering, cycling, fishing, watersports and golf. Some hotels offer activity packages, such as golf or fishing weekends. More traditional local sports such as *hound trailing* and *Cumberland Wrestling* can be found at agricultural shows.

Naturally with so much countryside, agriculture is one of the region's most important industries. A super place to take children is Heatherslaw Mill, near Ford (a delightful model village), a restored water-driven corn mill and agricultural museum. If you were a fan of the television series *One Man and His Dog*, then the skill of shepherd and dog can be seen at sheepdog trials and country shows.

The ancient crafts and customs of Northumbria provide a fascinating insight into the character of this lovely region. It is said that fact can be stranger than fiction, and you'll have fun exploring some of the local myths, from the tiny island of Lindisfarne to the church in the pretty village of Kirknewton, close to the Cheviots, where the sculptured *Adoration of the Magi* depicts the Wise Men wearing kilts!

A less well known feature of the region is that is has one of the liveliest arts scenes outside London. The Theatre Royal, Newcastle, is the third home of the Royal Shakespeare Company and a venue for other major touring companies. Throughout the region you can enjoy first class entertainment from open air Shakespeare to costumed pageants; from the Royal Ballet to Rock N Roll, from Mozart to music hall.

Warkworth Castle. Photo - Northumbria Tourist Board

Wherever you go, from the traditional pub in a tiny village to a top class hotel, you'll always find a warm welcome. The region is well served by trunk roads, high speed trains and airports. Please contact the Northumbria Tourist Board, address on previous page, for details.

Yorkshire

Yorkshire, so rich in history and tradition, boasts some of the country's most splendid scenery. For wide open spaces, visit the North York Moors with their 500 square miles of hills, dales, forest and open moorland, neatly edged by a spectacular coastline. Walking, cycling and pony trekking are ideal ways to savour the scenery; alternatively take the steam train from Pickering to Grosmont on the famous North Yorkshire Moors Railway.

Numerous greystone towns and villages dotted throughout the Moor2s are ideal bases from which to explore the countryside. From Helmsley, visit the ruins of Reivaulx Abbey, founded by Cistercian monks in the 12th century. In Hutton-le-Hole, the fascinating story of moorland life is told in the award-winning Ryedale Folk Museum. Likewise the Beck Isle Museum in Pickering provides a remarkable insight into the life of a country market town. A few miles down the road, you'll find Malton, once a Roman fortress, and a little further on, Castle Howard, (*see right*) the setting for *Brideshead Revisited*.

From the Moors to the Dales and a total change of scene. Wherever you go in the Dales, you'll come across visible reminders of the rich and changing past. In medieval days, solid fortresses were built to protect the area from marauding Scots, like Richmond, guarding on one side the Northern Dales and Middleham the other. Knaresborough, the home of the prophetess Mother Shipton, Ripley and Skipton all had their massive strongholds while Bolton Castle in Wensleydale once imprisoned Mary, Queen of Scots. The pattern of history is also enshrined in the great abbeys like Jervaulx Abbey, near Masham, where the monks first made Wensleydale cheese, Eastby Abbey on the banks of the river Swale, and the majestic ruins of Fountains Abbey (*below*) in the grounds of Studley Royal.

When exploring the Pennines, you will find history written across the landscape. For centuries sheep have grazed the uplands and cloth has been spun from their wool. The industrial revolution began here and, with the introduction of machinery, the mills sprang up. The fascinating story of England's Industrial Heritage can now be seen in the numerous craft centres and folk museums throughout West Yorkshire. To enjoy the countryside, take a trip on the steam hauled Keighley and Worth Valley Railway. Step off at Haworth, home of the Brontë sisters, a nd experience the rugged atmosphere of Wuthering Heights. Nor far from Haworth is Bingley, where the Leeds and Liverpool canal takes its famous uphill journey. In the past coal barges came this way, but nowadays holiday-makers in gaily painted boats have taken their place.

Moving into the East Riding, the scenery changes again. From the dramatic 400ft cliffs at Flamborough Head, sweeps south a forty-mile stretch of perfect sandy beach. Along this magnificent coastline, you will find the day and night entertainments of Cleethorpes and Bridlington, contrasting with the less boisterous attractions of Hornsea and Withernsea. From any of the seaside resorts it is an easy drive into the peaceful countryside of the Wolds, where you will find delightful old villages like Skidby, Thorngumbald, Fridaythorpe and Wetwang. The town of Beverley is a jewel of architectural heritage with its magnificent 13th-century minster and beautiful St Mary's Church, both set in a delightful lattice work of medieval streets and Georgian houses.

Back to the sea and to the city of Hull, you will find a lot has been happening: the Humber Bridge - the world's longest single span bridge at 1452 yards, and the colourful yacht haven, created from two abandoned city centre docks, to name but two. Hull's maritime history is recorded in the Museum.

No visit to the Northeast would be complete without savouring the delights of York. Wherever you turn within the city's medieval walls, you will find fascinating glimpses of the past. It can be seen in the splendours of the 600-year old Minster, the grim stronghold of Clifford's Tower, The National Railway Museum, the medieval timbers of the Merchant Adventurers Hall and the Jorvik Viking Centre which illustrates life in a 10th century Viking township. Throughout the city, statues and monuments remind you that this was where Constantine was proclaimed Emperor, Guy Fawkes was born and Dick Turpin met his end.

Grinkle Park Hotel

Easington, Saltburn-by-the-Sea,
Cleveland TS13 4UB
Tel: (01287) 640515; Fax: (01287) 641278
E-mail: grinkle.parkhotel@sixcretail.com
Website: www.grinklepark.co.uk

Grinkle Park is a hotel with a difference, for it is popular not only with traditional hotel guests but also with a large, local clientèle. Consequently evenings in the hotel's bar and lounge have a unique, informal atmosphere as lively local banter mixes with the conversation of guests relaxing after a day using the hotel's facilities or exploring the superb area in which the hotel is located. Nestled between Whitby and the North Yorkshire Moors, the hotel is set in 35 acres of attractive parkland and gardens abundant with rhododendrons and azaleas, a lake, peacocks and wildfowl. Inside a country house atmosphere prevails, with bedrooms all named after flowers or birds. Manager Jane Norton and her friendly staff are on hand to ensure that your visit is an enjoyable one. Golf on testing local courses, evenings at the theatre at Scarborough and Darlington, long walks on the moors and salmon and trout fsihing on the Esk are among the pleasures to be had nearby whilst staying at Grinkle Park.

Rates: Single room with breakfast from £86; Double room with breakfast from £105.
Leisure Breaks: 2-night breaks, dinner, b & b from £64 per pers per night, sharing.

- 20 en suite bedrooms, all with colour TV, direct-dial telephone, tea/coffee making facilities, hair-dryer, laundry service, radio/alarm, trouser press.
- 3-cse tdh dinner £21.50; lunch & spec. diets avail; last orders 9-9.30. pm.
- Two meeting rms 25 & 60. Parking for 120
- Croquet, tennis. Golf, fishing, riding, shooting nearby.
- & all major credit cards accepted.
- Open all year.

Guisborough 8, Saltburn-by-the-Sea 8, Whitby 10, Middlesbrough 18, London 262.

Horsley Hall

Eastgate, Weardale,
Co Durham DL13 2LJ
Tel: (01388) 517239; Fax: (01388) 517608
E-mail: hotel@horsleyhall.co.uk
Website: www.horsleyhall.co.uk

We are very pleased to welcome Horsley Hall into Signpost. It is a super hotel offering a warm and friendly welcome, comfortable, homely accommodation, good food and wine and the attentive personal service of owners Liz Curry and Derek Glass. Situated in a tranquil position on the old road south of the river Wear between Stanhope and Eastgate, the Hall is an elegant, three storey manor house with a history dating back to the 1600s and it has been tastefully renovated and developed to retain its historical character and ambience whilst at the same time offering the modern amenities required by today's guests. The Baronial Hall is a magnificent setting in which to enjoy Liz's expertly produced cuisine; the Drawing Room has fine furnishings and fabrics and stylish, relaxing decor, and each bedroom is furnished in the manor house style. This hotel is ideally located to explore Weardale - a designated Area of Natural Beauty - with attractions like the High Force Waterfall, Bowes Museum, Beamish, Derwent and Kielder reservoirs readily accessible.

Rates: Single room with breakfast from £47.50; Double room with breakfast from £70.
Leisure Breaks: 10% discount off accommodation rates midweek for stays of three days+ .

- 7 en suite bedrooms, all with colour TV, direct-dial telephone, tea/coffee making, hairdryer, laundry service, radio/alarm, trouser press. Non-smoking rooms available.
- 3-cse dinner £22.50; alc, lunch & spec. diets available; last orders 9.30. pm.
- Meeting room, capacity 65. Parking for 50.
- Fishing, designated cycling & jogging routes. Riding nearby.
- American Express & all major credit cards accepted.
- Open all year exc. Xmas/New Year.

Barnard Castle 14, Alston 16, Durham 18, Bishop Auckland 18, Newcastle 30, London 274.

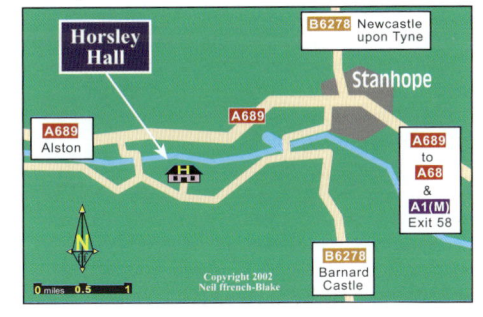

Headlam Hall Hotel & Restaurant

Headlam, Nr. Gainford, Darlington, Co Durham DL2 3HA
Tel: (01325) 730238; Fax: (01325) 730790
E-mail: admin@headlamhall.co.uk
Website: www.headlamhall.co.uk

This magnificent Jacobean manor house offers all that is best in country house accommodation. The Hall, built in the 17th century, has a rich history. The present owners, the Robinson family, took ownership in 1977 and have developed a super hotel, blending ancient and modern. There are 36 en suite individually furnished bedrooms, many with period furniture and some with four-posters. The restaurant is divided into four rooms, ranging from the elegance of the Victorian Room to the more modern warmth of the Patio Room. The Main Hall features an original carved oak fireplace and open staircase, and the Georgian drawing-room overlooks four acres of walled gardens featuring ancient beech hedges, colourful borders and a fishing lake. There is plenty at the hotel for the active guest - swimming, tennis and golf practice. Headlam is a good centre for touring Teesdale, Barnard Castle and Durham, and makes a wonderful spot for a leisure break.

Rates: Single room and breakfast from £75.00; double room inc. breakfast from £90.00.
Short Breaks: Min. 2 nights shared room, d, b & b pp per night Summer (May-Sept) fm £61; Winter (Oct-April) fm £57. Single room supplement +£15.

- 36 en suite bedrooms (inc 1 suite), all with d-dial telephone, colour TV+ satellite; hairdryer, laundry/valet service, tea/coffee making facilities, trouser press, radio/ alarm clock. ✂ & ♿ rms avail.
- Alc dinner; lunch & special diets avail. L.o. 2145
- Business services inc 4 meeting rooms to 100.
- Snooker, croquet, fishing, fitness centre, sauna, clay shooting, indoor swimming pool. Riding and golf 7 miles. Car parking for 80+.
- AMERICAN EXPRESS & major credit cards accepted.
- Open all year exc. Xmas Day.

Darlington 8, Bishop Auckland 9, Scotch Corner 10, Durham 19, London 246

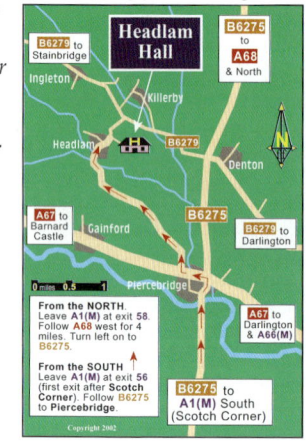

Seaham Hall Hotel & Oriental Spa

Lord Byron's Walk, Seaham,
Co Durham SR7 7AG
Tel: (0191) 516 1400; Fax: (0191) 516 1410
E-mail: reservations@seaham-hall.com
Website: www.seaham-hall.com

Occasionally a hotel opens which is magnificently different and steals the headlines. Seaham Hall is just such. Owners Tom and Jocelyn Maxfield and managing director Simon Rhatigan have invested enormous time and experience into developing Seaham Hall as a luxury hotel with a difference. Here is a hall which hosted Lord Byron's wedding in 1815 yet has been tastefully modernised to provide an unpretentious mix of 21st century design and technology with the high quality comfort and hospitality of a bygone age. Hospitality abounds - staff are professional, friendly and unstuffy and will welcome you personally to the hotel and show you to your suite. Each of these provides a pinnacle of comfort, style, panache, luxury and modern amenity - *'where internet meets intimate'* - in the words of the owners. The Oriental Spa has recently opened and is the first of its kind in Europe. Designed on *Feng Shui* principles, it aims to deliver state-of-the-art relaxation surrounded by original sculptures and works of art. Seaham is truly a first for the North-East!

Rates: *Suite room rate, inc. breakfast from £195; single occupancy £185 .*
Leisure Breaks*: Dinner inclusive rates are available at weekends throughout the year. Please call the hotel for details.*

● *19 suites, all with AC, direct dial telephone, colour TV+sat, hairdryer, laundry/valet service, minibar, 24-hour room/meal service, CD player, 100-channel music centre, radio /alarm clock, fax/ modem points, safe, ♿ & ⚡ rooms available.*
● *Tdh dinner £36; alc. lunch & special diets available; last orders 10 pm.*
● *4 meeting rms up to 120. Airport pickup.* P *100*
● *Fitness centre/gym, jacuzzi, sauna, massage, indoor pool in Spa opening mid-2002. Beauty salon.*
● *Visa, Diners & Mastercard accepted.* ● *Open all year*

Sunderland 5, Durham 11, Hartlepool 16, Newcastle 17, Scotch Corner 36, London 272.

Northumberland, Bamburgh

Waren House Hotel

Waren Mill, Belford, Northumberland
NE70 7EE
Tel: (01668) 214581; Fax: (01668) 214484
E-mail: enquiries@warenhousehotel.co.uk
Website: www.warenhousehotel.co.uk

Waren House is quite simply one of the best Country House hotels in the north-east. Set in six acres of gardens and woodland, it is a peaceful and tranquil centre from which to visit one of this country's most naturally beautiful and historic areas, largely unspoiled by tourism and commercialism. The castles of Bamburgh, Dunstanburgh, Alnwick and Warkworth are all easily accessible; there is a wealth of birdlife along miles of magnificent coastline, particularly at Budle Bay and Farne Islands and there is the Holy Island of Lindisfarne, the Cheviots and Scottish Borders near at hand. After a day out sightseeing, you can return to the quiet luxury of Waren House where owners Peter and Anita Laverack and their staff will pamper you. Bedrooms are decorated in various styles including Edwardian, Victorian, Oriental and French. The public areas are full of beautiful antiques and collectibles. In the evening, enjoy a gastronomic treat in the dining room and reflect on your good fortune. How many people speed by on the A1 without knowing the splendours that lie just off it both in this historic region in general and at Waren House in particular?

Rates: Single room and breakfast from £90; double room inc. breakfast from £120.
Bargain Breaks: 2 nights - 4-course dinner, room & breakfast from £152 per person standard room. For stay of 7+ nights, free upgrade standard➔ superior/superior➔ suite.

- 11 en suite bedrooms (inc 3 suites), all with direct dial telephone, colour TV; hairdryer, tea/coffee making facilities, trouser press.
- *Table d'hôte dinner £27.50; special diets available. Last orders 20.30.*
- *Business services inc meeting room to 20. Children over 14 welcome; dogs welcome by arrangement; conferences (boardroom) 20 max.*
- *Sea/river bathing, watersports. Tennis and golf two miles; riding five miles.* 15.
- & major credit cards accepted.
- Open all year;

Berwick 14, Alnwick 14, Newcastle 45, London 350.

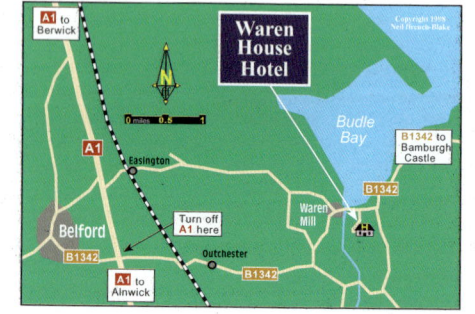

Matfen Hall Hotel & Golf Course

Matfen, Northumberland NE20 0RH.
Tel: (01661) 886500;
Fax: (01661) 886055
E-mail: info@matfenhall.co.uk
Website: www.matfenhall.co.uk
Winner: "Small Hotel of the Year" in the Excellence in England Award 2002.

Matfen Hall only became an hotel in 1999, yet is already regarded as one of the Northeast's most prestigious venues for golf and leisure breaks, conferences and weddings. Originally built in 1830, Sir Hugh and Lady Blackett have carefully restored the family seat set in beautiful Northumberland countryside with its own parkland landscape and 18-hole golf course. What impressed me was how well the Hall retains so much of its traditional style: the awe-inspiring Great Hall, elegant drawing room and impressive book-lined Library Restaurant retain the feeling of bygone luxury. They sit comfortably, however, with a modern reception area and Conservatory Bar, the latter overlooking the 18th green and providing an appetising all day menu. With Newcastle barely 20 minutes away and Northumberland's historic and coastal sites near at hand, Matfen offers a varied menu for that well-earned break.

Rates: Single room and breakfast from £97.50; double from £135. **Leisure Breaks:** two nts dinner, bed & breakfast £150 per pers + ex nts @£55 pp.

- 31 en suite bedrooms, all with d-d tel, colour TV+Sat, hairdryer, laundry service, tea/coffee making, 24-hr room service, trouser press, radio/alarm clock, fax/modem points. ✻ & ♿ rooms avail.
- The Library Restaurant ❀❀ tdh & alc, lunch & special diets available. Last orders 2130.
- Six meeting rooms, capacity to 120.
- Civil wedding licence. Car parking for 100.
- Golf. Fishing, riding, shooting, squash nearby.
- & all major credit cards accepted.
- Open all year.

Hexham 10, Newcastle 16, Carlisle 47, London 292.

North Yorkshire, Nr. Harrogate

The Sportsman's Arms Hotel & Restaurant

Wath in Nidderdale, Pateley Bridge, Harrogate, North Yorkshire HG3 5PP
Tel: (01423) 711306; Fax: (01423) 712524

The Sportsman's Arms Hotel and Restaurant nestles close to the river Nidd (on which it has fishing rights) at Wath in Nidderdale - a conservation village, and one of the most picturesque and unspoiled villages in a beautiful part of the Yorkshire Dales. Reached by a pack horse bridge and set in its own gardens, this attractive 17th century mellow sandstone building attracts you like a magnet. Once inside, the cosy lounges, log fires, bar and charming, softly lit restaurant exude warmth and this and the welcome and hospitality of owners Jane and Ray Carter will remain with you throughout your stay. The local reputation for the Sportsman's Arms is that it is a first class restaurant with bedrooms. However this is not fair to the bedrooms which are comfortable and tastefully decorated, retaining many original features. At the heart of the Sportsmans Arms, however, is the restaurant and the first class food and wine on offer. Working with the best fresh local game, fish and vegetables, the Sportsman's Arms provides a feast for its guests.

Rates: *Single occ. with breakfast from £50; double room with breakfast from £80.*
Leisure Breaks: *End Oct-end March Nidderdale Midweekers - 2 pers. sharing, min stay 2 nts, dinner, b & b £85 per person Sun-Thurs inclusive.*

- 12 en suite bedrooms (inc one suite), all with direct-dial telephone, colour TV; hairdryer, tea/coffee making facilities, 24-hour room service. ✹ & ♿ bedrooms available.
- A la carte dinner, lunch & special diets available; last orders 9 pm.
- Fishing, shooting. Car parking for 30 cars.
- Open all year (exc. Xmas Day).
- Visa, Mastercard, Switch cards accepted.

Harrogate 14, Skipton 20, Leeds 27, Leyburn 31, London 217.

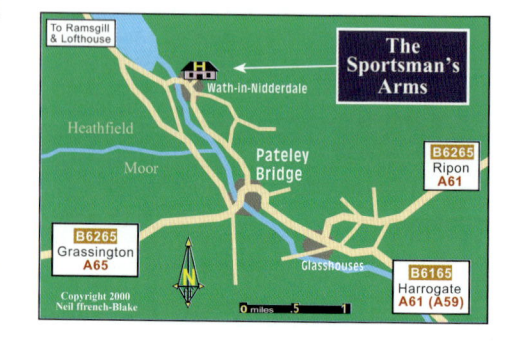

North Yorkshire, Harrogate   165

The Balmoral Hotel

Franklin Mount, Harrogate,
North Yorkshire HG1 5EJ
Tel: (01423) 508208; Fax: (01423) 530652
E-mail: info@balmoralhotel.co.uk
Website: www.balmoralhotel.co.uk

Jill Day and Julian Peck are continuing to develop the Balmoral's reputation as one of the best hotels in the elegant spa town of Harrogate. It is situated with its own on-site parking in award winning gardens away from the town centre and yet within walking distance of the conference centre, antique shops and art galleries of the town. The hotel has a good atmosphere, created by its impressive architecture, beautiful furnishings and antiques and the warmth of welcome provided by the hosts and their enthusiastic staff. Half of the 20 bedrooms have four-poster beds; the Windsor Suite on the ground floor offers accommodation of truly regal proportions for that special occasion but all rooms are comfortable and individual. The hotel's restaurant *Villa Toots*, provides excellent cuisine - another reason why the Balmoral is so popular with Signpost readers. It has been named as one of the Hotels of the Year 2002 by the *Which* Hotel Guide.

Rates: Single room with breakfast from £85, double with breakfast from £110.
Leisure Breaks: Short breaks from £55 per person per night , b & b. Celebration Champagne Breaks and Club & Spa Breaks - details on application.

- 21 en suite bedrooms (inc. 4 suites) all with direct dial telephone, colour TV, hairdryer, tea/coffee making, laundry service, radio/alarm, trouser press, 24-hr room/meal service.
- Tdh dinner £20; alc, lunch & special diets available; last orders 9.30 pm. Children welcome.
- Solarium, indoor pool and gym 1 mile; golf, tennis and riding nearby. Open all year. P 15.
- American Express, Mastercard, & Visa accepted.

Leeds/Bradford Airport 15, York 20, London 200.

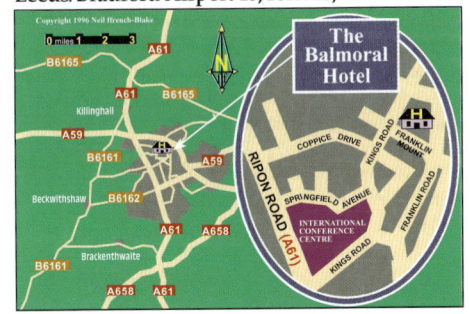

North Yorkshire, Hawes

Rookhurst Country House Hotel

West End, Gayle, Hawes,
North Yorkshire DL8 3RT
Tel: (01969) 667454; Fax: (01969) 667128
E-mail: rookhurst@lineone.net
Website: www.rookhurst.co.uk

Rates: Single/double/twin with breakfast from £90 per room.
Special Breaks: 2 nights or more Sun-Thurs, b & b from £80 per room per night. See our website.

- 5 en suite bedrooms, all with colour TV, hairdryer, minibar, tea/coffee making facilities, radio/alarm clock.
- Dinner from £20 per person. Parking for 5.
- Fishing, shooting, walking nearby.
- Visa, Mastercard, Delta accepted.
- Open all year.

Sedbergh 15, Leyburn 16, Kirkby Stephen 20, Kendal 26, Skipton 36, York 65, London 263.

To use an over-used, but in this case true, phrase, Richard and Judith Hynds welcome guests to share their home as well as their hotel. This superb country residence offers tranquillity, comfort and helpful, personal service. Judith conjures up appetising homemade specialities using fresh, local ingredients and Richard's wine knowledge and affability as a host will ensure that your stay will be a happy one. Set in its own attractive gardens with views over open countryside and the magnificent Wensleydale Fells, the hotel fronts the Pennine Way and is an ideal retreat for those who want to explore the delights of the Yorkshire Dales with their quaint market towns, wonderful walking and access to the famous Carlisle-Settle railway. After the exertions of the day, return to one of the five well-appointed bedrooms - I particularly liked the Attic Room (*pictured right*), accessed by a spiral wooden staircase. A visit to the hotel will certainly give you a Yorkshire break to remember.

North Yorkshire, Hawes 167

Simonstone Hall Country House Hotel

Hawes, North Yorkshire DL8 3LY
Tel: (01969) 667255; Fax: (01969) 667441
E-mail: hotel@simonstonehall.demon.co.uk
Website: simonstonehall.co.uk

This former hunting lodge of the Earls of Wharncliffe, where many leading political and social figures were entertained, has been beautifully restored to offer elegant accommodation, superb food, friendly service and hospitality. Set in magnificent countryside near the market town of Hawes in upper Wensleydale, it has spectacular views over the dale and surrounding fells. Seven of the individually designed bedrooms enjoy this panoramic view, whilst six have four poster beds. The elegant restaurant boasts a full à la carte menu with a wide range of wines, whilst the Game Tavern offers a varied choice of wholesome dishes. The comfortably furnished lounge, with its fine carved timber fireplace and great log fires in winter, is a peaceful haven for relaxation. Two further bedrooms and a new function room were added recently. The hotel is an excellent base from which to explore the beautiful scenery and many attractions of the Yorkshire Dales with their charming market towns, craft centres, castles and abbeys.

Rates: Single room with breakfast from £55. Double room including breakfast from £110.
Midweek Breaks: Prices on application.
● *20 en suite bedrooms, all colour TV, direct-dial telephone, hairdryer, tea/coffee making facilities; non-smoker bedrooms; dogs welcome some rooms.*
● *Two dining rooms; lunch & special diets available; last orders 8.30 pm.* 🅿 *30.* ● *Open all year.*
● *Licensed for civil weddings. Function room for 40 (conferences) or up to 70 (wedding receptions).*
● *Fishing, shooting. Major credit cards acc'd*
Leyburn 16, Kendal 26, Skipton 36, London 250

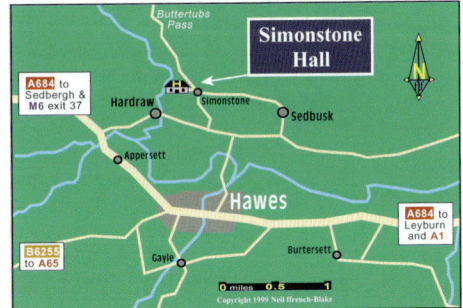

The Pheasant

Harome, Helmsley, N. Yorkshire YO62 5JG
Tel: (01439) 771241; Fax: (01439) 771744
AA★★★RAC

I have a very soft spot for The Pheasant - it was the first hotel I inspected for Signpost and it helped me to set a benchmark for others. Set in a delightful village, overlooking the village pond and millstream, it has been imaginatively created by the Binks family from a group of buildings on two sides of a courtyard. Inside the cosy oak beamed bar with log fire, the large tastefully decorated drawing room, and the cheerful orangery dining area combine to lend an air of warmth and comfort. Old fashioned in atmosphere the hotel might be, but the best of all modern amenities are also there. The hotel has a justifiably high reputation for food prepared by Mrs 'Tricia Binks using many ingredients from the hotel's own large garden and paddock. All the bedrooms and suites are brightly decorated in cottage style and face either the village pond or the courtyard and walled garden. There is also a charming 16th century cottage available 400 yards away in the village, with double bedroom and sitting room, serviced by the hotel staff with meals taken in the hotel. The Pheasant is a peaceful haven and an ideal base from which to explore this most beautiful part of Yorkshire, where there is so much to see and do.

Rates: Dinner, room and breakfast from £65 (1st Nov-mid-May); £67-£72 (high season) per person per day including VAT.

- 14 en suite bedrooms (1 ground floor), all with telephone, colour TV, tea/coffee making facilities; full central heating.
- *Last orders 8.00 p.m; bar meals (lunch); diets.*
- Children over 14 welcome; dogs by arrangement; conferences max. 12.
- <u>Own heated indoor swimming pool</u>; golf, tennis, riding, fishing all nearby.
- *Closed December, January and February.*
- & major credit cards accepted.

Helmsley 3, York 22, Scarborough 28, Leeds 48, Edinburgh 160, London 220.

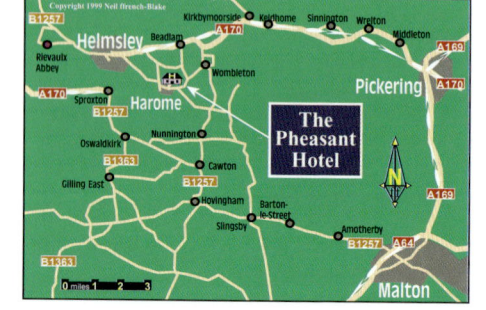

Lastingham Grange

Lastingham. Nr. Kirkbymoorside, York
YO62 6TH
Tel: (01751) 417345; Fax: (01751) 417358
E-mail: reservations@lastinghamgrange.com
Website: www.lastinghamgrange.com

Unique and incomparable was how one guest described this super hotel to me whilst on one of her numerous return stays. And it is easy to see why guests return time and again to this charming hotel situated on the edge of the Moors in the historic village of Lastingham, a peaceful backwater in the heart of the North Yorkshire Moors National Park. The old, stone-walled country house, built around a courtyard and set within 10 acres of attractive gardens, is owned and personally run by Mr. and Mrs. Dennis Wood. Their charming friendliness and hospitality sets the mood for all guests to feel at ease in this elegant and tasteful country home. The atmosphere is unhurried and peaceful, the south facing terrace providing a tranquil setting in which to relax and enjoy the beautiful rose garden. The welcoming hall, the spacious lounge with its open fire, the comfortable bedrooms with their impressive views, the excellent food, the attention to detail and the location make the Grange a perfect spot for a restful break.

Rates: Room and breakfast from £92.00 single; £175.00 double.
Leisure breaks: 2 nights or more, dinner, b & b, 2 sharing £215 per room per night. Also see website.

- 12 en suite bedrooms, all with bath and shower; direct-dial telephone, colour TV & radio, baby listening, trouser press, hairdryer, tea/coffee making.
- Table d'hôte dinner £33.75; lunch & special diets available; last orders 8.30 pm.
- Children welcome; adventure playground, drying room.
- Golf five miles; riding four miles.
- Open March to the beginning of December.
- AMERICAN EXPRESS & major credit cards accepted.

Malton 15, Scarborough 24, Thirsk 24, Whitby 26, York 33, London 232.

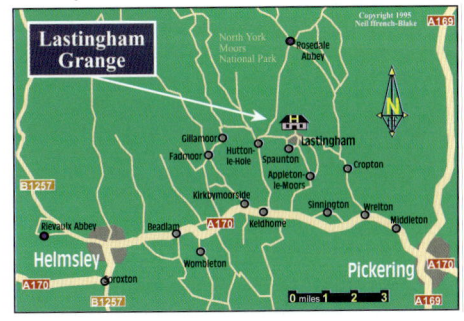

North Yorkshire, Monk Fryston/Pickering

Monk Fryston Hall Hotel

Monk Fryston, North Yorkshire
LS25 5DU
Tel: (01977) 682369;
Fax: (01977) 683544
E-mail: reception@monkfryston-hotel.com
Website: www.monkfryston-hotel.com

Frances Hodgson Burnett stayed at Monk Fryston several times and there is evidence that her *Secret Garden* was indeed that of the Hall. Today the 30-acre ornate garden, redesigned by Frances, Duchess of Rutland, includes a sunken paved patio, a lake and the early 20th century Lucerne Bridge, leading to the woodland park. It is populated by all sorts of wildlife! The hall dates back to 1500 and has a rich and colourful history. Cuisine is traditional English with a Mediterranean flavour. My dinner started with smoked haddock and welsh rarebit terrine followed by a chargrilled breast of chicken with a fresh asparagus and balsamic syrup. I awoke to look out onto a cherry blossom tree. The Hall is well placed for Leeds and York and provides a quiet, comfortable venue for a wedding or weekend break.

Rates: Single room with breakfast from £88; Double room including breakfast from £109.
Breaks: Min. 2-night stay, Mon-Thurs, dinner, b & b at £72.50 pppn sharing ; weekends £70 pppn.
- 30 en suite bedrooms (inc. 2 4-posters), all with col TV+sat, direct-dial telephone, tea/coffee making, hairdryer, laundry service, radio/alarm, fax/modem points, trouser press. ♿ rooms available.
- Last orders 2130; lunch & spec diets available.
- 3 meeting rms 50/16/14. 🅿 100. Open all year.
- Croquet, jogging. Golf, tennis, riding, pool nearby.
- & all major credit cards accepted.

A1 2m, Selby 8, Leeds 13, York 20, Hull 42, London 190

The White Swan Hotel & Restaurant

Market Place, Pickering, Ryedale, North Yorkshire YO18 7AA. Tel: (01751) 472288;
Fax: (01751) 475554
E-mail: welcome@white-swan.co.uk
Website: www.white-swan.co.uk

It is no surprise that this former 16th-century coaching inn was voted Hotel of the Year by the Yorkshire Tourist Board in 2000 and runner-up in 2001, for it is due to its consistently high standards that this charming hotel has a first class reputation. Owned and run by two generations of the Buchanan family since 1983, it has recently been refurbished throughout, whilst maintaining its original charm and character. The restaurant is very popular with locals, indicating how consistently good the food is, both lunchtime and evening menus offering a good choice of fresh food, complemented by an impressive wine list. Set in the middle of Pickering, this super small hotel offers good value for money and is well placed to explore this lovely part of Yorkshire.

Rates: Single room with breakfast from £60; Double room with breakfast from £90.
Leisure Breaks: 'Phone or see website for details of mid-week breaks, winter warmers & Jan 'sale'.
- 12 en suite bedrooms, all with colour TV, direct-dial telephone, tea/coffee making, hairdryer, laundry service, radio/alarm, trouser press, fax/modem.
- Alc dinner; lunch & diets avail; last orders 9pm
- 2 mtg rms 25 ea. 🅿 35. Barber/beauty salon nearby.
- Golf, fishing, riding, sailing, tennis, shooting nearby.
- Visa & Mastercard accepted.

Malton 8, Helmsley 13, Scarborough 16, Whitby 20, York 25, Bridlington 31, London 213.

North Yorkshire, Scarborough

The Royal Hotel Scarborough

St Nicholas Street, Scarborough
North Yorkshire YO11 2HE
Tel: (01723) 364333; Fax: (01723) 500618
E-Mail: royalhotel@englishrosehotels.co.uk
Website: www.englishrosehotels.co.uk

The famous historic Royal Hotel, built at the peak of Regency elegance in the 1830s, has always been a centre piece of Scarborough, one of England's earliest resort towns. Regular visitors have included Sir Winston Churchill and Charles Laughton. It is now being refurbished by English Rose Hotels and will be fully restored to its former glory by 2003. The ground floor is already complete with the magnificent staircase in the entrance hall an inspiring sight that sets the mood of eager anticipation for the remaining restoration. Bedrooms are being refurbished to the highest standard and guests will be able to enjoy individually designed rooms which will be a subtle blend of traditional style with modern features. The health, leisure and beauty centre has been updated to provide state-of the-art facilities for guests young and old. Located in the heart of Scarborough, the hotel is within easy reach of all the town's attractions. The town makes a good base for visiting Castle Howard, Whitby, York and other local attractions.

Rates: Single room with breakfast from £55; double inc. breakfast from £110.

● *134 en suite bedrooms (inc 20 family rooms & 7 suites) all with TV+ satellite, direct-dial telephone, hairdryer, laundry service, radio/alarm clock, tea/coffee making, trouser press;* ♿ *rooms available.*
● *Restaurant table d'hôte £22.50. Cafe Bliss - new continental-style coffee shop. A la carte, lunch & special diets available; last orders 9.30 pm*
● *Indoor pool, fitness centre/gym, sauna, steam room, solarium.*
● *Full business services inc. conference/banqueting rooms to 400.*
● *& all major credit cards accepted.*
● *Open all year.*

Pickering 16, Whitby 18, Driffield 21, Malton 24, York 40, London 213.

Wrea Head Country House Hotel

Barmoor Lane, Scalby, Scarborough
North Yorkshire YO13 0PB
Tel: (01723) 378211; Fax: (01723) 355936
E-mail: wreahead@englishrosehotels.co.uk
Website: www.englishrosehotels.co.uk

This elegant Victorian country house, built in 1881, stands prominently in 14 acres of wooded and landscaped grounds and gardens on the edge of the famous North Yorkshire Moors National Park. The mood for the hotel is set immediately on entry via the superb oak panelled hall and its inglenook fireplace, antiques and paintings making it apparent that this is a quiet, elegant retreat with character and charm. The newly refurbished library, the cosy corners, the conservatory and the terrace with its panoramic views of the gardens, urge you to relax and let the troubles of the world pass you by. Or, if you wish to be more active, take advantage of the hotel's ideal location for exploring 'Heartbeat' country or the distinctive Yorkshire heritage coastline with its fascinating resorts like Robin Hood's Bay, Whitby and of course Scarborough, famed for its beaches, cricket, music and theatre. And on your return to the hotel, relax again with an apéritif before dinner in the Four Seasons restaurant.

Rates: Single room with breakfast from £60.00; double inc. breakfast from £120.00
Leisure Breaks: 2 nights dinner b & b from £65 per person per night, based on 2 sharing.

- 20 en suite bedrooms all with TV, direct-dial telephone, hairdryer, laundry service, radio/alarm clock, tea/coffee making facilities, trouser press.
- Table d'hôte dinner £24.95. A la carte, lunch & special diets available; last orders 9.15 pm.
- 2 meeting rooms for up to 60. Car parking for 100.
- Indoor swimming pool, golf one mile.
- AMERICAN EXPRESS & all major credit cards accepted.
- Open all year

Scarborough
2½, **Whitby**
17, **Pickering**
18, **York** 36,
London 216.

The Coniston Hotel

Coniston Cold, Skipton,
North Yorkshire BD23 4EB
Tel: (01756) 748080; Fax: (01756) 749487
E-mail: info@theconistonhotel.com
Website: www.theconistonhotel.com

Warmth of welcome and helpfulness of staff are among the many things you will remember about your stay at this award winning hotel. Located just outside the small village of Coniston Cold in the Yorkshire Dales, the hotel was designed to provide reasonable cost, high standard accommodation within the Coniston Hall Estate. This has 1200 acres of undulating countryside around a 24-acre lake and has facilities for leisure and business guest alike. The proprerty is run by the Bannister family and it is their active involvement and determination to apply high standards that sets the tone. There are three dining areas -Macleod's Bar , Winston's Bistro and Oliver's Restaurant. The converted 17th century barn, which is *Winston's Bistro* has been awarded an AA and provides Yorkshire fare with international influences as well as the estate's own seasonal game and fish. Private dining or meeting is catered for in the Cygnet, Bewick or Swan rooms. Coniston is an excellent spot for a private sporting party, a celebration or for business entertaining.

Rates: *Single room with breakfast from £76.00; double inc. breakfast from £87.00*
Leisure Breaks: *Dinner, bed & breakfast, min. 2-night stay £60 per person per night sharing rm.*

● 40 en suite bedrooms all with TV + satellite, direct-dial telephone, hairdryer, laundry service, tea/coffee making, 24-hr room serv, fax/modem points, trouser press. ✄ & ♿ rooms available.
● Tdh dinner £21.50. A la carte, lunch & special diets available; last orders 9.30 pm.
● 4 meeting rooms, 10-55 people. ᴾ 120. Open all year
● Fishing, shooting, archery, off road driving, hovercraft, horse driving, mountain biking.
● & all major credit cards accepted.

Skipton 7, Settle 7, Burnley 22, Harrogate 28, Leeds 33, York 45, London 224.

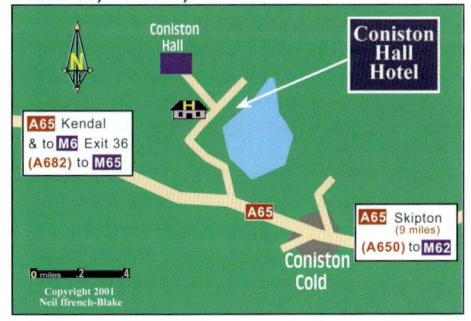

North Yorkshire, Skipton

Crab Manor Hotel

Asenby, Thirsk, North Yorkshire
YO7 3QL
Tel: (01845) 577286; Fax: (01845) 577109
E-mail: reservations@crabandlobster.co.uk
Website: www.crabandlobster.com

Crab Manor was recommended to me as "sumptuously different - a unique experience" and I can think of no better way of describing this very popular and successful hotel. General manager Mark Spenceley and staff provide not only a friendly welcome but a stay you are unlikely to forget. Each of the 11 individually decorated bedrooms allows you to sample the luxury of some of the world's most famous hotels. The list is impressive - *The Waldorf Astoria, Raffles,* the *Cipriani, Turnberry, Sharrow Bay, Sandy Lane Bardados* are just some of the luxurious styles in the superb Georgian Manor House; three further rooms are in the authentic tropical beach house annexe. Despite all the luxuries, good food remains at the heart of Crab Manor's reputation. Fine dining is available in the Manor Room restaurant or less formally but equally deliciously in the famous Crab and Lobster, which is in the hotel's grounds. Ideally located for visiting the Yorkshire Dales and Moors, Harrogate and York, Crab Manor offers an experience not to be missed.

Rates: Single room with breakfast from £110 weekends:double inc. breakfast from £130.00
Gourmet Dinner Breaks: 5-cse gourmet dinner + b & b for 2 people sharing £170 per night per rm.

- 11 en suite bedrooms all with TV + satellite, direct-dial telephone, hairdryer, laundry service, tea/coffee making facilities.
- Dinner from £15.50 à la carte; last orders 9.15 pm.
- 2 meeting rooms, 12 & 24 pax. Large P
- Airport pickup by arrangement.
- Golf, jacuzzi, sauna/solarium on premises.
- & all major credit cards accepted.
- Open all year

Thirsk 5,
Ripon 5,
Whitby 17,
York 24,
Leeds 37,
London 222.

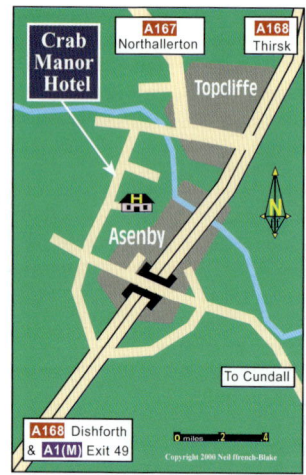

North Yorkshire, Whitby

Dunsley Hall Country House Hotel

Dunsley, Whitby, North Yorkshire
YO21 3TL
Tel: (01947) 893437; Fax: (01947) 893505
E-mail: reception@dunsleyhall.com
Website: www.dunsleyhall.com

This fine country house was converted into an hotel in 1987 and has evolved into a haven for visitors from all over the world. It offers traditional comfort and excellent food along with period charm and peaceful serenity, blended with modern elegance and leisure facilities. There are 18 en-suite bedrooms, all individually furnished, two with four-poster beds and two with private sitting areas. The public rooms contain a wealth of historic features, with original oak panelling, stained glass windows, fascinating fireplaces and other period gems. The hotel is within brisk walking distance of the Heritage Coast and is well located for exploring the North Yorkshire National Park, the seafaring towns of Whitby and Scarborough, historic York, Castle Howard and TV's *Heartbeat* country. After a day's exploration, relax in one of the elegant restaurants. In the Visitors's Book when I stayed, I noticed the following comment: *"Of the 50 hotels visited this year, this was by far the best!"*

Rates: Single room with breakfast from £69.85; double inc. breakfast from £109.70 inc. VAT.
Leisure Breaks: Weekend breaks from £145 pp, dinner b & b.

- 18 en suite bedrooms all with TV, direct-dial telephone, hairdryer, laundry service, radio/alarm clock, tea/coffee making facilities, safety deposit box, trouser press.
- A la carte dinner, lunch & special diets available; last orders 9.30 pm.
- 2 meeting rooms for up to 100. P 40
- Croquet, fitness centre, sauna/solarium, indoor pool, tennis at hotel. Fishing, golf, bathing, sailing, riding all within 3 miles. ● Open all year.
- American Express, Mastercard, Visa Switch accepted

Whitby 3, Scarborough 22, Middlesbrough 27, Pickering 23, York 49, London 235

Middlethorpe Hall

Bishopthorpe Road, York, North
Yorkshire YO23 2GB
Tel: (01904) 641241; Fax: (01904) 620176

E-mail: info@middlethorpe.com
Website: www.middlethorpe.com

A William & Mary country house built in 1699 and once the home of the famous diarist Lady Mary Wortley Montagu, Middlethorpe is one of the finest hotels of the Northeast. It has been immaculately restored to its original elegance and style by Historic House Hotels - the decor, furnishings, antiques and pictures consistent with the period of the house and providing luxury that it would be difficult to surpass. It is set in 20 acres of its own mature gardens and parkland. Guests can enjoy the pleasures of a walled garden, the white garden, a small lake, some magnificent trees and the original ha-has. The classically panelled dining room overlooks the gardens and the food - justifiably of AA ❀❀❀ standard - offers traditional excellence in contemporary English cooking with a good selection of wines. In keeping with the rest of the hotel, bedrooms are beautifully designed. Facing the hall a subtly extended pair of Edwardian cottages hides a Health & Fitness Spa. The Hall is an obvious choice for racegoers and the historic City of York is two miles distant.

Rates: Single room with breakfast from £129.50; double from £194.00.
Leisure Breaks: November-March Champagne Break from £125 pppn min. 2 nights, 2 sharing. July-Aug Summer Break fm £125 pppn min 2 nts.

- 30 en suite bedrooms (inc 7 suites) with TV, direct-dial telephone, hairdryer, laundry service, trouser press. ● Open all year.
- Table d'hôte dinner £36-45; à la carte, lunch & special diets available. Last orders 9.45 pm
- 2 meeting rooms, cap'y 56; 🅿75. Airport pickup
- Croquet, fishing, fitness centre/gym, jacuzzi, jogging track, massage, sauna, indoor swimming pool, beauty salon, gardens. Golf & riding 5 miles.
- Children over 8 years welcome. Sorry, no dogs.
- Visa, Mastercard & Switch accepted.

York 2, Leeds 22, Manchester 70, Edinburgh 194, London 207.

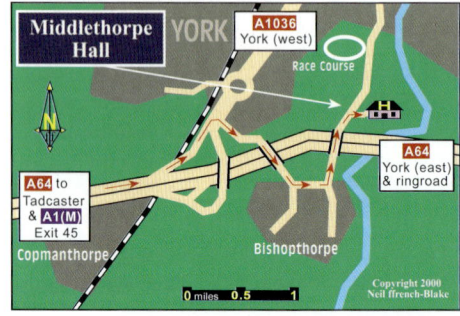

North Yorkshire, Nr. York

The Parsonage Country House Hotel

Escrick, York, North Yorkshire YO19 6LF
Tel: (01904) 728111;
Fax: (01904) 728151
E-mail: reservations@parsonagehotel.co.uk
Website: www.parsonagehotel.co.uk

The Escrick Estate dates back to Viking times, with the Lascelles family owning it in the Middle Ages. The building then became a rectory and today has a relaxed yet stylish country house ambience. Set in 6 acres of landscaped gardens and woodland, it provides a peaceful haven only four miles from the historic city of York. Its 46 comfortable, individually designed bedrooms are either in the main house, the Coach House or the Cottage. This year a further block of rooms was added at the back of the hotel. The hotel's homely drawing room is warmed by log fires in winter and the spacious conservatory is a friendly place to relax with afternoon tea or with a light snack. The AA ●● Lascelles Restaurant has gained a well deserved local reputation for imaginative cooking and well presented dishes. The hotel also has a civil wedding licence and can host receptions and meetings.

Rates: Single room with breakfast from £75; Double room including breakfast from £95.
Leisure Breaks: Jan/Feb 2003 & July/Aug mid-week 2-nights dinner, b & b £110 per pers sharing Weekend breaks thr't year £140 per rm d,b&b 2 nts

- 46 en suite bedrooms (inc. 1 suite), all with colour TV, direct-dial telephone, tea/coffee making, hairdryer, laundry service, trouser press. 24-hr room serv, fax/modem points. ✄ & ♿ rooms avail.
- Alc dinner; lunch & diets avail; last orders 2115
- 4 meeting rooms - 150 max. ₽100
- Solarium. Golf, tennis, riding nearby.
- [AMERICAN EXPRESS] & all major credit cards accepted.
- Open all year.

York 4, Selby 9, Kingston-upon-Hull 43, Leeds 31, London 199.

Signpost Guide 2003
Wales

Fact File
Illustrated Guide to HistoricHouses, Gardens & Sites
Diary of Events

Hotels in	PAGE
Aberconwy & Colwyn	183
Carmarthenshire	186
Gwynedd	188
Monmouthshire	194
Pembrokeshire	197
Powys	199

Wales

Llynnau Cregennen

Mid Wales is a land of dramatic contrasts in which you can enjoy the considerable pleasures of both coast and countryside. It is an area of immense natural beauty with a wide variety of scenery, each season bringing its own particular enhancement. With well over half the Snowdonia National Park lying in Mid Wales, some of the beauty is unsurpassed. The region has high mountains with breathtaking views, large attractive lakes and rambling green hills.

There is no more relaxing way of enjoying nature's wonders than on horseback. Both the regular rider and novice will find superb pony trekking country. An alternative means of seeing the countryside is by taking a ride on one of the Great Little Trains. When various industries began to develop in Mid Wales, a need for transport arose. This demand was met by a network of small railways. There are five such narrow gauge railways, most of them dating back to the last century, operating in the region - now making Mid Wales a must for all steam enthusiasts. Throughout Mid Wales a network of well surfaced roads lead towards remote uplands, winding along the contours of the slopes. These are the Cambrian 'mountains, Wales' magnificent backbone, the upland region where hamlets and farms nestle into the folds of seemingly endless hills. In this area farming life is centred around a series of small towns which often stand at an important crossroads or a ford in the river. They are linked by splendidly scenic mountain roads or old drovers' ways along which cattle were once driven to market. Llanidoes, with its 16th century market hall built of stout timber, stands almost at the centre of Wales, and at the confluence of the Severn and Clywedog Rivers.

In Mid Wales life inland revolves around the historic market towns and the old spa centres, while the coastline is punctuated by small fishing villages and popular seaside resorts. The western districts are strongholds of Welsh culture where the language is in everyday use.

The west of the region has over a hundred miles of coastline. Expansive, sandy beaches, spectacular estuaries and rugged cliffs leading down to secluded coves make this an ideal area for a holiday. It is not surprising to discover that Mid Wales has always had a seafaring tradition. In bygone days schooners sailed all over the world from the little ports of Aberaeron, Aberdyfi, Aberystwyth, Barmouth and New Quay.

Ffestiniog Railway

The harbours are still bustling and active but with a different type of craft.

To the East are the Welsh Marches with their traditional half-timbered black and white buildings. Despite being so close to England, the borderlands of Powys maintain much of their Welsh character and tradition. Many centuries ago this area was governed by the Marcher Lords on behalf of the king. Further back in time, Offa, an 8th century Saxon king, built a massive dyke to keep marauding Welsh forces out of his kingdom. Traces of these large earthworks can be seen along the border, forming the basis of the Offa's Dyke Trail, a long distance walkway of 168 miles. At Knighton a special Heritage Centre illustrates the significance of the Dyke.

The whole of Mid Wales has a colourful and exciting history and this is reflected in the many ancient buildings and other monuments which are to be seen. The struggle to keep Wales independent from the influence of numerous invaders has been a constant theme throughout history. This is evident in ruined castles such as Harlech Castle and Castell-y-Bere. Powys Castle, the home of "Clive of India" is on the other hand beautifully maintained, together with its outstanding gardens. Other popular attractions are the industries which reflect the Welsh rural life. These small industries such as woollen weaving in traditional patterns, pottery, and craft work, reflect a harmonious bond between people and environment which is typical of Mid Wales.

For those wishing to learn more of the area's history there are a number of museums and interpretative centres in the region. Historical artifacts can be seen at displays in Llandrindod Wells, Llanidoes, Machynlleth, Aberystwyth, Tre'r Ddol, Newtown and Welshpool. At Llandrindod Wells a display on the *Spas of Wales* has been opened. There is also an opportunity to "take the water" in the original Pump Room, refurbished in the Edwardian style.

Wales

North Wales has been attracting holiday visitors for over two hundred years, - Wordsworth, Samuel Johnson, Turner, Nelson, George Burrows, Bismarck and Wellington have all come to the area. Nowadays we still attract artists, poets, politicians and sailors but the range of accommodation and attractions make North Wales a perfect venue, whatever your choice of holiday.

Our hotels, restaurants and inns are continually improving their standards and now compare with the best in Britain; added to this we have the unfair advantage of some of the most impressive scenery in the world. Snowdonia is justly famous for its magnificent mountains, lakes and forests, but the Hiraethog Mountains in the North East, the Berwyns, south of Llangollen and the beautiful river valleys of the Conwy, Clwyd, Dee and Glaslyn have a magic of their own. The variety of the scenery is what impresses first time visitors. Within six miles of Llandudno - our largest resort - you can find the peace of the Carneddau, one hundred square miles of beautiful mountain moorland, dotted with Neolithic trackways, standing stones, bronze age sites and beautiful lakes, without a single road crossing it (except the old Roman road from Caerhun to Carnarfon).

The past surrounds you in North Wales. You can trace the history of man in these parts from the Neolithic tombs of 6,000 years ago, to the Iron Age hill forts that were inhabited when the Roman legions came, then through the cells and abbeys of the early Celtic church to the Nonconformist chapels of the 19th century so admired by Sir John Betjeman.

The 12th century Welsh castles and 13th century castles of the Plantagenets reflect a more turbulent time, but what masterpieces of military architecture they left us - Conwy, Carnarfon, Rhuddlan, and Beaumaris are breathtaking in their size and splendour, while the Welsh keeps of Dolwyddelan, Dinas Bran and Dolbadarn will appeal to more romantic souls. Medieval towns such as Conwy and Ruthin, the splendid Elizabethan and Jacobean farmhouses and the tiny country cottages show the ordinary side of life in the 16th, 17th and 18th centuries. The Industrial Revolution brought changes to North Wales, most of which are now featured in our tourist trade. Slate was the major industry; now you can explore the slate caverns at Blaenau Ffestiniog or Glyn Ceiriog or see the Quarry Museum at Llanberis. Most of the Great Little Trains of Wales were first used to carry slate from the mines to the harbours, the one notable exception being the Snowdon Mountain Railway.

As soon as you cross the border into Wales, the look of the countryside changes, the road signs seem unpronounceable and you are met by warm hospitable people. The language, music and heritage of Wales add a special dimension to a holiday in our wonderful country. *Croeso* is the word for Welcome - you will hear it often.

Cardiff, Wales' capital is essentially a young city, even 'though its history dates back many centuries. The development of its docks during the Industrial Revolution for the export of Welsh iron and coal was the basis of its prosperity. Cardiff Castle is part Roman fort, part medieval castle and part 19th-century mansion. Its Chaucer Room has stained glass windows depicting The Canterbury Tales. Its Summer Smoking Room has a copper, brass and silver inlaid floor. The castle is the present home of the Welsh Assembly. The National Museum of Wales houses a wealth of exhibits, from impressionist paintings to examples of Swansea porcelain. To the East, near Newport is Caerleon, which was the site of the Roman fortress of Isca, built in AD75. Further East, on the Monmouth-Chepstow road is Tintern Abbey, one of the finest relics of Britain's monastic age. It was founded in the 12th century by Cistercian monks, rebuilt in the 13th-century and sacked by Henry VIII during the Dissolution of the Monasteries. Offa's Dyke, part of an 168-mile rampart built by King Offa of Mercia in the 8th century to keep the Welsh out, and now a noted walk, runs past Tintern's portals. To the northwest of Cardiff is the late 19th-century Castell Coch (Red Castle), a mixture of Victorian Gothic and fairytale styles. Well preserved is 13th-century Caerphilly Castle, with its famous leaning tower.

Further West, outside Port Talbot, the visitor comes to Margam Country Park, 850 acres including an Iron Age hill fort, a restored abbey church with windows by William Morris, Margram Stones Museum with stones and crosses dating from the 5th-11th centuries and the main house with its 327-ft long orangery.

Threecliff Bay

The Gower Peninsula, west of Swansea is a secluded world of its own, with limestone cliffs, remote bays and miles of golden sands. It is the 'Riviera' of South Wales. Sites not to miss here include the late 13th-century Weobley Castle, the ruins of Threecliff Bay and Gower Farm Museum with its 100-yr old farm memorabilia. Near Carmarthen is Dylan Thomas' village of Laugharne, in whose churchyard he is buried. The rugged Pembroke coast is guarded on its Western rim by Britain's smallest city - St David's, whose cathedral was founded by the eponymous saint in the 8th century, although the present building is believed to date from the 12th century.

WALES

Historic Houses, Gardens & Parks

Aberconwy & Colwyn
Chirk Castle, Bodelwyddan
Bodrhyddan Hall, Rhuddlan
Bodnant Garden, Tal-y-Cafn
Colwyn Leisure Centre

Anglesey
Plas Newydd, Llanfairpwll

Glamorgan
Castell Cochi, Tongwynlais, Cardiff
Cosmeston Lakes Country Park & Medieval Village
Dyffryn House & Gardens, St. Nicholas, Nr. Cardiff Llanerch Vineyard, Pendoylan

Gwynedd
Bryn Bras Castle, Llanrug, Nr. Llanberis
Parc Glynllifon, Nr. Caernarfon
'Y Stablau', Gwydyr Forest Park, Llanrwst

Monmouthshire
Bryn Bach Park, Tredegar
Caldicot Castle & Country Park, Nr. Newport
Llandegfedd Reservolr, Pontypool
Tredegar House, Newport

Neath & Port Talbot
Margam Park, Port Talbot

Pembrokeshire
Manor House Wildlife & Leisure Park, Tenby
Tudor Merchant's House, Quay Hill, Tenby

Wrexham
Erddig Hall, Wrexham

Walks & Nature Trails

Aberconwy & Colwyn
Llyn Brenig Visitor Centre, Corwen

Anglesey
Bryntirion Open Farm, Dwyran
South Stack Cliffs Reserve & Elfins Tower Information Centre,Holyhead

Blaenau Gwent
Festival Park, Ebbw Vale

Carmarthenshire
Gelli Aur Countly Park, Llandeilo

Flintshire
Greenfield Valley Heritage Park, Holywell
Logger Heads Country Park, Nr Mold

Gwynedd
Coed-y-Brenin Forest Park & Visitor Centre, Ganllwyd, Dolgellau
The Greenwood Centre, Port Dinorwic

Parc Padarn, Llanberis
Tyn Llan Crafts & Farm Museum, Nr. Porthmadog

Merthyr Tydfil
Garwnant Visitor Centre, Cwm Taf

Neath & Port Talbot
Alan Forest Park & Countryside Centre, Port Talbot
Gnoll Country Park, Neath

Pembrokeshire
Bwlch Nant Yr Arian Forest Visitor Centre, Ponterwyd
Llysyfran Reservoir & Country Park, Nr. Haverfordwest
Pembrey Country Park, Pembrey

Powys
Brecon Beacons Mountain Centre, Nr. Libanus
Gigrin Farm & Nature Trail, Rhyader
Lake Vyrnwy RSPB Reserve & Information Centre
Ynys-Hir Reserve & Visitor Cenne, Machynlleth

Vale of Glamorgan
Bryngarw Country Park, Nr. Bridgend

Wrexham
Ty Mawr Country Park, Cefn Mawr

Historical Sites & Museums

Aberconwy & Colwyn
Bodelwyddan Castle
Carreg Cennen Castle, Trapp, Llangollen
Denbigh Castle
Valle Crucis Abbey, Llangollen

Cardiganshire
Museum of the Welsh Woollen Industry, Llandysul

Carmarthenshire
Castell Henllys Iron Age Hillfort, Crymych

Flintshire
Flint Castle & Twon Walls
Rhuddlan Castle, Nr. Rhyl

Glamorgan
Aberdulair Falls, Vale of Neath, Neath
Caerphilly Castle
Cardiff Castle
Castell Coch, Cardiff
Cefn Coed Colliery Museum, Crynant, Neath
National Museum of Wales
Welsh Folk Museum,Cardiff

Gwynedd
Beaumaris Castle
Caernarfon Castle
Conwy Castle

Cymer Abbey, Dc'gellau
Dolbadarn Castle, Llanberis
Dolwyddelan Castle
Harlech Castle
Llanfair Slate Caverns, Nr. Harlech
The Lloyd George Museum, Llanystumdwy, Criccieth
Penrhyn Castle, Bangor

Monmouthshire
Chepstow Castle, Chepstow
The Nelson Museum & Local History Centre
Penhow Castle, Nr. Newport
Raglan Castle
Tintern Abbey, Tintern

Pembrokeshire
Castle Museum & Art Gallery, Haverfordwest
Kidwelly Castle
Manorbier Castle, Nr. Tenby
Milford Haven Museum, The Docks, Milford Haven
Picton Castle, Haverfordwest
Pembroke Castle
St Davids Bishop's Palace

Powys
Powys Castle & Museum, Welshpool
Tretower Court & Castle, Crickhowell

Entertainment Venues

Aberconwy & Colwyn
Felin Isaf Water Mill, GlanConwy
Llyn Brenig Visitor Centre, Cerrigydrudion

Anglesey
Anglesey Bird World, Dwyran/ Sea Zoo, Brynsiencyn

Cardiganshire
James Pringle Weavers of Llanfair P.G.
The Llywenog Silver-Lead Mines, Nr Aberystwyth

Flintshire
Afonwen Craft & Antique Centre, Nr. Mold

Gwynedd
Alice in Wonderland Visitor Centre, Llandudno
Butlins Starcoast World, Pwllheli
Ffestiniog Railway, Porthmadog
Maes Artro Tourist Village
Llanbedr Penmachno Woollen Mill, Nr. Betws-y-Coed
Portmeirion Village, Nr. Porthmadog
Sygun Copper Mine, Beddgelert
Snowdon Mountain Railway, Llamberis
Trefriw Woollen Mills, Trefriw
Welsh Gold, Dolgellau
Welsh Highland Railway, Porthmadog

Wales

Neath & Port Talbot
Margam Park, Port Talbot
Penscynor Wildlife Park, Cilfrew, Nr. Neath

Pembrokeshire
Oakwood Park Theme Park, Narberth

Powys
Dan-yr-Ogof Showcaves, Abercraf
Welshpool & Llanfair Light Railway
Welsh Whisky Visitor Centre, Brecon

Rhondda Cynnon Taf
Rhondda Heritage Park

Dolbadarn Castle

DIARY OF EVENTS

February

2-3*. **Swansea Antiques Fair,** Brangwyn Hall, Swansea.
22. **RFU Wales v England.** Millennium Stadium, Cardiff

March

2. **Football: Worthington Cup Final.** Millenium Statdium.
22. **RFU 6 Nations. Wales v Ireland.** Millennium Stadium.
29. **RFU Six Nations. Wales v France.** Millenium Statdium.

May

17. **Football. FA Cup Final.** Millenium Stadium, Cardiff
7 & 26. **Racing at Chepstow.**
10-12*. **Llangollen International Jazz Festival.** Var. venues, Llangollen, Denbigh
30-8.6*. **Hay Festival.** Hay-on-Wye, Powys/Herefords.

June

1-9*. **St David's Cathedral Festival.** St David's, Pembs
16-22*. **Cardiff Singer of the World Competition.** St David's Hall, Cardiff

July

July. **Cardiff International Festival.** Var. venues, Cardiff.
7-13*. **Llangollen International Singer & Musical Eisteddfod** Royal Int'l Pavilion, Llangollen, Denbighshire
19-27*. **Fishguard Int'l Music Festival.** Various venues.
19-3.8. **Abergavenny Festival.** Var venues, Abergavenny, Mon
21-24. **Royal Welsh Show.** Showground, Llanelwedd, Builth Wells, Powys. Wales' Premier Agricultural Show.
25-27*. **Monmouth** Festival.
26-27*. **The Big Cheese.** Caerphilly. Folk dancing, theatre

August

1-3. **The BIG Weekend.** Cardiff Festival, Civic Centre, Cardiff
2-9 **Royal National Eisteddfod.** Var ious locations, Meifon, Powys.
8-10. **Brecon Jazz Festival.** Var. venues, Brecon, Powys
9*. **Chepstow Agricultural Show.** Chepstow, Monmouths.
12-13. **Anglesey County Show** Holyhead, Isle of Anglesey.
12-14*. **Pembrokeshire County Show.** Showground, Haverfordwest.
14 & 25. **Racing at Chepstow.**
16-24*. **Llandrindod Wells Victorian Festival.** Old Town Hall, Llan' Wells, Powys.
27. **Vale of Glamorgan Agric'l Show,** Fonmon, Barry, Glam

September

1-8*. **Barmouth Arts Festival.** Dragon Theatre, Barmouth, Gwynedd.
21-27*. **North Wales International Music Festival.** St Asaph Cathedral. Denbighshire.

October

4-5. **Brecon Beacons Food Festival.** Brecon, Powys.
17-1.11*. **International Festival of Music Theatre.** Various theatres, Cardiff.
18-19*. **Swansea Antiques Fair.** Brangwyn Hall, The Guildhall, Swansea

November-December

1.11*. **Portmeirion Antiques Fair.** Var. venues, Portmeirion
7-9. **Network Q Rally of Great Britain.** Cardiff.
8.11 **Tote Silver Trophy Hurdle.** Chepstow, Monmouths.
14-23.11*. **Mid-Wales Beer Festival.** Various locations in/near Llanwrtyd Wells, Powys
23.11*. **Anglesey Winter Show** Showground, Holyhead, Ang
1.12*. **Royal Welsh Agricultural Winter Fair.** Llanelwedd, Powys
26.11. **Coral Welsh National Chase.** Chepstow, Monmouths.

(* = provisional dates)
For further information, contact:

TOURIST BOARD

Wales Tourist Board
Brunel House, 2 Fitzalan Road,
Cardiff CF2 1UY.
Tel: 01222 499909
Website: www.visitwales.com

St Tudno Hotel

Promenade, Llandudno
North Wales LL30 2LP
Tel: (01492) 874411;
Fax: (01492) 860407
E-mail: sttudnohotel@btinternet.com
Website: www.st-tudno.co.uk
Winner *AA Wine Award for Wales 2000*. AA Red Stars. RAC Gold Ribbon

Situated at the far end of Llandudno's fine promenade, opposite the pier, the St Tudno is one of Wales' leading hotels and has won many prestigious awards. Owners Martin and Janette Bland not only supervise every aspect of this first class hotel, but together with their charming and efficient staff, they make you feel instantly at home and very welcome. The Garden Room Restaurant, with lime green and primrose decor, is one of the prettiest in Wales. The cuisine has earned three AA rosettes. Excellent bar meals are also available at lunchtime. The lounges have a Victorian theme with comfortable chairs and restful colours. Bedrooms are individually decorated, the ones on the front being the most prestigious. Nice touches include a welcoming quarter bottle of wine, a fresh pint of milk, Villeroy & Boch china, bathrobes, and Molton Brown toiletries. Alice Liddell, better known as Lewis Carroll's Alice in Wonderland, stayed here in 1861. St Tudno is ideally situated for visits to Snowdonia, Conwy & Caernarfon Castles and Bodnant Gardens. Llandudno itself has good shops and fun pubs and has enjoyed something of an investment boom in recent years, helped by the opening of the A55 trunk road, bringing Liverpool within an hour's drive.

Rates: Single room with breakfast from £70; double room with breakfast from £90.
Winter breaks: Two nights, dinner, bed & breakfast from £98 per person based on 2 sharing.(3.11.02-4.4.03). **Summer Breaks:** From £134 per person. Exc. Xmas & Bank Holidays.

● 19 en suite bedrooms, all with telephone, satellite TV + complimentary video library, radio/alarm, hairdryer, laundry/valet service, minibar, tea/coffee making. ✻ rooms available.
● 5-cse alc dinner Garden Room £36; lunch, diets available. Last orders 9.30 pm (Suns 9 pm).
● Indoor swimming pool, sea bathing. Sailing, squash, tennis, dry ski-ing 1/2 mile. Riding 5 miles. ● Open all year.
● American Express & major credit cards accepted.
Bangor 19, Betws-y-Coed 19, Holyhead 43, Liverpool 65, London 243.

The Groes Inn

Tyn-y-Groes, Nr. Conwy LL32 8TN
Tel: (01492) 650545; Fax: (01492) 650855
E-mail: thegroesinn@btinternet.com
Website: www.groesinn.com

There has been an inn in this spot since 1573 when The Groes was on the main coach route between London and Holyhead/Ireland. The Groes Inn is a true family-run hostelry, whose decor reflects the personality of the hosts: from stone cats lounging in the fireplace to the inn's collection of Victorian hats and shields. There is even a display of saucy Victorian postcards, but no jukeboxes or gaming machines! Cuisine specialises in local delights: Conwy crab, mussels and plaice and oysters from the sea around Anglesey. Bread is crusty and homemade. Puddings are another delight with a selection of homemade ice creams. The extensive wine list has a good selection of half bottles. Classic Welsh cheeses are also on offer. Bedrooms are smartly decorated, each one differently; some have four-posters, others dormer windows. All have magnificent views, either of the foothills of Snowdonia or of the Conwy valley. There is a private suite - The Gallery - for that special celebration. The Groes Inn is the perfect spot for a short Welsh Break and is ideally placed for visiting Conwy Castle, Bodnant Gardens & Snowdonia.

Rates: Single room with breakfast from £68; double room with breakfast from £85.
Special breaks: 2 nights, dinner, bed & breakfast 2 sharing from £53 per person per night.

- 14 en suite bedrooms (inc. 4 suites), all with d-dial telephone, colour TV, radio/alarm clock, hairdryer, tea/coffee making, safe, trouser press, ✕ & ♿ rooms available.
- 3-cse tdh dinner £25; alc, lunch & diets available. Last orders 9 pm.
- Meeting room for 20. Car parking for 150
- Fishing, golf, watersports, sailing, shooting, indoor pool, tennis, riding, mountain walking nearby.
- & major credit cards accepted.
- Open all year.

Conwy 3,
Llandudno 6,
Betws-y-Coed 15, Chester 50,
Liverpool 65,
London 243.

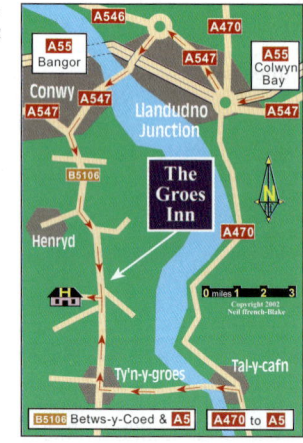

Sychnant Pass House

Sychnant Pass Road,
Conwy LL32 8BJ
Tel/Fax: (01492) 596868
E-mail: bresykes@sychnant-pass-house.co.uk
Website: www.sychnant-pass-house.co.uk

Set in the foothills of the Snowdonia National Park and just over one mile from the medieval town of Conwy with its Edward 1st castle and less than three miles form the beach, Sychnant Pass House is ideally situated. The area is one of rural beauty and serenity with unfenced roads, roaming sheep and wild ponies. It is a haven for walkers with the North Wales coastal path just a stroll away. Locally the amenities include golf, sailing, paragliding and horse riding. There are excellent beaches, and Conwy Castle, Penryn Castle and Bodnant Gardens are nearby. The house stands in two acres of lawns and gardens with a stream running through. It borders the Pensychnant Nature Reserve and buzzards, herons and foxes are just some of the visitors to the garden. The house itself is pet and children friendly. Three of the comfortable bedrooms are ground floor (good for canine exercise!) and all are named after T S Eliot's Old Possum's Book of Cats: *Grumbuskins, Cat Morgan, Macavity* and so on. There are three suites with four-posters and sitting rooms. If travelling *'en famille'* sofa beds can be provided. Public rooms are spacious with comfortable sofas; there is a 200-strong video library and the dining room is cheerful with pine chairs. It has an excellent local reputation, uses much local produce and the soda bread is home made. The house (not *hotel*) is run very much as a home by Graham and Bre Carrington-Sykes who fell in love with the area when on a visit. It is easy to see why and any Signpost guest is bound also to feel the Conwy magic!

- *10 en suite bedrooms (inc. 3 suites), all with colour TV+video, radio/alarm clock, hairdryer, tea/coffee making, safe, iron + board, fridge, safety deposit box, rooms available.*
- *3-cse tdh dinner £21.95; alc & spec. diets available. (Rest't closed Mondays). Last orders 8.30 pm.*
- *Beach, golf, sailing, riding nearby. welcome.*
- *Visa, Mastercard & Switch accepted.*
- *Closed 14 December-13 February.*

Conwy 2, Llandudno 6, Betws-y-Coed 18, Chester 47, Liverpool 62, London 240.

Rates: *Single room with breakfast from £50; double inc. breakfast £70-110.*

Glanrannell Park Country House Hotel

Crugybar, Nr. Llanwrda,
Carmarthenshire SA19 8SA.
Tel: (01558) 685230; Fax: (01558) 685784
E-mail: enquiry@glanrannellpark.co.uk
Website: www.glanrannellpark.co.uk

Since taking over the hotel two years ago Richard and Lucy Golding have worked tirelessly to keep Glanrannell at the top of the South-West Wales hospitality index - and they have succeeded admirably! My stay here was memorable - an excellent dinner where the menu was 'proposed' rather than 'prescribed'. My spacious, freshly decorated room overlooked the lake and there was no telephone to disturb the peace. My hosts recommended an energetic 4-mile walk down the enchanting Cothi valley. This lies between the Cambrian mountains and the Brecon Beacons and is one of west Wales' best kept secrets. The hotel nestles here in 23 acres of parkland. Nearby are the goldmines at Pumsaint, the 12th century Tally Abbey and Felin Newydd, a functioning watermill. For birdwatchers, cyclists, walkers, pony-trekkers and fishermen, this is indeed a paradise. The hotel can arrange for guests to fish club waters for *Sewin* (sea trout) on the river Towy. An enchanting, very private, spot.

Rates: Single room with breakfast from £46; double room with breakfast from £80.
***Leisure Breaks** & special discounted winter breaks available. Please 'phone for details.*

- 7 en suite bedrooms with radio, hairdryer.
- 3-cse dinner £20 (pre-booking necessary) packed lunch available; P 10.
- Fishing, riding, walking. Golf nearby.
- Mastercard & Visa accepted.
- Open all year

Llanwrda 7,
Lampeter 12,
Llandeilo 9,
Swansea 34,
London 225.

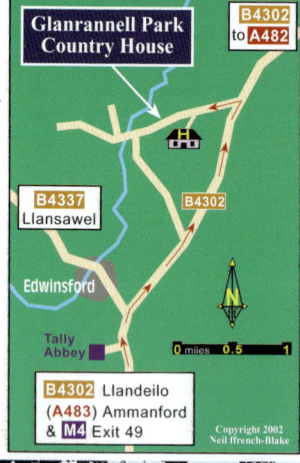

Ty Mawr Country Hotel

Brechfa, Carmarthenshire SA32 7RA
Tel: (01267) 202332; Fax: (01267) 202437
E-mail: info@tymawrhotel.co.uk
Website: www.tymawrhotel.co.uk

Ty Mawr is a peaceful rural retreat dating from the 15th century and now family-run by John and Pearl Richardson. Downstairs exposed stone walls, polished floors, old beams, log fires and cosy corners give it an intimacy all of its own. The refurbished bedrooms blend the best of the old with the 21st century - William Morris-style décor, Victorian claw-footed central standing baths and wide screen televisions with DVDs. There is plenty of choice on the evening menu. We had a warm chicken liver and bacon salad followed by seared breast of duck with warm cranberry and caramelised onion. John is a genius with local ingredients and the desserts and Welsh cheeseboard are equal treats. With the spectacular Dynefwr and Aberglasney Gardens, the National Botanic Garden of Wales, the castles of Pembroke, Kidwelly, Carreg Cennen and Llansteffan and the Llyn Brianne dam close at hand, there is plenty to see in the area, if you can tear yourself away from this hideaway in the beautiful Cothi valley, only 30 minutes form Swansea and 15 from the M4.

Rates: Single room with breakfast from £55; double room with breakfast from £88.
Leisure Breaks: £10 per night disc. for stays of two nights or more on dinner, b & breakfast basis.

- 5 bedrooms (4 en suite), all with wide-screen TV + DVD, radio/aram clock, hairdryer, laundry service, minibar, bathrobes, tea/coffee making.
- 5-cse dinner £26; Sunday lunch available; spec. diets available; last orders 9.30 pm.
- Meeting room for 20. 20.
- Fishing, riding, walking, tennis, shooting, river bathing nearby. Golf 10 miles.
- Major credit cards accepted.
- Open all year.

A48/M4 extension 10m, Carmarthen 13, Llandeilo 17, Swansea 29, London 212.

Trefeddian Hotel

Aberdovey (Aberdyfi), LL35 OSB
Tel: (01654) 767213; Fax: (01654) 767777
E-mail: enquiries@trefwales.com
Website: www.trefwales.com

The Trefeddian Hotel stands in its own grounds, away from the main road, and is one mile west of Aberdovey, a village with many attractions, fast becoming a centre for many outdoor activities. For example, special sailing instruction can be arranged. The directors, Mr & Mrs John Cave and Mr & Mrs Peter Cave, are responsible for the running of this first class family hotel, and are constantly making improvements. Recently a top floor consisting of eight large new bedrooms was added; this year several bedrooms at the front have been refurbished and landings widened. The lounges are spacious, relaxing and peaceful and have also recently been refurbished. The bedrooms, with views of Cardigan Bay, are comfortable and elegantly decorated. The menus offer a good choice of interesting and nicely presented dishes, complemented by a well chosen wine list. The Trefeddian faces a four-mile stretch of sandy beach and overlooks the golf course, where the hotel can obtain reduced green fees, with the ever changing view of the sea beyond. The courtesy and efficiency of the staff create a happy atmosphere.

*Rates: Bed, breakfast and dinner from £69 per person. **Leisure Breaks:** Spring and Autumn less 5%. January 3 night specials. Festive season Breaks 23 Dec-2 January. Please ring for details.*

- 59 en suite bedrooms, all with telephone, colour TV, radio, hairdryer, laundry/valet service, tea/coffee making facilities. Lift to all floors. Hotel suitable for movement of wheelchair. Car parking for 80.
- 3 self-catering properties (to 8 pers). Garaging.
- 5-course table d'hôte dinner £23.75; children's menu, lunch & special diets avail; last orders 8.45
- Billiards/snooker, indoor games, pitch & putt, watersports, solarium, indoor swimming pool, tennis, children's play area. Fishing, riding, sailing/boating, clay shooting nearby.
- Mastercard & Visa accepted. ● Open all year.

Machynlleth 11, Dolgellau 24, Shrewsbury 68, Chester 70, London 215.

Penhelig Arms

Aberdovey (Aberdyfi), LL35 0LT
Tel: (01654) 767215;
Fax: (01654) 767690
E-mail: penheligarms@saqnet.co.uk
Website: www.penheligarms.com

Standing beside the Penhelig Harbour, where ocean-going schooners were built many years ago, the Penhelig Arms, with superb views across the Dyfi estuary, is of specific historical interest. The major part was built in the 1700s and was known then as *Y Dafarn Fach* (The Little Inn). In the 19th century, Charles Dickens is reputed to have stayed here. Today the hotel's reputation continues to grow, thanks to its acclaimed cuisine, backed up by proprietor Robert Hughes' carefully chosen wine list, and because of the appeal of the bedrooms. These are either 'traditional' in the original inn building or 'large superior' in the recently converted *Bodhelig* annexe. The hotel has retained its essential appeal to locals, too. The Fishermans Bar is always busy! Aberdovey has an 18-hole golf course and the RSPB bird sanctuary across the estuary is home to more than 60 bird species.

Rates: single room, dinner, bed & breakfast, from £62; double - dinner, b & b from £56 per person.
Short Breaks: Dinner, b & b from £112 pp 2 nights

● 14 en suite bedrooms, all with telephone, colour TV, radio, hairdryer, tea/coffee making.
● Golf (reduced green fees available weekdays - exc. Aug - handicap certificate required), sailing, sea bathing. Fishing, birdwatching, climbing nearby.
● Visa, Mastercard, Switch, Connect accepted.
● Open all year.

Directions: At Eastern end of village, by station. **Dolgellau** 24, Machynlleth 11, Shrewsbury 68, London 215.

Penmaenuchaf Hall

Penmaenpool, Dolgellau LL40 1YB
Tel: (01341) 422129
Fax: (01341) 422787
E-mail: relax@penhall.co.uk
Website: www.penhall.co.uk

The e-mail address says it all - 'relax at Penhall' and I did! My room was called *Vaughan* and as well as a spacious bathroom, it had a tempting minibar, a bed that was hard to get out of and a superb view of the gardens, with not another house in sight! Lorraine Fielding and Mark Watson are 'hands-on' hosts, Mark giving advice in the AA oak-panelled restaurant and Lorraine looking after the front of house. Built in 1860, Penmaenuchaf overlooks the Mawddach estuary. A ramble or cycle along the old railway line which used to bring visitors from Euston to Fairbourne is a great way to take in this beauty spot. You can then return to the hotel on the smartly resurfaced drive to explore its own 21 acres of terraced gardens and woodlands and admire the sunken rose garden. An excellent centre for exploring Snowdonia.

Rates: single occupancy, with breakfast, £75-£115; double inc. breakfast £116-£176.
Leisure Breaks: Please visit our website - address left

● 14 en suite bedrooms, all with d-dial telephone, colour TV, radio, hairdryer, laundry service, tea/coffee making, 16-hr room service, fax/modem points, minibar. rooms available.
● Snooker, croquet, fishing (trout & salmon free to residents). Golf, watersports, shooting, squash, tennis, riding nearby. ● Meeting room for 20.
● & all major credit cards accepted.
● Open all year. **Dolgellau** 2, Barmouth 6, Machynlleth 15, Shrewsbury 62, London 209.

Hotel Portmeirion

Portmeirion, Gwynedd LL48 6ET
Tel: (01766) 770000; Fax: (01766) 771331
E-mail: hotel@portmeirion-village.com
Website: www.portmeirion-village.com

Portmeirion Hotel and Village was the unique creation of Sir Clough Williams-Ellis 75 years ago. His ambition was to develop a beautiful location without spoiling it. The hotel enjoyed a celebrated clientèle from the start: George Bernard Shaw, Bertrand Russell and H G Wells were habitués; Noel Coward wrote *Blithe Spirit* here during two weeks in 1941. In 1966 it was the setting for the cult television series *The Prisoner*, starring Patrick Mc Goohan. Today the village has matured and brings to mind a piece of Tuscany on the Welsh coast. As such, it provides an enchanting escape from today's busy life. Bedrooms are either in the main hotel (*pictured above*), or spread throughout the cottages that make up the village. Further rooms and suites are in Castell Deudraeth (*see opposite page*). I chose the village and was accommodated in *Neptune One* - a yellow ochre towered cottage approached via a stone staircase. The village has shops selling pottery, local produce, books and ice cream; there is a Hair & Beauty Salon and the 70 acre sub-tropical gardens surrounding the village, known as *The Gwilt* should not be missed.

Rates: Single room with breakfast from £116; double inc. breakfast from £147.
Leisure Breaks: 2 night breaks, dinner, bed & breakfast from £102 per person per night. 3 nights for two also available in winter from £102 pppnt.

- 40 en suite rooms (inc. 12 suites & 4 family rooms), all with colour TV + sat, d-dial telephone, hairdryer, laundry service, tea/coffee making, minibar, radio/alarm clock, fax/modem points, 24-hr room service, trouser press.
- 3-cse tdh dinner £35; alc, lunch & spec, diets available; last orders 9 pm.
- Outdoor pool, massage, jacuzzi, sea bathing. Fishing & golf 2 m; water-sports, riding, shooting, sailing nearby.
- Barber shop/beauty salon.
- Open all year.
- 3 meeting rooms, capacity 100. Ample P.
- AMERICAN EXPRESS & all major credit cards accepted.

Porthmadog 3, Betws-y-Coed 24, Dolgellau 26, Shrewsbury 88, London 245.

Castell Deudraeth

Portmeirion, Gwynedd LL48 6ET
Tel: (01766) 770000; Fax: (01766) 771331
E-mail: hotel@portmeirion-village.com
Website: www.portmeirion-village.com

Castell Deudraeth, opened in 2001, is very different. It has 11 bedrooms, two dining areas, a meeting room and walled garden. Beneath its Grade II listed 19th-century exterior, it is bold and contemporary in style. Bedrooms are furnished with king or queen size beds, whirlpool baths, real flame gas fires, oak floors with underfloor heating and wide screen TVs with DVDs. The interiors fuse traditional Welsh materials such as slate and oak with cutting edge design featuring unusual finishes such as burnt and fumed oak and acid patinated zinc. This leads to a simple, clean yet high quality finish. Dining choice is either the Castell's informal brasserie or the restaurant at the main hotel (*see left*). It was always part of Sir Clough Williams-Ellis' plan that the Castell would form part of the enchanting village, and this dream has now become a reality. There is nothing quite like it in Wales. Quiet woods surround the castle but the views over the bay are stunning. The main village is a gentle 5-minute walk away.

Rates: Single room with breakfast from £161; double inc. breakfast from £192.
Leisure Breaks: 2 night breaks, dinner, bed & breakfast from £102 per person per night. 3 nights for two also available in winter from £102 pppnt.
- 11 en suite rooms (inc. 4 suites & 2 family rooms), all with colour TV + sat & DVD, d-dial telephone, hairdryer, laundry service, tea/coffee making, minibar, radio/alarm clock, fax/modem points, 24-hr room service, trouser press.
- 3-cse tdh dinner £30; alc, lunch & spec. diets available; last orders 9.45 pm. ● Open all year.
- Outdoor pool, massage, jacuzzi, sea bathing. Fishing & golf 2 m; watersports, riding, shooting, sailing nearby. ● Barber shop/beauty salon.
- Meeting room, capacity 25. Ample P.
- & all major credit cards accepted.

Porthmadog 3, Betws-y-Coed 24, Dolgellau 26, Shrewsbury 88, London 245.

Gwynedd, Nr. Dolgellau

Bontddu Hall Hotel

Bontddu, Nr. Dolgellau, Gwynedd
LL40 2SU
Tel: (01341) 430661; Fax: (01341) 430284
E-mail: Reservations@bontdduhall.co.uk
Website: www.bontdduhall.co.uk

Bontddu Hall, wonderfully situated in three acres of landscaped grounds, overlooks fine views of the Mawddach Estuary and famous Cader Idris range of mountains. The unspoilt charm of this attractive Victorian mansion has always made it a favourite of mine. Both Churchill and Roosevelt stayed in the hotel before the war and both have rooms named after them. You will enjoy excellent food from an interesting country house evening dinner menu, dishes are varied and nicely served. Salmon and lobster are a speciality when available. A special carvery lunch is served on Sundays and an appetizing brasserie menu on other days. The furniture, pictures, colour schemes and flowers are all reminiscent of a country house and the hotel has been completely refurbished. All bedrooms are very comfortable and nearly all have estuary and mountain views. In the Lodge, above the main drive are some additional rooms with balconies and exceptional views. I can only recommend a visit and you will want to return.

Rates: Room and breakfast from £62.50 (single), £100-£115 (double/twin), inclusive of VAT. Weekly demi-pension £450 per person; four-poster suites for romantics £160.
Leisure Breaks: Any two consecutive nights half board from £140-£160 per person inc. service & VAT. Extra nights pro rata.

● 20 en suite bedrooms, all with telephone, colour TV, clock radio, hairdryer, tea/coffee making facilities; central heating; night service to midnight.
● Late meals to 9.30p.m.; diets; children welcome; dogs welcome.
● Sea bathing, golf and riding all five miles; gold mine nearby.
● Mastercard, Diners & Visa credit cards accepted. ● Open March to October.
Barmouth 5, Dolgellau 5, Aberystwyth 35, Caernarfon 50, Birmingham 110, London 235.

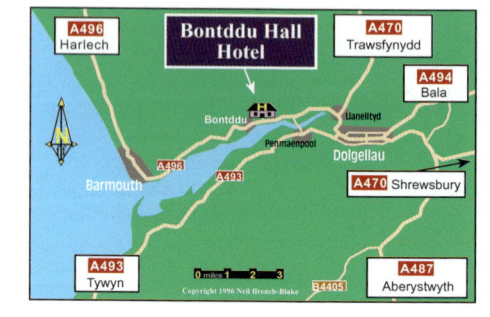

Plas Bodegroes
Restaurant with rooms

Nefyn Road, Pwllheli, Gwynedd LL53 5TH
Tel: (01758) 612363; Fax: (01758) 701247
E-mail: gunna@bodegroes.co.uk
Website: www.bodegroes.co.uk

Plas Bodegroes (possibly meaning *Rosehip Cottage* in English) is described as a *Restaurant with Rooms* but this could be said to underestimate the rooms which are enchanting. Ours was called *Tresi Aur* (Laburnum) and others are similarly named after flowers and shrubs of the area. We approached it via a charming wisteria and rose-clad courtyard. But it is undoubtedly the dining experience which brings guests from as far away as Liverpool and Birmingham to Plas Bodegroes. Chris and Gunna Chown were in the vanguard of the Culinary Revolution of North Wales, having earned the first Michelin star there. For 2003 they have been nominated *Good Food Guide Restaurant of the Year*. All dishes are prepared to order, making use of succulent local seafood and their Welsh lamb and beef is second to none. Herbs and vegatables are supplied from the house's own gardens. Their intention to let the *fresh* taste of these ingredients shine through. The Llyn peninsula is studded with sandy coves and is ideal for walking. Snowdonia is within easy reach.

Rates: Single with breakfast from £45; double inc. breakfast from £90.
Midweek Breaks: Any two consecutive nights, Tues-Fri, dinner, bed & breakfast £140-£180 per person for two nights.

- 11 en suite bedrooms, all with d-dial telephone, colour TV, clock radio, hairdryer. ✄ rms available.
- 3-cse tdh dinner £32.50 (not Mondays); Sunday lunch available; spec. diets by arrangement; last orders 9 pm.
- Golf, watersports & sailing one mile. Fishing, shooting, riding nearby.
- Mastercard, Switch & Visa accepted.
- Open mid-February to mid-November.

Pwllheli 2, Porthmadog 16, Caernarfon 23, Aberystwyth 75, Chester 91, London 263.

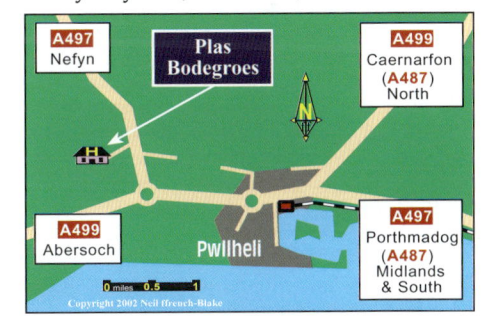

Allt Yr Ynys Country Hotel

Walterstone, Nr. Abergavenny
(Herefordshire) HR2 0DU
Tel: (01873) 890307; Fax: (01873) 890539
E-mail: allthotel@compuserve.com
Website: www.allthotel.co.uk

Allt Yr Ynys sits astride the Monmouthshire/Herefordshire border and is centred on a beautifully preserved medieval 16th-century manor house. The Elizabethan Lord Burleigh owned the house at the end of the 16th century and there are many original features still visible: moulded ceilings, oak panelling and beams, a cider press and even a priest's hole. Most bedrooms are in the converted stables and outbuildings and the hotel nestles in stunning countryside at the foot of the majestic Black Mountains and on the fringes of the Brecon Beacons National Park. The award-winning restaurant serves 'modern British cuisine' and, unusually for a country house hotel, there is an indoor swimming pool and jacuzzi. When we stayed, there was a 'team building' course in action. I am sure many of the delegates will return as leisure guests to explore further this spectacular Border country. The hotel has a civil wedding licence and its Elizabthan Knot Garden is also a popular place for couples to 'tie the knot'.

Rates: single room with breakfast from £65. Double inc breakfast from £85.
Special Breaks: Min. 2 nights from £57.50 per person per night in shared room, inc 3-cse dinner.

- 19 en suite bedrooms (inc 2 suites & 2 family rooms), all with d-dial telepehone, TV & radio, laundry service, tea/coffee making facilities, fax/modem points, trouser press. ♿ rooms available.
- Alc restaurant; lunch & spec. diets available; last orders 9.30 pm.
- Two meeting rooms, capacity 120. Ample 🅿.
- Fishing, jacuzzi, river bathing, massage, sauna, indoor swimming pool. Golf, ballooning, cycling, sailing, tennis, riding nearby.
- AMERICAN EXPRESS & all major credit cards accepted.
- Open all year.

Abergavenny 7, Hereford 20, Ross-on-Wye 22, Brecon 27, London 140.

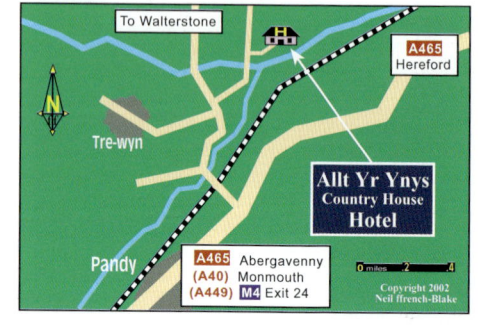

Llansantffraed Court Hotel

Llanvihangel Gobion, Nr. Abergavenny, Monmouthshire NP7 9PA
Tel: (01873) 840678; Fax: (01873) 840674
E-mail: reception@llch.co.uk
Website: www.llch.co.uk

Llansantffraed Court stands at the Gateway to Wales and its site dates back to the 12th century. The present house is William & Mary in style and stands in 19 acres of private parkland, complete with ornamental lake. It has been an hotel since the 1920s and guests are welcomed as if to a comfortable home by present owner Mike Morgan. Inside the hotel is exquisitely furnished to give a sense of homely yet spacious luxury. Good food is at the centre of the operation and the restaurant has two AA 🌹🌹. The menu changes daily and makes use of fresh local produce, complimented by a good selection of fine wines. Each of the 21 spacious bedrooms is furnished differently and each commands a view either towards the Sugar Loaf mountain northwards, the majestic Black Mountains to the west, Great Skirrid ridge to the east or Clytha Castle to the South. Llansantffraed Court is an excellent base for exploring the Wye Valley and the Border Country. The Forest of Dean and the Brecon Beacons are also near at hand.

Rates: single room with breakfast from £72. Double inc breakfast from £90.
Short Breaks: Min. 2 nights from £70 per person per night, sharing, dinner, bed & breakfast.

- 21 en suite bedrooms (inc 1 suite & 1 family room), all with d-dial telephone, col TV+ sat, hairdryer, laundry service, minibar, tea/coffee making, fax/modem points, trouser press, radio/alarm clock, sate, 24-hr room service. ✄ & ♿ rooms available. Lift.
- Court Restaurant 3-cse tdh dinner £29.50; alc, lunch & spec. diets available; last orders 8.45 pm.
- Three meeting rooms, capacity 400. 🅿 250.
- Fishing, croquet, putting green, jogging, river bathing, shooting, riding. Tennis, squash, golf nearby.
- & all major credit cards accepted.
- Open all year.

Abergavenny 6, Monmouth 10, Ross-on-Wye 20, Cardiff 27, London 135.

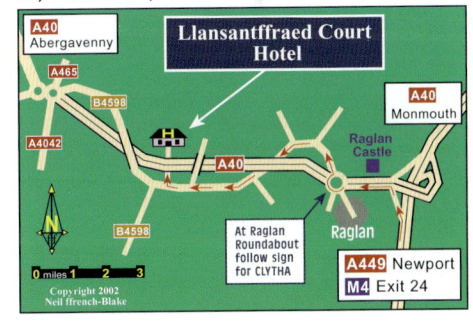

Glen-Yr-Afon House Hotel

Pontypool Road, Usk, Monmouthshire NP15 1SY. Tel: (01291) 672302/673202; Fax: (01291) 672597
E-mail: enquiries@glen-yr-afon.co.uk
Website: www.glen-yr-afon.co.uk

One of the first things that the visitor will notice about the Glen-Yr-Afon is the friendliness and efficiency of owners Jan and Peter Clarke and their staff who believe in a "hands on" approach. Guests' every needs are anticipated. Only five minutes' walk from the pleasant market town of Usk, the hotel is situated on the Pontypool road with an agreeable river walk opposite. An excellent base from which to explore South Wales and only half an hour from the motorway. Glen-Yr-Afon is an imposing and elegant Victorian house retaining many original features, yet sympathetically updated by Jan and Peter. 28 elegantly decorated bedrooms boast bathrooms with wonderfully large baths. The bridal suite again reflects the impeccable taste of the owners. The oak-panelled air-conditioned restaurant offers an excellent choice of à la carte dishes, imaginatively presented with generous helpings and a well-chosen wine list. Business people and wedding parties are well catered for with a function suite seating 140, whilst the charming library is the venue for anniversaries, dinner parties and smaller functions for up to 20 people. This year the hotel has made available to guests, for a small charge, the services of a chauffeur-driven Mercedes Vito.

Rates: Single room with breakfast from £63 +VAT. Double with breakfast from £82+VAT. **Leisure Breaks:** *Any two days sharing room, dinner, bed & breakfast per person £105.*

- 28 en suite bedrooms (inc 2 family suites), all with TV+sat, radio, d-dial telephone, laundry service, tea/coffee making. ✄ bedrooms.
- Last orders for dinner 21.00. Special diets available
- Croquet, fishing, golf, gliding, grass skiing - nearby.
- Full business services and 2 conference rooms for total of 140 guests. AV equipment available. ● Open all year.
- Car parking for 100 cars. ♿ facilities. ● Limousine service.
- ● & major credit cards accepted. **Newport 10, Monmouth 13, Cardiff 22, Bristol 30, Gloucester 39, London 136** .

Penally Abbey

Penally, Nr. Tenby, Pembrokeshire
SA70 7PY.
Tel: (01834) 843033; Fax: (01834) 844714
E-mail: penally.abbey@btinternet.com
Website: www.penally-abbey.com

Penally Abbey is a fine country house rich in character and old world charm, where many celebrities have stayed. Standing in five acres of gardens and woodlands with magnificent views over Caldey Island and Carmarthen Bay, it exudes an air of peace and tranquility that belies its monastic past. The hotel stands on the site of a 6th-century abbey and there is a ruined medieval chapel and a wishing well in the garden. Bedrooms, either in the main house or in the adjoining coach house, are individually and originally furnished with antiques, many having four posters. Dining is a romantic candle-lit affair, making use of the best local produce when in season. Afterwards guests can relax with a game of snooker or play the piano in the drawing room. There is a lot to see and do in this corner of Wales. Tenby has a sheltered harbour, Georgian and Regency houses, medieval castle ruins, town walls and a 13th century church. Tenby golf course is almost opposite the hotel and the Pembrokeshire Coastal Path passes nearby.

Rates: Single room with breakfast from £98. Double with breakfast £126-£146. Dinner, bed & breakfast from £93 per person per night.
Leisure Breaks: Any two nights, 2 people sharing, dinner, bed & breakfast per person £174.

- 17 en suite bedrooms with colour TV, radio, direct-dial telephone, laundry service, tea/coffee making facilities.
- 3-cse tdh dinner £30. Special diets catered for. Last orders 9 pm.
- Indoor swimming pool, snooker, croquet. Golf, sea bathing, riding, shooting, fishing, nearby.
- & major credit cards accepted.
  - Open all year. ● Sorry, no pets.

Tenby 2, Pembroke 11, Haverfordwest 18, Carmarthen 29, Swansea 57, London 241.

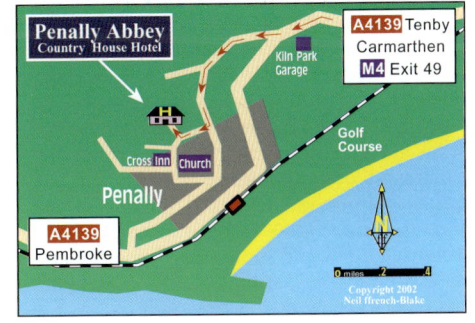

Warpool Court Hotel

St. Davids, Pembrokeshire SA62 6BN
Tel: (01437) 720300; Fax: (01437) 720676
E-mail: warpool@enterprise.net
Website: www.warpoolcourthotel.com

The Warpool Court is in a wonderful position overlooking the wild Atlantic and within a few minutes' walk of the famous St. David's Cathedral. This splendid country house hotel, with its unique collection of antique tiles, has been recommended by Signpost for a long time. It is owned by Peter Trier and managed by the very professional and 'hands-on' host Rupert Duffin. You can be assured of good food, gracious living and a warm welcome. The colour schemes are soft and restful and the staff cheerful and efficient. The two restaurant has a high reputation for good food, backed by a fine selection of well chosen wines. My salmon and crab starter, was the best I had had anywhere in 2002. Salmon is smoked on the premises, crab and lobster are caught at the nearby village of Solva. The lounge bar provides a relaxed atmosphere for that pre-dinner drink and post-dinner coffee. There are numerous outdoor activities available: walking the Pembrokeshire Coastal Path, near the hotel, bird watching, golf and surfing.

Rates: *Room and breakfast from £77 (single), £132 (twin/double) inclusive of VAT.*
'Country House Breaks' *(2 -5 nights out of season d,b&b from £84 pppn; 6+ nights from £76 pppn). Full Christmas and New Year packages.*

- 25 en suite bedrooms all with telephone, colour TV, baby listening, tea/coffee making facilities; family rooms.
- Last orders 9.15 p.m.; lunch & special diets available; children welcome; dogs accepted.
- Table tennis, gymnasium and sauna, pool table, heated covered swimming pool (Apr-Oct), all weather tennis court, 9 hole golf course nearby (2 miles); sea bathing; sandy beaches; lovely walks.
- & major credit cards accepted.
- Open February-December.

Fishguard 16, Haverfordwest 16, Carmarthen 46, Severn Bridge 130, Birmingham 177, London 264

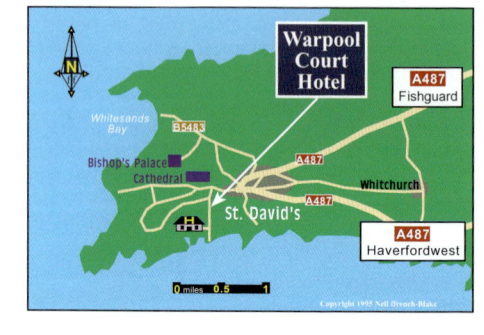

Peterstone Court
Llanhamlach, Brecon, Powys
LD3 7YB
Tel: (01874) 665387;
Fax: (01874) 665376
E-mail: info@peterstone-court.com
Website: www.peterstone-court.com

Peterstone Court is an impressive Georgian manor set back from the A40, whose origins can be traced back to Norman times. The hotel changed hands in 2002 and the new owners are doing an excellent refurbishment job. There are just eight luxurious guest suites, high-ceilinged and furnished with antiques in the main building, and four charming split level studios in the adjoining, recently converted, stable block. Bedroom extras include a glass of sherry, a cassette player, videos and bathrobes. Gourmet dining is either in the Terrace Bistro with panoramic views over the river Usk towards the Brecon Beacons or in the Usk dining room. In the cellar is a small gym, sauna and jacuzzi while outside is a swimming pool. The hotel is also popular for weddings and meetings.

Rates: Single room with breakfast from £98; double inc b'ast fm £109. Major c.cards accd.
Leisure Breaks: 2 nights, dinner, b & b, 2 people sharing £150 per night; 3 nights £144 per night. [Ad]
- 12 en suite bedrooms (inc 2 family) all with d-d telephone, colour TV+ video, fax/modem points, hairdryer, laundry service, tea/coffee making facilities, radio/alarm, trouser press.
- Tdh dinner fm £24.95; lunch & diets avail. L.o.9 pm
- Fitness centre/gym, jacuzzi, outdoor pool, solarium. Fishing, golf, shooting, riding nearby.
- 3 meeting rooms, cap'y 130. ₽ 45.● Open all yr

Brecon 2, Builth Wells 17, Abergavenny 18, Hay-on-Wye 18, London 163.

Caer Beris Manor
Builth Wells, Powys LD2 3NP
Tel: (01982) 552601;
Fax: (01982) 552586
E-mail: caerberismanor@btinternet.com
Website: www.caerberis.co.uk

Caer Beris was until recently the home of Lord Swansea, although there was a manor on the site as long ago as 1093. Peter and Katharine Smith took over the property in 1988 and have converted it into a secluded country house hotel. It sits in 27 acres of parkland on the banks of the river Irfon and is the perfect escape from the pressures of the modern world. Each bedroom, including four-posters, has its own style. The oak panelling in the award-winning restaurant dates back to Tudor Times. Dishes such as fillet of Welsh black beef with a marrow and tarragon sauce or Canon of Welsh lamb with cranberries and calvados are typical choices. The wine list stretches to over 150 bins and the malt whisky collection is extensive. Fishing is available at the hotel and riding, birdwatching, golf, as well as the beauties of the Brecon Beacons are all on the doorstep.

Rates: Single room with breakfast from £54.50; double inc breakfast fm £87. [Ad]
Leisure Breaks: Any 2 nights, dinner, b & b £55 per person. Open all year.
- 23 en suite bedrooms all with telephone, colour TV+ satellite, hairdryer, laundry service, tea/coffee making facilities, radio/alarm. ♿ rms available.
- Tdh dinner fm £13.95; lunch & diets avail. L.o.2130
- Fishing, fitness centre, river bathing, sauna, shooting, riding, birdwatching. Golf, tennis nearby.
- Business services inc 3 mtg rooms to 100. ₽ 50.
- ● & major credit cards accepted. Brecon 16, Ross-on-Wye 49, Aberystwyth 51, London 171.

Gliffaes Country House Hotel

Crickhowell, Powys NP8 1RH
Tel: 0800 146719; Fax: (01874) 730463
E-mail: calls@gliffaeshotel.com
Website: www.gliffaeshotel.com

The clockfaces on the four sides of the Gliffaes' tower show four different times. No, not the hour in Tokyo, London, New York and Sydney, but a symbol of the 'timelessness' of the hotel. It has the aura of a private house or fishing lodge where visitors are treated, not as customers, but as valued 'guests'. Although renowned for its fishing with over three miles reserved primarily for guests to fish for salmon and wild brown trout, Gliffaes also offers tennis, golf putting, croquet and fabulous walks in the 33 acres of exotic shrubs and trees which surround the hotel. The Brecon Beacons offer many other activities nearby. Exercise is recommended in order to make room for the award-winning cuisine. The hotel has two spacious sitting rooms and a sun room opening onto the terrace. Light lunches can be taken here as well as afternoon tea, which is best described as a trencherman's dream, with plenty of home made cakes! Bedrooms are priced according to size and views, all being comfortable and full of character. This year the four largest bedrooms overlooking the river have been completely refurbished to the highest standard. The Brabners' daughter and son-in-law Susie and James Suter - the third generation - now run the hotel.

Rates: Single room with breakfast from £57; double/twin with breakfast from £69. **Leisure breaks:** *Short stay and weekly rates on application.*

- 22 en suite bedrooms all with direct-dial telephone, colour TV, tea/coffee making facilities and baby listening.
- Children welcome; dogs (but not in hotel).
- Late meals by arrangement; diets.
- TV room; meeting rooms for conferences up to 16
- 3½ miles of salmon & wild brown trout fishing; tennis, walks; putting & golf practice net; croquet; billiards. Golf, riding, shooting, sailing & boating all nearby.
- Open all year.
- Diners, Mastercard & Visa accepted.

Crickhowell 3½ miles, Abergavenny 10, London 160.

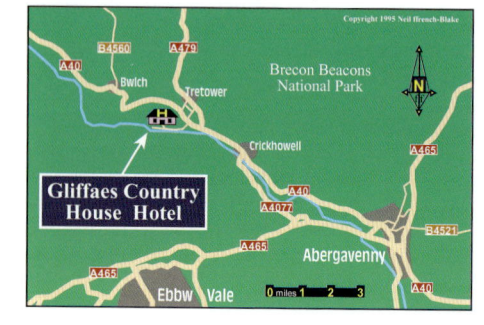

Milebrook House Hotel

Milebrook, Knighton, Powys
LD7 1LT. Tel: (01547) 528632;
Fax: (01547) 520509
E-mail: hotel@milebrook.kc3ltd.co.uk
Website: www.milebrookhouse.co.uk

Milebrook is the 'first hotel in Wales', approaching from Ludlow on the A4113. The 18th century house sits in three acres on the banks of the river Teme. Formal gardens, including both indigenous and exotic trees and plants, herbaceous borders and a croquet lawn lead down to the river. The kitchen garden provides many of the vegetables served in the award-winning restaurant. Hosts Beryl and Rodney Marsden take great trouble with their guests, Beryl in the kitchen and Rodney on hand to give advice on local places of interest and nearby fishing opportunities. Indeed there is much to see in this wild border country - march castles, historic Ludlow and a stretch of the Offa's Dyke path. Bedrooms are well appointed and comfortable. A new wing of four deluxe rooms was opened in 1996 by Sir Wilfred Thesiger, who used to live in the house from 1922-1939 and still visits regularly.

Rates: Single room with breakfast from £56; double inc. breakfast from £86
Leisure Breaks: Any 2 nights, dinner, b & b from £117 per person. Open all year.

- 10 en suite bedrooms all with telephone, colour TV, hairdryer, laundry service, tea/coffee making facilities, radio/alarm. ♿/✱ rms available.
- *Tdh dinner fm £23.50; lunch & diets avail. L.o.2030*
- *Fishing from hotel. Golf, squash, indoor pool, tennis, riding nearby.*
- *Business services inc meeting room for 14.* 🅿 20
- *& major credit cards accepted.* **Knighton 2, Ludlow 12, Hereford 31, Shrewsbury 35, London 162**

Lasswade Country House Hotel

Llanwrtyd Wells, Powys LD5 4RW. Tel: (01591) 610515;
Fax: (01591) 610611
E-mail: rstevens@messages.co.uk
Website: www.lasswadehotel.co.uk

Roger and Emma Stevens bought Lasswade in 2002 and are busy putting their stamp on it. Roger is an award-winning chef, previously from London, who also teaches cooking. A Lasswade dinner menu might start with *terrine of duckling and pork served with apricot and ginger* and might follow with *Slow roast shoulder of local lamb* or a *baked fillet of Milford cod*. Local and organic sources are used wherever possible. Bedrooms are light and airy, with high ceilings, and decorated in pretty floral patterns and with Welsh pine furniture. Breakfast is taken in the conservatory with views over the surrounding countryside and dinner in the Regency Dining Room. This is a totally unspoiled area in the Heart of Wales, lying between the Brecon Beacons and Radnor Forest. It is famous for a variety of wild birds, including the Red Kite.

Rates: Single room with breakfast from £45; double inc. breakfast from £68.
Leisure Breaks available throughout the year, some themed. Please contact hotel for details.

- 8 ✱ en suite bedrooms all with colour TV & radio, hairdryer, tea/coffee making facilities.
- *3-cse tdh dinner £19.95; spec. diets avail. L.o. 2130.*
- *Sauna. Riding 1/4 mile; golf 10m, fishing 12m.*
- *Meeting room for 12.* 🅿 8. ● *Open all year.*
- *Visa, Mastercard, Switch, JCB accepted.*

Llandovery 11, Builth Wells 13, Rhayader 21, Brecon 24, Carmarthen 39, London 185.

Lake Vyrnwy Hotel

Lake Vyrnwy, Llanwddyn,
Powys SY10 0LY
Tel: (01691) 870692; Fax: (01691) 870259
E-mail: res@lakevyrnwy.com
Website: www.lakevyrnwy.com

The Lake Vyrnwy Hotel enjoys one of the best locations in Britain. It sits high in the hills of the Berwyn range, in the midst of a 24,000 acre estate, overlooking the man-made lake, created to supply water to Liverpool in the last century. The peace, tranquillity and remarkable views that surround this unique hotel provide the perfect setting for a relaxing stay. Built in 1890 from locally quarried stone, the hotel is full of character, retaining the traditional atmosphere of a country fishing lodge, with expansive armchairs, a well stocked library and board games. It is a walker's paradise and many other country pursuits are on hand: classic fly fishing on the lake, game and clay shooting and bird watching, to name but a few. After a day's activity, you can enjoy the award-winning cuisine, whose emphasis is on fresh ingredients sourced locally and game from the surrounding estate. Then retire to your individually decorated and spacious bedroom (some have four posters and some jacuzzis) ready to wake up to the stunning view again in the morning.

Rates: *Single room with breakfast from £90; double/twin with breakfast from £120.*
Leisure breaks: *Min. 2-night stay, dinner, bed & breakfast fm £150 per night per couple, sharing.*

- 35 en suite bedrooms (inc 1 suite) all with d-dial telephone, colour TV, hairdryer, laundry service, fax/modem points, tea/coffee making. ⌘ rms avail.
- 3-cse tdh dinner £27.50; lunch & diets available. Last orders 9.15 pm.
- *Three meeting rooms, capacity up to 120.* ▣ 70.
- *Snooker, lake fishing; tennis, walks, clay shooting, quad trekking, archery, tennis, sailing. Golf 10m*
- & major credit cards accepted.
- Open all year.

Llanfyllin 10, Dolgellau 27, Shrewsbury 35, Birmingham 90, Manchester 103, London 204.

Vale of Glamorgan, Nr Bridgend

The Coed-Y-Mwstwr Hotel

Coychurch, Nr. Bridgend,
Vale of Glamorgan CF35 6AF
Tel: (01656) 860621; Fax: (01656) 863122
E-mail: enquiries@coed-y-mwstwr.com
Website: www.coed-y-mwstwr.com

Coed-Y-Mwstwr (*Whispering Trees* in English) is an exceptionally well situated country hotel set in 17 acres of woodland on a Welsh hillside. Recent investment has enhanced its position as one of the leading hotels of South Wales. Built in 1888, the house first became an hotel in 1965. Each luxurious bedroom is distinctly decorated and there are nice touches: a teddy bear on each bed and a fluffy dog to place outside your door if you do not wish to be disturbed! Fine dining with the finest Welsh ingredients is available in the Eliot restaurant (remember to leave room for one of their 'special desserts') or lighter fare in the lounge. There is a separate conference or (wedding) reception wing. With its outdoor swimming pool, and, from this year, health and beauty centre, and with golf next door, tennis courts and other country pursuits near at hand, there is nowhere better than Coed-Y-Mwstwr to recharge the batteries. Staff are charming and helpful and once visited, you are sure to want to come again.

Rates: *Single room with breakfast from £95; double/twin with breakfast from £135.*
Leisure breaks: 2 nights dinner, bed & breakfast + complimentary golf, 2 sharing, from £70 pp pnt.

- 28 en suite bedrooms (inc 2 suites) all with d-dial telephone, colour TV+sat, fax/modem points, hairdryer, laundry service, tea/coffee making, radio/alarm clock, 24-hr room service. Non-smoking rooms available.
- 3-cse tdh dinner £22.95; alc, lunch & diets available. Last orders 10 pm.
- Four meeting rooms, capacity up to 150. P 100.
- Fitness centre/gym, golf, sauna, outdoor swimming pool, tennis. Fishing, shooting, archery by arr't.
- American Express & major credit cards accepted.
- Open all year.

Bridgend 2, M4 junc. 35 - 3, Pontypridd 16, Cardiff 18, Swansea 21, London 168.

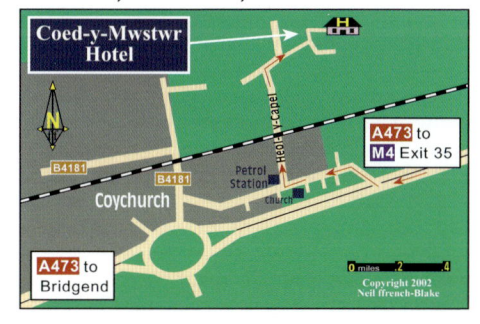

Egerton Gray Country House Hotel

Porthkerry, Nr. Rhoose, Cardiff
CF62 3BZ, Vale of Glamorgan
Tel: (01446) 711666; Fax: (01466) 711690
E-mail: info@egertongray.co.uk
Website: www.egertongray.co.uk

Egerton Gray is a small but very private Country House Hotel nestling in a secluded valley with views down to the sea. It has seven acres of lush garden, which includes a croquet lawn. In the 19th century it was a rectory and private home and it still has this aura, with a library, an intimate panelled dining-room (formerly a billiard room) as well as a private dining-room. Bedrooms are cheerfully decorated, one having a four-poster and one an Edwardian bathroom. The award winning restaurant serves excellent country house recipes and our breakfast of local sausages and home made fishcakes was memorable. There is a nice walk through the hotel's grounds down to the Porthkerry Country Park. The hotel is well positioned for Cardiff Airport and City and the Glamorgan Heritage Coast starts just west of it. The Museum of Welsh Life at St Fagan's is nearby and there are two golf courses in Barry, one within walking distance!

Rates: *Single room with breakfast from £89.50; double/twin with breakfast from £95.*
Short breaks *available, dinner, bed & breakfast, min. two nights from £55 per person per night.*

- 10en suite bedrooms (inc 2 suites) all with d-dial telephone, colour TV, hairdryer, laundry service, fax/modem points, tea/coffee making, radio/alarm clock, safe. ✽ rooms available.
- 2-cse tdh dinner from £13.50; lunch & diets available. Last orders 9.15 pm.
- Two meeting rooms, capacity up to 40. ℙ 60.
- Croquet. Golf, sea bathing, tennis nearby.
- & major credit cards accepted.
- Open all year.

Cardiff Airport 1, Barry 3, Cardiff 10, Cowbridge 10, London 160.

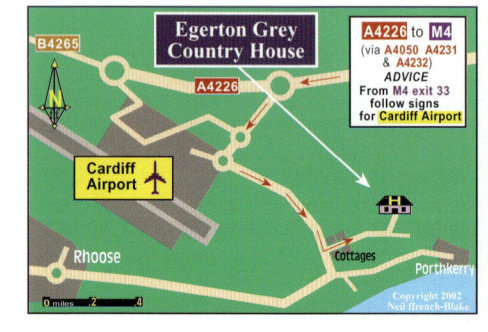

Signpost Guide 2003

Scotland

Fact File
Illustrated Guide to
Historic Houses, Gardens & Sites
Diary of Events

Hotels in	PAGE
Aberdeenshire	212
Argyll & Bute	213
Dumfries & Galloway	
	215
East Lothian	216
Edinburgh	217
Fife	218
Glasgow	219
Highland	220
Perth & Kinross	226
Scottish Borders	230

Scotland

Historic Houses, Gardens & Parks

Aberdeenshire
Castle Fraser & Garden, 4m N of Dunecht
Crathes Castle & Garden, Nr Banchory
Cruickshank Botanic Gardens, Aberdeen University
Darnside Herb Garden, Benholm by Johnshaven
DrumCastle & Garden, by Banchory
Duff House, Banff
Duthie Park & Winter Gardens, Aberdeen
Fasque, Fettercain
Fyvie Castle
Haddo House, Tarves
James Cocker & Sons, Rosegrowers, Aberdeen
Leith Hall & Garden, Kennethmont, Huntly
Pitmedden Garden & Museum of Farming by Ellon

Angus
Duntrune Demonstration Garden, Dundee
House of Dun, 3m W of Montrose

Argyll & Bute
Ardnaiseig Gardens, 22m E of Oban
Arduaine Garden, 20m S of Oban
Barguillean Garden, 3m W of Taynuilt
Brodick Castle, Garden & Country Park, Isle of Arran
Torosay Castle & Gardens, 1^1/$_2$m SSE of Craignure, Isle of Mull

City of Edinburgh
Dalmeny House, By South Queensferry
The Georgian House, Charlotte Sq., Edinburgh
Gladstone's Land, Royal Mile, Edinburgh
House of the Binns, 15m W of Edinburgh
Hopetoun House, W of South Queensferry
Inveresk Lodge Garden, 6m E of Edinburgh
Malleny Garden, Balerno, W of Edinburgh
Royal Botanic Gardens, Edinburgh

City of Glasgow
Greenbank Garden, Clarkston, Glasgow

Dumfries & Galloway
Drumlanrig Castle & Country Park, 3m N of Thornhill Galloway House Gardens, Garlieston
Maxwelton House, 13m NE of Dumfries
Meadowsweet Herb Garden, Castle Kennedy, Stranraer
Threave Garden, Castle Douglas

East Ayrshire
Dean Castle & Country Park, Kilmarnock

Fife
Balcaskie House & Gardens, 2m W of Pittenween
Cambo Gardens, 1m S of Kingsbarns
Earlshall Castle & Gardens, 1m E of Leuchars
Falkland Palace & Gardens, 11m N of Kirkcaldy
Hill of Tarvit Mansionhouse & Garden, 2m S of Cupar
Kellie Castle & Garden, 3m N of Pittenween
Sir Douglas Bader Garden for the Disabled, Duffus Park

Highland
The Achiltibuie Hydroponicum
Balmacara Estate & Lochalsh Woodland Garden, Kyle of Lochalsh
Dunrobin Castle, Gardens & Museum, Golspie, Sutherland
Dunvegan Castle, Isle of Skye
Inverewe Garden, by Poolewe
Oldwick Castle, Wick

Moray
Brodie Castle, 4m W of Forres

Perth & Kinross
Bell's Cherrybank Gardens, Perth
Blair's Castle, 7m NNW of Pitlochry
Branklyn Garden, Perth
Cluny House Gardens, 3^1/$_2$ m from Aberfeldy
Edzell Castle & Garden, 6m N of Brechin
Magginch Castle Gardens, 10m E of Perth
Scone Palace, 2m NE of Perth

Scottish Borders
Bowhill, 3m W of Selkirk
Dawyck Botanic Garden, Stobo
Floors Castle, Kelso
Kailzie Gardens, 2m E of Peebles

Stirlingshire
Culcreuch Castle & Country Park, Fintry

South Ayrshire
Culzean Castle & Country Park, 4m W of Maybole

West Lothian
Suntrap (Garden) Gogarbank, 6m W of Edinburgh

Walks & Nature Trails

Aberdeenshire
Aden Country Park, Mintlaw
Braeloine Visitor Centre, Glen Tanar, by Aboyne
Bullers of Buchan, Cruden Bay
Forview Nature Reserve, Newburgh

Angus
Monikie Country Park, 10m N of Dundee

Argyll & Bute
Carsaig Arches, on shore 3m W of Carsaig, Isle of Mull
King's Cave, shore, 2m N of Blackwaterfoot
Lauder Forest Walks, 3m S of Strachur, Glenbranter
Puck's Glen, 5m W of Dunoon

Dumfries & Galloway
Caerlaverock National Nature Reserve, S of Dumfries

City of Edinburgh
Cammon Estate, NE off Queensferry Road, Edinburgh

East Ayrshire
Muirshiel Country Park, 9m SW of Paisley

East Lothian
John Muir Country Park, Dunbar

Fife
Scottish Deer Centre, £m W of Cupar

Highland
Abriachan Garden Nursery Walk, Loch Ness
Aultfearn Local Walk, Kiltarlity
Dalabil Glen, between Tarskavaig & Ostair, Isle of Skye
Falls of Foyers Woodland Walks
Farigaig Forest Trails
Forestry Walk, between Ardvasar & Aird of Sleat, Isle of Skye
Glen Affric Forest Walks
Plodda Falls Scenic Walk
Reelig Forest Walks, W of Inverness
The Trotternish Ridge, Isle of Skye

Perth & Kinross
Queen's View Centre, Loch Tummel, 6m NW of Pitlochry
St Cyrus National Nature Reserve, Nether Warburton

Scottish Borders
Jedforest Deer & Farm Park, Camptown
Pease Dean, Nr. Cockburnspath

Scotland

Stirlingshire
Gartmorn Dam Country Park & Nature Reserve, by Sauchie

Historical Sites & Museums

Aberdeenshire
Aberdeen Maritime Museum - Provost Ross's House
Ballindalloch Castle
Balmoral Castle, Crathie
Braemar Highland Heritage Centre
Brodie Castle, Forres
Castle Fraser, Nr Inverurie
Colgarff Castle, Strathdon
Crathie Church, Crathie
Dallas Dhu Distillery, Forres
Kings College Chapel & Visitor Centre
Provost Skene's House, Aberdeen
St Michael's Cathedral, Old Aberdeen

Angus
Angus Folk Museum, Glamis
Arbroath Abbey
Barrie's Birthplace, Kirriemuir
Glamis Castle, 5m SW of Forfar

Argyll & Bute
Bonawe Iron Works, Nr Taynuilt
David Livingstone Centre, Blantyre
Doon Valley Heritage, 2m S of Patna
Duart Castle, Isle of Mull
Inverary Castle & Gardens
Kilmory Castle Gardens, Lochgilphead
The Old Byrem, Dervaig, Isle of Mull
Rothesay Castle, Isle of Bute
Souter Johnnie's Cottage, Kirkoswald

City of Edinburgh
Craigmillar Castle, 2.5m SE of Edinburgh
Edinburgh Castle
Georgian House
John Knox House
National Gallery of Scotland
Palace of Holyrood House
St Giles Cathedral

City of Glasgow
Kelvingrove Art Gallery & Museum
Museum of Transport
Gallery of Modern Art
Glasgow Cathedral
Hunterian Gallery
The Burrell Collection
People's Palace, Glasgow

Dumfries & Galloway
Burns House, Dumfries
Caerlaverock Castle, 8m SE of Dumfries
Carlyle's Birthplace, Ecclefechan
Dumfries Museum & Camera Obscura, Dumfries
Maclellan's Castle, Kirkcudbright
Mill on the Fleet Heritage Centre, Gatehouse of Fleet New Abbey
Cornmill, 8m S of Dumfries
Sweetheart Abbey, New Abbey
Threave Castle, 3m E of North Berwick

East Ayrshire
Weaver's Cottage, Kilbarchan, 12m SW of Glasgow

East Renfrewshire
Coats Observatory, Paisley

East Lothian
Dirleton Castle & Garden, 7m W of North Berwick
Preton Mill a Phmtassie Doocot, 23m E of Edinburgh
Tantallon Castle, 3m E of North Berwick
The Heritage of Golf, Gullane

Fife
Aberdour Castle
Balgonie Castle, by Markinch
Inchcolm Abbey (via ferry from S Queensferry)
St Andrew's Cathedral
St Andrew's Castle

Highland
Castle Grant, Grantown-on-Spey
Cawdor Castle, 5m N of Nairn
Colbost Folk Musuem, Isle of Skye
Culloden Battlefield, 5m N of Inverness
Dornoch Cathedral
Durness Visitor Centre
Eilean Donan Castle, 9m E of Kyle of Lochalsh
Fort George, 10m W of Nairn
Giant MacAskill Museum, Dunvegan, Isle of Skye
Glen Coe Visitor Centre, 17m S of Fort William
Glenfinnan Monument, Lochaber, 18m W of Fort William
Hugh Miller's Cottage, Cromarty, 22m NE of Inverness
Leckmeln Shrubbery & Arboretum, Nr Ullapool
Lochinver Visitor Centre
Piping Centre, Borreraig, Isle of Skye
Skye Museum of Island Life, Kilmuir, Isle of Skye
Urquart Castle on Loch Ness, Nr Drumnadrochit

Moray
Elgin Cathedral

Perth & Kinross
Atholl Country Collection, Blair Atholl
Black Watch regimental Museum, Balhousie Castle, Perth
Doune Castle, 8m S of Callander
Killiekrankie Visitor Centre, 3m N of Pitlochry Loch Leven Castle, via ferry from Kinross

Scottish Borders
Dryburgh Abbey, 5m SE of Melrose
Robert Smail's Printing Works, Innerleithen
Hermitage Castle 5m NE of Newcastleton
Jedburgh Abbey
Jim Clark Memorial Trophy Room, Duns
Melrose Abbey
Smallholm Tower, 6m W of Kelso

South Ayrshire
Bachelor's Club (re: Robert Burns), Tarbolton
Burns Cottage & Museum, 2m S of Ayr

South Lanarkshire
Gladstone Court Museum, Biggar
John Buchan Centre, 6m E of Biggar

Stirlingshire
Inchmahoune Priory, Lake of Mentieth
National Wallace Monument, $1^{1}/_{2}$ m NNE of Stirling

West Dunbartonshire
Dumbarton Castle
The Hill House, Helensburgh

West Lothian
Linlithgow Palace
Blackness Castle, 4m NE of Linlithgow

Entertainment Venues

Aberdeenshire
Alford Valley Railway, Alford
Fowlsheugh RSPB Seabird Colony
Glenshee Ski Centre, Cairnwell by Braemar
Holyneuk Bird Park, Nr Macduff
Loch Muick & Lochnagar Wildlife Reserve, Crimond
North East Falconry Centre, Cairnie, by Huntly
Peterhead Fish Market
Royal Lochnagar Distillery, Crathie
St Cyrus National Nature Reserve, by Montrose
Storybook Glen, Maryculter
Ugie Fish House, Peterhead

Scotland

Angus
Discovery Point, Dundee

Argyll & Bute
Ardnamurchan Natural History & Visitor Centre, Nr. Glenborrowdale
Antartex Village, Balloch
Balloch Castle Country Park, at S end of Loch Lomond
Glenbart Abbey Visitor Centre, 12m NW of Campbeltown
Glenfinnart Deer Farm, Ardentinny
Inverawe Smokery, Bridge of Awe
Isle of Mull Wine Company, Bunesan
Kelburn Country Centre, between Lairgs & Fairlie
Mull Railway, Craignure
Mull Little Theatre, Dervaig
Tobermory Distillery Visitor Centre

City of Edinburgh
Camera Obscura, Castlehill
Edinburgh Clan Tartan Centre, Leith
Crabbie's Histonc Winery Tour, Great Junction Street
Edinburgh Crystal Visitor Centre, Penicuik
Kinloch Anderson Heritage Room, Leith
National Gallery of Scotland, The Mound
The Scottish Whisky Heritage Centre, Royal Mile

Dumfries & Galloway
Old Blacksmith's Shop Centre, Gretna Green
Robert Burns Centre, Dumfries

Fife
Deep sea World, North Queensferry

Highland
Aviemore Centre
Castle Grant, Grantown-on-Spey
Clan Donald Visitor Centre at Armadale Castle
Dulsie Bridge
Glen Ord Distillery, Muir of Ord 
Highland Folk Museum, Kingussie
Loch Ness Centre, Drumnadrochit
Made in Scotland Exhibition of Crafts, Beauly
The Malt Whisky Trail, Speyside
Rothiemurchas Estate, Nr. Aviemore
Skye Oysters, Loch Harport
Speyside Heather Centre, Grantown
Strathspey Steam Railway, Nr. Aviemore
Talisker Distillery, Loch Harport
Torridon Countryside Centre, 9m SW of Aberdeen

North Lanarkshire
The Time Capsule, Monklands, Coatbridge

Perth & Kinross
Beatrix Potter Garden & Exhibition, Brinham
Caithness Glass (Perth), Inveralmond
Crieff Visitors' Centre
Rob Roy & Trossachs Visitor Centre, Callander

Scottish Borders
Borders Wool Centre Nr. Galashiels
Peter Anderson of Scotland Cashmere Woollens Mill & Museum, Galashiels
St. Abb's Head, 2m N of Coldingham

Stirlingshire
Bannockburn Heritage Centre, 2m S of Stirling
Blair Drummond Safari & Leisure Pk
Village Glass, Bridge of Allan

DIARY OF EVENTS

January

1-31. **Vaughan Bequest of Turner Watercolours.** National Gallery of Scotland, Edinburgh
15-2.2. **Celtic Connections.** Glasgow's annual celebration of Celtic music. Var. venues.
25. **Robert Burns Day** - celebrations throughout Scotland for national poet.
28. **Up Holly AA**. Traditional Viking Fire festival, Lerwick, Shetland.
30-2.2. **Yonex Scottish National Badminton Championships.** Bells Sports Centre, Perth.

February

2-16. **123rd Exhibition of Scottish Watercolours.** Dundee
15. **6-Nations Rugby Cup.** France v England. Murrayfield, Edinburgh.
22-March 15. **Inverness Music Festival.** Var. venues Inv'ness
12&22. **Racing** at Musselburgh

March

7-9. **Braemar Telemark Festival.** Braemar, Aberdeenshire.
8. **6-Nations Rugby.** Scotland v Wales. Murrayfield, Edinbr'
15-16. **Scottish Badminton Masters**. Cockburn Centre, Glasgow.
20-5.4. **Glasgow International Comedy Festival**. Glasgow.
29. **Scotland v Iceland**. Football. Hampden Park, Glasgow
29. **Scotland v Italy.** Rugby Int'l, Murrayfield, Edinburgh.
30. **Edinburgh Dolls House & Miniature Fair**. South Queensferry, West Lothian.

April

10-13. **Glasgow Art Fair 2003.** George Square, Glasgow.
11-22. **Edinburgh International Science Festival.** Var.
11-12. **Scottish Grand National.** Ayr Racecourse, Ayr.
20-26. **St Andrews Golf Week** St Andrews, Fife.
26-3.5. **Pitlochry Golf Week.** Pitlochry Golf Course, Perths'

May

May. **Orkney Folk Festival.** Var. venues. Orkney.
1-5*. **16th Isle of Bute Jazz Festival.** Var. venues, Bute.
2-5*. **Spirit of Speyside Whisky Festival.** Various venues, Speyside, Grampian
24-25. **Atholl Highlanders Parade & Highland Games.** Blair Castle, Blair Atholl.
31. **Football: Tennents Scottish Cup Final.** Hampden Park, Glasgow.

June

1. **Borders Vintage Automobile Club Historic Motoring Extravaganza.** Gordon, Berwickshire.
19-22. **Royal HighlandShow** Ingliston, Edinburgh.
25-27.7. **Bard in the Botanics.** Glasgow.
27-6.7. **Glasgow International Jazz Festival.** Various venues, Glasgow.

July

July. **Scottish Traditional Boat Festival.** Portsoy, Aberdeensh'
1-7. **12th World Kendo Championships.** Glasgow.
8-18. **The Skye Festival.** Teangue, Isle of Skye.
12. **Alva Highland Games.** Alva, Clackmannanshire.
14-19. **Aberdeen Internationl Football Festival.** Aberdeen.
16. **Luss Highland Gathering.** Luss, Dunbartonshire.
24. **Mull Highland Games.** Tobermory, Isle of Mull.
25-3 Aug*. **Edinburgh International Jazz & Blues Festival.** Various venues.

August

August. **Dundee Flower & Food Festival.** Var, Dundee.
August. **Hebridean Maritime Festival.** Stornoway, I o Lewis
1-23. **Edinburgh Military Tattoo.** Edinburgh Castle.
2. **Aboyne Highland Games.** Aboyne, Aberdeenshire.
3-25. **Edinburgh Festival Fringe.** Var. venues, Edinbrgh
10. **Perth Highland Games.** Var. venues, Perth.
9-25. **Edinburgh Int'l Book Festival.** Charlotte Square Gdns
10-24*. **Edinburgh Int'l Film Festival.** Filmhouse Theatre.
10-30. **Edinburgh International Festival.** Prestigious multi-arts festival, Edinburgh
14. **Ballater Highland Games.** Ballater, Aberdeenshire.
16. **World Pipe Band Championships.** Glasgow.

September

September. **Largs Viking Festival.** Largs, Ayrshire.
Sept. **Talisker, Skye & Lochalsh Food & Drink Festival.**
12-14. **Borders Festival of Jazz & Blues.** Hawick, Borders.
28. **Granite City Festival of Highland Dancing.** Aberdeen.

October

10-17. **Royal National MOD** Var venues, Stornoway, I o Lewis
17-19. **The Knit, Stitch & Creative Crafts Show.** Edinburgh.

November

5. **Inverness Grand Bonfire & Fireworks Party.** Inverness.
27-30*. **St Andrews Week.** Var. venues, St Andrews, Fife

December

6-6 Jan*. **Winter Wonderland.** Princes St Gardens East, Edin'
31. **Stonehaven Fireball Festival.** High St, Stonehaven, Aberdeenshire.

*Denotes provisional date

For further details contact:
The Scottish Tourist Board, 23 Ravelston Terrace, Edinburgh EH4 3EU.
Tel: 0131 332 2433

Blair Castle, Blair Atholl

Glasgow & Edinburgh

Glasgow, Scotland's 'second capital' is one of the liveliest and most cosmopolitan destinations in Europe. The city has been reborn as a centre of style and vitality, set against a backdrop of outstanding Victorian architecture. It was *European City of Culture 1990* and in 1999 *UK City of Architecture and Design*. Glasgow boasts world famous art collections, some of the best shopping in the UK outside London and the most vibrant nightlife in Scotland. A 'must see' is the Art Nouveau splendour of Scotland's best known architect Charles Rennie Mackintosh, whose inimitable style adorns attractions such as The Lighthouse, Glasgow School of Art , House for an Art Lover and the Hunterian Gallery. Glasgow Art Gallery & Museum displays a unique collection of European art and a famous array of European arms and armour.

Art and culture are important in Glasgow life with its many galleries and museums - most with free admission. The choice of over 20 includes the world's first Museum of Religion, the renowned Burrell Collection and the contemporary Gallery of Modern Art. Glasgow Cathedral is built on or near the site of a chucrh built in the 6th century by St Mungo, said to be the founder of Glasgow. The Museum of Transport has a showroom of Scottish-built cars and the Clyde Room of ship models. The People's Palace, in Glasgow's East End is a social history museum covering the city's history since 1175. It has a purse and ring which once belonged to Mary, Queen of Scots.

No visit to the city would be complete without experiencing the city's shopping with high street stores, designer labels and speciality outlets to explore, and welcome pit-stops available in the cafes around The Italian Centre, Merchant Square or the Gallery of Modern Art. Glasgow's Botanic Gardens, with its unique Fern Collection and herb garden, should also not be missed.

Glasgow's revitalised riverside offers numerous options for leisure and entertainment, including the city's newest attraction, the £75m Glasgow Science Centre. This exciting development is an attractive titanium-clad complex which includes an IMAX cinema, a science mall and the unique engineering feat of the 100m tall Glasgow Tower, Scotland's tallest building, with panoramic views over the city.

Edinburgh is the jewel in Scotland's crown. The jewel has many facets: classical architecture piled on hilltops, tree-filled valleys, sweeping Georgian crescents, medieval cobbled closes, graceful bridges soaring across chasms, green parks, sudden views of the sea from street corners. Scotland's capital city has been dubbed The Athens of the North. Its centre-piece is of course The Castle which dominates the city from its volcanic rock. It as the traditional home of Scottish kings and queens and now the Scottish Crown Jewels are kept in the Old Royal Palace where Mary Queen of Scots gave birth to the future James VI of Scotland, James I of England. At the other end of the Royal Mile in the old city is Holyroodhouse, Her Majesty the Queen's official residence when in Edinburgh. Mary Queen of Scots lived here from 1561-1567 and today the picture gallery has portraits of 89 Scottish kings.

Also in the Old Town is John Knox House, home of Scotland's religious reformer and St Giles Cathedral, the high kirk of Edinburgh, with its famous Crown Spire, dating from the 15th century.

The 18th-century New Town, north of Prince's Street is the largest single area of Georgian architecture in Europe. It has been officially recognised by the EU as a valuable part of the European heritage. Edinburgh's blessing has been the manner in which distinguished architects, particularly in the 18th & 19th centuries, endowed the city with a wealth of meritorious buildings, both public and private, and made use of the city's contours. Georgian House, in Charlotte Square, has rooms furnished as they might have been in the city's Golden Age - 1796. Nearby the West Register House has a fascinating collection of documents from Scotland's past.

Today the highlight of Edinburgh's cultural year is the Festival, taking place in August, which is the largest pan-arts festival in the world. As well as the official festival, there are over 500 'fringe' events where many of today's leading actors and comedians have cut their teeth, and also now a literary festival. The Scottish Parliament, the first devolved one for 300 years, opened in the new Holyrood House in 1999.

Aberdeenshire, Aberdeen/Ballater

Ardoe House Hotel

Blairs, South Deeside Road,
Aberdeen AB12 5YP
Tel: (01224) 867355;
Fax: (01224) 861283
E-mail: reservations@ardoe.macdonald-hotels.co.uk
Website: www.macdonaldhotels.co.uk/ardoe

Built in 1878 in Scottish Baronial style, Ardoe House is situated within its own beautifully landscaped grounds with magnificent views over the river Dee and open countryside. It has the style of an elegant country mansion with all modern comforts. Some bedrooms have ISDN/Modem lines and the fare available in the hotel's ◎◎ award-winning restaurant will suit even the most critical palate. The hotel's extensive conference and banqueting facilities and its proximity to Aberdeen make it an ideal venue for both business and pleasure and a good base from which to explore North East Scotland. Aberdeen City Centre and Rail Station are only ten minutes away and Aberdeen International Airport 30 minutes. Ardoe is an ideal gateway for touring Royal Deeside with Balmoral only 40 miles upstream. A new leisure centre opend in 2000 with pool, spa, aerobics studio, gym and beauty salon.

Rates: Mid-week from £80 single, £90 double.
Leisure Breaks: at weekends & certain mid-week dates accomm. from £130 per person 2-night stay inc dinner, b&b. Third night accom only free to Signpost readers on production of 2002 guide.
- 112 en suite bedrooms (inc 3 suites) all with satellite TV, d-dial telephone, hairdryer, laundry/valet service, tea/coffee making, 24-hr room service, radio/alarm, trouser press. ✂ & ♿ rms avail.
- ◎◎ Restaurant. A la carte, lunch & special diets available; last orders 9.45. 10 meeting rooms to 500
- Croquet, fitness centre, indoor pool, spa, tennis.
- & major credit cards accepted. **Aberdeen 3**, Braemar 50, Inverness 112, Edinburgh 125.

Darroch Learg Hotel

Braemar Road, Ballater,
Aberdeenshire AB35 5UX
Tel: (013397) 55443;
Fax: (013397) 55252

E-mail: nigel@darrochlearg.co.uk
Website: www.darrochlearg.co.uk

No visitor to Royal Deeside could choose a more comfortable base from which to explore this special part of Scotland with its clan history, well preserved castles, pretty gardens, famous fishing rivers and neat, prosperous little country towns. Darroch Learg, a late Victorian pink granite mansion, was built on a south-facing slope in four acres of natural oak woodland. *Darroch* in Gaelic means oakwood and *Learg* means sunny or south-facing. The views from the hotel, which is in two buildings, are very special, most bedrooms overlooking the Dee valley towards Lochnagar and the Grampians. For over 40 years the Franks family have presided over the hotel's fortunes and it has received many accolades for warmness of welcome and excellence of food and wine.

Rates: Single with breakfast from £65; double with breakfast from £125. *Leisure Breaks*: 3 days+ packages available Feb-April & November.

- 18 en suite bedrooms with colour TV, radio, d-dial telephone, hairdryer, laundry service, tea/coffee making, trouser press. ✂ rooms available.
- 3-course tdh dinner £35. Lunch & special diets available. Last orders 2100. Car parking 15.
- Riding, fishing, golf, clay shooting nearby. 🐕
- & major credit cards accepted. ● Closed Xmas & 9-28 January.

Balmoral 7, Aberdeen 42, Perth 67, Edinburgh 111, London 483.

Taychreggan Hotel

Kilchrennan, Taynuilt, Argyll
PA35 1HQ
Tel: (01866) 833211;
Fax: (01866) 833244
E-mail: info@taychregganhotel.co.uk
Website: www.taychregganhotel.co.uk

A seven mile drive down Glen Nant on the B845 from Taynuilt brings you to the solitude of Taychreggan, nestled on the shores of Loch Awe in 40 acres of garden and woodland. The proprietors have indulged in a love of art by hanging contemporary works in all public rooms and bedrooms. Adjoining rooms with wonderful loch views have been named after the famous 18th century travellers and men of letters Dr Samuel Johnson and his friend James Boswell who stayed here after their tour of the Highlands. A welcome addition this year is the full-sized billiard table in its specially designed room. All this blends happily with the antique furniture in this 350-year old former Drovers' Inn. The courtyard now boasts a conservatory, adding to the bar with its 80+ malt whiskies and trophies of locally caught giant fish. Grassy banks of rhododendrons and bluebells reach down to the lochside with convenient sitting places along the way. Two boats rest by the jetty for fishermen or adventurous hotel guests. With a fine reputation for food and wine, this is the perfect place for total escape and self-indulgence.

Rates: *Standard double/twin room from £130 per night.* **Special Breaks:** *Two nights, dinner, bed & breakfast from £185 per person and Hogmanay House Party Breaks from £350 per person.*

- *19 en suite bedrooms, (inc 4-posters & 1 suite) all with d-dial telephone, hairdryer, laundry facility, tea/coffee making.*
- *Bar lunches 12.30-2 pm; dinner 7.30-8.45 pm.*
- *Billiards, fishing, croquet, boating.*
- *Two meeting rooms to 25. Ample parking.*
- *& major credit cards accepted.*
- *Open all year.*

Oban 18, Crianlarich 37, Glasgow 87, Edinburgh 117.

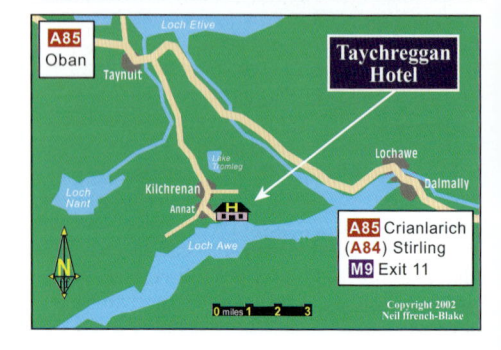

Argyll, by Tarbert 213

Balinakill Country House Hotel

Clachan, By Tarbert, Argyll PA29 6XL
Tel: (01880) 740206; Fax: (01880) 740298
E-mail: info@balinakill.com **Website**: www.balinakill.com

Scotland is full of unexplored corners where entrepreneurs of the industrial revolution built baronial country houses. Balinakill is one of these, built by Sir William MacKinnon, founder of the British East India Steam Navigation Company. High ceilings and huge windows fill the house with light and upper floor windows offer impressive views to the islands of Islay. Angus and Susan Macdiarmid bought it with much of the original furniture. Some bedrooms, which have the bonus of open fires, have gigantic carved hardwood wardrobes, unusual bedheads and quirky en suite bathrooms where claw-footed baths and antique nickel-plated towel rails sit alongside modern plumbing. Fine panelling in the corridors and the sitting room and rugs give the feeling of a comfortable home. Angus is a chef born on the Isle of Harris and knows where to source the finest Scottish ingredients. Susan looks after the front of house with modest charm. The Kintyre peninsula is an area of great historical interest with neolithic stones, iron age forts, keeps and castles. Walkers can see many of these from Forestry Commission pathways.

*Rates: Single inc breakfast from £40; double from £80. **Special Breaks** available Autumn and Spring. Please 'phone for details.*

- 11 en suite rooms, all with radio/TV, telephone, hairdryer, tea/coffee making facilities, trouser press. ✂ rooms available.
- 3-cse tdh dinner £22.95; alc, lunch and special diets available. Last orders 9 pm.
- Fishing, sea/river bathing, shooting, trail riding/ trekking, golf nearby.
- Meeting room for 40. Car parking for 40.
- Visa, Mastercard, Delta & Switch accepted.
- Open all year.

Tarbert 10, Lochgilphead 24, Campbeltown 24, Glasgow 93, Edinburgh 135.

Dumfries & Galloway - Castle Douglas

Balcary Bay Country House Hotel

Auchencairn, Nr. Castle Douglas, Dumfries & Galloway DG7 1QZ
Tel: (01556) 640217/640311
Fax: (01556) 640272
E-mail: reservations@balcary-bay-hotel.co.uk
Website: www.balcary-bay-hotel.co.uk

A winding lane leads from Auchencairn to this enchanting hotel, which has views over Balcary Bay to Hestan Island and the Solway Firth. The hotel stands in three acres of its own grounds on a safe beach. Its cuisine has an excellent local reputation, specialities including Galloway beef, Balcary Bay salmon, West Coast Scallops and grilled wild boar sausages. At lunchtime the conservatory offers a lighter alternative or sandwiches can be served in the lounge. Bedrooms are spacious, airy and quiet, either overlooking the bay or the quiet land-side garden. Each has a welcoming tartan teddy bear! The area is rich in shoreline and forest walks, five golf courses are nearby as are numerous National Trust houses and gardens. This relatively undiscovered area of southwest Scotland is warmed by the Gulf Stream and remains mild all year round.

Rates: Single with breakfast from £61; double from £108. **Spring & Autumn Breaks:** 3rd March-19th May (exc. Easter) and 1st Oct-mid Nov 2 days from £54 pp per night, dinner, b&b; 4 days from £52 pppn; 7 days from £48 pppn.

- 20 en suite bedrooms, all with TV, telephone, radio & TV, hairdryer, tea/coffee making facilities. Trouser press, iron, drying room on request. & access.
- 4 cse tdh dinner £25.75. A la carte & lunch available.; last orders 8.30 pm.
- Children welcome. Baby listening. Dogs welcome.
- Open March-end November.
- AMERICAN EXPRESS & major credit cards accepted.

Dalbeattie 7,
Dumfries 21,
Gatehouse 19,
Glasgow 90,
Edinburgh 91.

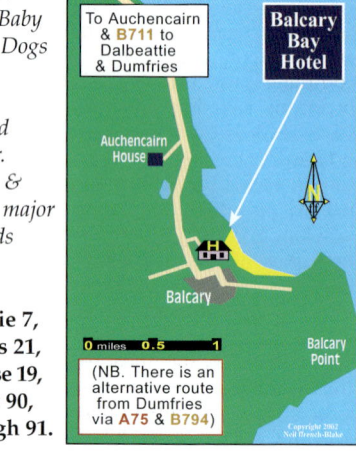

(NB. There is an alternative route from Dumfries via A75 & B794)

Greywalls Hotel

Muirfield, Gullane, East Lothian
EH31 2EG
Tel: (01620) 842144; Fax: (01620) 842241
E-mail: hotel@greywalls.co.uk
Website: www.greywalls.co.uk

This lovely hotel enjoys views over the Firth of Forth and Muirfield golf course. Its architecture, history, atmosphere and award-winning restaurant combine to make a stay at Greywalls a very pleasurable experience. The then holiday home was created by the architect of New Delhi, Sir Edwin Lutyens, in 1901 and later the leading Scottish architect Sir Robert Lorimer added a wing, making Greywalls a unique co-operation between two eminent designers, as well as being the only complete Lutyens house in Scotland. The beautiful walled garden has been attributed to Gertrude Jekyll. One famous visitor was King Edward V11 and his outside lavatory is now transformed into a charming bedroom aptly named the *King's Loo*. Greywalls became a hotel in 1948 and the same family, which has now owned it for over seventy years, continue to impart the atmosphere of a private house to their guests. This shows in the bedrooms and the wood panelled library with its open fire - probably one of the finest rooms in this home from home. The bar is cosy and the sun room a delight. Simon Burns presides over the acclaimed restaurant. The kitchen produces modern British cuisine using the best of Scottish produce. The cool green dining-room overlooks Muirfield golf course. Greywalls is a perfectly enchanting place and the hotel's particular magic has few equals.

Rates: *Single room including breakfast from £120; double room with breakfast from £200.*
Leisure Breaks: *Spring & autumn breaks available.*

● 23 en suite bedrooms with satellite TV, radio, direct-dial telephone, hairdryer, laundry service.
● Last orders for dinner 21.00. Meeting room with capacity for 20 guests; secretarial services.
● Golf, tennis (hard court & grass court), croquet. Airport pick-up. Ample car parking.
● & major credit cards accepted. Open April-October.

Haddington 7½, Edinburgh 18, Berwick-upon-Tweed 45, Glasgow 62, London 377.

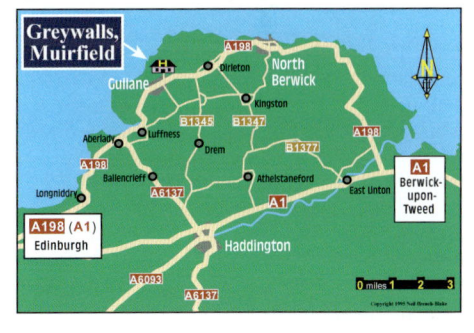

Prestonfield House

Priestfield Road, Edinburgh EH16 5UT
Tel: (0131) 668 3346; Fax: (0131) 668 3976
E-mail: info@prestonfieldhouse.com
Website: www.prestonfieldhouse.com

Prestonfield House must be one of the most attractive capital city hotels in Britain. When Sir William Bruce, the architect responsible for extending the Royal Palace of Holyrood in the 17th century, had finished his work there, he accepted a commission to build a small country house for a rich merchant, Sir James Dick, who was then Lord Provost of Edinburgh. Now only five minutes from the city centre, this unique renaissance-style building, which once sat in lands stretching as far as Edinburgh Airport, is now bordered by an 18-hole golf course and has fine views over Arthur's Seat. Much of the original heavy plasterwork remains on the ceilings and the *Leather Room*, which was originally the principal bedroom of the house, is uniquely decorated with panels of embossed leather and makes a charming sitting room, warmed by a log fire. One of the smaller dining rooms has delicate painted panels of Italian pastoral scenes. Other delights are the multitude of varied prints hanging in the bedrooms and corridors. A discreet new wing gives the hotel 31 spacious bedrooms, but there is always the choice of sleeping in *The Cupid Room* with a flying Cupid over the bed! The staff are helpful and friendly and the chef, Jim Ford, has been at the hotel for four years and is firmly established as one of the city's foremost cooks. Prestonfield is the most charming hideaway, a peaceful retreat from the buzz of city life and an ideal place from which to explore the history of Edinburgh.

Rates: Single/double/twin £145-£225

● 31 en suite bedrooms (inc 2 suites) all with colour TV, direct-dial telephone, hairdryer, trouser press, laundry service, tea/coffee making facilities, radio/alarm clock, fax/modem points, 24-hr room service. ✖ & ♿ rooms available.
● Tdh & alc dinner in Old Dining Room. Lunch & special diets available. Last orders 10 pm.
● 6 meeting rooms, cap'y 800. 🅿 200.
● 🆎 & major credit cards accepted.
● Open all yr.

City centre 2,
Haddington 15,
Glasgow 45
London 375.

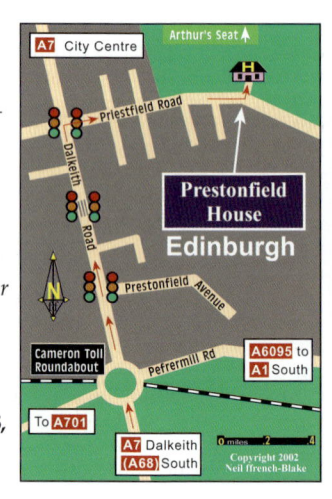

Balbirnie House

Balbirnie Park, Markinch,
Glenrothes, Fife KY7 6NE
Tel: (01592) 610066; Fax: (01592) 610529

E-mail: info@balbirnie.co.uk
Website: www.balbirnie.co.uk

A delightful Georgian house dating from 1777, Balbirnie is now a quite unique multi-award winning hotel which combines understated luxury with superb service and outstanding value. Bedrooms are large and luxurious, furnished with antiques and with many fine touches: a welcome letter from the family owners, a decanter of sherry, 20" TV, bathrobes, welcome fruit and 'tablet' and many trappings of a luxury hotel. At dinner my locally caught *fruits de mer* main course was excellent and throughout we were looked after by friendly, but not over-solicitous, staff. Afterwards we relaxed with a Malt in the Library Bar. Dinner is now served in the newly built *Orangery*. The hotel is the centrepiece of a 416-acre park featuring specimen trees and a rare collection of rhododendrons. There is a par 71 golf course in the park (the hotel was named *Golf International Hotel of the Year* in 1998) and other activities are on offer in the grounds. The hotel offers *Pampered Weekend*, *Champagne* and *Golfing Enthusiasts* breaks as well as being a good centre for corporate entertainment. An exceptional haven for those on business or pleasure wanting easy access to Edinburgh (half an hour away), Perth, the Fife coast and golf courses.

Rates: *Single room inc. breakfast from £130; double from £190.*
Pampered Weekend Breaks: *dinner, b&b+tea £95 pppn sharing.* **Golf Breaks** *fm £120 pppn*

- 30 en suite bedrooms with radio/TV + SKY, telephone, hairdryer, laundry service, 24-hour room service.
- Table d'hôte dinner £31.50; lunch & special diets available; last orders 9 pm.
- Golf (71 par own course), croquet, woodland walks & jogging trails at hotel. Clay pigeon shooting, off track driving, fishing, motor racing, game shooting, riding nearby. Ample car parking.
- Conferences to 250. A/V material available.
- Open all year.
- & all major credit cards accepted.

Glenrothes 2,
Perth 23,
St Andrews 20,
Dundee 26,
Stirling 37,
Edinburgh 35.

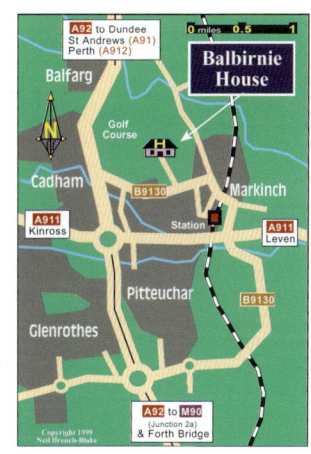

Saint Jude's

190 Bath Street, Glasgow G2 4HG
Tel: (0141) 352 8800; Fax: (0141) 352 8801
E-mail: info@saintjudes.com
Website: www.saintjudes.com

Robert Paterson, the owner and creator of St Jude's, has provided central Glasgow with a small, elegant hotel which is a welcome alternative to the more familiar, larger establishments. The early Victorian townhouse, with its glass cupola illuminating the central staircase, has been cleverly converted. The six bedrooms are uncluttered but have all the electronic extras required by today's guest. The Restaurant, under the care of Australian chef Martin Teplitzky, serves an eclectic mix of modern European dishes as well as the best Scottish beef and lamb. The walls are hung with the dramatic works of young Scottish artists. The Bar, encompassing design influences from throughout the 20th century, has been described as post-modern and retro-futurist. It is a subtly stylish, timeless but quirky space and serves beers, cocktails and snacks. The Club Room, with its skylit roof, provides the perfect space for private dinner parties, lunches, receptions and meetings, with space for up to 35 people. The transformation of Glasgow from Victorian boom-town through post-war deprivation to modern renaissance has given the city a new vitality. Saint Jude's is ideally positioned for exploring the city's nightlife, museums and shops.

Rates: Single room and breakfast from £90; double room inc. breakfast from £110.
Special Breaks: Stay Saturday and get Sunday night for half price if dining in the restaurant Sun.

● 6 double en suite bedrooms with King size beds (twins available), television, tea/coffee making, hairdryer, radio/alarm clock, laundry service, fax/modem points, minibar.
● Tdh from £17.50. Alc, lunch & spec. diets available. Last orders 10.30 pm. Meeting room for 25.
● & major credit cards accepted.
● Open all year.

Glasgow Airport 10, Edinburgh 45, London 388.

Gleddoch House Hotel & Country Estate

Langbank, Renfrewshire, Nr. Glasgow
PA14 6YE.   Tel: (01475) 540711;
Fax: (01475) 540201
E-mail: info@gleddochhouse.co.uk
Website: www.gleddochhouse.co.uk

Gleddoch House and its 260-acre estate was once the home of the shipping baron Sir James Lithgow. It is the ideal base from which to explore scotland's famous sights and attractions and is uniquely situated for Glasgow Airport and City Centre, with other major cities and motorways within easy range. Each of the individually styled bedrooms offers picturesque views of either the Clyde Estuary, the surrounding estate or the gardens. The Garden restaurant has achieved international recognition for its high standard of cuisine, prepared by the award winning chef. The Morning Room and Conservatory provide a perfect setting in which to relax and enjoy the comfort and tranquility of a byegone era. Guests may choose from a unique range of leisure facilities - 18 hole par 72 golf course, shooting, riding and off-road driving. The hotel also caters for for conferences and wedding receptions. Personal service is guaranteed and excellent cuisine and hospitality are provided by a personable and professional staff.

Rates: *Single room & breakfast from £99; double inc. breakfast from £150.*
Golf & Leisure Breaks: *Details on request.*

- 39 en suite bedrooms (inc 4 suites), all with colour TV+satellite, airconditioning, d-dial telephone, hairdryer, laundry service, tea/coffee making, 24-hr room/meal service, trouser press, radio/alarm clock. ✂ rooms available.
- Table d'hôte dinner £35. Alc, lunch & special diets available. Last orders 10 pm.
- Business services inc 6 meeting rooms to 150.
- Car parking for 100. Airport pickup by arrang't
- Croquet, fitness centre, golf, jogging track, sauna, shooting, indoor swimming pool, off road driving. Car rental & airport pickup by arr't. 🅿 200. Open all year.
- & all major credit cards accepted.

Greenock 7, Paisley 10, Glasgow 14 Edinburgh 39

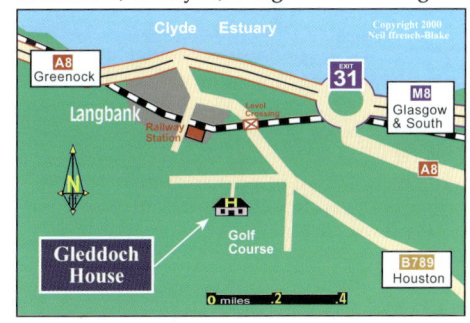

Highland, Boat of Garten

The Boat

Deshar Road, Boat of Garten,
Inverness-shire PH24 3BH
Tel: (01479) 831258; Fax: (01479) 831414
E-mail: info@boathotel.co.uk
Website: www.boathotel.co.uk

The Boat is a striking name for an hotel on the north-western fringes of the Cairngorm mountains but in Victorian times this was the terminus where passengers alighted to be ferried across the river Spey by chain ferry to holiday in the Nethybridge area. No longer a 'railway hotel', the Boat still sits alongside the old station buildings whence the Strathspey Steam Railway runs daily to Aviemore, now manned by earnest, uniformed volunteers. The hotel's new young owners have given the hotel a bright, fresh look, influenced not a little by their own experience of living in the Far East. The relaxing soft colours of the Residents' Lounge which overlook the sloping garden is the perfect place to curl up with a good book. The dining room, with its deep blue walls hung with vibrant Picasso and other modern prints, is a peaceful setting for Tony Alcott and his team's award-winning cuisine. There are several distilleries close by, also the RSPB's Osprey Centre, a championship golf course and some wonderful hill walks.

Rates: *Single room with breakfast from £52.50; double room inc. breakfast from £105.*

- 30 en suite bedrooms (inc. 2 family), all with direct dial telephone, colour TV, radio/alarm clock, tea/coffee making, laundry service, hairdryer. Non-smoking rooms available.
- Alc dinner; special diets available; last orders 9 pm
- Meeting room for up to 45. Parking for 33 cars.
- Billiards at hotel. Golf, fishing, tennis $^1/_2$ mile. Sailing, shooting, watersports, riding nearby.
- Visa, Mastercard, Switch, Delta accepted.
- Closed three weeks in January.

Carrbridge 3, Aviemore 5, Grantown-on-Spey 10, Inverness 26, Edinburgh 129.

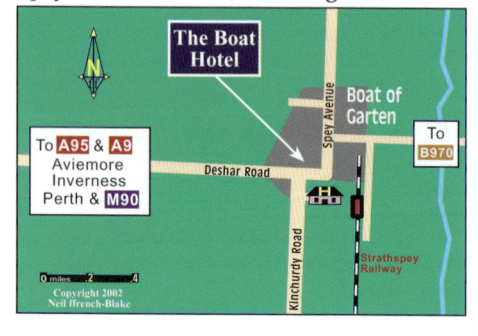

Culloden House Hotel

Inverness, Highland IV2 7BZ
Tel: (01463) 790461); Fax: (01463) 792181
E-mail: info@cullodenhouse.co.uk;
Website: www.cullodenhouse.co.uk

Culloden House is a handsome Adam style Georgian country house with a tradition of lavish hospitality stretching back hundreds of years. Bonnie Prince Charlie spent his last night before the fateful Battle at Culloden House. Today the long serving Scottish resident staff are on hand at all times to extend a warm welcome to all visitors - *Ceud Mi'le Fai'lte!* The house is decorated with magnificent Adam plasterwork and fireplaces and furnished to the highest standard. Every bedroom is individually decorated, many with fireplaces and four-posters and come with every luxury. The newly refurbished *Tartan Wing* and the *Garden Pavilion* in the grounds offer the discerning guest suite and junior suite accommodation. Dinner is announced by a piper on the lawn and prepared by award-winning chef Michael Simpson. A private dining room is also available. The extensive wine cellar is complemented by a large selection of single malt whiskies. Leisure facilities include a two-tee, net golf driving range and a Spa is planned. Situated in 40 acres of elegant lawns and parkland, just 3 miles from the centre of Inverness, Culloden represents the highest standards in Highland hospitality.

Rates: Room and breakfast from £195 (one single room - £155). **Leisure breaks** *- November 1st -April 30th - rates on application.*

- 28 en suite bedrooms, all with direct dial telephone, TV (+satellite), tea/coffee making, laundry service, music/radio/alarm, trouser press, hair-dryer. Eight non-smoking rooms inc 4 junior suites in Garden Pavilion. Car parking for up to 60 cars.
- Table d'hôte 4 cse dinner £35; alc, lunch & special diets catered for; last orders 9 pm.
- Meeting room up to 28 delegates. Ample **P**
- Tennis, sauna, croquet, boules, golf net driving tee at hotel. Shooting, fishing, 4x4 off-road driving by arrangement. Golf, watersports nearby.
- Major credit cards accepted.
- Open all year.

Inverness 3, Airport 5, Nairn 13, Aberdeen 104, Dundee 131, Edinburgh 158, London 532

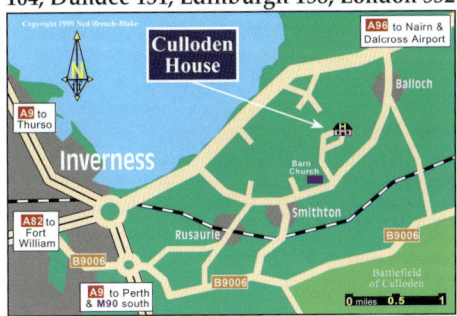

Hotel Eilean Iarmain

Sleat, Isle of Skye, Highland IV43 8QR
Tel: (01471) 833332; Fax: (01471) 833275
E-mail: hotel@eileaniarmain.co.uk
Website: www.eileaniarmain.co.uk

The Isle of Skye was first mentioned in a travel guide when a Sarah Murray sailed there in an open boat from the Isle of Rhum in 1800. The island is a must for all Scotland lovers, access easy with a new bridge and ferries. In a sheltered bay in the south of the island, Hotel Eilean Iarmain (also known as Isle Ornsay Hotel) overlooks sea, islands and mountains. One of Stevenson's white lighthouses stands guard on a rocky outcrop, seagulls wheel overhead and otters play in the shallows. Fishing boats with fresh seafood come to the pier where Flora Macdonald came as a captive after rescuing Prince Charles Edward Stuart. Today the hotel has antique furniture and pretty fabrics, pine panelling and open fires in public rooms. The former stables have been converted into four charming suites and another building is an art gallery in summer. There is trout fishing, as well as shooting, on the 2000-acre estate. Local fiddlers, pipers and *clarsach* (Gaelic Harp) players sometimes play in the public bar. Menus are based on locally caught seafood, shellfish, game and oysters from the hotel's own beds. Organic vegetables are used where possible. The hotel has won many awards including Joint Best Hotel of the Year (*Relais Routiers*) and Most Romantic Hotel.

Rates: *Single with breakfast from £90; double inc. breakfast from £100; suites from £180.*
Leisure Breaks: *Autumn & Winter breaks available - details on application.*

- 16 bedrooms (inc 4 enchanting suites) all with good facilities and dressing gowns.
- 3 course dinner £25. Last orders 8.45 pm.
- Fishing, shooting, stalking, riding nearby.
- Small seminars catered for. ● Golf 20 miles.
- Honeymooners welcomed.
- & major credit cards accepted.
- Open all year inc. Xmas & New Year.

Skye Road Bridge 13, Portree 34, Inverness 85, Edinburgh 210.

The Cross

Tweed Mill Brae, Kingussie,
Highland PH21 1TC
Tel: (01540) 661166
Fax: (01540) 661080
E-mail: relax@TheCross.co.uk;
Website: www.thecross.co.uk

Travelling North from Perth to Inverness, it is easy to miss the villages of Newtonmore and Kingussie, with their sturdy grey granite houses lining the main streets. Kingussie has another surprise. On the banks of the Gynock burn, which runs into the river Spey, there is an old water-powered tweed mill, which has been sympathetically converted into a nine-bedroom hotel nestling in a four-acre native woodland garden. The owners, Tony and Ruth Hadley, have created an hotel of great individuality. The residents' lounge on the first floor is open beamed and airy, dominated by a large locally crafted table of wych elm and containing an eclectic collection of modern art and traditional pieces. The bedrooms are freshly decorated with roomy bathrooms. Some overlook the burn whose soothing murmur makes for tranquil sleep on a summer's night. Ruth, a master chef, presides in the kitchen. The restaurant has won three AA rosettes and a *Which Hotel Guide* Award in 2001. Our five-course menu delighted the palate: sweet West Coast *squatties* (squat lobsters) with a Thai dressing, a tiny taster of fresh tomato and mint soup, a smoked fishcake on a tomato base, followed by Oriental breast of duck or a simply fried fillet of Scottish beef. The choice of a pear and butterscotch tart or the chocolate pavlova was a difficult one and we had to forego the wonderful cheeseboard. Tony, a careful and attentive host, matches his wife's menus with a fine, worldly wine list. This is a peaceful restaurant with rooms, where the guest is made to feel really welcome in a most discreet way.
Aviemore 12, Inverness 41, Perth 73, Edinburgh 117.

Rates: Dinner, bed & breakfast £115 per person.
Leisure Breaks: Two nights, dinner, b & b £95 pppn.
Occasional wine weekends. Please call for details.

- 9 en suite bedrooms, all with direct dial telephone, colour TV, tea/coffee making, hairdryer. ✗ rms avail.
- Table d'hôte 5 cse dinner £37.50; special diets catered for; last orders 8.30 pm. ☺☺☺ AA P12 cars
- Golf, shooting, fishing, sailing, tennis, riding nearby.
- Visa, Mastercard, Delta, Switch cards accepted.
- Open 2nd March - 30 November.

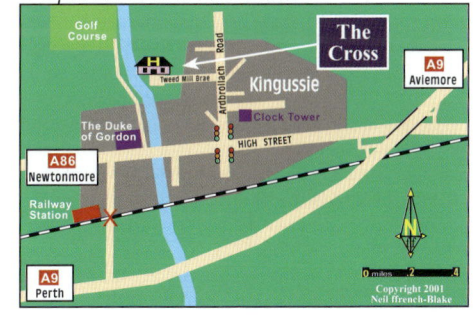

Portland Arms Hotel

Lybster, Caithness, Highland KW3 6BS
Tel: (01593) 721721; Fax: (01593) 721722
E-mail: info@portlandarms.co.uk
Website: www.portlandarms.co.uk

Driving into Lybster, the prospect of stern grey stone houses is immediately arrested by the proud frontage of the Portland Arms. It sits at the crossroads of Telford's Parliamentary Road and Quatre Bras Street, named by General Sinclair (this is Sinclair country) to commemorate the opeing of the Battle of Waterloo. As soon as you enter the porch, a warm feeling envolopes you. This newly refurbished hotel provides all the stylish comfort you could wish for. The informal *Jo's Kitchen*, with its huge Aga centre-stage and farmhouse feel, serves country food 'just like it used to be'. The Bistro Bar and more formal Library offer the same good food and a varied evening menu using the best of local Scottish produce. The drawing room with its huge sofas and many books is the perfect place for after-dinner chat. From Lybster, the archeological sites of Caithness can be explored, John O' Groats visited and day trips can be taken to the magical island of Orkney. Seabirds throng the cliffs, seals abound offshore, deserted sandy beaches invite walkers and moorlands beckon. This is a very special and unspoiled corner of Scotland, full of surprises for the inquisitive traveller.

Rates: *Single room with breakfast from £50; Double £75; Exec double £90; Family room £95.*
Leisure breaks: *Stay for a 3 night break for £130 per person dinner, b & b and get the last night b & b FREE if dinner taken in hotel on 3rd night.*

- 22 en suite bedrooms, all with direct dial telephone, colour TV, hairdryer, laundry service, radio/alarm clock, tea/coffee making, trouser press, safe, fax/modem points. ✂ & ♿ rooms available.
- Alc dinner; lunch & special diets catered for; last orders 9 pm. 2 meeting rooms 2-200. 🅿 for 25.
- Shooting, fishing, sailing, golf, watersports nearby. Special activity breaks organised by hotel.
- AMERICAN EXPRESS & major credit cards accepted.
- Open all year.

Wick 14, Helmsdale 24, Thurso 28, John O' Groats 31, Inverness 94, Edinburgh 251.

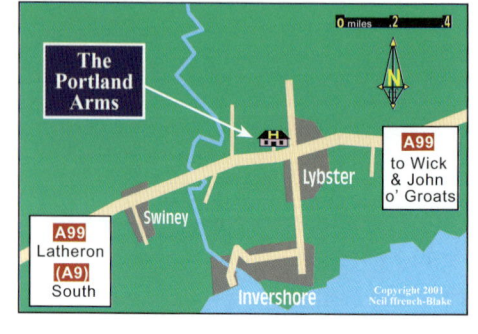

Eddrachilles Hotel

Badcall Bay, Scourie, Sutherland
IV27 4TH. Tel: (01971) 502080;
Fax: (01971) 502477
E-mail: enq@eddrachilles.com
Website: www.eddrachilles.com   AA ★★ 72%

Escape to the peace and tranquillity of this former manse, comfortably refurbished to maintain the character of former times. Both à la carte and fixed price offer excellent home cooking, with Aberdeen Angus beef, local fish as well as delicious home made desserts. The wine list offers a selection of over 60 bins and, for after dinner drinking, choose from a selection of over 80 malts. The north of Scotland is unique for its remote and untouched beauty. You can explore it from quiet, single-track roads, or walks over beaches, cliffs and hills. Nearby Handa Island is a famous bird sanctuary and boat trips across the short stretch of water can be made from Tarbet. The shore is within walking distance of the hotel. Guests are encouraged to record unusual birds or beasts sighted in the hotel's leather-bound log "Nature Observed".

Rates: Room and breakfast from £40.00; dinner, room and breakfast from £52.00. (inc VAT.) **Leisure Breaks** *- reduced rates for stays of 3, 6 or 10 days.*

- 11 en suite bedrooms (4 on ground floor), all with TV, hospitality tray, iron & hairdryer.
- Last orders for dinner 8. 00 p.m; bar lunches available; special diets by arrangement.
- Children of 3 + welcome. ● Sailing/boating; fishing
- Hotel closed November-February inclusive.
- Switch, Visa and Mastercard accepted.

Ullapool 40, Thurso 95, Inverness 98, Edinburgh 245.

Ben Loyal Hotel

Main Street, Tongue, Sutherland
IV27 4XE. Tel: (01847) 611216:
Fax; (01847) 611212
E-mail: benloyalhotel@btinternet.com
Website: www.benloyal.co.uk

After three years of hard work, Paul and Elaine Lewis have established the Ben Loyal as a bright and comfortable hotel. Surrounded by some of the most dramatic scenery in Scotland, guests are offered diversions such as woodcock shooting, hind stalking, clay pigeon shooting and brown trout fishing on peaty highland lochs, as well as spectacular walks. Most bedrooms, the residents' lounge and the dining room have views of Ben Hope, the northernmost Munro and Ben Loyal, towering above the valley that lies beyond the vast sandy estuary of the Kyle of Tongue. Chef Liz presides in the all-female kitchen and menus in the AA ◉ dining room are tantalising and offer local oysters and lobster (to order), fresh fish and venison. Elaine greets her guests in the dining room and is a mine of local information. There is a games room and family corner.

Rates: Single room with breakfast from £25; double inc. breakfast from £50. Open all year.

- 11 en suite bedrooms, all with colour TV, d-dial telephone, radio/alarm, hairdryer, tea/coffee making, safe. ✂ rooms available.
- 4-cse tdh dinner £26.50; a/c, lunch in bar, diets avail.
- Meeting room for 40, Parking for 20 cars.
- Indoor games, pool table. Fishing, bathing, game shooting locally. Riding 12 miles. Children welcome
- Visa, Mastercard & Switch cards accepted.

Lairg 38, Thurso 43, Inverness 101, Edinburgh 257.

Cairn Lodge Hotel

Orchil Road, Auchterarder, Perthshire
PH3 1LX
Tel: (01764) 662634; Fax: (01764) 664866
E-mail: e-mail@cairnlodge.co.uk
Website: www.cairnlodge.co.uk

Alex and Michele Macdonald are proud of their new extension which blends well with the existing building. As official booking agents for the Gleneagles Golf Course, the hotel can book tee times or organise golfing breaks. Dining is either in the AA ●● Capercaille Restaurant or the less formal Jubilee Bar. Smoked marlin and chicken piri piri with spiced couscous sit happily between more conventional choices of Scottish beef and game on the menu. All this is backed up by a comprehensive wine list with a good house wine, and a good selection of malt whiskies. There is also a vegetarian and childrens' menu and at weekends high teas and traditional Sunday lunch are on offer. As well as golf, there is shooting and riding at nearby Gleneagles and other local attractions include Drummond Castle with its Italianate formal gardens and the Glenturret Distillery. Scone Palace is nearby and guests can walk to the many antique shops and galleries of Auchterarder village (known as *The Lang Toon*).

Rates: Single room and breakfast from £65; double room with breakfast from £100.
Leisure breaks at certain times of year. For full details, please see our website.

- 11 en suite bedrooms (inc 4 suites), all with colour TV, d-dial telephone, hairdryer, laundry service, radio/alarm, trouser press, tea/coffee making, fax/modem points.
- 3-cse tdh dinner £29.50; lunch & special diets available; last orders 9.30 pm. **P** *for 50*
- *Meeting room for 20. Airport pickup available.*
- *Golf, shooting, riding nearby.*
- Visa, Switch, Delta cards accepted.

Crieff 9, Perth 14, Stirling 15, Glasgow 45, Edinburgh 55.

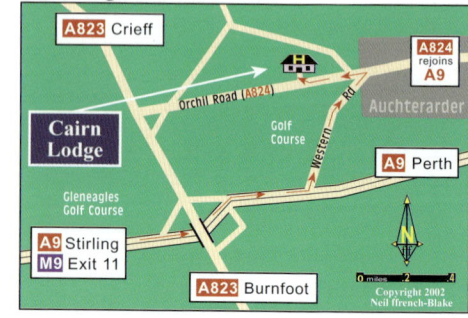

Perth & Kinross, Lochearnhead/St Fillans

Monachyle Mhor
Balquhidder, Lochearnhead,
Perthshire FK19 8PQ
Tel: (01877) 384622;
Fax: (01877) 384305
E-mail: info@monachylemhor.com
Website: www.monachylemhor.com

An absolutely enchanting place, six miles up Loch Voil west of Balquhidder, in whose church Rob Roy is buried and where chamber music concerts are now held on Summer Sunday evenings. Our inspector was torn between keeping Monachyle a secret for his private enjoyment or bringing it to the attention of discerning Signpost readers. Owned by the Lewis family, son Tom is in charge of the much acclaimed kitchen. Specialities include Scottish West Coast Lemon Sole, Mallaig Scallops and Perthshire beef. Puddings are home made and our fluffy scrambled egg and smoked salmon breakfast, with fresh scones, was equally memorable. Bedrooms and public rooms are furnished like a private house, with some in outside barns and cottages. Small wonder that Scots come from as far away as Glasgow to sample the peace and quiet and good food here.

Rates: Single room with breakfast from £50. Dble inc. breakfast from £65. Visa, Mastercard accepted

● 10 en suite bedrooms, 8 with colour TV, all with telephone, hairdryer, tea/coffee making facilities, music/radio/alarm clock. Non smoker bedrooms available. Two self-catering cottages.
● Table d'hôte £30; à la carte, lunch & special diets available; last orders 8.45 pm. ◎◎ Restaurant
● No pets or disabled facilities. ● Closed January.
● 2000 acre estate. Private fishing, red deer stalking and grouse moor in season. Loch bathing.

Callander 17, Lochearnhead 10, Glasgow 53, Edinburgh 62

The Four Seasons Hotel
St Fillan's, Perthshire PH6 2NF. Tel: (01764) 685333;
Fax: (01764) 685444
E-mail: info@thefourseasonshotel.co.uk
Website: www.thefourseasonshotel.co.uk

Andrew Low, an experienced local hotelier, took over the Four Seasons recently and is busy bringing the standard of public and bedrooms up to that of the acclaimed AA ◎◎ restaurant. The hotel has its own jetty and slipway on Loch Earn and St Fillans is an excellent centre for sailing and watersports. It also has its own 9-hole golf course and this part of Perthshire is superb walking country. Ben Vorlich, a 3000+ ft Munro, can be approached from the south side of the loch. The Four Seasons has two restaurants: the acclaimed *Meall Reamhar* (High Hills), which specialises in local 'Taste of Scotland' dishes and the less formal Tarken Room. As well as the main hotel, there are six smart chalets in the grounds, providing privacy for couples with children. The Four Seasons provides a wonderful base for exploring Perthshire and the Heart of Scotland.

Rates: Single occupancy from £35; double/twin rooms from £70. Open Easter to Jan 3rd.
Leisure breaks: 3 nights for the price of two on dinner, b & b basis, acc. to season & availability.

● 12 en suite bedrooms, all with colour TV, d-dial telephone, hairdryer, laundry service, radio/alarm clock, trouser press, tea/coffee making. ✹ rms avail
● Table d'hôte £26.50; lunch & special diets avail. last orders 9.30 pm. ● Two mtg rms, cap 40. ▣ 30
● Fishing, sailing, bathing from hotel. 9-hole golf course one mile; watersports one mile.
● Mastercard, Visa accepted.

Perth 30, Stirling 30, Glasgow 56, Edinburgh 65.

Kinnaird

**Kinnaird Estate, Dalguise,
Nr. Dunkeld, Perthshire PH8 0LB
Tel: (01796) 482440; Fax: (01796) 482289**
E-mail: enquiry@kinnairdestate.com
Website: www.kinnairdestate.com

In the beautiful wooded valley of the river Tay, in a magnificent 9000 acres of spectacular Perthshire countryside, sits one of Scotland's most unique hotels: Kinnaird. The estate comprises the original Edwardian mansion plus eight charmingly furnished, individual, 'satellite' cottages. Whether it be the warmth and comfort of the Cedar Room, with its deep cushioned sofas and club chairs or in the lovely old frescoed panelled dining room, Constance Ward and General Manager Douglas Jack and their superb and highly efficient team will pre-empt your every need. The house, which dates back to the 1770s, has been furnished almost entirely with fine and rare pieces of antique furniture, china and pictures. Dining at Kinnaird is a gourmet's delight, with an experienced chef presenting seasonal menus, backed up by a well stocked wine cellar. In the daytime, guests may fish for trout or salmon on the Tay or on one of the three lochs of the estate, play tennis, croquet or bowls, shoot clay pigeon, play golf locally or just walk for miles through the majesty surrounding countryside. A truly unforgettable place.

Rates: Single/double room inc. breakfast £255.
Leisure Breaks: Jan 5- 11 May 2003, all rooms are £295 dinner, b & b for two. For 2+ night stay, price becomes £250 per night inc VAT.

- 9 en suite bedrooms (inc 1 suite), all with colour TV+Sat, direct-dial telephone, hairdryer, laundry service, radio/alarm clock, trouser press.
- *Tdh dinner £50; lunch & special diets available; last orders 9.30 pm. Children over 12 welcome.*
- *Two meeting rooms, capacity 12. Parking for 20*
- *Snooker, croquet, bowls, tennis, shooting, fishing. Golf nearby.*
- *Closed Mon/Tues/Wed January/February.*

Visa & Mastercard accepted.

Pitlochry 7,
Dunkeld 7,
Aberfeldy 10,
Perth 14,
Edinburgh 58.

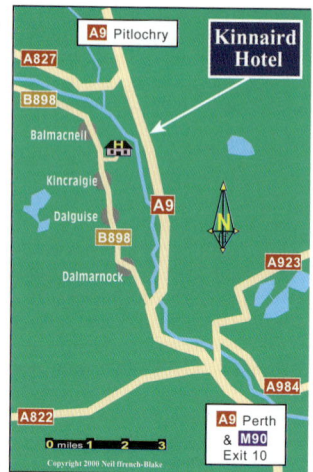

Perth & Kinross, Spittal of Glenshee

Dalmunzie House Hotel

Spittal of Glenshee, Blairgowrie,
Perthshire PH10 7QG
Tel: (01250) 885224; Fax: (01250) 885225
E-mail: dalmunzie@aol.com Web: www.dalmunzie.com

If you are looking for perfect peace and quiet or for a sporting holiday, this impressive country house, hidden away in the hills, is an excellent venue. Dalmunzie has been in the Winton family for many years, and is now looked after by Simon and Alexandra, whose care and attention result in a well run house, personal service, and a happy atmosphere. The sitting rooms, cosy cocktail bar and spacious bedrooms are all in excellent decorative order, well furnished and comfortable, and log fires and central heating ensure warmth in every season. In the AA dining room, which has won the Game Cookery Award from the Scottish Association for Country Sports, the varied table d'hôte dishes are well cooked and feature traditional Scottish fare, accompanied by a carefully chosen wine list. This family owned sporting estate can organise almost any shooting holiday, whilst other field sports, trout fishing, walking and climbing also beckon. Dalmunzie have their own 9 hole golf course available for guests. Nearby Glenshee offers well organised skiing for all abilities, and for those wishing to explore on wheels, there are quiet roads and much to see.

Rates: Room and breakfast from £45 per person, weekly rates from £427 per person, full board. During the ski season, dinner, bed and breakfast from £58-£71.
Leisure Breaks: Dinner, bed & breakfast Jan-April 2 nights from £116 & 5 nights from £255. From April-October 3 nights, dinner, b&b fm £180.

- 18 bedrooms (1 for the disabled, 16 en suite).
- Last dinner orders 8.30 p.m.; light bar lunches; special diets on request.
- Children welcome; dogs accepted; conferences to 20.
- Games room; bar billiards; 9 hole golf course; tennis; shooting/fishing (trout/salmon; own rainbow trout stocked loch); skiing in Glenshee; pony trekking; mountain bikes.
- Closed December. Mastercard & Visa accepted.

Perth 35, Dundee 37, Braemar 15, Blairgowrie 20, Edinburgh 78, London 453.

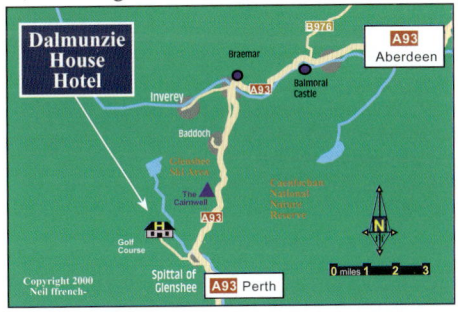

Scottish Borders - St Boswells

Dryburgh Abbey Hotel

St Boswell's, Melrose TD6 ORQ
Tel: (01835) 822261; Fax: (01835) 823945
E-mail: enquiries@dryburgh.co.uk
Website: www.dryburgh.co.uk

Dryburgh Abbey Hotel is owned and managed by the Grose family, who also own Thurlestone in Devon, another Signpost hotel. I was very impressed by Dryburgh. It sits atop a hill rising above the Tweed in an area of outstanding natural beauty. The ruins of Dryburgh Abbey, Sir Walter Scott's last resting place, are in the grounds. Inside the hotel is comfortable without frills or fuss. Yet everything you want for a relaxing stay is here: spacious bedrooms named after salmon flies: *Silver Wilkinson, Hairy Mary, Roger's Fancy*; two dining-rooms, the Tweed Restaurant, overlooking the river, or the Courtyard Bar bistro. Menus change daily to reflect the abundance and quality of local produce. From freshly caught salmon to haggis in a whisky cream sauce or roast rack of border lamb, all meals are prepared with style and imagination. The wine list boasts over 150 vintages. Dryburgh is very popular for business events and there was a wedding going on when I stayed. What a romantic start to married life! As well as being able to arrange shooting in season, the hotel can book salmon or trout fishing on 14 beats of the Tweed. There are 14 golf courses nearby, plenty of sites of interest and an indoor pool in the hotel.

Rates: Single room & breakfast from £45; double inc. breakfast from £90.
Leisure Breaks: Dinner, bed & breakfast from £55 per person 5th Dec-16 March. Weekend breaks.

- 38 en suite bedrooms, all with colour TV, telephone, hairdryer, laundry service, tea/coffee making facilities, 24-hr room/meal service, trouser press, radio/alarm clock. Deluxe, half-tester, four-poster and tower suites also available. ♿ facilities.
- Table d'hôte 4-cse dinner £26. A la carte, lunch & special diets available. Last orders 9.15 pm.
- Business services inc 2 meeting rooms 20/150 cap
- Car parking for 100. Airport pickup by arrang't
- Croquet, fishing, shooting, indoor swimming pool, tennis. Golf 3m, riding 4m, off-road driving 25m.
- American Express & Visa, Mastercard accepted
- Open all year.

Melrose 4, Hawick 17, Newcastle-upon-Tyne 66, Glasgow 79, Edinburgh 39.

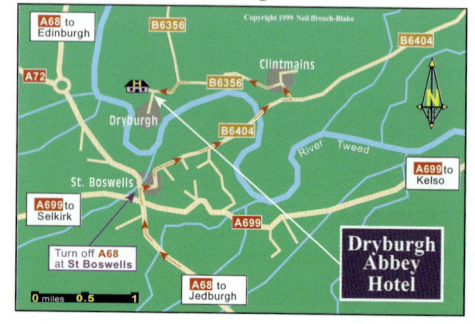

Signpost Guide 2003
Channel Islands

Fact File
Illustrated Guide to Historic Houses, Gardens and Sites
Diary of Events

Hotels in	PAGE
Guernsey	236
Herm	239
Jersey	240
Sark	242

The Channel Island of Guernsey - a veritable haven for the holidaymaker. A modern airport, excellent harbour, hotels and guest houses with every amenity. A thriving tourist industry which encourages and welcomes visitors, and rewards them with all the comforts associated with up-to-date civilised living.

But existing alongside the evidence of today's lifestyle are customs and traditions that have resisted change. Large chunks of Guernsey's intricate and chequered history blend harmoniously with the present. This is all part of Guernsey's unique character; the present is built around the past rather than unceremoniously trampling upon it.

For the visitor who is ignorant of Guernsey's history, it would seem also that the island cannot decide whether it is French or British! In St. Peter Port, for example, street names are displayed in both English and French, and the town retains a definite air of an ancient Norman seaport. Now and again throughout the island, one can catch snatches of conversations spoken in Guernsey *patois*, which the uninitiated could forgivably mistake for French.

The French/British connection is in itself unusual. Geographically closer to France, but essentially a "British" Island, Guernsey was once under the domination of the Norman dukes, who in turn were vassals of the French king. William II of Normandy, crowned William I of England in 1066, established the connection with England and subsequent events have established the Channel Islands as part of the dominion of the Kings of England, but never part of their kingdom.

An air of the past, a French flavour - the visitor cannot ignore these influences. St. Peter Port, a flourishing commercial centre with its busy harbour, still preserves its past identity, with its buildings of traditional Guernsey granite and its unspoilt skyline. And from the castle ramparts throughout the summer season booms the noonday gun, after a ceremony that is fascinating to witness.

Guernsey has many unique attractions for the visitor. The Little Chapel is the smallest chapel in the world, and lavishly decorated with pottery and shells, has room for only five people inside. Victor Hugo, the famous French author, lived in exile for 15 years on Guernsey, and his house is an extravagant monument to his life and work. Guernsey has a host of museums, a butterfly centre, zoo, aquarium, craft centre and a variety of fascinating archaeological sites as well as a fine leisure centre which caters for all the main sports. Add to this Guernsey's spectacular cliff walks and beautiful countryside and the visitor will find that all tas-tes are catered for.

As is to be expected, Guernsey is famed for a number of traditional dishes and delicacies, not the least of which is the *Guernsey Gache*, a sort of fruit loaf still popular on the island. It can be purchased in a number of shops, and many people have their own, special recipes, but perhaps the most intriguing place to purchase it is in the Old Guernsey Market, held on Thursdays in St. Peter Port. Traditionally dressed stall holders sell all manner of island-produced wares from freesia corms, to the beautifully made, oiled-wool Guernseys for which the island is so famous.

St Peter Port

There is much to fascinate the holidaymaker in Guernsey; one could spend many return visits delving into traditions, customs and folklore alone. The islanders, proud of their heritage and keen to share it, afford the warmest of welcomes.

Historic Houses, Gardens & Parks

Candle Gardens, St Peter Port, G'y
Castle Cornet & Maritime Museum, Guernsey
Eric Young Orchid Foundation, Trinity, Jersey
Fantastic Tropical Gardens, St. Peter's Valley, Jersey
Grande Marais Koi Farm, Vale, G'y Howard David Park, St. Helier, Js'y
Jersey Flower Centre, St. Lawrence
Jersey Lavender Farm St. Brelade
La Mare Vineyards, St. Mary, Jsy
La Seigneurie, Island of Sark Samares Manor, St Clement, Jsy
St. Ouen's Manor Grounds, St Ouen, Jersey
Saumarez Manor, St Martin's, Guernsey
Specialist Gardens at Castle Cornet, Guernsey
Sunset Carnation Nurseries, St. Ouen's Bay, Jersey

Walks & Nature Trails

Grandes Rocques, Guernsey
Guided nature walks - Jersey's Coastal Walks:
  i) Grosnez to Sorel
  ii) Sorel to Bouley Bay
  iii) Bouley Bay to St. Catherine's
Le Catioroc Nature Trail & L'Eree Port Soif Nature Trail, Guernsey
Shingle Bank Portinfer, Guernsey
The Saumarez Nature Trail & Park Walk, starting at Cobo Bay, Guernsey
St Peter Port to St Martin's Point Walk, Guernsey

Historical Sites & Museums

La Valette Underground Military Museum, St. Peter Port, Guernsey
German Occupation Museum, St. Peter Port, Guernsey
Guernsey Aquarium, Havelet Bay
Guernsey Museum & Art Gallery, St Peter Port
National Trust of Guernsey Folk Museum, Saumarez Park 
Fort Grey Shipwreck Museum, St. Saviours, Guernsey
Battle of Flowers Museum, St Ouen, Jersey
Elizabeth Castle, St Aubin's Bay, Jersey
Faldouet Dolmen, Gorey, Jsy
German Underground Hospital, St. Lawrence, Jersey 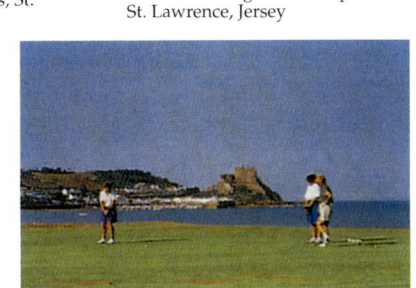
Grosnez Castle & La Pinacle, Les Landes, Jersey
Hamptonne Country Life Museum, St. Lawrence, Jersey
The Hermitage St Helier, Jersey
La Hougue Bie, Grouville, Jersey
Island Fortree Occupation Museum, St. Helier, Jersey
Jersey Motor Museum
The Living Legend, St Peter, Jersey
Mont Orgueil Castle, Gorey, Jersey
The Pallot Heritage Steam Museum, Trinity, Jsersey
St. Peter's Bunker Museum, St. Peter, Jersey

Entertainment Venues

Fort Regent Leisure Centre, St Helier, Jersey
Guernsey Bird Sanctuary, St Andrew's
Jersey Butterfly Centre, St Mary
Jersey Shire Horse Farm & Museum, St Ouen
Jersey Pottery, Gorey Village
Jersey Zoo, Trinity
Le Friquet Butterfly Centre, Castel, Guernsey
Oatlands, Guernsey's craft Centre, St Sampson's

Channel Islands 233

DIARY OF EVENTS

January-February

19-26.1. **Guernsey Open Bowls Tournament.** Guernsey Bowls Stadium.
9-16.2. **Jersey Comedy Festival.** Various venues.

March

21-24. **Spring Garden Festival.** Var venues, Jersey.
28-30* **International Guernsey Masters Swim Meet**, Beau Sejour Leisure Centre, SPPOrt

April

18-19. **Easter Athletics, Badminton & Hockey.** Guernsey.
13-20. **Spring Walking Week.** Contact Jersey Tourism.

May

2-4*. **Int'l Guernsey Masters Swim Meet.** Beau Sejour Ctre
3-10. **International Arts Festival.** Jersey
3-5. **First Active Gaelic Football 7s Tournament.** Port Soif, Guernsey.
9. **Liberation Day.** From German occupation. St Peter Port, Guernsey.
10-18. **Jersey International Food Festival.** Var. venues.
24-26. **Country Fayre.** Jersey.

June

1-6. **Guernsey Regatta.** Guernsey Yacht Club.
1-9. **Floral Guernsey Show.** Cambridge Park, St Peter Port
6-8. **Jersey Festival of Mot'rg**
8. **Guernsey Classic Vehicle Show & Guernsey Mini Owners Club Show.**

Saumarez Park, St Peter Port.
9-11. **Jersey Wild Week -Bugs, Bats, Birds & Buttercups.** June*. **Jersey Maritime Festival.**
28-4.7. **Guernsey Natwest Island Games.**
28-29. **Guernsey Rowing Club Little Russell Regatta.**

July

7. **Le Viaer Marchi.** Traditional festival with songs, dance, arts etc. Sausmarez Park, Guernsey.
5-11. **Jersey Garden Festival.**
12-13. **North Regatta.** St Sampson's Harbour, Guernsey.
25. **Harbour Carnival.** St Peter Port, Guernsey.
26-27*. **Sark Water Carnival.**
26-2.8. **St Peter Port Carnival,** Guernsey.

August

14-15. **Jersey Battle of Flowers**
6-7. **South Show.** Guernsey.
16-17. **Al Fresco Film Feast.** St Helier, Jersey.
16. **Lions Club Donkey Derby.** Saumarez Park, Gnsy.
20-21. **North Show/Battle of Flowers.** Saumarez Park, Guernsey.
27-31. **Horse of the Year Show.** Guernsey.

September

11*. **International Air Display** Jersey.
11. **Battle of Britain Air Display.** St Peter Port, Gnsey.

13-14. **Guernsey Petanque Open**. Catel, Guersnsey.
13-15. **32 Guernsey Int'l Air Rally.** Aero Club, Guernsey.
21-29. **Guernsey Int'l Bridge Congress**. Beau Sejour Centre

October/November

3-5.10. **Guernsey Lily Intl Amateur Film Festival.**
3-5.10. **Guernsey Jazz Festival.** Var. venues, St Peter Port
6-10.10. **Autumn Wild Week - Waters & Woodland**. Jersey.
19.10. **29th International Chess Festival.** Peninsula Hotel, Vale, Guernsey
27-21.10*. **Family Fun Week.** Jersey.
30-2.12. **Guernsey Volleyball Open**. Beau Sejour Leis Ctre

*dates to be confirmed
For further details contact:

TOURIST BOARDS

States of Guernsey Department of Tourism and Recreation, PO Box 23, St. Peter Port, Guernsey, Channel Islands GY1 3AN. Tel: 01481 723552. www.jersey.com

Jersey Tourism. Liberation Sq, St Helier, Jersey E1 1BB, Channel Islands. Tel: 01534 500700. www.guernseytouristboard.com

Jersey

The island of Jersey has something to offer everyone, but there's a lot more for children than just the obvious attractions of sun, sea and sand. Its wealth of sporting facilities, historic sites and animal centres make it an ideal spot for family holidays, and even offer children and parents the chance to get away from each other once in a while.

If you really can't bear to tear yourself away from the sea, there are all kinds of watersports available around the island and Jersey Tourism can provide a comprehensive list of surfing, sailing and water-ski clubs.

But if the children want to go it alone, there's no need for parents to worry. *The Wind & Water Windsurfer School* at St. Aubin offers a 5-hour windsurfing course for beginners from the age of nine upwards, using a small lightweight rig for younger pupils. Tuition is by fully qualified instructors.

Youngsters who prefer riding a horse to a surfboard are well catered for by the island's numerous riding stables, several of whom are also pleased to welcome unaccompanied helpers. Prices average £9 an hour for a hack, £10-12 for a lesson and hard hats can usually be provided, so there's no need to squeeze one into the hand-luggage.

A number of sports centres and pleasure parks offer

a variety of activities from weight-training to table tennis, go-karts to snooker, but perhaps the best known of them all is Fort Regent - the huge sports and leisure complex housed in the Napoleonic fortress overlooking St. Helier.

When the family is tired of having fun and fancies a little gentle education, there is no shortage of historical sites to interest visitors of all ages. Elizabeth Castle in St. Aubin's Bay was begun in the reign of Queen Elizabeth I and has been re-fortified throughout the centuries right up until the First World War. Open only during the summer months, the castle is reached across the bay from St. Helier by an amphibious vehicle service using a World War II landing craft.

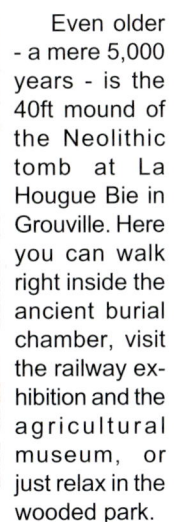

Even older - a mere 5,000 years - is the 40ft mound of the Neolithic tomb at La Hougue Bie in Grouville. Here you can walk right inside the ancient burial chamber, visit the railway exhibition and the agricultural museum, or just relax in the wooded park.

Those who like natural history will enjoy a visit to the Kempt Tower Interpretation Centre on the Five Mile Road at St. Ouen. A converted Martello tower, it contains displays and artefacts relating to the special characteristics of Jersey's "mini national park". Open every afternoon from June to September.

Animal lovers of all ages are well catered for on the island. Heatherbrae Farm in St. John offers visitors the chance to learn all about milk production and watch the 50-strong herd of pure bred Jersey cows during afternoon milking. There's also a fascinating Shire Horse Farm in St. Ouen and, for the very large to the very small, a butterfly farm at the Haute Tombette.

Finally, no animal lover can afford to miss the unique collection of endangered species at the Jersey Wildlife Preservation Trust established 33 years ago by naturalist Gerald Durrell in Trinity.

Jersey may measure a mere nine miles by five, but

La Corbière lighthouse, Jersey, where a siren is soundeed at high tide.

it is packed with interesting things to see and do - for the young in years and the young at heart!

La Favorita Hotel

Fermain Bay, Guernsey GY4 6SD
Tel: (01481) 235666; Fax: (01481) 235413
E-Mail: info@favorita.com
Website: www.favorita.com

The warmth of the welcome from proprietors Helen and Simon Wood and their staff sets the tone for your stay at La Favorita. Nothing will be too much trouble to ensure that you have a relaxed and memorable stay at this one time country house, now a fully licensed successful hotel which combines original character and charm with modern extensions and facilities. Set in the attractive wooded valley that leads down to Fermain Bay and within walking distance of St Peter Port, the hotel enjoys beautiful views over the valley and sea. The 33 bedrooms are comfortable with all modern amenities and the restaurant has a good reputation for traditional English cooking. As a less formal alternative the Coffee Shop serves snacks and lighter meals. The other public rooms and extensive leisure facilities make La Favorita a veritable 'favourite' for a relaxing break in whatever season. The hotel can also help with travel arrangements, car hire and in pointing out to visitors the many delights of the island.

Rates: Single room inc. breakfast from £48; double room with breakfast from £80.
Romantic Breaks including travel, car hire, champagne and roses from around £200(2 nights).
Walking Holiday Breaks inc travel, guidebooks, maps and bus rover ticket from ca. £300 (4 nights).

- 33 en suite non smoking bedrooms (inc 5 family rooms), all with colour TV, radio, hairdryer, laundry/valet service, tea/coffee making, baby listening.
- 4-cse table d'hôte menu £16.25; à la carte, lunch & special diets available; last orders 9 pm.
- Meeting room to 80; car parking for 30; airport pickup by arrangement. Facilities for the disabled.
- Indoor swimming pool, jacuzzi, sauna. Fishing, sea, sailing, clay shooting, tennis, riding and walking all nearby.
- Open March - December.

Diners, Visa & Mastercard accepted.

St Peter Port 2 miles.

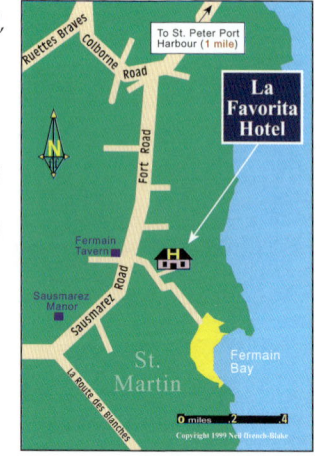

Bella Luce Hotel & Restaurant

Moulin Huet, St. Martins, Guernsey
GY4 6EB
Tel: (01481) 238764; Fax: (01481) 239561
E-Mail: info@bellalucehotel.guernsey.net
Website: www.bellalucehotel.guernsey.net

The Bella Luce is one of the most attractive hotels and restaurants on the lovely island of Guernsey. Originally a 12th century manor house, it is set in its own well tended and colourful gardens with an abundance of flowers and wonderful hanging baskets. New proprietor, John Cockcroft, who had been the General Manager for ten years, and his staff take great pride in running this hotel to ensure their guests' maximum contentment. All the public rooms are attractively furnished and very comfortable. The lounge bar, with its oak beamed ceiling, has a warm and friendly atmosphere, and is the ideal place in which to enjoy either a drink or a dish chosen from the extensive bar lunch menu. The freshly prepared food served in the restaurant is excellent, with a delicious choice of dishes from either the table d'hôte or à la carte menus. To accompany these, there is a comprehensive wine list to suit all palates. The hotel is well located in a peaceful and tranquil setting in St Martin's just two miles from the beautiful "capital" of Guernsey, St. Peter Port, with the island's magnificent cliffs and coastal scenery providing breathtaking views.

Rates: Room and breakfast £30-£55; dinner, room and breakfast £44-£70.
Leisure breaks available 1st November-1st April, £30 per person per night for b & b.

- *31 en suite bedrooms (4 ground floor), all with direct dial telephone, colour TV, room service; baby listening; hairdryer.*
- *Last orders for dinner 9.45p.m.; bar meals; special diets.*
- *Children welcome; dogs accepted at management's discretion.*
- *Outdoor heated swimming pool (May-September); sauna; solarium.*
- *Open all year; major credit cards accepted.*

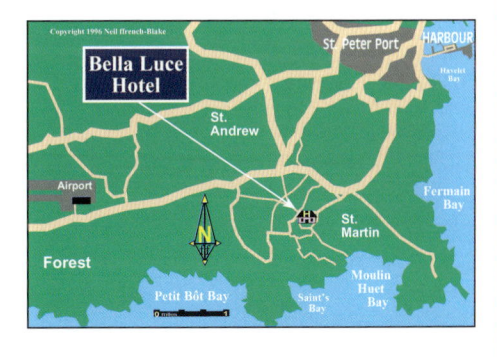

Guernsey, Castel

La Grande Mare Hotel, Golf & Country Club

Vazon, Castel, Guernsey
GY5 7LL
Tel: (01481) 256576
Fax: (01481) 256532
E-mail: hotellagrandemare@gtonline.net
Website: www.lgm.guernsey.net

Whatever your reason for visiting Guernsey - business, pleasure, a short break or a family holiday, La Grande Mare, with its beachside location and multiple leisure activities, should be high on your short list of places to stay. The hotel, spa and golf courses are family owned and run with attention to detail and guests' comfort and enjoyment the top priority. Spacious bedrooms have the finest linen sheets and are fitted out to a high standard. Dinner is of the highest calibre and can either be taken in the formal restaurant whose westerly aspect enjoys spectacular sunsets or during the summer *al fresco* on the timber balcony beside the pool. Alternatively a snack meal is available in the conservatory. Within yards of the hotel is recreation of many kinds: a leisurely picnic by the lake, a walk or jog on the Vazon bay beach (one of the longest on the island), a supervised workout in the gym, a swim in either the indoor or outdoor pool, a game of tennis on the all-weather court, a sauna, jacuzzi, or any form of watersport. For the golfer, there is an 18-hole course set in 110 acres of parkland. It also caters for Corporate and Society Days with PGA tuition and a very well-stocked tax-free golf shop. Just 15 minutes from the airport and St Peter Port, La Grande Mare is a hotel with a lot to offer in comfort and style to visitors of all ages.

press, modem points, 24-hr room service, safe. ✻ & ♿ rooms available. ● Open all year.
● 3-cse tdh dinner £19.95; alc, lunch & spec diets available; last orders 9.30 pm. Meeting room for 30.
● Croquet, fishing, fitness centre/gym, golf, jacuzzi, sauna, out-and indoor swimming pools, tennis. Riding, sailing, squash, shooting nearby.
● & all major credit cards accepted.

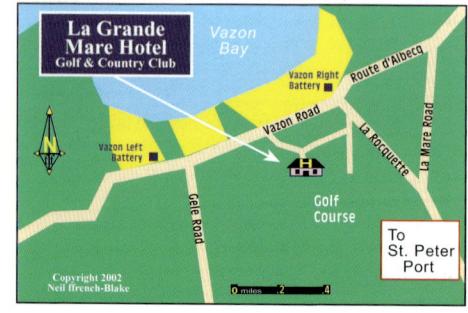

Rates: *Single/double/twin room with breakfast from £84.*
Leisure Breaks *of many sorts available: gourmet, golf, romantic, chill-out. See our tariff for details.*
● 25 en suite bedrooms (inc 14 suites), all with satellite TV, hairdryer, direct-dial telephone, radio/alarm, tea/coffee making, laundry service, trouser

The White House Hotel

Herm Island, via Guernsey GY1 3HR
Tel: (01481) 722159; Fax: (01481) 710066
E-mail: hotel@herm-island.com
Website: www.herm-island.com

Herm is a 20-minute boat journey from Guernsey and is the smallest of the Channel Islands. There are no cars and Herm's magic starts to work as soon as you are greeted on the quayside: the pretty harbour houses the island's three shops and the Ship Inn. Nearby is the castellated manor, where the owners of the island, the Heyworths, live and where you will find the island's school and 10th century chapel. There are bracing cliff walks and beautiful unspoiled beaches, wild flowers and clear landscapes for painting. As the gentle chugging of a tractor heralds the arrival of your luggage, you know the White House Hotel is special. After all, how many hotels can boast an island as their garden, a harbourside setting and such spectacular sea views? Where else could you enjoy shellfish so fresh in the award-winning restaurant? Tradition is cherished at the White House Hotel. You are assured of a warm welcome and friendly service from Jonathan Watson and his staff. In the 39 delightful bedrooms, you'll find private bathrooms and baby listening but no televisions, clocks or telephones. Children have always been welcome, with a popular high tea for junior diners. The hotel encourages you to unwind and the island is perfect for that away-from-it-all break.

Rates: *Dinner, bed & breakfast from £61 per person per night. Saturday night gourmet menu.*
Leisure Breaks: *Bluebells in Bloom Spring Break to end-May (exc Easter) £142 pp two nights inc boat fare, wine & flowers.*

- 39 en suite bedrooms with hairdryer, radio, baby listening, tea/coffee making. Non-smoker bedrooms available.
- Last orders for dinner 9 pm. Special diets and lunch available.
- Croquet, fishing, tennis, bathing, sailing, outdoor swimming pool.
- Open April 4-Oct 12th.
- Visa, Master-, Euro, Switch accepted.

Jersey, St Peter's/Gorey

Greenhills Country Hotel & Restaurant

St Peter's Valley, Jersey JE3 7EL
Tel: (01534) 481042;
Fax: (01534) 485322
E-mail: greenhills@messages.co.uk

What a discovery! This 17th century country house is one of the most delightful small hotels in Jersey. Set in award winning gardens and nestled attractively in the tranquil heart of St Peter's Valley, the hotel has retained its character and features to ensure that guests experience the unique atmosphere and intimacy of a period country house. The 31 comfortable and traditionally styled bedrooms have a 'cottagey' atmosphere but with all modern amenities. Cuisine is British with continental influences, the accent being on fresh local seafood. Add to this comfortable public rooms and a sheltered swimming pool and you have a perfect hideaway. Personal and unpretentious hospitality from owner Peter Bromley and his staff will ensure that you'll want to keep the Greenhills secret to yourself!

Rates: Single room with breakfast from £52; double inc breakfast from £104.

● 31 en suite bedrooms (inc suites), all with colour TV, radio, direct-dial telephone, hairdryer, laundry service, trouser press.
● 4 cse table d'hôte from £19.50. A la carte, lunch & special diets available. Last orders 9.00 pm
● Conference room & car parking for 40. Airport pickup by arrangement.● Open April 27-18th Oct.
● & major credit cards accepted. <u>Directions:</u> Fm St Helier take A1, then A11 to St Peter's Valley. 4 miles out turn rt on C112; hotel signed on left.

The Moorings Hotel & Restaurant

Gorey Pier, Jersey JE3 6EW
Tel: (01534) 853633;
Fax: (01534) 857618
E-mail: reservations@themooringshotel.com
Website: www.themooringshotel.com

The Moorings is one of the most popular hotels and restaurants on the beautiful island of Jersey, both for its visitors and for its residents. Its position is unique, bridging the centuries. It nestles between the walls of Elizabethan Gorey Castle and the waterfront. It provides a haven for those who enjoy good food and wine combined with an individual and sensitive service in homely and comfortable surroundings. The bustling quayside is still used for the traditional fishing industry, alongside local shops. The pretty harbour, once the centre of Jersey's oyster industry, is alive with colour and movement throughout the day. Several times daily ferries arrive and depart for local French ports. This is a great centre not only for shopping but also for walking, cycling, golf, sailing, fishing, watersports, tennis and riding may be found in the surrounding area.

Rates: Single room including breakfast from £41.50. Double room with breakfast from £83.
Winter Breaks available 1st Nov-31st March. Full Xmas programme inc. hire car. Details on appn.

● 15 en suite bedrooms with TV, direct-dial telephone; hairdryer, trouser press, radio/alarm clock, tea/coffee making facilities. Open all year.
● Restaurant, two bars, alfresco dining area lounge; last orders 10.15 pm; Alc, lunch & dinner, special diets available. Corporate rates, conference facilities.
● Fishing, golf, watersports, riding, sailing, tennis, cycling nearby.
● & Visa, Mastercard, Switch accepted.

Hotel L'Horizon

St Brelade's Bay, Jersey JE3 8EF
Tel: (01534) 743101; Fax: (01534) 746269
E-mail: hotellhorizon@jerseymail.co.uk
Website: www.hotellhorizon.com

Without doubt one of the premier hotels in the Channel Islands, L'Horizon nestles at the centre of the superb St Brelade's Bay in the beautiful island of Jersey. Its magnificent south facing location ensures that it has one of the best beachside positions on the island. For many, the secret of its success is the combination of the superb beachside position and the internal luxury expected of a top rated hotel. Tastefully furnished throughout, there are a number of areas for guests to sit and relax within the comfort of the hotel or on the long front terrace overlooking the golden sands. Many of the comfortable and spacious bedrooms and suites also have uninterrupted views of the scenic bay from their private balconies. Guests can further enjoy the view from one of three distinctive restaurants: the acclaimed traditional, elegant Crystal Room, the intimate Grill or the less formal Brasserie. The active will enjoy the Health & Leisure Club whilst, further afield, golf, riding, coastal walks and countless places of interest can be recommended by the helpful management and staff of this first class hotel.

Rates: *Single room with breakfast from £120; double inc breakfast from £170.*
Leisure Breaks: *available for each season.*

- 107 en suite bedrooms (inc 5 suites), all with colour TV+satellite, direct-dial telephone, minibar, hairdryer, laundry service, 24-hr room/meal service, trouser press, safe. ♿ *rooms available.*
- *Tdh dinner £29. A la carte, lunch & special diets available. Last orders 10 pm.*
- *Business services inc. 3 meeting rooms. Airport pickup & car rental by arrangement.* 🅿 *121.*
- *Fitness centre, jacuzzi, sauna, steam rooms and large indoor heated swimming pool. Golf, tennis, sea fishing, watersports, sailing, riding, cycling, scuba diving nearby.* ● *Open all year.*
- *Diners, Mastercard, Switch & Visa cards accepted.*

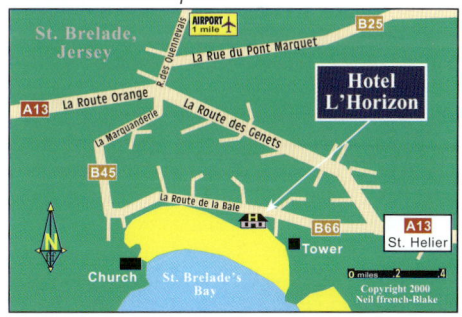

Hotel Petit Champ

Sark, Channel Islands GY9 0SF
Tel: (01481) 832046; Fax: (01481) 832469

E-mail: hpc@island-of-sark.co.uk
Website: www.island-of-sark.co.uk

The island of Sark is truly unique. It retains a feudal constitution dating back to the reign of Elizabeth I, has its own government, no income tax and is home to just 550 residents. It is also a natural, car free and tranquil retreat for people who enjoy beautiful walks, breathtaking scenery and a refreshing break from the modern world. The Hotel Petit Champ is a reflection of all that with its secluded position and views to the sea. Here, under the expert supervision of the resident proprietors Chris and Caroline Robins, is a true gem of an hotel with a country house atmosphere and 10 cosy en suite bedrooms, some of which have balconies. There are three sun-lounges as well as a peaceful library lounge. Drinks before dinner are taken in the intimate bar and then guests repair to the candlelit restaurant renowned for its good cuisine with local lobster and crab dishes as specialities. A solar heated swimming pool nestles in the natural setting of an old quarry and forms a perfect sun trap. The

Hotel Petit Champ, set in the island magic of Sark, is truly enchanting and the spell draws visitors back for holidays year after year.

Rates: Single room including breakfast and dinner from £53.50. Double room with breakfast and dinner from £51.50 per person.

- 10 en suite bedrooms. Hairdryers available.
- 5-course table d'hôte dinner £19.25; à la carte, lunch & special diets available. Last orders 20.30.
- Putting green and solar heated outdoor swimming pool, garden walks, boat trips, horse & carriage tours. Nearby sea fishing, tennis, billiards, badminton.
- All-inclusive holidays with travel available.
- Diners, Mastercard, Visa & Switch accepted. ● Open April- early October.

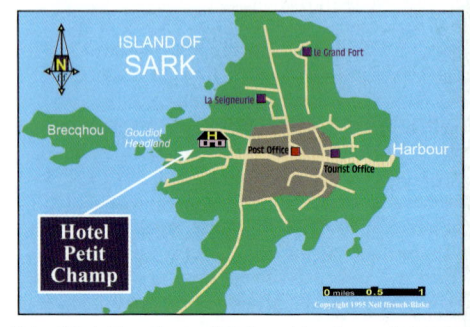

Signpost Guide 2003
Ireland

Fact File
Illustrated Guide to Historic Houses, Gardens and Sites
Diary of Events

Hotels in	PAGE
Co. Cork	248
Co. Donegal	250
Co. Dublin	251
Co. Galway	254
Co. Kerry	255
Co. Offaly	260
Co. Tipperary	262

Ireland

Houses, Gardens & Parks - North
Andress House, Co Armagh
The Argory, Co Armagh
Castle Coole, Co Fermanagh
Castle Ward, Co Down
Cratlow Woods House, Co Down
Downhill, Londonderry
Florence Court, Co Fermanagh
Gray's Printing Press, Strabane, Co Tyrone
Hezlett House, Co Londonderry
Mount Stewart House, Garden & Temple
Rowallane Garden, Saintfield, Down
Springhill, Moneymore, Co Londonderry

Templetown Mausoleum, Co Antrim
Wellbrook Beetling Mill, Cookstown, Co Tyrone

Historical Sites & Museums - North
Carrickfergus Castle, Carrickfergus, Co Antrim
City Hall, Belfast
Devenish Island, Lough Erne
Giant's Causeway, Nr Coleraine, Co Antrim
Glen of Glenariff, NE of Ballymena
Slieve Gullion, Newry, Co Down
Stormont Castle, Belfast
Ulster Museum, Belfast

DIARY OF EVENTS - THE NORTH

January
16-19*. **Holiday World.** Kings Hall, Balmoral, Belfast.

February
26-Mar 8. **Ballymoney Drama Festival.** Ballymoney Borough Council, Ballymoney, Co Down

March
11-18. **Celtic Spring Festival.** St Patricks Week.Var.Londonderry
15-18. **St Patrick's Day Celebrations.** Armagh, Ballycastle & Downpatrick.
19-30*. **Between The Lines 2003.** Int'l literary festival. Crescent Arts Centre, Belfast.

April
2-5. **Bangor Choral Festival.** Var. venues, Bangor, Co Down.
10-12. **Knit, Stitch & Creative Crafts Show.** Barnett Pk, Belfast.

May
1-11. **Cathedral Quarter Arts Festival.** Belfast north city c'tre.
14-16. **Balmoral Show.** Kings Hall, Balmoral, Belfast.
17-24. **Ballyclare May Fair Festival.** Var, venues, Ballyclare.
17-1.6*. **Belfast Summerfest 2002.** Entertain't. Var ven, Belfast

June
June*. **Shankill Community Festival.** Shankill, Belfast.
6-8. **Walled City Festival.** City Centre & Waterside Area, Londonderry.
29-30. **Northern Ireland Game & Country Fair.** Galgorm Castle, Ballymena, Co Antrim.
20-22*. **Galway Hooker Regatta.** Portaferry, Co Down.
Mid-June*. **Enniskillen Air Show.** Enniskillen, Co Ferm'gh

July
July*. **Rostrevor Harp Festival.** Carlingford Lough, Co Down.
4-6. **American Independence Day Celebrations.** Ulster American Folk Park, Omagh.
16. **Aughnagloy Horse Fair.** Aughnagloy, Co Tyrone.
18-19. **Ulster Traction Engine Rally.** Ballymena, Co Antrim.
19-25. **Northern Ireland Milk Cup.** Coleraine, Co Londonderry.

August-November
1-10.8. **Féile an Phobail Community Festival.** West Belfast.
1-31Aug. **Ould Lammas Fair.** Ballycastle, Co Antrim BT54
5-7*. **Appalachian & Bluegrass Music Festival.** Ulster American Folk Park, Omagh.
13-14.9. **European Heritage Open Days.** Var. venues Belfast
31.10-16.11. **Belfast Festival at Queens.** Queen's Univ, Belfast.
27.11-7.12. **Cinemagic Int'l Film Festival for Young People.** Var venues throughout N Ireland.

Historic Houses Gardens - Republic
Annes Grove Gardens, Castletownroche
Ayesha Castle, Killiney, Co Dublin
Bantry House, Bantry, Co Cork
Birr Castle Demesne, Co Offaly
Blarney Castle & Blarney House, Blarney, Co Cork
Bunratty Castle & Folk Park, Bunratty, Co Clare
Carrigglass Manor, Longford, Co Longford
Castletown House, Cellbridge, Co Kildare
Cloghan Castle, Banagher, Co Clare
Colnalis House, Castlerea, Co Roscommon
Craggaunowen - The Living Past - Kilmurry, Co Clare
Dunguaire Castle, Kinvara, Co Galway
Dunloe Castle Hotel Gardens, Beaufort, Killarney, Co Kerry
Emo Court, Portlaoise, Co Leix
Fernhill Garden, Sandyford, Co Dublin
Fota Wildlife Park, Fota Island, Carrigtwohill, Co Cork
Glin Castle, Glin, Co Limerick
GPA Bolton Library, Cashel, Co Tipperary
Japanese Garden, Tully, Co Kildare
Johnstown Castle Demesne, Wexford, Co Wexford
The James Joyce Tower, Sandycove, Co Dublin
The John F Kennedy Arboretum, New Ross, Co Wexford
Knappogue Castle, Quin, Co Clare
Kylemore Abbey, Kylemore, Connemara, Co Galway
Lismore Castle, Lismore, Co Waterford
Lissadell, Sligo
Lough Gur Visitor Centre, Lough Gur, Co Limerick
Lough Rynn Estate & Gardens, Mohill, Co Leitrim
Malahide Castle, Malahide, Co Dublin
Mount Congreve Gardens, Nr. Waterford
Mount Usher Gardens, Ashford, Co Wicklow
Muckross House & Gardens, Killarney, Co Kerry
National Botanic Gardens, Glasnevin, Dublin 9
Newbridge House, Donabate, Co Dublin
Phoenix Park, Dublin
Powerscourt Gardens & Waterfall, Enniskerry, Co Wicklow
Powerscourt Townhouse Centre, 59 South William St, Dublin 2
Riverstown House, Glanmire, Co Cork
Royal Hospital, Kilmainham, Co Dublin
Russborough, Blessington, Co Wicklow

*For further information, contact: The Northern Ireland Tourist Board
St Anne's Court, 59 North Street, Belfast BT1 1NB. Tel: (02890) 231521; Fax: (02890) 240960*

DIARY OF EVENTS

Slane Castle, Slane, Co Meath
Strokestown Park House, Strokestown, Co Roscommon
Swiss Cottage, Chir, Co Tipperary
Thoor Ballylee, Gort, Co Galway
Timoleague Castle Gardens, Bandon, Co Cork
Tullynally Castle, Castlepollard, Co Westmeath

Historical Sites & Museums

Augustinian Priory (14thC), Kells, Co Kilkenny
Blarney Castle & Stone, Co Cork
Castle (State Apartments), Dublin
Christ Church Cathedral, Dublin
Cliffs of Moher & O'Brien's Tower, Lahinch, Co Clare
Glengarrif, 8m N of Bantry, Co Cork
Grianan of Eilach Fort, 18m NE of Letterkenny, Co Galway
Jerpoint Abbey ruins, 12m SE of Kilkenny, Co Kilkenny
Lough Corrib/Claregalway, Galway, Co Galway
Lough Gill/Lough Colgath, Sligo, Co Sligo
Lynch's Castle, Galway, Co Galway
Mellifont Abbey, Drogheda, Co Louth
Monasterboice, Drogheda, Co Louth
Monastic City/St Kervin's Church, Glendalough, Co Wicklow
Municipal Art Gallery/Hugh Lane Gallery, Dublin
Museum of Modern Art, Kilmainham, Dublin
National Gallery, Dublin
National Museum, Dublin
Ring of Kerry, Killarney, Co Kerry
St Ann's Shandon Church, Cork
St Canice's Cathedral, Kilkenny, Co Kilkenny
St Patrick's Rock (Rock of Cashel), Co Tipperary
Sheehans Pt, remains of Carhan House, Waterville, Co Kerry   Timoleague Franciscan Abbey, Courtmacsherry, Co Cork
Trinity College Library, Dublin
Tulla Church, 10m E of Ennis, Co Clare
Writers' Museum, Dublin

January

26-2.3. **Dublin Boat Show.** Main Hall, Royal Dublin Soc'y.

March

8. **6-Nations Cup Ireland v France.** Lansdowne Rd, Dublin.
15-17. **St Patrick's Festival.** Nationwide (Day = 17th)
10-18*. **Bridge House Irish Festival.** Bridge House Hotel, Tullamore, Co Offaly *(see page 261 of this guide)Irish food,drink&c*
14-17. **International Band Festival.** Var. venues Limerick
30. **6-Nations Cup. Ireland v England.** Lansdowne Rd, Ballsbridge, Dublin 4.

April

18-22.**West of Ireland Amataur Open Golf Championship.** Inniscrone, Co Sligo
29-3.5. **Punchestown Festival Meeting.** Racecourse.Co Kildare

May

1-4. **Cork International Choral Festival.** City Hall, UCC, Triskel Arts Centre, Cork.
2-4. **Bray Jazz Festival,** Wicklow
3-4.**Heineken Kinsale Rugby 7s by the Sea**, Kinsale, Co Cork
6-17. **All Ireland Drama Festival.** Dean Crowe Theatre, Athlone. Co Westmeath.
9-12*.**Murphy's International Mussel Fair.** Bantry, Co Cork.

*Provisional Date. For further information, contact **Bord Failte** (Irish Tourist Board, Baggot Street Bridge, Dublin 2. Tel: 1 602 400060; Fax: 1 475 8046. Website: www.bordfailte.com

June

2-3. **Murphys Cat Laughs Comedy Festival.** Kilkenny City.
2. **East of Ireland Open Golf Championship,** Co Louth.
16-18.**Bloomsday Festival** James Joyce Centre & oth ven, Dublin
29. **Budweiser Irish Derby.** The Curragh, Co Kildare.

July

10-13. **Anglo Irish Bank Garden Heaven.** RDS, Dublin.
15-27. **Galway Arts Festival.** Var. venues, Galway City.
27-28.**Yeats Int'l Summer School.** Memorial Bldg, Douglas Hyde Bridge, Sligo.
28-3.8. **Galway Festival Meeting.** Galway Racecourse

August

6-10. **Kerrygold Horse Show** RDS Showground, Dublin 4.
10-12. **Puck Fair.** Irish Festival, Killorglin, Co Kerry.
8-17. **Kilkenny Arts Festival.** Var. venues, Kilkenny.
22-26.**Rose of Tralee Festival.** Var. venues, Tralee, Co Kerry.

September

9. **All Ireland Hurling Final.** Croke Park, Dublin.
20-Oct 5. **Waterford Int'l Festival of Light Opera.** Theatre Royal, Waterford.
12-14. **Clarenbridge Oyster Fest.** Clarenbridge, Co Galway.
25-28. **Galway Oyster Festival**
29-11.10.**Dublin Theatre Festival.** Major theatres, Dublin.

October

25-28*. **Guinness Cork Film Festival.** Cork Opera Hse, Cork.
16-Nov 2. **Wexford Festival Opera,** Theatre Royal Wexford
23-27.**PMPA Ideal Homes Exhib Exhib** RDS, Ballsbridge, Dublin 4
28. **All Ireland Football Final.** Croke Park, Dublin.

Circuit of Ireland

Ireland is roughly 300 miles long from the north coast of Donegal to the south coast of County Cork and about 170 miles wide from Dublin on the east coast to the west coast of County Mayo. Dublin and Belfast have fine airports. Car ferries run from Holyhead to Dun Laoghaire, Fishguard and Pembroke to Rosslare, Swansea to Cork, and Stranraer in Scotland to Larne in Northern Ireland. As well as the established Aer Lingus routes from the UK to Eire, in recent years Ryanair have greatly increased their route network and now fly from Bournemouth, Bristol, Birmingham, Cardiff, Leeds/Bradford, Stansted, Liverpool, Manchester and Edinburgh regularly to the Republic and at very low cost (from £40 per head one way). Once arrived at your Irish entry port, you will find helpful and reasonably priced car hire firms ready to help you.

One of the most attractive reasons for choosing Ireland as a country for scenery, sport and ports of call, is the freedom of its roads. They are not infested by monster juggernauts, exasperating queues and long delays at junctions. So the driver proceeds in peace enjoying the view of the country without wondering if he's likely to be mown down by some rushing madman. Be warned, 'though, that road surfaces are not always as smooth as in Britain, so cars tend not to live to a ripe old age.

Ireland, North or South, has a huge choice for people of varied interests. Fishing, of course, the Dublin Horse Show, racing, splendid golf courses, unpolluted sands, ancient relics, and all sorts of magnificent coastal scenery like the tremendous Cliffs of Moher on the west coast, Blarney Castle near Cork where you can kiss the stone and supposedly be rewarded with exceptional eloquence. The Giant's Causeway, easily reached from Portrush in County Antrim, and its thousands of basalt columns which are certainly one of the most curious geological formations in the world. As a similar formation is found in the Scottish Island of Staffa on the west coast of Scotland, it has been suggested that these formations may extend and meet under the Irish Sea.

Now a few hints on how to see the West of Ireland. Whether you start from Dublin, Rosslare or Cork, from a viewing point it's better to follow the sun round, in other words left handed keeping to the coast. Starting at Rosslare you can visit the famous crystal glass factory at Waterford; in nearby Middleton, the home of Irish whisky, you can tour a distillery. Wexford has a famous Opera Festival and Heritage Park, bringing Irish history to life. County Cork and County Kerry are generally reckoned to provide the finest and most varied scenery. Cork is Ireland's second city, home of *Murphy's* stout and the famous jazz festival. The road from Cork gives one a taste of the mountains ahead, Killarney follows, a veritable wonderland of mountains and lakes many with odd names like the *MacGillicuddy Reeks* 3,414' which include the highest peaks in Ireland. There are first class hotels in the town and several most excellent ones a few miles west. One could spend a fortnight exploring this wonderful and beautiful area alone.

From Killarney to Waterville, a noted fishing town with several first class and friendly hotels. Limerick and Galway are the main cities of Ireland's West Coast; the latter famous for its annual Race Meeting and Oyster Festival. In nearby Connemara you will find the world famous marble, and see the equally famous wild Connemara ponies. Next to County Mayo where the soft pastel shades of the mountains and clouds appeal to the artist and photographer. In the Oughterard, Clifden, Newport and Westport area have some charming family run hotels of special merit.

Southwest of Westport the 2,510' high hump of *Croagh Patrick* (near Knock) attracts yearly pilgrimages up its stony flanks and unfortunately now is apt to be trippery with tourists sometimes outnumbering pilgrims. County Donegal is famed for its Atlantic Drive and has one of the least polluted coasts in Europe.

From here one turns east into Londonderry and then to Portrush and its golf courses and the Giant's Causeway near Bushmills. The Antrim coast road south to Belfast affords sea and land views while a more exciting hilly road from Bally Castle takes in Carrick-a-Rede whose cliffs and suspension bridge are well worth a visit. In Dungannon you can visit and purchase the famous Tyrone Crystal.

Elegant Ireland
...simply the best

Elegant Ireland represents a number of top quality properties, ranging from cosy, one bedroom cottages to large, fully staffed and self catering castles.

Our properties are available for exclusive use, usually for one week or more. They represent the best in each category and location. Some of the larger houses offer a daily dinner, bed & breakfast service, when not rented.

As a leading incoming tour operator, we offer a full ground handling service, including chauffeur/self-drive cars, customised itinerary and tour design.

With Elegant Ireland, Reality Surpasses Expectation

ELEGANT IRELAND
15 Harcourt Street, Dublin 2, Ireland. Tel + 353 1 475 1632/475 1665
Fax: + 353 1 475 1012   e mail info@elegant.ie   Website www.elegant.ie

ITOA

Maryborough House Hotel

Maryborough Hill, Douglas, Cork
Tel: (021) 436 5555; Fax: (021) 436 5662
E-mail: maryboro@indigo.ie
Website: www.maryborough.com

The Maryborough is a charming old world mansion at the centre of natural parkland with majestic oaks, rhododendrons and an outstanding collection of shrubs and plants. Every room has views of these outstanding gardens. The 18th century core building has been restored to preserve all the original Georgian features: high stuccoed ceilings, gracious curved staircases with antique furniture to match. The Garden Room connects the old mansion with the new wing and leads to the 21st century amenities - banqueting and conference areas, state-of-the-art leisure club, swimming pool, and to the contemporary restaurant which serves an exciting mixture of modern flavours and styles, created where possible from fresh local produce. Douglas is a pleasant suburb of Cork, handy for the airport and ferry port, close to the city centre and road network, yet Maryborough provides an oasis of old world elegance, mixed with new world efficiency. A good business or holiday hotel for those embarking on a tour of southwest Ireland.

Rates: Single room inc. breakfast from €138; double room inc. breakfast from €140.
Bargain Breaks: Weekend breaks - 2 nights b&b + one dinner from €152 per person sharing.

● 79 en suite bedrooms, all with colour TV+ satellite, direct dial telephone, hairdryer, laundry/ service, tea/coffee making facilities, 24-hr room service, trouser press. Non-smoker and disabled bedrooms available. ● Closed 24-26 Dec.
● Table d'hôte dinner €32; à la carte, lunch & special diets available. Last orders 10 pm.
● Eight meeting rooms, capacity 5-500. Airport pickup. Car parking 300. Car rental.
● Billiards/snooker, croquet, gymnasium, jacuzzi, massage, sauna, indoor swimming pool, tennis. Fishing, golf, watersports, sailing, riding nearby.
● & all major credit cards accepted
Cork 3, Airport 5, Killarney 51, Dublin 157

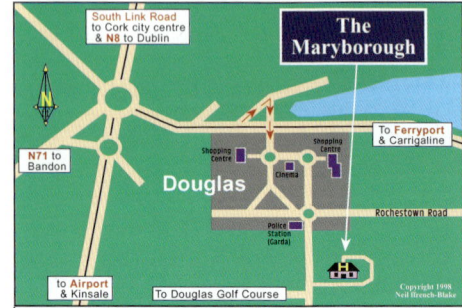

Note: the Euro (€) became the official currency of the Irish Republic on 1.1.02. 1€ = £ sterling 0.66.

Co Cork, Midleton/Shangarry

Ballymaloe House

Shanagarry, Co Cork
Tel: (021) 465 2531;
Fax: (021) 465 2021
E-mail: res@ballymaloe.ie
Website: www.ballymaloe.com

Ballymaloe is a large family farmhouse, still with its 14th century keep, situated on a 400-acre farm 20 miles east of Cork city. It has become well known throughout the British Isles and the USA for the high standard of its accommodation and cuisine. To stay here is to savour all the charm of Irish country living at its best, as exemplified by the spacious public rooms graced by modern Irish paintings and by the large comfortable drawing room where you can relax in front of a roaring log fire. The bedrooms are full of character and are cosy, traditionally furnished or more modern depending on whether they are in the main "home" or in one of the outbuildings. The Craft Shop, Ballymaloe Cookery School in Shanagarry, the restaurant in the Crawford Art Gallery in Cork City are all also run by members of the Allen family. The cuisine in the hotel has won many plaudits. Vegetables are home grown and fish is fresh from Ballycotton nearby.

Rates: Double/twin room including breakfast €180-260. **Special winter rates:** Nov 1-Feb 28 on request. Closed Dec 23-27.

● 33 en suite bedrooms all with d-dial telephone, hairdryer, laundry service, iron;
● Table d'hôte €55. lunch & special diets available; last orders 21.30. Unlimited car parking.
● Croquet, small golf course, outdoor swimming pool, children's play area. Fishing, watersports, sea bathing, riding, tennis, golf courses nearby. Baby sitting
● AMERICAN EXPRESS & major credit cards accepted. **Cork** 25, **Waterford** 64, **Limerick** 91, **Dublin** 163.

Castle Murray House Hotel

St John's Point, Dunkineely, Co Donegal
Tel: (00353) 74 97 37022; Fax: 74 97 37330
E-mail: castlemurray@eircom.net
Website: www.castlemurray.com

Castle Murray House is a compact small Country House Hotel and Restaurant enjoying a magical location overlooking McSwyne's Bay and the exceptionally scenic surrounding countryside. The reception area, lounge and dining room enjoy this view from large picture windows, the floodlit ruins of McSwyne's Castle providing a dramatic backdrop at night. The hotel restaurant specialises in seafood and has a live lobster tank to select from! The hotel is two minutes from the shore and four kms from the beach. There is much to see and do in the area: the fishing port of Killybegs, Donegal Town with its many craft shops, Donegal Castle and Glenveigh National Park, home to one of the biggest red deer herds in Ireland. Local activities include Deane's Open Farm and Equestriuan Centre, golf at Narin/Portnoo course, scuba diving, sea fishing, boat chartering and Waterworld at Bundoran.

Rates: Single room including breakfast €71-85; double room with breakfast €96-128.
Leisure Breaks: 3 nights bed & breakfast - 15% discount; five + nights = 25% disc. Low season only.

- 10 en suite bedrooms with colour TV; direct-dial telephone, hairdryer, tea/coffee making facilities.
- 3 course à la carte dinner from €30; Sunday lunch from €22.50. Special diets available. Last orders 9.30 pm.
- Fishing, jogging track, sea bathing, boating. Golf and riding nearby. Pets welcome.
- *Open all year exc mid-January-mid February.*
- *Visa, Mastercard & Laser credit cards accepted.*

Killybegs 5, Donegal 18, Ballyshannon 33, Londonderry 48, Dublin 182.

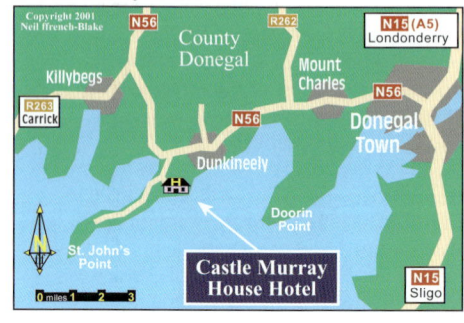

Co Dublin, Dublin 251

Longfields Hotel

10 Fitzwilliam Street Lower, Dublin 1
Tel: (00353-1) 676 1367;
Fax: (00353-1) 676 1542
E-mail: info@longfields.ie   website: www.longfields.ie

The Georgian Doors of Dublin are an established visual attraction in souvenir poster form. A prime example is No 10 Fitzwilliam Street Lower, part of the longest unbroken line of Georgian houses in Ireland and home to Longfields, one of Dublin's most distinguished small hotels. A quiet haven for the visitor, Longfields is an ideal base for forays into the capital's prime shopping streets, such as Grafton Street, for bargain hunting in antique and curio shops, for cinemas and theatres and for Dublin's numerous art galleries and museums - all are within easy walking distance. The city's main burgeoning Bohemian quarter of Temple Bar is ten minutes' walk, as are St Stephens Green and Trinity College. Attention to detail and personal service are the hallmarks of Longfields. This is seen in the elegantly furnished bedrooms and reception area and perhaps best exemplified in the restaurant. Affectionately known as *No 10* to to the business lunch set, it has received excellent reviews.

Rates: Single room including breakfast €145-185; double room with breakfast €215-255. [Ad]

- 26 en suite bedrooms (inc 2 suites) all with colour TV, d-dial telephone, hair-dryer, laundry service, 24-hr room/meal service, fax/modem points, radio/alarm clock.
- 3-cse tdh dinner €50 +12.5% sc; lunch avail; last orders 10 pm. Open all year.
- Visa, Mastercard & Diners accepted.

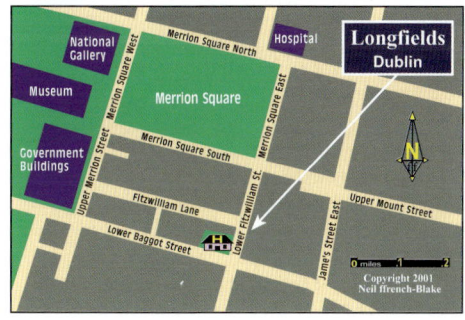

Number 31

31 Leeson Close, Dublin 2
Tel: (00353-1) 676 5011; Fax: 676 2929
E-mail: number31@iol.ie
Website: www.number31.ie

The brochure for No 31 describes it as *'one of Dublin's best-kept secrets'*, and your inspector has to agree that he was immensely surprised and delighted by the location, standard of accommodation and welcome which all guests receive. An award winning guesthouse in the heart of Georgian Dublin, it is the former home of leading architect Sam Stephenson. Set almost in the epicentre of Dublin, St Stephen's Green, owners Deirdre and Noel Comer have made No 31 into a haven of quiet good taste, tranquillity and greenery. There are 18 en suite bedrooms, all large, comfortable and spacious. The beds are firm and comfortable and the furnishings blend with the house, long lined expensive curtains covering the Georgian windows. Being so central, Number 31 does not provide dinner, but a breakfast the size of many dinners, with excellent fresh ground coffee. The helpful staff will park your car for you, relieving you of the worry of clampers and ever vigilant wardens. No 31 is extremely comfortable, quiet and a great find in central Dublin. Children over the age of 10 are welcome. Parents with younger children may be worried about the abundance of fine furniture and paintings. No 31 is within walking distance of Dublin's art galleries, fashionable shops, museums and top restaurants.

Rates: Single room including breakfast from €67; double room with breakfast €71-118.

● 20 en suite bedrooms (inc 2 suites) all with colour TV, direct-dial telephone, hair-dryer, safety deposit box, tea/coffee making facilities. Non-smoking bedrooms available.
● Car parking for 16.
● Children over 10 welcome.
● Open all year
● Visa, Mastercard accepted.

Glenogra House

64 Merrion Road, Dublin 4.
Tel: (01) 668 3661; Fax (01) 668 3698
E-mail: glenogra@indigo.ie
Website: www.glenogra.com

Seamus and Cherry McNamee have very carefully developed an ideal guesthouse with 13 beautifully furnished rooms. A finely appointed Edwardian residence opposite the Royal Dublin Society (RDS) and Four Seasons Hotel, it is close to the city centre, bus routes and the Sandymount DART station, and minutes walk from the US embassy and many fine restaurants. Breakfast has always been regarded as the essential foundation for a good day by the hosts and afternoon tea by the fire is just what is needed after a day's shopping or sightseeing in central Dublin. Bedrooms are smartly decorated in harmony with the period residence. Glenogra is a Four Star Irish Tourist Board guesthouse, ideal for business or leisure travellers looking for good value near to the centre of Dublin. A ✼ house.

Rates: *Single room inc. breakfast €70-85; Double room with breakfast €105-115.*

- 13 en suite bedrooms with radio, colour TV+ satellite, direct-dial telephone, hairdryer, laundry service, trouser press. A non-smoking house.
- Airport pick-up & car rental by arr't.
- & all major credit cards accepted.

Derrynane Hotel

Caherdaniel, Ring of Kerry,
Co. Kerry. Tel: (066) 947 5136;
Fax: (066) 947 5160
E-mail: info@derrynane.com
Website: www.derrynane.com

Derrynane lies amidst some of the most spectacular scenery in Ireland. Offering guests all the pleasures of an elegant modern hotel, the Derrynane boasts a wealth of seaside and country pursuits. The area is a walkers' paradise with the Kerry Way and The Mass Path on the doorstep, hills to climb and secluded coves and beaches to visit. Hotel facilities include a gym, sauna, steam room and tennis court. There is plenty to do in the area: boat trips to the Skelligs to see early Christian dwellings, sea, stream or lake fishing and championship golf at the Waterville and Ring of Kerry courses. In the evening you can return to enjoy a sumptuous meal in the restaurant where fresh fish is a speciality. Derrynane is an ideal spot for a family activity holiday with sporting tuition available nearby.
Cahersiveen 18, Kenmare 30, Killarney 35, Cork 100, Dublin 231.

Rates: *Single room with breakfast from €70; double room with breakfast from €100.*
Bargain Breaks: *Special packages inc. dinner available throughout season based on stay length.*

- 70 en suite bedrooms with satellite TV, d-dial telephone, hairdryer, radio/alarm, tea/coffee making.
- 3-cse tdh dinner €35; alc/diets avail; last ord 2100.
- Fishing, fitness centre, golf, indoor games, jogging, beach,watersports, massage, sauna, sailing, outdoor swimming pool, tennis, riding.
- & all major cards accepted.
- Closed October-Easter.

Renvyle House Hotel

Renvyle, Commemara, Co Galway
Tel: (00353) [0] 95 43511;
Fax: (00353) [0] 95 43515
E-mail: renvyle@iol.ie   Website: www.renvyle.com

Renvyle has been a country house hotel since 1883 and has played host since then to many famous guests: Augustus John, WB Yeats and Winston Churchill among them. The first sign that greets you as you arrive says *"Stress Free Zone"* and so it proved to be for our inspector, with mobile 'phones refusing to work! The hotel sits beside its own lake on a promontory jutting into the Atlantic. Dogs are welcome, so the hotel appeals to country people in sensible shoes and festooned with all sorts of sporting paraphernalia. Here you can go for long walks, play golf, tennis and croquet, swim, ride from the hotel stables, fish in the hotel lake, climb mountains or explore the nearby islands. It is the sort of place that people visit for a week in order to completely unwind. There are open fires, a library for quiet reading, a conservatory which in summertime is a lovely place for tea and scones, and a large welcoming restaurant, serving excellent cuisine, based on fresh local produce -notably Connemara lamb, game and fresh fish, with a wine cellar to match. No wonder the place was packed when we stayed!

Rates: *Single room with breakfast from €80; double inc. breakfast from €140.*
Leisure Breaks: *Minimum 3-day Sun-Thursday break from €180 per person to include 3 nights b & b with two full dinners.*

● 65 en suite bedrooms (inc. family roms), all with radio, satellite TV, telephone, hairdryer, laundry service, trouser press, fax/modem points. ♿ rms avail.
● 5-cse tdh dinner €40; lunch & special diets available; last orders 9.30 pm.
● Snooker, croquet, fishing, golf, indoor games, beach, sailing (10 km), outdoor swimming pool, tennis, riding. ● 2 meeting rooms, capacity 120.
● Mastercard , Visa & Diners accepted.
● Open all year. 🅿 100 cars.

Clifden 14, Westport 37, Castlebar 48, Galway 63, Dublin 198.

Co Kerry, Killarney

Hotel Europe

Killarney, Co. Kerry
Tel: (064) 31900; Fax: (064) 32118
E-mail: sales@kih.liebherr.com Website: www.iol.ie/khl

Space, grace and elegance are but a few of the words which would describe this modern hotel set overlooking Killarney's lakes and mountains. All the rooms are bright and airy, beautifully furnished with a perfect blend of antique and modern and the elegance is enhanced by the quiet efficiency of the staff. There are superb views from the restaurant where the most delicious Irish and international cuisine can be enjoyed, with local fish, lobster and smoked salmon as specialities. The hotel is the right choice for an active holiday. Some of Ireland's most beautiful and famous golf courses are within easy reach of the hotel. The spectacular surrounding countryside also provides opportunities for tennis, swimming, pony trekking, cycling and hiking. The hotel itself has an excellent fitness centre and children can entertain themselves in the playroom or ride the hotel's own Hafflinger ponies. Hotel Europe is the ideal place to relax after an invigorating day exploring some of Ireland's finest countryside.

Rates: Single /double twin room with breakfast from €228.
Leisure Breaks: Details on application

- 206 en suite bedrooms (inc. 8 suites), all with satellite TV, telephone, radio, hairdryer, laundry service, 24-hour room/meal service.
- 4-cse table d'hôte €50; à la carte, lunch & special diets available; last orders 9.30 pm.
- Biliards/snooker, fishing, golf adjacent, indoor swimming pool, fitness centre, free riding, boating, indoor tennis. Watersports, fishing & squash nearby. Shooting by arrangement.
- American Express, Diners, Mastercard & Visa accepted.
- Open March-November.

Tralee 22, Kenmare 24, Cork 54, Limerick 69, Shannon 84, Rosslare 172, Dublin 189.

Hotel Dunloe Castle
Killarney, Co. Kerry
Tel: (064) 44111; Fax: (064) 44583
E-mail: sales@kih.liebherr.com   Website: www.iol.ie/khl

Like its sister hotel, the Europe, Dunloe Castle is a modern hotel set in the most fabulous gardens leading to the ruins of the old castle itself. The park is host to a remarkable award-winning botanical collection of rare flowers and plants as well to grazing Hafflinger horses. Inside the hotel, the furnishings and decor are faultless, inviting and comfortable and, whilst every facility is provided for meetings and conferences, the keynote is an atmosphere in which to relax and unwind. The restaurant serves the most delicious food with the accent on local specialities. The surrounding countryside is famous for walking, fishing and riding, with tennis and swimming on the premises. What could be more rewarding than to dine here after, let us say, a day playing golf opposite the hotel or one of the numerous famous courses nearby, fishing or perhaps walking up the Gap of Dunloe? This is the outdoor sportsman's paradise, the gourmet's heaven and the holiday maker's *Shangri-La*, all packaged into one superb venue.

Rates: Single/double/twin room with breakfast from €190.

● 110 en suite bedrooms (inc. one suite), all with satellite TV, direct-dial telephone, hairdryer, laundry service, 24-hour room service.
● Table d'hôte dinner €50; lunch & special diets available; last orders 9.30 pm.
● Free river fishing, golf adjacent, jogging track, complimentary riding & tennis, indoor swimming pool. Historical gardens, sailing, squash nearby. Shooting by arrangement.
●   Diners, Mastercard & Visa accepted.
● Open May - October.

Tralee 25, Kenmare 27, Cork 57, Limerick 69, Shannon 84, Rosslare 172, Dublin 189.

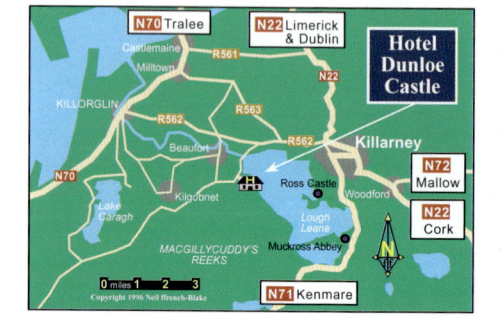

Co Kerry, Killorglin 257

Hotel Ard Na Sidhe

Caragh Lake, Killorglin, Co. Kerry
Tel: (066) 979105; Fax: (066) 979282
E-mail: sales@kih.liebherr.com **Website**: www.iol.ie/khl

It is a pity to call this an hotel, for at Ard Na Sidhe (*The House of the Fairies*), one is a guest in an elegant country house. Warmly furnished, it has that welcoming atmosphere that so many hotels try to emulate but few seem to achieve. Built in 1880 with fabulous award-winning gardens sloping down to the lake, the house offers a tranquillity rarely found today. It has valuable antiques, open fires and a magnificent, mature garden which has twice won first prize in the Irish National Gardens Competition. You can read, go for walks, paint, dream or simply 'switch off' in this idyllic setting. For those seeking a more active holiday, the environs provide more sporting activities than almost any comparable area in Europe; golf (nine courses within a 30-mile readius), fishing and hill trekking to name a few. Whilst Ireland is a relaxing country, even a leisurely tour is tiring. Any visit to the southwest and the Ring of Kerry would be incomplete without staying here for at least a couple of days to recharge the batteries.

Rates: Single/double/twin room with breakfast from €185.

● 19 en suite bedrooms, all with telephone, hairdryer.
● Table d'hôte dinner €50. Special diets available; last orders 9.00 pm
● Leisure facilities available at sister hotels Dunloe Castle and Hotel Europe in Killarney (see previous pages)
● American Express, Diners, Mastercard & Visa accepted.
● Open May - October.

Killarney 12, Tralee 16, Limerick 66, Cork 64, Dublin 207.

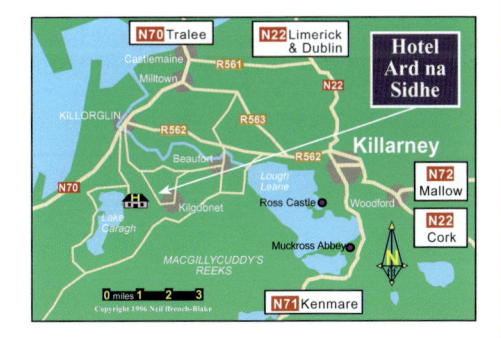

Please note that when dialling into the Republic of Ireland from the UK or USA, numbers should be prefaced by +353, and the first zero omitted.

Caragh Lodge

Caragh Lake, Killorglin, Co Kerry
Tel: (066) 976 9115; Fax: (066) 976 9316
E-mail: caraghl@iol.ie   Website: www.caraghlodge.com

With Kerry airport just a short drive away, the Ring of Kerry just a mile and the golden beaches of Dingle Bay just four miles away, the location of this gracious house, right on the edge of Caragh Lake, makes it ideal for a short break or longer stay to explore the area. Relaxation and quality are the keywords here. Spacious rooms are all equipped with modern facilities, period furnishings and antiques. Many overlook the gardens with their colourful displays of rare sub-tropical shrubs and plants - rhododendrons, camellias, and azaleas - to the lake beyond. Owner Mary Gaunt personally supervises the kitchen, where freshly caught wild Kerry salmon and lamb and home grown vegetables are used where possible. Views from the dining room and lounge towards McGillycuddy's Reeks are breathtaking. This area of Kerry is a golfer's paradise with more than 10 courses nearby. It is also an ideal base for fishermen with the lake and two rivers on the doorstep. Ghillies and necessary permits can be arranged. The Gaunts are most hospitable hosts and you will certainly want to return to this charming spot.

Rates: Single room with breakfast from €130; double room with breakfast from €180.

- 15 en suite bedrooms (inc 1 suite) with direct-dial telephone, hairdryer, radio/alarm.
- Alc dinner; last orders 8.30 pm. Special diets catered for.
- Fishing, sauna on site. Golf & riding four miles.
- Meeting rooms for 12. Parking for 25.
- & all major credit cards accepted.
- Open May - mid-October.

Killorglin 3, Killarney 16, Limerick 66, Cork 66, Dublin 216.

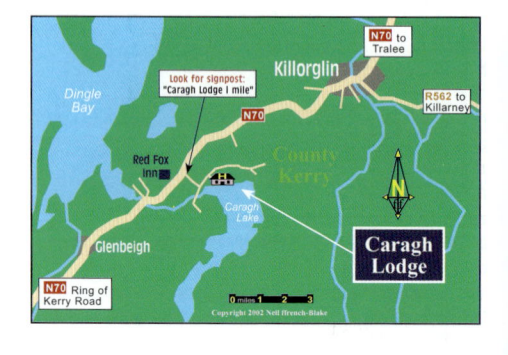

Parknasilla Great Southern Hotel

Sneem, Co Kerry
Tel: (064) 45122; Fax: (064) 45323

E-mail: res@parknasilla.gsh.ie
Website: www.parknasilla.com

The Great Southern Hotel has featured in Signpost for many years, and I was intrigued to return to it recently and find it even more inviting. It is one of the leading hotels of ireland's southwest. Parknasilla is luxurious 19th century building standing in 300 acres of sub-tropical gardens. The setting is majestic and the hotel blends easily with its parkland surroundings which offer a 9-hole golf course, horse riding and much more. The interior is impressive too - lots of public rooms and an especially fine upper conservatory corridor with comfortable seats and splendid views over the bay. The stylish *Pygmalion*Restaurant, patronised by George Bernard Shaw, enjoys the same outlook whilst the library, the billiard room and the *Doolittle Bar* are in quiet contrast to the bustling main lounge. The roomy bedrooms have sparkling bathrooms and all modern facilities. The hotel has recently celebrated its centenary and makes an ideal jumping off point from which to explore the beauties of south-west Ireland: the villages of west Cork, the Ring of Kerry and the Killarney National Park.

Rates: *Single room with breakfast from €92; double room with breakfast from €152.*
Bargain Breaks: Two nights, one dinner, low season, from €95 per person. Ad

- *84 en suite bedrooms with satellite TV, direct-dial telephone, hairdryer, trouser press, laundry service, 24 hr room/meal service. ⅟ rooms available*
- *Last orders for dinner 2045. Spec diets available*
- *Snooker, indoor games, jacuzzi, sauna, indoor swimming pool, jogging track, watersports, riding, fishing, shooting, tennis, 9-hole golf course, clay pigeon shooting, archery, pétanque.*
- *Full business services inc 2 meeting rooms for 50*
- AMERICAN EXPRESS *Visa, Diners & Mastercard accepted.*
- *Closed January/February.* P *75.*

Kenmare 16, Cork 80, limerick 100, Dublin 216

Co. Offaly, Nr. Birr

Kinnitty Castle

Kinnitty, Birr, Co Offaly
Tel: (0509) 37318;
Fax: (0509) 37284
E-mail: kinnittycastle@eircom.net
Website: www.kinnittycastle.com

The history and background of Kinnitty Castle is like a short history of Ireland. It has its roots in fable, has frequently succumbed to attack and has risen with pride from its own ashes. The present phoenix arose after destruction in 1929. Why is this resplendent Gothic edifice standing in woodlands on the slopes of the Slieve Bloom Hills such a centre of interest? First the sheer size and beauty of the estate is enough to engender four of the seven deadly sins; secondly its strategic position in the centre of Ireland, 1½ hours from Dublin, Limerick and Galway; thirdly - its wealth of wildlife and game make it a paradise for almost every country pursuit; and there is now a fourth attraction - a dedication to good food and wine. The hotel has recently undergone a £3 million refurbishment which puts it among Ireland's leading luxury hotels.

Rates: *Single room with breakfast from €133; double room inc. breakfast from €288.*
Leisure Breaks: *weekends 2 nights b & b + 1 dinner pp sharing from €220; midweek from €160 pp.*
● 37 en suite bedrooms (inc 4 four-posters), all with direct-dial telephone, hairdryer, 24-hr room service, radio/alarm clock. Open all year.
● Table d'hôte dinner ca €42. Lunches & spec diets avail; last orders 9.30 pm. ● 4 meeting rms to 250.
● Jacuzzi, massage, sauna, shooting, tennis, riding, hunting, archery, quad bikes at hotel. Fishing and golf nearby. Airport pickup on request
● & major credit cards accepted.

Moneyguyneen House

Kinnitty Castle Demesne,
Kinnitty, Nr Birr, Co. Offaly
Tel: (0509) 37337;
Fax: (0509) 37389
E-mail: moneyguyneenhouse@eircom.net
Website: www.moneyguyneenhouse.com

Moneyguyneen Country House is situated at the foothills of the Slieve Bloom Mountains. Nestling in the centre of 145 acres of lush rolling parkland, Moneyguyneen House possesses an ambience that has more in common with a private house filled with family and friends, than a hotel. Originally the dower house to Kinnitty Castle (*see above*) when the O'Carrolls of Ely were in residence, having changed hands over the years, it now forms part of the the Kinnitty Castle Demesne. Boasting 12 beautiful bedrooms, a comfortable dining room and drawing room, Moneyguyneen is a haven for the most discerning guest who will appreciate both the beauty of the surrounding demesne and the finest of Irish hospitality. The spirit will be lifted and the soul soothed by a few days' relaxation in a house you may now call home.

Rates: *Single room with breakfast from €80; double room inc. breakfast from €110.*
Special midweek breaks: *2 nights B & b + one evening meal €100 per person.*

● 12 en suite bedrooms, all with d-dial telephone.
● Table d'hôte dinner €30. Lunches & spec diets avail; last orders 9.30 pm.
● Jacuzzi, massage, sauna, shooting, tennis, riding, hunting, archery, quad bikes at nearby Kinnitty Castle. Fishing and golf nearby.
● & major credit cards accepted. ● Open all year

Co. Offaly, Tullamore

Bridge House Hotel

Tullamore, Co Offaly
Tel: (0506) 22000;
Fax: (0506) 25690
E-mail: info@bridgehouse.com
Website: www.bridgehouse.com

The Bridge House in Tullamore town centre, is renowned for hospitality, good food and service. It has 72 bedrooms, complete conference facilities and a state of the art Leisure Club with beautiful swimming pool, deck area, unique outdoor hydrotherapy spa pool, gymnasium and aerobics studio. World club golf is available in the hotel, where you can play many of the world's great golf courses, such as the Belfry and Valderama, in virtual reality. There are two real championship courses nearby including Tullamore Golf Club and Esker Hills. Ryder Cup 2006 Venue, the K-Club, is only 45-50 minutes away. Bridge House has two restaurants and three in-house bars which have won awards including the Black & White Millennium Award for Best Hotel Bar in Ireland. There is also an impressive coffee shop, carvery, pool bar and private dining rooms. A grand chandelier dominates the spectacular entrance and foyer, hanging over a beautiful marble stairway, leading to the balcony foyer, conservatory and pool bar. The Bridge House Hotel is an ideal base to tour Clonmacnoise, the Grand Canal, the Slieve Bloom Mountains, Birr Castle Gardens and the Giant Telescope, the Jealous Wall at Belvedere, Tullamore Dew Heritage Centre, Lockes Distillery Museum or for horse racing at Kilbeggan. The hotel has its own car park. The Bridge Shopping Centre and 6-screen cinema are located just across from the hotel.

Birr 8, Athlone 28, Limerick 58, Dublin 79.

Rates: Single room with breakfast €95; double room inc. breakfast €170. **Midweek Breaks:** *2 nights, dinner, b & b from €140 per person. Major credit cards accepted.*

● 72 en suite bedrooms (inc 3 suites), all with aircon, d-dial telephone, TV+satellite, hairdryer, laundry service, safe, minibar, tea/coffee making, 20-hr room/meal service, radio/alarm, & rms avail.
● Tdh dinner from €30; alc, lunch & diets available. Last orders 9.30 pm.
● ₽50. Airport pickup.
● Full business services inc. meeting rooms to 500.
● Fitness centre/gym, indoor games, jacuzzi, massage, sauna, indoor pool at hotel. Fishing, shooting, riding, tennis & golf nearby.
● Open all year

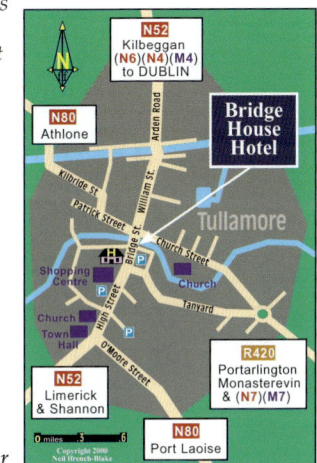

The Horse and Jockey Inn

N8 Main Road, Nr. Thurles, Co Tipperary
Tel: (0504) 44192; Fax: (0504) 44747
E-mail: horseandjockeyinn@tinet.ie
Website: www.horsejockeyinn.com

If you are at all interested in equestrian sports, be it racing, hunting or just hacking or if you just appreciate the beauty of horses, then this is the place for you! This inspector has to confess that he had driven past the Horse & Jockey many times without entering..... now that he has, he will return time and time again. The visitor should not be put off by the location of the Horse & Jockey on a great traditional crossroads of Ireland, North/South and East/West. It has been trading for over 250 years. Recently the owner, a quiet and charming soul, has refurbished the whole building - adding on bedrooms to create a blend of luxury and unspoiled friendliness. My room was very comfortable, and the bathroom had big brass taps, fluffy white towels and many little luxuries. I spent a long time looking at the many equestrian pictures and memorabilia on the walls of the public rooms. Well known jockeys and trainers gaze down from the dining room walls - Mick Kinane, Enda Bolger, Charlie Swan, Jamie Spenser and Aidan O'Brien to name just a few. You might even find yourself sitting next to one of them as several of Ireland's leading racecourses, training yards and studs are nearby. There are books and old photographs to look at in the hotel's comfortable sitting rooms. There is even an hotel shop with designer clothes, local pottery and jewellery.

Rates: Single room inc. breakfast from €75; double inc. breakfast from €140.

● *33 en suite rooms with direct-dial telephone, satellite TV, hairdryer, laundry service, tea/coffee making, radio/alarm clock, safe, trouser press. Non-smoker and disabled bedrooms available.*
● *A la carte restaurant; lunch & special diets available. Last orders 9.45 pm. Hotel shop.*
● *& major credit cards accepted.*
● *Open all year.*

Thurles 5, Cashel 9, Limerick 47, Dublin 87.

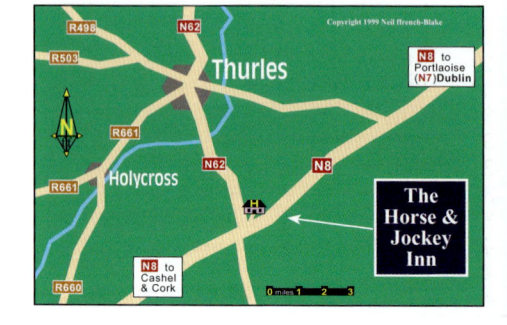

HOTELS WITH SPORTING AND CONFERENCE FACILITIES
Below we list Signpost hotels who can offer Golf, Conference Facilities, Fishing & Shooting, Civil Wedding Licenses, Swimming Pools, Fitness Centres/Gyms, Tennis and those who accept pets.

Hotels with Golf (own course or special arrangements with an adjacent course)

Page	Hotel
8	Meudon Hotel, Cornwall
17	Thurlestone Hotel, Devon
21	Woolacombe Bay Hotel, Devon
34	Knoll House, Studland Bay, Dorset
41	Chewton Glen, New Milton, Hants
43	Priory Bay Hotel, Isle of Wight
63	Beauport Park, Hastings, E Sussex
70	Coulsdon Manor, Surrey
121	The Dormy House, Broadway, Worcs
163	Matfen Hall Hotel, Northumberland
174	Crab Manor, Thirsk, Yorkshire
188	Trefeddian Hotel, Gwynedd
203	Coed-Y-Mwstwr, Vale of Glamorgan
215	Greywalls, Gullane, East Lothian
216	Prestonfield House, Edinburgh
217	Balbirnie House, Glenrothes, Fife
219	Gleddoch House Hotel, Nr Glasgow
220	The Boat Hotel, Inverness-shire
226	Cairn Lodge Hotel, Perthshire
229	Dalmunzie House Hotel, Perthshire
238	La Grande Mare Hotel, Guernsey
249	Ballymaloe House, Co. Cork
253	Derrynane Hotel, Co Kerry
254	Renvyle House Hotel, Co. Galway
255	Hotel Europe, Killarney, Co. Kerry
256	Hotel Dunloe Castle, Co. Kerry
54	The Leonard Hotel, London W1
57	De Vere Cavendish St James, London
62	Lansdowne Hotel, Eastbourne, Sussex
63	Beauport Park, Hastings, Sussex
64	Flackley Ash Hotel, Peasmarsh, Sussex
67	Eastwell Manor, Ashford, Kent
69	Stade Court, Hythe, Kent
70	Coulsdon Manor, Surrey
72	Bingham Hotel, Richmond, Surrey
73	Richmond Hill Hotel, Surrey
74	Oatlands Park, Weybridge, Surrey
80	The Inn at Woburn, Bedfordshire
98	Santo's Higham Farm, Derbyshire
107	Hare & Hounds, Tetbury, Glos
107	De La Bere Hotel, Cheltenham, Glos
108	Feathers hotel, Ledbury, Herefords
109	Branston Hall Hotel, Nr. Lincoln
110	Olde Barn Hotel, Grantham, Lincs
112	Fawsley Hall, Northanptonshire
116	Feathers Hotel, Ludlow, Shropshire
119	Charlecote Pheasant, Warwickshire
120	Stratford Victoria, Warwickshire
121	The Dormy House, Worcestershire
134	Armathwaite Hall, Cumbria
137	The Wordsworth Hotel, Cumbria
144	Low Wood Hotel, Cumbria
147	Etrop Grange, Manchester Airport
149	Lancaster House Hotel, Lancaster
151	Grand Hotel, Lytham, Lancashire
160	Headlam Hall, Darlington, Durham
161	Seaham Hall, Co Durham
163	Matfen Hall, Northumberland
170	Monk Fryston Hall, Nr. Selby, Yorks
171	Royal Hotel, Scarborough, Yorks
175	Dunsley Hall, Whitby, North Yorks
177	The Parsonage Hotel, Nr. York
190	Portmeirion Hotel, Gwynedd
194	Allt-Yr-Ynys, Monmouth/Herefords
195	Llansantffraed Court, Monmouths
196	Glen-Yr-Afon House Hotel, Monmouths
199	Caer Beris Manor, Powys
199	Peterstone Court, Nr. Brecon, Powys
202	Lake Vyrnwy Hotel, Powys
211	Ardoe House, Aberdeen
216	Prestonfield, Edinburgh
217	Balbirnie House, Fife
222	Hotel Eilean Iarmain, Isle of Skye
230	Dryburgh Abbey, Scottish Borders
248	Maryborough House, Co Cork
254	Renvyle House Hotel, Co Galway
260	Kinnitty Castle, Co. Offaly
261	Bridge House Hotel, Co Offaly

Hotels with Conference Facilities
(for 60+ delegates)

Page	Hotel
9	Polurrian Hotel, Cornwall
10	Hannafore Point Hotel, Cornwall
11	Queen's Hotel Penzance, Cornwall
12	Garrack hotel, St Ives, Cornwall
14	The Berry Head Hotel, Devon
15	Royal Beacon Hotel, Devon
16	The Cottage Hotel, Hope Cove, Devon
17	Thurlestome Hotel, Devon
19	Lewtrenchard Manor, Devon
21	Woolacombe Bay Hotel, Devon
22	Hunstrete House, Nr Bath, Somerset
24	Walnut Tree, Bridgwater, Somerset
30	Monkey Island Hotel, Berkshire
31	Taplow House Hotel, Berkshire
32	Norfolk Royale, Bournemouth, Dorset
33	Manor Hotel, Dorchester, Dorset
38	Springfield Country Hotel, Dorset
39	Eastbury Hotel, Sherborne, Dorset
40	Essebourne Manor Hotel, Hampshire
41	Chewton Glen, New Milton, Hants
45	Cotswold Lodge Hotel, Oxford

Hotels with Fishing (✓ = + game shooting)

8	Meudon Hotel, Cornwall	
19	Lewtrenchard Manor, Devon	✓
20	Tides Reach Hotel, Devon	
30	Monkey Island Hotel, Berkshire	
68	Walletts Court, Nr. Dover, Kent	
80	The Mill House, Bedfordshire	
84	Petersfield House Hotel, Norfolk	
95	Izaak Walton Hotel, Derbyshire	
102	Peacock Hotel, Rowsley, Derbyshire	
103	Swan Hotel, Bibury, Gloucestershire	
110	Olde Barn Hotel, Grantham, Lincs	
113	Langar Hall, Nottinghamshire	
117	Overton Grange, Ludlow, Shropshire	
118	Soulton Hall, Shropshire	✓
130	Lovelady Shield, Cumbria	
134	Armathwaite Hall, Cumbria	✓
137	The Wordsworth Hotel, Cumbria	
138	Dale Head Hall, Cumbria	✓
139	Derwentwater Hotel, Cumbria	
142	Gilpin Lodge, Cumbria	
143	Linthwaite House, Cumbria	
144	Low Wood Hotel, Cumbria	
159	Horsley Hall, Co. Durham	
160	Headlam Hall Hotel, Co. Durham	✓
164	The Sportsman's Arms, Yorkshire	✓
176	Middlethorpe Hall, Yorkshire	
167	Simonstone Hall, Yorkshire	✓
173	The Coniston Hotel, Yorkshire	✓
186	Glanrannell Park, Carmarthenshire	
189	Penmaenuchaf Hall, Gwynedd	
194	Allt-Yr-Ynys Hotel, Monmouths	✓
195	Llansantffraed Court, Monmouths	✓
199	Caer Beris Manor, Powys	✓
200	Gliffaes Cntry Hse Hotel, Powys	✓
202	Lake Vyrnwy Hotel, Powys	✓
201	Milebrook House, Powys	
212	Taychreggan Hotel, Argyll	
213	Balinakill Hotel, Argyll	
219	Gleddoch House Hotel, Nr Glasgow	✓
225	Eddrachilles Hotel, Highland	
227	Monachyle Mhor, Perthshire	✓
227	The Four Seasons, Perthshire	
228	Kinnaird, Perthshire	✓
229	Dalmunzie House Hotel, Perthshire	✓
230	Dryburgh Abbey, Scottish Borders	
249	Ballymaloe House, Co Cork	
250	Castle Murray House, Co Donegal	
253	Derrynane Hotel, Co Kerry	
254	Renvyle House, Co Galway	
255	Hotel Europe, Killarney, Co Kerry	
256	Hotel Dunloe Castle, Co Kerry	
258	Caragh Lodge, Co Kerry	
259	Parknasilla Gt Southern, Co Kerry	

Hotels Licensed for Civil Weddings

22	Hunstrete House, Bath, Somerset
30	Monkey Island Hotel, Berkshire
31	Taplow House Hotel, Berkshire
33	Manor Hotel, Dorchester, Dorset
39	The Eastbury Hotel, Dorset
40	Esseborne Manor, Andover, Hants
41	Chewton Glen, Hampshire
43	Priory Bay Hotel, Isle of Wight
67	Eastwell Manor, Ashford, Kent
72	The Bingham Hotel, Richmond-u-T
73	Richmond Gate Hotel, Surrey
74	Oatlands Park Hotel, Surrey
82	Redcoats Farmhouse Hotel, Herts
83	Gissing Hall, Diss, Norfolk
84	Petersfield House, Norfolk
86	Broom Hall Cntry Hotel, Norfolk
95	Izaak Walton Hotel, Derbyshire
96	Riverside House Hotel, Derbyshire
100	Riber Hall, Derbyshire
101	East Lodge Hotel, Derbyshire
102	Peacock Hotel, Rowsley, Derbyshire
103	Swan Hotel, Bibury, Gloucestershire
105	Charingworth Manor, Gloucestershire
110	Olde Barn Hotel, Grantham, Lincs
111	Falcon Hotel, Northamptonshire
112	Fawsley Hall, Northamptonshire
113	Langar Hall, Nottinghamshire
114	Cockcliffe Cntry Hse, Nottingham
117	Overton Grange Hotel, Shropshire
121	Dormy House Hotel, Worcestershire
130	Lovelady Shield Hotel, Cumbria
137	The Wordsworth Hotel, Cumbria
141	Sharrow Bay Hotel, Cumbria
143	Linthwaite House Hotel, Cumbria
145	The Samling, Windermere, Cumbria
147	Etrop Grange Hotel, Manchester
159	Horsley Hall, Co Durham
160	Headlam Hall, Darlington, Durham
163	Matfen Hall Hotel, Northumberland
167	Simonstone Hall, North Yorkshire
170	Monk Fryston Hotel, Yorkshire
172	Wrea Head Country Hotel, Yorks
175	Dunsley Hall, Whitby, North Yorks
177	The Parsonage Hotel, Nr. York
189	Penmaenuchaf Hall, Gwynedd
190	Portmeirion Hotel, Gwynedd
192	Bontddu Hall Hotel, Gwynedd
194	Allt-Yr-Ynys Hotel, Monmouthshire
195	Llansantffraed Court, Monmouths
197	Penally Abbey, Pembrokeshire
198	Warpool Court Hotel, Pembrokeshire
200	Gliffaes Country Hse Hotel, Powys
202	Lake Vyrnwy Hotel, Powys
211	Ardoe House Hotel, Aberdeen
219	Gleddoch House Hotel, Nr. Glasgow

Hotels by Facilities 265

221	Culloden House Hotel, Inverness
228	Kinnaird, Perthshire
229	Dalmunzie House Hotel, Perthshire
250	Castle Murray Hotel, Co. Donegal

Hotels with Swimming Pools
(🕏 = indoor)

9	Polurrian Hotel, Cornwall
10	Hannafore Point, Cornwall
11	Queen's Hotel, Cornwall 🕏
12	Garrack Hotel, St Ives, Cornwall 🕏
14	The Berry Head, South Devon 🕏
17	Thurlestone Hotel, South Devon
20	Tides Reach Hotel, South Devon
21	Woolacombe Bay Hotel, North Devon
22	Hunstrete House, Somerset
32	Norfolk Royale, Dorset
34	Knoll House Hotel, Dorset
38	Springfield Country Hotel, Dorset
41	Chewton Glen, Hampshire + 🕏
63	Beauport Park, East Sussex
64	Flackley Ash Hotel, East Sussex 🕏
65	Rye Lodge, Rye, East Sussex 🕏
66	The Brickwall Hotel, East Sussex
67	Eastwell Manor, Ashford, Kent + 🕏
68	Walletts Court, Dover, Kent 🕏
70	Coulsdon Manor, Surrey
71	Chase Lodge, Kingston, Surrey 🕏
73	Richmond Hill/Gate Hotels, Surrey
83	Blakeney Hotel, Norfolk 🕏
86	Broom Hall Hotel, Norfolk 🕏
105	Charingworth Manor, Glos 🕏
107	De la Bere Hotel, Gloucestershire 🕏
108	The Feathers, Ledbury, Herefords 🕏
109	Branston Hall, Lincolnshire 🕏
110	Olde Barn Hotel, Grantham, Lincs 🕏
117	Wynnstay Hotel, Shropshire
119	Charlecote Pheasant, Warwickshire
133	Appleby Manor Hotel, Cumbria
134	Armathwaite Hall, Cumbria 🕏
142	Gilpin Lodge, Cumbria 🕏
144	Low Wood, Cumbria 🕏
137	The Wordsworth Hotel, Cumbria 🕏
150	Chadwick Hotel, Lancashire 🕏
151	The Grand Hotel, Lytham, Lancs 🕏
160	Headlam Hall, Co Durham
161	Seaham Hall, Co Durham
168	The Pheasant, Harome, N Yorks 🕏
171	Royal Hotel, Scarborough, Yorks 🕏
172	Wrea Head Hotel. Yorkshire 🕏
175	Dunsley Hall, North Yorkshire 🕏
176	Middlethorpe Hall, Yorkshire 🕏
188	Trefeddian Hotel, Gwynedd 🕏
194	Allt-Yr-Ynys, Monmouthshire 🕏
183	St Tudno Hotel, Aberconwy & Colwyn 🕏
197	Penally Abbey, Pembrokeshire 🕏
190	Portmeirion Hotel, Gwynedd
198	Warpool Court, Pembrokeshire 🕏

199	Peterstone Court, Powys
203	Coed-Y-Mwstwr, Vale of Glamorgan
211	Ardoe House, Aberdeenshire 🕏
219	Gleddoch House Hotel, Nr. Glasgow 🕏
237	Bella Luce Hotel, Guernsey
238	La Grande Mare Hotel, Guernsey + 🕏
239	The White House, Herm, C I
241	Hotel L'Horizon, Jersey 🕏
242	Hotel Petit Champ, Sark, C I
248	Maryborough House, Co. Cork 🕏
249	Ballamaloe House, Co Cork
254	Renvyle House, Co Galway
253	Derrynane Hotel, Co. Kerry
255	Hotel Europe, Killarney, Co. Kerry 🕏
256	Hotel Dunloe Castle, Co Kerry 🕏
259	Parknasilla Gt Southern, Co Kerry
261	Bridge House Hotel, Co. Offaly 🕏

Hotels with Fitness Centres/Gyms

9	Polurrian Hotel, Cornwall
10	Hannafore Point, Cornwall
12	Garrack Hotel, St Ives, Cornwall
17	Thurlestone Hotel, South Devon
20	Tides Reach Hotel, South Devon
21	Woolacombe Bay Hotel, North Devon
34	Knoll House Hotel, Dorset
38	Springfield Country Hotel, Dorset
41	Chewton Glen, Hampshire
54	The Leonard Hotel, London W1
64	Flackley Ash Hotel, East Sussex
67	Eastwell Manor, Ashford, Kent
68	Walletts Court, Dover, Kent
70	Coulsdon Manor, Surrey
74	Oatlands Park Hotel, Surrey
73	Richmond Hill/Gate Hotels, Surrey
83	Blakeney Hotel, Norfolk
105	Charingworth Manor, Gloucestershire
107	De la Bere Hotel, Gloucestershire
108	The Feathers, Ledbury, Herefordshire
109	Branston Hall, Lincolnshire
110	Olde Barn Hotel, Grantham, Lincs
117	Wynnstay Hotel, Shropshire
120	Stratford Victoria, Warwickshire
121	The Dormy House, Worcestershire
133	Appleby Manor Hotel, Cumbria
134	Armathwaite Hall, Cumbria
137	The Wordsworth Hotel, Cumbria
149	Lancaster House, Lancashire
150	Chadwick Hotel, Lancashire
151	The Grand Hotel, Lytham, Lancs
160	Headlam Hall, Co Durham
161	Seaham Hall, Co Durham
174	Dunsley Hall, North Yorkshire
176	Middlethorpe Hall, Yorkshire
189	Warpool Court, Pembrokeshire
199	Caer Beris Manor, Powys
199	Peterstone Court, Powys

Hotels by Facilities

203	Coed-Y-Mwstwr, Vale of Glamorgan	194	Allt-Yr-Ynys Hotel, Monmouthshire
211	Ardoe House, Aberdeenshire	195	Llansantffraed Court, Monmouthshire
238	La Grande Mare Hotel, Guernsey	192	Bontddu Hall, Gwynedd
241	Hotel L'Horizon, Jersey	202	Lake Vyrnwy Hotel, Powys
248	Maryborough House, Co. Cork	211	Ardoe House, Aberdeenshire
253	Derrynane Hotel, Co. Kerry	211	Darroch Learg Hotel, Aberdeenshire
255	Hotel Europe, Killarney, Co. Kerry	214	Balcary Bay Htl, Dumfries & Galloway
260	Kinnitty Castle, Co. Offaly	216	Prestonfield House, Edinburgh
261	Bridge House Hotel, Co. Offaly	219	Gleddoch House Hotel, Nr. Glasgow
		222	Hotel Eilean Iarmain, Highland
		227	The Four Seasons Hotel, Perthshire
		229	Dalmunzie House Hotel, Perthshire

Hotels who accept pets (can be charged)

Hotels with tennis courts

8	Meudon Hotel, Cornwall		
12	Garrack Hotel, Cornwall		
20	Tides Reach, Salcombe, Devon	9	Polurrian Hotel, Cornwall
22	Hunstrete House, Nr. Bath, Somerset	17	Thurlestone Hotel, Devon
25	Crown Hotel, Exford, Somerset	21	Woolacombe Bay Hotel, Devon
37	Plumber Manor, Dorset	22	Hunstrete House, Nr. Bath, Somerset
39	Eastbury Hotel, Sherborne, Dorset	34	Knoll House, Studland Bay, Dorset
39	Beachleas Hotel, Dorset	36	Manor House, Studland Bay, Dorset
43	Priory Bay Hotel, Isle of Wight	37	Plumber Manor, Dorset
58	Basil Street Hotel, London SW1	38	Springfield Country House, Dorset
64	Flackley Ash Hotel, East Sussex	40	Esseborne Manor, Hampshire
66	The Brickwall Hotel, East Sussex	41	Chewton Glen, Hampshire
66	Little Hemingfold Hotel, E Sussex	63	Beauport Park, East Sussex
67	Eastwell Manor, Ashford, Kent	70	Coulsdon Manor, Surrey
71	Chase Lodge, Surrey	83	Gissing Hall, Norfolk
84	Petersfield House Hotel, Norfolk	100	Riber Hall, Derbyshire
85	Elderton Lodge, Norfolk	105	Charingworth Manor, Gloucestershire
87	Wentworth Hotel, Suffolk	107	Hare & Hounds, Gloucestershire
95	Izaak Walton hotel, Derbyshire	119	Charlecote Pheasant, Warwickshire
98	Biggin Hall, Derbyshire	121	Dormy House, Worcestershire
100	Riber Hall, Matlock, Derbyshire	130	Lovelady Shield Hotel, Cumbria
102	Peacock at Rowsley, Derbyshire	134	Armathwaite Hall, Cumbria
109	Lake Isle Hotel, Uppingham, Leics	138	Dale Head Hall, Cumbria
110	Olde Barn Hotel, Grantham, Lincs	144	Low Wood, Cumbria
111	Falcon Hotel, Northamptonshire	160	Headlam Hall, Co Durham
112	Fawsley Hall, Northamptonshire	175	Dunsley Hall, Whitby, Yorkshire
111	Windmill at Badby, Northanptonshire	188	Trefeddian Hotel, Gwynedd
114	Cockcliffe Cntry Hse, Nottinghamshire	198	Warpool Court, Pembrokeshire
113	Langar Hall, Nottinghamshire	200	Gliffaes Cntry Hse Hotel, Powys
118	Soulton Hall, Shropshire	202	Lake Vyrnwy Hotel, Powys
115	Old Vicarage Hotel, Shropshire	203	Coed-Y-Mwstwr, Vale of Glamorgan
123	Cottage in the Wood, Worcestershire	211	Ardoe House, Aberdeenshire
121	Dormy House Hotel, Worcestershire	215	Greywalls Hotel, East Lothian
128	Broxton Hall, Cheshire	221	Culloden House, Inverness-shire
139	Derwentwater Hotel, Cumbria	228	Kinnaird, Perthshire
130	Lovelady Shield, Cumbria	229	Dalmunzie House Hotel, Perthshire
133	Appleby Manor, Cumbria	238	La Grande Mare, Guernsey
147	Etrop Grange, Manchester Airport	239	The White House, Herm, C.I.
162	Waren House, Northumberland	248	Maryborough House, Co Cork
163	Matfen Hall Hotel, Northumberland	249	Ballymaloe House, Co Cork
165	Balmoral Hotel, Harrogate, Yorkshire	254	Renvyle House, Co Galway
167	Simonstone Hall, Yorkshire	255	Hotel Europe Killarney, Co Kerry
170	Monk Fryston Hall, Yorkshire	259	Parknasilla Gt Southern, Co Kerry
170	White Swan, Pickering, Yorkshire	260	Kinnitty Castle, Co Offaly
183	St Tudno Hotel, Conwy	261	Bridge House, Co Offaly
185	Synchant Pass House, Conwy		

LOCATION INDEX
ENGLAND
THE WEST COUNTRY

Location	Hotel	Page
Cornwall		
Falmouth	Meudon Hotel	8
Lizard Peninsula	Polurrian Hotel	9
West Looe	Hannafore Point Hotel	10
Penzance	Queens Hotel	11
St Ives	The Garrack Hotel	12
Devon		
Beaworthy	Blagdon Manor	13
Brixham	The Berry Head Hotel	14
Exmouth	The Royal Beacon Hotel	15
Hope Cove	The Cottage Hotel	16
Kingsbridge (Thurlestone)	Thurlestone Hotel	17
Okehampton (Sourton)	Collaven Manor Hotel	18
Okehampton (Lewdown)	Lewtrenchard Manor	19
Salcombe	Tides Reach Hotel	20
Woolacombe	Woolacombe Bay Hotel	21
Somerset		
Nr. Bath	Hunstrete House	22
Bath	Windsor Hotel	23
Bridgwater	Walnut Tree Hotel	24
Exford	The Crown Hotel	25

CENTRAL SOUTHERN ENGLAND

Location	Hotel	Page
Berkshire		
Maidenhead	Monkey Island Hotel	30
Maidenhead	Taplow House Hotel	31
Dorset		
Bournemouth	Norfolk Royale Hotel	32
Dorchester	The Manor Hotel	33
Studland Bay	Knoll House Hotel	34/35
Studland Bay	Manor House Hotel	36
Sturminster Newton	Plumber Manor	37
Wareham	Springfield Country Hotel	38
Sherborne	Eastbury Hotel	39a
Wimborne Minster	Beechleas Hotel	39b
Hampshire & Isle of Wight		
Andover	Esseborne Manor Hotel	40a
Brockenhurst	Whitley Ridge Hotel	40b
New Milton	Chewton Glen	41
Winchester	The Winchester Royal	42
Seaview, Isle of Wight	Priory Bay Hotel	43

Location	Hotel	Page
Oxfordshire		
Clanfield	The Plough	44
Oxford	Cotswold Lodge Hotel	45
Bledington	The King's Head Inn & Restaurant	46a
Wiltshire		
Nr. Salisbury	Howard's House Hotel	46b

LONDON & THE SOUTH

Location	Hotel	Page
London		
W1	The Ascott Mayfair	53
W1	The Leonard	54a
W1	10 Manchester Street	54b
W1	The Montcalm	59b
SW1	De Vere Cavendish St James	57
SW3	The Beaufort	55
SW3	Parkes Hotel	56
SW3	Basil Street Hotel	58
SW5	20 Nevern Square	60
SW7	Five Sumner Place	59a
SE5	The Clarendon Hotel, Blackheath	61a
BW3	The Langorf	61b
East Sussex		
Eastbourne	The Lansdowne Hotel	62
Hastings	Beauport Park Hotel	63
Peasmarsh	Flackley Ash Hotel	64
Rye	Rye Lodge Hotel	65
Battle	Little Hemingfold Hotel	66a
Sedlescombe	The Brickwall Hotel	66b
Kent		
Ashford	Eastwell Manor	67
Dover	Walletts Court	68
Hythe	Stade Court Hotel	69
Surrey		
Cobham	Cedar House Hotel	75a
Coulsdon	Coulsdon Manor Hotel	70
Kingston-upon-Thames	Chase Lodge Hotel	71
Richmond-upon-Thames	The Bingham Hotel	72
Richmond-upon-Thames	The Richmond Gate Hotel	73a
Richmond-upon-Thames	The Richmond Hill Hotel	73b
Weybridge	Oatlands Park hotel	74
West Sussex		
Arundel	Burpham Country House Hotel	75b

Location *Hotel* *Page*

EAST OF ENGLAND

Bedfordshire
Nr. Bedford | The Mill House | 80a
Woburn | The Inn at Woburn | 80b

Cambridgeshire
Cambridge | Arundel House | 81

Hertfordshire
Hitchin | Redcoats Farmhouse Hotel | 82

Norfolk
Blakeney | The Blakeney Hotel | 83a
Diss | Gissing Hall | 83b
Horning | Petersfield House Hotel | 84
Norwich | Georgian House Hotel | 85a
Thorpe Market | Elderton Lodge | 85b
Nr. Thetford | Broom Hall Country Hotel | 86

Suffolk
Aldeburgh | The Wentworth Hotel | 87
Southwold | The Swan | 88

THE HEART OF ENGLAND

Derbyshire
Alfreton | Santo's Higham Farm | 98b
Ashbourne | Izaak Walton Hotel | 95
Ashford-in-the-Water | Riverside House Hotel | 96
Bakewell | The Croft Country House Hotel | 97a
Biggin-by-Hartington | Biggin Hall | 98a
Hope | Underleigh House | 99a
Matlock | The Red House Country Hotel | 99b
Matlock | Riber Hall | 100
Rowsley | East Lodge Country House Hotel | 101
Rowsley | The Peacock Hotel | 102
Shottle, Nr. Belper | Dannah Farm Country Guest House | 97b

Gloucestershire
Bibury | The Swan Hotel | 103
Bourton-on-the-Water | The Dial House | 104
Nr. Cheltenham | Hotel De La Bere | 107a
Chipping Campden | Charingworth Manor | 105
Chipping Campden | The Malt House | 106
Tetbury | The Hare & Hounds Hotel | 107b

Herefordshire
Ledbury | The Feathers Hotel | 108

Location	Hotel	Page
Leicestershire		
Uppingham (Rutland)	The Lake Isle	109a
Lincolnshire		
Nr. Grantham	The Olde Barn Hotel	110
Nr. Lincoln	Branston Hall Hotel	109b
Northamptonshire		
Nr. Daventry	Fawsley Hall	112
Nr. Daventry	The Windmill at Badby	111a
Nr. Northampton	The Falcon Hotel	111b
Nottinghamshire		
Langar	Langar Hall	113
Nottingham	Cockcliffe Country House Hotel	114
Shropshire		
Nr. Bridgnorth	The Old Vicarage	115
Ludlow	The Feathers Hotel	116
Nr. Ludlow	Overton Grange Hotel	117a
Oswestry	Wynnstay Hotel	117b
Wem	Soulton Hall	118
Warwickshire		
Charlecote, Nr. Stratford	The Charlecote Pheasant	119
Stratford upon Avon	Stratford Victoria	120
Worcestershire		
Broadway	Dormy House Hotel	121
Little Malvern	Holdfast Cottage Hotel	122
Malvern Wells	The Cottage in the Wood	123

THE NORTH WEST

Location	Hotel	Page
Cheshire		
Nr. Chester	Broxton Hall	128
Nr. Macclesfield	Sutton Hall	129
Cumbria		
Nr. Alston	Lovelady Shield Hotel	130
Ambleside	Rothay Manor Hotel	131
Ambleside	Waterhead Hotel	132
Appleby-in-Westmoreland	Appleby Manor Country House Hotel	133
Bassenthwaite Lake	Armathwaite Hall	134
Bassenthwaite Lake	The Pheasant Inn	135
Grange-over-Sands, Cartmel	Aynsome Manor	136
Grasmere	The Wordsworth Hotel	137
Keswick	Dale Head Hall Lakeside Hotel	138
Nr. Keswick	Derwentwater Hotel	139
Nr. Keswick	Scafell Hotel	140
Ullswater	Sharrow Bay Country House Hotel	141
Windermere	Gilpin Lodge	142
Windermere	Linthwaite House Hotel	143
Windermere	Low Wood	144
Windermere	The Samling	145
Windermere	The Wild Boar	146

Location	Hotel	Page
Greater Manchster		
Manchester Airport	Etrop Grange Hotel	147
Lancashire		
Chorley	The Pines Hotel	148
Lancashire	Lancaster House Hotel	149
Lytham St Annes	The Grand Hotel	151
Lytham St Annes	Chadwick Hotel	150a
Poulton-le-Fylde	Singleton Lodge	150b

YORKSHIRE & THE NORTH EAST

Location	Hotel	Page
Cleveland		
Saltburn-by-the-Sea	Grinkle Park	158
Co. Durham		
Nr. Bishop Auckland	Horsley Hall	159
Gainford, Darlington	Headlam Hall Hotel	160
Seaham, Durham	Seaham Hall	161
Northumberland		
Bamburgh	Waren House	162
Matfen	Matfen Hall	163
North Yorkshire		
Harrogate	The Balmoral	165
Hawes	Rookhurst Country House Hotel	166
Hawes	Simonstone Hall	167
Helmsley	The Pheasant, Harome	168
Lastingham	Lastingham Grange Hotel	169
Pateley Bridge	The Sportsman's Arms	164
Pickering	The White Swan	170b
Scarborough	The Royal Hotel	171
Nr. Scarborough	Wrea Head Country House Hotel	172
Ne. Selby	Monk Fryston Hall	170a
Skipton	Coniston Hall Lodge	173
Thirsk	Crab Manor	174
Whitby	Dunsley Hall	175
York	Middlethorpe Hall	176
York	The Parsonage, Escrick	177

WALES

Location	Hotel	Page
Carmarthensire		
Nr. Llanwrda	Glanrannell Park	186
Brechfa	Ty Mawr Country Hotel	187
Conwy		
Nr. Conwy	The Groes Inn	184
Nr. Conwy	Synchnant Pass House	185
Llandudno	St Tudno Hotel	183

Location	Hotel	Page
Gwynedd		
Aberdovey	Trefeddian Hotel	188
Aberdovey	Penhelig Arms	189a
Dolgellau	Penmaenuchaf Hall	189b
Nr. Dolgellau	Bontddu Hall Hotel	192
Porthmadog	Portmeirion Hotel	190
Portmadog	Castell Deudrach	191
Pwllheli	Plas Bodegroes	193
Monmouthshire		
Nr. Abergavenny	Allt-Yr-Ynys Country Hotel	194
Nr. Abergavenny	Llansantffraed Court Hotel	195
Usk	Glen-Yr-Afon House	196
Pembrokeshire		
St David's	Warpool Court Hotel	198
Tenby	Penally Abbey	197
Powys		
Nr. Brecon	Peterstone Court	199a
Builth Wells	Caer Beris Manor	199b
Crickhowell	Gliffaes Country House Hotel	200
Knighton	Milebrook House	201a
Llanwrtyd Wells	Lasswade Country House Hotel	201b
Llanddyn	Lake Vyrnwy Hotel	202
Vale of Glamorgan		
Nr. Bridgend	Coed-Y-Mwstwr Hotel	203
Porthkerry	Egerton Gray Country House Hotel	204

SCOTLAND

Aberdeenshire		
Aberdeen	Ardoe House Hotel	211a
Ballater	Darroch Learg Hotel	211b
Argyll & Bute		
Kilchrenan by Taynuilt	Taychreggan Hotel	212
Tarbert	Balinakill Country House Hotel	213
Dumfries & Galloway		
Auchencairn	Balcary Bay Hotel	214
East Lothian		
Gullane	Greywalls Hotel	215
Edinburgh	Prestonfield House	216
Fife		
Glenrothes	Balbirnie House	217

Location	Hotel	Page
Glasgow	Saint Jude's	218
Nr. Glasgow	Gleddoch House Hotel	219
Highland		
Boat of Garten	The Boat	220
Inverness	Culloden House	221
Kingussie	The Cross	223
Lybster	The Portland Arms	224
Scourie	Eddrachilles Hotel	225a
Skye	Hotel Eilean Iarmain (Isle Ornsay)	222
Tongue	Ben Loyal Hotel	225b
Perth & Kinross		
Auchterarder	Cairn Lodge	226
Balquhidder	Monachyle Mhor	227a
Nr. Dunkeld	Kinnaird	228
St Fillan's	Four Seasons Hotel	227b
Spittal of Glenshee	Dalmunzie House Hotel	229
Scottish Borders		
St Boswell's	Dryburgh Abbey	230

CHANNEL ISLANDS

Guernsey		
Castel	La Grande Mare Hotel	238
Fermain Bay	La Favorita	236
St Martin's	Hotel Bella Luce	237
Herm	The White House Hotel	239
Jersey		
Gorey	The Moorings Hotel & Restaurant	240b
St Brelade	Hotel L''Horizon	241
St Peter	Greenhills Hotel	240a
Sark	Hotel Petit Champ	242

IRELAND

Ireland, various locations	Elegant Ireland	247
Co. Cork		
Douglas	Maryborough House	248
Shanagarry	Ballymaloe House	252b
Co. Donegal		
Dunkineely	Castle Murray House Hotel	250

Co. Dublin
Dublin	Longfields	251
Dublin	Number 31	252
Dublin	Glenogra House	253a

Co. Galway
Renvyle	Renvyle House Hotel	254

Co. Kerry
Caherdaniel	Derrynane Hotel	253b
Killarney	Hotel Europe	255
Killarney	Hotel Dunloe Castle	256
Killorglin	Ard-na-Sithe Hotel	257
Killorglin	Caragh Lodge	258
Sneem	Parknasilla Great Southern	259

Co Offaly
Birr	Kinnitty Castle	260a
Birr	Moneyguyneen House	260b
Tullamore	Bridge House Hotel	261

Co. Tipperary
Thurles	Horse & Jockey Inn	262

Goff's Business Hotel Guide 2002

- 200 hotels for the business traveller
- Colour photographs
- Location maps
- Meeting facilities
- Online Booking

www.goffsguide.co.uk

PRIORY PUBLICATIONS LTD

GOFF'S Business Hotel Guide is the business companion to Signpost.

It features over 300 business hotels in the UK, with over 150 enhanced entries and maps, enabling the business traveller to budget accurately. The website features over 650 hotels which can be viewed and booked on line at *www.goffsguide.co.uk*.

"Worth its space in the glove compartment for executives clocking up hefty mileages" - Executive Travel Magazine

"Turns business travel into a pleasure" - What's New in Marketing

"Handy Guide for Travellers" - DTI 'In Business Now'

Now available for £3.50 (inc p & p) from the address below

Syresham, Brackley, Northants NN13 5HH
Tel: (01280) 850603; Fax: (01280) 850576
E-mail: info@goffsguide.co.uk; web: www.goffsguide.co.uk

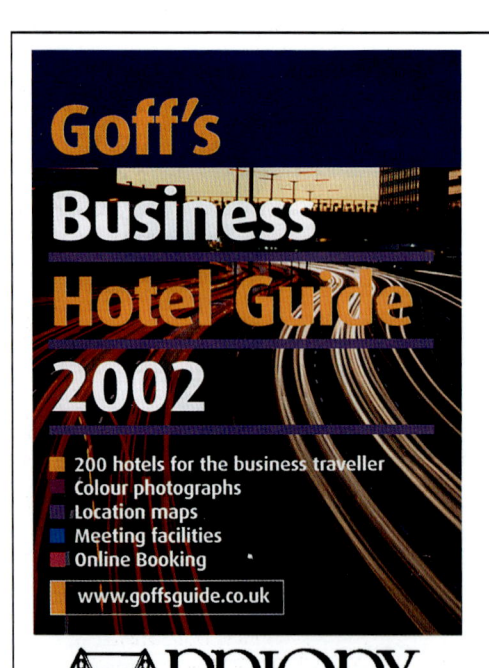

ALPHABETICAL INDEX OF HOTELS

Allt-Yr-Ynys Country House Hotel 194
Appleby Manor Country Club Hotel 133
Ardoe House Hotel, Aberdeen 211
Ard-na-Sithe Hotel, Killorglin 257
Armathwaite Hall, Bassenthwaite Lake 134
Arundel House Hotel, Cambridge 81
Ascott, Mayfair, the 53
Aynsome Manor Cntry Hse Hotel 136
Balbirnie House, Glenrothes 217
Balinakill Country House Hotel, Tarbert 213
Balcary Bay Hotel, Auchencairn 214
Ballymaloe House, Shanagarry 249
Balmoral, the, Harrogate 165
Basil Street Hotel, The, London SW3 58
Beaufort, the, London SW3 55
Beauport Park Hotel, Hastings 63
Beechleas Hotel, Wimborne Minster 39
Bella Luce Hotel, Guernsey 237
Ben Loyal Hotel, Tongue 225
Berry Head Hotel, Brixham 14
Biggin Hall, Nr. Buxton 98
Bingham Hotel, Richmond-upon-Thames 72
Blagdon Manor Hotel, Ashwater 13
Blakeney Hotel, the 83
The Boat, Boat of Garten 220
Bontddu Hall Hotel, Dolgellau 192
Branston Hall Hotel, Lincoln 109
Brickwall Hotel, Sedlescombe 66
Bridge House Hotel, Tullamore 261
Broom Hall Country Hotel, Nr. Thetford 86
Broxton Hall Country House Hotel 128
Burpham Country House Hotel 75
Caer Beris Manor, Builth Wells 199
Cairn Lodge, Auchterarder 226
Caragh Lodge, Killorglin 258
Castle Murray House Hotel 250
Cedar House Hotel, Cobham 75
Castell Deudrath, Porthmadog 191
Chadwick Hotel, Lytham St Annes 150
Charingworth Manor 105
Charlecote Pheasant Hotel 119
Chase Lodge Hotel, Kingston-on-Thames 71
Chewton Glen, New Milton 41
Clarendon Hotel, London SE3 61
Cockcliffe Country House Hotel 114
Coed-Y-Mwstwr Hotel, Nr. Bridgend 203
Collaven Manor, Okehampton 18
Coniston Hall Lodge, Skipton 173
Cotswold Lodge Hotel, Oxford 45
Cottage Hotel, Hope Cove 16
Cottage in the Wood, the, Malvern Wells 123
Coulsdon Manor, Coulsdon 70
Crab Manor, Nr. Thirsk 174
Croft Country House Hotel, Bakewell 97
Cross, the, Kingussie 223
Crown Hotel, Exford 25
Culloden House , Inverness 221
Dale Head Hall Lakeside Hotel 138
Dalmunzie House Hotel, Glenshee 229
Dannah Farm, Shottle 97
Darroch Learg, Ballater 211
De La Bère Hotel, Nr. Cheltenham 107
Derrynane Hotel, Caherdaniel 253

Derwentwater Hotel, Nr. Keswick 139
De Vere Cavendish, the, London W1 57
Dial House Hotel, Bourton-on-the-Water 104
Dormy House Hotel, Broadway 121
Dryburgh Abbey, St Boswell's 230
Dunloe Castle, Killarney 256
Dunsley Hall, Whitby 175
Eastbury Hotel, Sherbourne 39
East Lodge Hotel, Rowsley 101
Eastwell Manor, Ashford 67
Eddrachilles Hotel, Scourie 225
Egerton Gray Hotel, Porthkerry 204
Eilean Iarmain Hotel, Skye 222
Elderton Lodge, Thorpe Market 85
Elegant Ireland 247
Esseborne Manor, Nr. Andover 40
Etrop Grange, Manchester 147
Europe Hotel, Killarney 255
Falcon Hotel, The, Nr Northampton 111
Favorita, La, Guernsey 236
Fawsley Hall Hotel, Nr. Daventry 112
Feathers, the, Ledbury 108
Feathers, the, Ludlow 116
Five Sumner Place, London SW7 59
Flackley Ash Hotel, Rye 64
Four Seasons Hotel, St Fillans 227
Garrack Hotel, St Ives 12
Georgian House Hotel, Norwich 85
Gilpin Lodge Country House Hotel 142
Gissing Hall, Nr. Diss 83
Glanrannell Park, Crugybar 186
Gleddoch House, Langbank 219
Glenogra House, Dublin 253
Glen Yr Afon House Hotel, Usk 196
Gliffaes Country Hotel, Crickhowell 200
Grand Hotel, Lytham St Anne's 151
Greenhills Hotel, Jersey 240
Greywalls Hotel, Gullane 215
Grinkle Park Hotel, Saltburn 158
Groes Inn, Nr. Conwy 184
Hannafore Point Hotel, West Looe 10
Hare & Hounds,Tetbury 107
Hawkstone Park, Weston-u-Redcastle 112
Headlam Hall Hotel, Gainford 160
Holdfast Cottage, Little Malvern 122
Horizon,L', Hotel, Jersey 241
Horsley Hall, Weardale 159
Horse & Jockey Inn, Thurles 262
Howard's House Hotel, Nr. Salisbury 46
Hunstrete House, Nr. Bath 22
Inn at Woburn, the 80
Izaak Walton Hotel, Nr Ashbourne 95
Kings Head Inn, Bledington 46
Kinnaird, by Dunkeld 228
Kinnitty Castle, Birr 260
Knoll House Hotel, Studland Bay 34/35
La Grande Mare Hotel, Guernsey 238
Lake Isle Hotel & Restaurant, Uppingham 109
Lake Vyrnwy Hotel, Llanddyn 202
Lancaster House, Lancaster 149
Langar Hall, Nr. Nottingham 113
Langorf Hotel, Hampstead NW3 61
Lansdowne Hotel, Eastbourne 62

Index

Lasswade Cntry Hse Hotel, Llanwrtyd Wells 201
Lastingham Grange Hotel, Kirkbymoorside 169
Leonard, the, London W1 54
Lewtrenchard Manor, Nr. Okehampton 19
Linthwaite House Hotel, Windermere 143
Little Hemingfold Hotel, Nr. Battle 66
Llansantffraed Court, Nr. Abergavenny 195
Longfields Hotel, Dublin 251
Lovelady Shield, Nr. Alston 130
Low Wood, Windermere 144
Malt House, the, Chipping Campden 106
Manor Hotel, Dorchester 33
Manor House Hotel, Studland Bay 36
Maryborough House, Douglas 248
Matfen Hall, Northumberland 163
Meudon Hotel, Falmouth 8
Middlethorpe Hall, York 176
Milebrook House, Knighton 201
Mill House, the, Nr. Bedford 80
Monachyle Mhor, Balquhidder 227
Moneyguyneen House, Birr 260
Monk Fryston Hall, Nr. Selby 170
Monkey Island Hotel, Nr. Maidenhead 30
Montcalm, the, London W1 59
Moorings Hotel & Restaurant, Jersey 240
Norfolk Royale, Bournemouth 32
Number 31, Dublin 252
Oatlands Park, Weybridge 74
Olde Barn Hotel, Nr, Grantham 110
Old Vicarage, Nr. Bridgnorth 115
Overton Grange, Nr. Ludlow 117
Parkes Hotel, Londond SW3 56
Parknasilla Great Southern, Sneem 259
Parsonage, the, Escrick 177
Peacock Hotel, the, Rowsley 102
Penally Abbey, Tenby 197
Penhelig Arms, Abverdovey 189
Penmaenuchaf Hall, Dolgeallau 189
Petersfield House Hotel, Horning 84
Peterstone Court, Nr Brecon 199
Petit Champ Hotel, Sark 242
Pheasant, the, Helmsley 168
Pheasant Inn, Bassenthwaite Lake 135
Pines Hotel, Chorley 148
Plas Bodegroes, Pwllheli 193
Plough at Clanfield, Nr. Faringdon 44
Plumber Manor, Sturminster Newton 37
Polurrian Hotel, Lizard Peninsula 9
Portland Arms, Lybster 224
Portmeirion Hotel, Porthmadog 190
Prestonfield House, Edinburgh 216
Priory Bay Hotel, Seaview 43
Queen's Hotel, Penzance 11
Redcoats Farmhouse Hotel, Hitchin 82
Red House Country Hotel, Matlock 99
Renvyle House, Renvyle 254
Riber Hall, Matlock 100
Richmond Gate Hotel, Richmond-upon-Thames . 73
Richmond Hill Hotel, Richmond-upon-Thames .. 73
Riverside Hotel, Ashford in the Water 96

Rookhurst Country House Hotel, Hawes 166
Rothay Manor Hotel, Ambleside 131
Royal Beacon Hotel, Exmouth 15
Royal Hotel, the, Scarborough 171
Rye Lodge Hotel, Rye 65
Saint Jude's, Glasgow 218
St Tudno Hotel, Llandudno 183
Samling, the, Windermere 145
Santo's Higham Farm, Alfreton 98
Scafell Hotel, Nr. Keswick 140
Seaham Hall, Nr. Durham 161
Sharrow Bay C'ntry Hse Hotel, Ullswater 141
Simonstone Hall, Hawes 167
Singleton Lodge, Poulton-le-Fylde 150
Soulton Hall, Wem 118
Sportsman's Arms, Harrogate 164
Springfield Country Hotel, Wareham 38
Stade Court Hotel, Hythe 69
Stratford Victoria, Stratford-upon-Avon 120
Sutton Hall, Macclesfield 129
Swan, the, Southwold 88
Swan Hotel, Bibury 103
Synchnant Pass House, Nr. Conwy 185
Taplow House, Nr, Maidenhead 31
Taychreggan Hotel, Kilchrenan 212
Ten Manchester Street, London W1 54
Thurlestone Hotel, Thurlestone 17
Tides Reach Hotel, Salcombe 20
Trefeddian Hotel, Aberdovey 188
Twenty Nevern Square, London SW5 60
Ty Mawr Country Hotel, Brechfa 187
Underleigh House, Hope 99
Walletts Court, St Margaret-at-Cliff 68
Walnut Tree Hotel, Bridgwater 24
Waren House, Bamburgh 162
Warpool Court Hotel, St David's..........................198
Waterhead Hotel, Ambleside................................132
Wentworth Hotel, The, Aldeburgh.........................87
White House, Herm 239
White Swan, Pickering..170
Whitley Ridge Country House Hotel.....................40
Wild Boar, Crook..146
Winchester Royal, the,...42
Windmill at Badby, the, Daventry........................111
Windsor Hotel, Bath...23
Woolacombe Bay Hotel...21
Wordsworth Hotel, Grasmere...............................137
Wrea Head Cntry Hse Hotel..................................172
Wynnstay Hotel, Oswestry...................................117

Other Signpost Approved Partners

American Express Europe..7
Robert Barry & Co 51

Signpost Advantage Card 2003 EDITION

The Signpost Advantage Card is supplied free of charge to purchasers of the book on receipt of this form.

It entitles the bearer to a 10% discount on room rates (only) quoted in this book in those hotels who have an [Ad] printed beside their prices. This is according to availability and at the discretion of the hotelier. It applies only to accommodation - not to meals or extras. Some hotels may offer a room upgrade instead.

Please fill in the coupon below and return to Priory Publications Ltd, PO Box 24, Brackley, Northamptonshire NN13 5BR, to receive your free Advantage Card.

I have purchased* Signpost 2003/Country Inns of Great Britain & Iraland 2003 and would like to apply for a free Advantage Card.

Name_____

Postal Address_____

_____Date_____

E-mail address: _____

NB: Readers who have not yet *purchased* a copy of Signpost should fill in and mail the card on the following pages, ticking the box for an Advantage Card.

SIGNPOST ADVANTAGE CARD

General Terms and Conditions

A. Advantage Cards are not interchangeable, must be signed as above and only give benefit to the signatory of the card

B. 10% discount may be granted on presentation of the card on accommodation only.

C. As an alternative to a 10% discount, a hotel may offer a free room upgrade.

D. Cards are valid from the time of purchase of *Signpost/Premier Hotels of Great Britain and Ireland* (the USA title) until 31 December 2003.

E. Readers should state at the time of booking that they are Signpost Advantage card holders and should check the advantages the establishment is offering.

F. Only the Signpost establishmen with an [Ad] printed by their room rates in this guide are taking part in the Advantage Card promotion.

G. Advantage cardholders can also book on line, quoting their card no via *www.signpost.co.uk*. Prices on participating hotels' home pages on our website are similarly flagged.

H. Benefits will not apply at Christmas, New Year and Bank Holiday periods; also at certain peak periods at individual hotels, e.g. at the time of York or Cheltenham Races in hotels local to such events.

I. Cardholders with e-mail will receive our regular Special Offers e-newsletter but their names will NOT be passed to any other marketing organisation.

Priory Publications Ltd, Syresham, Brackley, Northants NN13 5HH
Tel: 01280 850603; Fax: 01280 850576

MAP SECTION

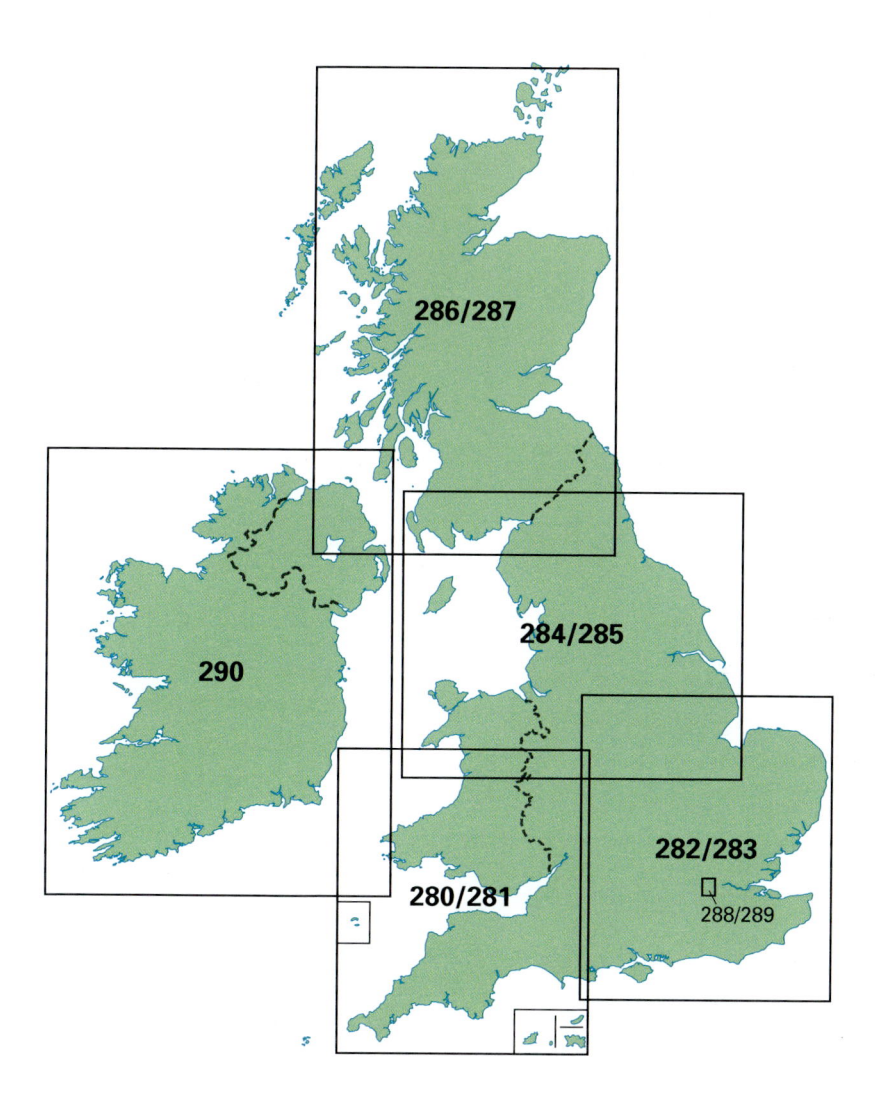

286/287

284/285

290

282/283

280/281   288/289

Numbers in black ovals on the following maps denote page numbers of Signpost approved hotels. Turn to these pages for full details of accommodation in the area where you are looking.

Maps designed and produced by GEOprojects (UK) Ltd., Reading. RG1 4QS. © GEOprojects (UK) Ltd.

1. CITY OF WOLVERHAMPTON
2. WALSALL
3. DUDLEY
4. SANDWELL
5. BIRMINGHAM
6. NEATH & PORT TALBOT
7. RHONDDA CYNON TAFF
8. MERTHYR TYDFIL
9. CAERPHILLY
10. BLAENAU GWENT
11. TORFAEN
12. BRISTOL

281

Legend

1. CITY OF DERBY
2. CITY OF LEICESTER
3. CITY OF WOLVERHAMPTON
4. WALSALL
5. DUDLEY
7. SANDWELL
7. BIRMINGHAM
8. SOLIHULL
9. COVENTRY

283

284

1. NORTH TYNESIDE
2. NEWCASTLE UPON TYNE
3. GATESHEAD
4. SOUTH TYNESIDE
5. SUNDERLAND
6. HARTLEPOOL
7. DARLINGTON
8. STOCKTON-ON-TEES
9. MIDDLESBROUGH
10. REDCAR & CLEVELAND
11. CITY OF KINGSTON UPON HULL
12. CITY OF STOKE-ON-TRENT
13. CITY OF DERBY
14. CITY OF LEICESTER

286

287

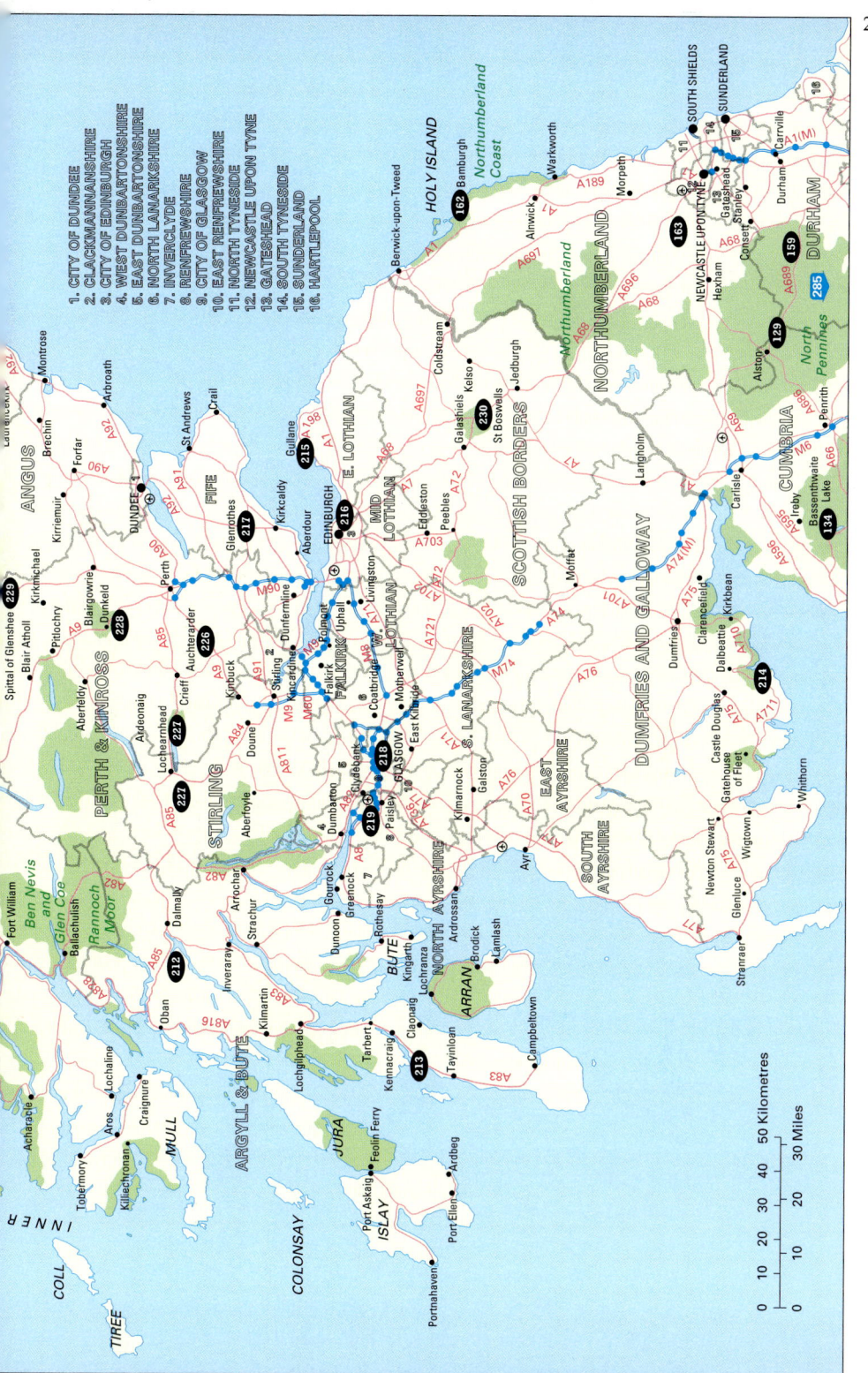

1. CITY OF DUNDEE
2. CLACKMANNANSHIRE
3. CITY OF EDINBURGH
4. WEST DUNBARTONSHIRE
5. EAST DUNBARTONSHIRE
6. NORTH LANARKSHIRE
7. INVERCLYDE
8. RENFREWSHIRE
9. CITY OF GLASGOW
10. EAST RENFREWSHIRE
11. NORTH TYNESIDE
12. NEWCASTLE UPON TYNE
13. GATESHEAD
14. SOUTH TYNESIDE
15. SUNDERLAND
16. HARTLEPOOL

288

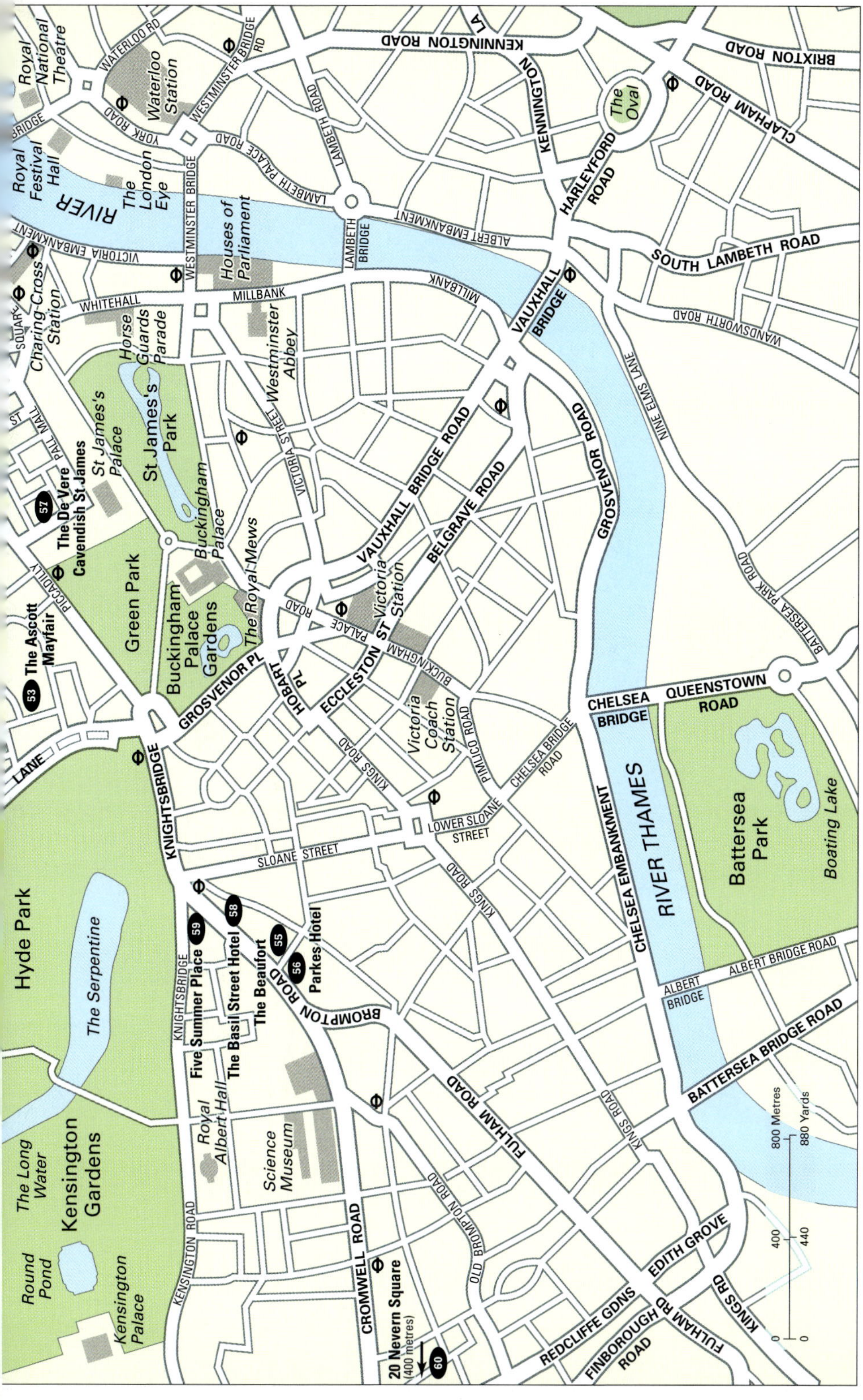
Hyde Park
The Serpentine
Kensington Gardens
The Long Water
Round Pond
Kensington Palace
Royal Albert Hall
Science Museum
KENSINGTON ROAD
KNIGHTSBRIDGE
CROMWELL ROAD
BROMPTON ROAD
OLD BROMPTON ROAD
FULHAM ROAD
20 Nevern Square
(400 metres)
60
59
Five Summer Place
58
The Basil Street Hotel
55
The Beaufort
56
Parkes Hotel
53
The Ascott Mayfair
57
The De Vere Cavendish St James
LANE
PICCADILLY
Green Park
Buckingham Palace Gardens
Buckingham Palace
The Royal Mews
St James's Palace
St James's Park
Horse Guards Parade
Charing Cross Station
PALL MALL
ST
SQUARE
WHITEHALL
Westminster Abbey
Houses of Parliament
MILLBANK
WESTMINSTER BRIDGE
WESTMINSTER BRIDGE RD
VICTORIA EMBANKMENT
RIVER
The London Eye
Royal Festival Hall
BRIDGE
Royal National Theatre
WATERLOO RD
Waterloo Station
YORK ROAD
LAMBETH PALACE ROAD
LAMBETH ROAD
LAMBETH BRIDGE
ALBERT EMBANKMENT
KENNINGTON ROAD
KENNINGTON LA
KENNINGTON
The Oval
HARLEYFORD ROAD
BRIXTON ROAD
CLAPHAM ROAD
SOUTH LAMBETH ROAD
WANDSWORTH ROAD
VAUXHALL BRIDGE
VAUXHALL BRIDGE ROAD
BELGRAVE ROAD
VICTORIA STREET
Victoria Station
GROSVENOR PL
HOBART PL
ECCLESTON ST
BUCKINGHAM PALACE ROAD
Victoria Coach Station
PIMLICO ROAD
KINGS ROAD
SLOANE STREET
LOWER SLOANE STREET
CHELSEA BRIDGE ROAD
GROSVENOR ROAD
NINE ELMS LANE
BATTERSEA PARK ROAD
CHELSEA BRIDGE
QUEENSTOWN ROAD
CHELSEA EMBANKMENT
RIVER THAMES
Battersea Park
Boating Lake
ALBERT BRIDGE ROAD
ALBERT BRIDGE
BATTERSEA BRIDGE ROAD
EDITH GROVE
REDCLIFFE GDNS
FINBOROUGH ROAD
FULHAM RD
KINGS RD
800 Metres
880 Yards
400
440
0

290

SEND FOR YOUR FREE BROCHURES

TO RECEIVE THE BROCHURE OF ANY HOTEL FEATURED IN THIS 64th EDITION, SIMPLY PUT THE APPROPRIATE PAGE NUMBERS IN THE BOXES BELOW AND RETURN THE CARD TO US. ALTERNATIVELY E-MAIL US ON info@signpost.co.uk UP TO 12 PAGE NUMBERS AND YOUR NAME AND ADDRESS.

PLEASE LIST IN PAGE ORDER

NAME (Mr/Mrs/Miss)..(CAPITALS PLEASE)

ADDRESS..

....

....POSTCODE..

E-MAIL ADDRESS..

SIGNPOST
PRIORY PUBLICATIONS LTD
PO BOX 24
BRACKLEY
NORTHAMPTONSHIRE NN13 5BR

AFFIX STAMP

SIGNPOST - COLOUR HOTEL GUIDE 2003
ORDER FORM

No. of copies	Price	Total
	£10.95	
For postage per copy to....		
UK and Europe, add £1.55		
Outside Europe Airmail, add £5		
Total (inc. carriage)		
Please include an Advantage Card		

TO SIGNPOST, PRIORY PUBLICATIONS LTD, SYRESHAM, BRACKLEY, NORTHANTS NN13 5HH (Fax: 01280 850576)

I enclose cheque in the sum of £_____
made payable to Priory Publications Ltd, or

I wish to pay by Visa/Master Card/Amex; please charge to my account. My card number is (13 or 16 digits):

Signature   Expiry date   /

Name (on card)

Address

Postcode

Please deliver to:

NAME..

ADDRESS ....

....

....POSTAL CODE......................

SIGNPOST - COLOUR HOTEL GUIDE 2003
ORDER FORM

No. of copies	Price	Total
	£10.95	
For postage per copy to....		
UK and Europe, add £1.55		
Outside Europe Airmail, add £4		
Total (inc. carriage)		
Please include an Advantage Card		

TO SIGNPOST, PRIORY PUBLICATIONS LTD, SYRESHAM, BRACKLEY, NORTHANTS NN13 5HH (Fax: 01280 850576)

I enclose cheque in the sum of £_____
made payable to Priory Publications Ltd, or

I wish to pay by Visa/Master Card/Amex; please charge to my account. My card number is (13 or 16 digits):

Signature   Expiry date   /

Name (on card)

Address

Postcode

Please deliver to:

NAME..

ADDRESS ....

....

....POSTAL CODE......................

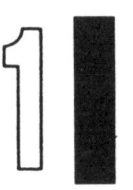

Business Reply Service
Licence no: **NH 0504**

SIGNPOST
PRIORY PUBLICATIONS LTD
PO BOX 24
BRACKLEY
NORTHAMPTONSHIRE NN13 5BR

Business Reply Service
Licence no: **NH 0504**

SIGNPOST
PRIORY PUBLICATIONS LTD
PO BOX 24
BRACKLEY
NORTHAMPTONSHIRE NN13 5BR